SPAIN: DICTATORSHIP TO DEMOCRACY

Spain:
Dictatorship to Democracy

RAYMOND CARR
and
JUAN PABLO FUSI AIZPURUA

London
GEORGE ALLEN & UNWIN
Boston   Sydney

First published in 1979

GEORGE ALLEN & UNWIN LTD
40 Museum Street, London WC1A 1LU

© George Allen & Unwin (Publishers) Ltd, 1979

British Library Cataloguing in Publication Data

Carr, Raymond
  Spain.
  1. Spain – History – 1939–1975 2. Spain – History
  – Civil War, 1936–1939 3. Spain – History – 1975–
  I. Title   II. Fusi, Juan Pablo
  946.082   DP270   78–41081
  ISBN 0-04-946012-9

Typeset in 10 on 11 point Times by Red Lion Setters, Holborn, London
and printed in Great Britain
by Unwin Brothers Ltd, Old Woking, Surrey

PREFACE

This book consists of two distinct parts. Chapters 1 to 6 discuss the political, economic and social evolution of modern Spain. We then discuss the tensions within the Franco regime and proceed to a political narrative which concentrates on the period from the crisis of Francoism (*c.* 1969) up to the elections of 1977 and the government of Señor Suárez. Those who wish to follow political events can therefore begin with Chapter 7. To make this possible we have consciously indulged in some repetition.

Certain preteritions and points of emphasis are also conscious. We have throughout concentrated rather on the regime than on the role of the opposition. Similarly Franco's foreign policy does not concern us directly. Both aspects of Francoism will be the work of two distinguished British scholars.

We could not hope to cover all aspects from the running of the railways to the social security system. We have therefore preferred to concentrate on selected issues. We are aware that we have not, for instance, dealt with municipal government, important because this was the aspect of government which touched the average Spaniard most directly.

We are also aware of the difficulties of writing on culture. Inevitably a short chapter verges on a catalogue. In Spain — whether this is to Spain's advantage or not is another question — an intellectual elite enjoys a prestige and influence unthinkable in England. This is a paradox in a country where what we call the 'culture of evasion' is deeply rooted. Moreover we are aware that in seeking to map a general landscape we have neglected writers of distinction, particularly poets, and whole areas — psychology, philosophy and the natural sciences.

Finally we would wish to caution alike against Napoleon's verdict that Spaniards are no different from Neapolitans and other European peoples, and the advertising slogan of Francoism that 'Spain is different'. If we talk of the economic difficulties of the present in Spain, other countries suffer from the effects of the oil crisis, inflation and chronic unemployment. Steel and shipbuilding are in trouble not only in Spain. Spain has its culture of evasion, its TV civilisation, its consumer society; so have other nations. If the advance of the permissive society disconcerts the right and the puritans in Spain, we have our Mrs Whitehouse. If Spain's cities and rivers are polluted, so they are in other industrial societies — though these societies have had a longer time to cure the consequences of urbanisation.

What is peculiar to Spain is the celerity and the abruptness of the jump into modernity after forty years of official, traditional Catholic conservatism; the cultural shock of the sudden end of the *atraso*, that social and cultural lag which has so long obsessed Spanish thinkers. It is somehow symbolic of this catching-up process, which does not always catch up in time, that the striptease joints of Madrid employ girls who cannot find employment in Europe where that particular mode is no longer quite the flourishing concern it was. *Per ardua ad vacua.*

The Epilogue is prophecy. Since jobbing historians are not trained in political divination, it must be read with due caution.

R. C.
J. P. F.

CONTENTS

CHRONOLOGICAL TABLE OF EVENTS

1892		Birth of Francisco Franco Bahamonde at El Ferrol (Galicia)
1898		Defeat of Spain by USA and end of Spanish colonial empire
1923		Military coup of General Primo de Rivera
1931	14 April	Proclamation of Second Republic
1933	29 October	Right wins general election
1936	16 February	Left wins general election
	17–18 July	Civil War begins
1939	1 April	Civil War ends
1940	16 October	Serrano Suñer appointed Foreign Minister
1942	3 September	Serrano Suñer dismissed
1943	17 March	Cortes opens
1945	19 March	Don Juan's Lausanne Manifesto against Franco
	17 July	Spaniards' Charter promulgated (*Fuero de los Españoles*)
1946	12 December	UN recommends diplomatic boycott of Spain
1951	1 March	Barcelona strike
1952	16 May	End of rationing in Spain
1953	27 August	Concordat with Vatican signed
	20 September	Base Agreement between USA and Spain signed
1955	14 December	Spain admitted to UN
1956	February	Student troubles; dismissal of Ruiz Giménez and Fernández Cuesta
1957	25 February	Franco forms sixth government, including the technocrats of Opus Dei
1958	17 May	Principles of National Movement presented to Cortes
1959	22 July	Stabilisation Plan announced
1961	15 May	Encyclical *Mater et Magistra*
1962	9 February	Spain requests negotiations with EEC
	April–June	Workers' and students' agitation State of emergency in Basque provinces and Asturias
	5–6 June	Spanish opposition participates in Munich meeting

	10 July	Seventh government
1963	20 April	Execution of Grimau
	28 December	First Development Plan
1964	30 September,	'Twenty-five years of peace'
	30 October	campaign: protest of intellectuals against repression in the Asturian mining strikes
1965	11 February	Eighth government
	23–25 February	Student demonstrations in Madrid. Five professors dismissed from university
1966	18 March	Fraga Iribarne's Press Law
	22 November	Organic Law of State presented to Cortes
	14 December	Referendum on Organic Law
1967	21 September	Admiral Carrero Blanco appointed Deputy Head of Government
1968	28 March–6 May	Madrid University closed
	21 December	Members of Carlist (Bourbon-Parma) family expelled from Spain
1969	24 January–25 March	State of emergency in Spain
	22 July	Franco presents Juan Carlos as his successor
	29 October	Ninth government dominated by Opus Dei
1970	3–28 December	Burgos Trial of ETA
1971	1 October	National homage to Franco in Madrid
	19 October	CC OO leaders arrested
	11 November	Third Development Plan announced
1972	6–8 January	Clashes in Madrid University
	10 March	Workers riot in El Ferrol
1973	8 June	Carrero Blanco appointed Prime Minister
	20 December	Carrero Blanco assassinated
	29 December	Arias Navarro appointed Prime Minister
	29 December	Main leaders of CC OO sentenced to 12–20 years in prison
1974	12 February	Arias announces 'opening' of the regime
	28 February	Bishop of Bilbao put under house arrest
	2 March	Execution of Puig Antich, Catalan anarchist
	9 July	Franco taken seriously ill
	19 July–2 September	Franco hands over power to Juan Carlos
	29 July	Opposition forms Democratic Junta

	13 September	Twelve people killed in Madrid bomb explosion attributed to ETA
	29 October	Dismissal of 'liberal' Minister of Information, Pío Cabanillas
	23 December	New Law of Political Associations
1975	February	Wave of strikes
	April	State of emergency in the Basque country
	June	Moderate opposition forms the Platform of Democratic Convergence
	August	New Anti-Terrorist Law, following months of terrorist activity
	21 September	Five ETA and FRAP members executed. Protests all over Western Europe
	20 November	Franco dies
	22 November	Juan Carlos crowned King
	4 December	Arias confirmed as Prime Minister
	13 December	Arias forms new government including reformists Fraga, Areilza, Garrigues
1976	January–February	Largest ever wave of strikes
	28 January	Arias presents his programme to Cortes
	3 March	Five workers killed in clashes with police in Vitoria
	26 March	Opposition unites in Democratic Co-ordination
	15 April	First legal congress of the Socialist union (UGT) in 40 years
	9 June	New Law of Associations approved by Cortes
	1 July	Arias resigns
	3 July	Adolfo Suárez appointed Prime Minister
	30 July	Government grants a partial amnesty
	10 August	Suárez dines with Socialist leader, Felipe Gonzalez
	8 September	Suárez meeting with military authorities
	10 September	Government announces new Law of Political Reform
	16 November	Cortes approves Law of Political Reform, which re-establishes democracy in Spain
	5 December	27th Congress of the Socialist party, the first held in Spain for 40 years
	15 December	Referendum on Law of Political Reform. Abstentions: 22.6%. Yes: 94.2%. No: 2.6%.

1977	23–28 January	Ten people die in Madrid 'Tragic Week'
	2 March	Eurocommunist summit in Madrid
	7 April	Movement dismantled
	9 April	Suárez legalises Spanish Communist party
	12–14 May	Six people killed in new wave of violence in the Basque country
	15 June	First democratic elections held since 1936
	22 July	New parliament opens
	29 September	*The Generalitat* (self-government of Catalonia) re-established. Josep Tarradellas returns to Spain as new Catalan president on 23 October
	15 October	New amnesty announced
	25–27 October	Government and opposition sign the Pact of Moncloa
	December	Regionalist unrest in Basque provinces, Galicia and Andalusia
	30 December	Pre-autonomy given to the Basque provinces
1978	January	Unrest in Spanish jails
	17 February	A Socialist, R. Rubial, becomes President of the Basque General Council (pre-autonomy self-government)
	February–March	CC OO win syndical elections
	24 February	First serious ministerial crisis after the 1977 election
	19–23 April	Communists hold first legal congress for 40 years. 'Leninism' rejected
	5 May	Debates on new Constitution begin
	8–13 July	Serious incidents in the Basque country
	21 July	Two senior officers killed by ETA
	6 September	Suàrez visits Cuba and Venezuela
	October–December	Worst ever ETA offensive
	14 October	Police mutiny in Bilbao
	31 October	Constitution approved by Congress and Senate
	17 November	"Operation Galaxia" disclosed
	6 December	Referendum on Constitution
	27 December	Constitution sanctioned by the King

GLOSSARY OF POLITICAL TERMS

ACNP (Asociación Católica Nacional de Propagandistas) A Catholic lay organisation founded in 1904, dedicated to penetrating the political and intellectual elite. Leading spirit Angel Herrera (b. 1886), editor of the Catholic daily *El Debate* and promoter of Acción Popular

AP (Alianza Popular) A conservative, right-wing party founded in the autumn of 1976 by former Franco ministers led by M. Fraga Iribarne

Asamblea de Cataluña Unitary body of the Anti-Francoist Catalan opposition launched in clandestinity in 1971

Carlists Classic right-wing Catholic party in Spain. Rejected the 'liberal' monarchy of Alfonso XIII in favour of the claims of the descendants of Don Carlos (1785–1855). Majority of its activists concentrated in Navarre where its militia (the *requetés*) was recruited. Fused with the Falange in April 1937

CDC (Convergencia Democrática de Catalunya) A centre-left Catalan nationalist party created in 1974 by Jordi Pujol

CEDA (Confederación Española de Derechas Autónomas) Founded March 1933. A nation-wide confederation of Catholic right-wing parties, the core of which was Acción Popular. It had a 'left' which professed social-Catholic doctrine but was essentially a party of the conservative right committed to the corporate state

CGV (Consejo General Vasco) The autonomous Basque government set up in December 1977

CNT (Confederación Nacional de Trabajo) The anarcho-syndicalist trades union founded in 1910. Believed in 'direct action' against employers, rejecting political action and electoral participation. CNT leadership deserted apoliticism to join the Popular Front government in November 1936. CNT strength lay in Catalonia (particularly Barcelona), in the Levante and Aragon, and appealed to the landless labourers of Andalusia

CC OO (Comisiones Obreras – Workers' Commissions) Illegal trade unions formed by Communists, Catholics and left-wing Marxists. Appeared in late 1950s. Legalised 1977. Now a Communist-led trade union

CNC (Confederación Nacional de Combatientes) Right-wing Francoist association of former Civil War combatants, led by J. A. Girón de Velasco

CSUT (Confederación Sindical Unitaria de Trabajadores) A left-wing Marxist trade union federation formed in 1976 after a split in CC OO

EDC (Esquerra Democrática de Catalunya) Liberal Catalan party created in 1975; led by Professor Trías Fargas

EIA (Party of the Basque Revolution) An offspring of ETA. Created in 1977

ETA (Euzkadi Ta Askatasuna) Clandestine revolutionary organisation formed in 1959 by those who considered the PNV (q.v.) too moderate. Responsible for terrorism, including the assassination of Admiral Carrero Blanco (December 1973)

Falange Española A grouping of authoritarian Nationalist parties under the leadership of José Antonio Primo de Rivera, son of the 'dictator'. After his execution (November 1936) Falange led by Manuel Hedilla. The nearest approach to a Fascist party in Spain. Grew rapidly in early months of the Civil War and in April 1937 fused by Franco with the Carlists to form the FET de las JONS – the only political 'party' in Franco Spain

FLP (Frente de Liberación Nacional) Left-wing student organisation influential in the 1960s

FDP (Federación Popular Democrática) A Christian-Democrat group led by José Ma. Gil Robles

FRAP (Frente Revolucionario Antifascista Patriótico) One of the factions of the revolutionary left which emerged after 1968. Involved in terrorist activities after 1973

Fuerza Nueva Neo-Fascist party led by Blas Piñar

Generalidad The autonomous government of Catalonia set up by the Statute of 1932

GRAPO (Grupo Revolucionario Antifascista Primero Octubre) Left-wing terrorist group created in 1976

HOAC (Hermandad Obrera Acción Católica) Catholic workers' organisation opposed to the Francoist 'vertical' syndicates and very active in the late 1950s

ID (Izquierda Democrática) Christian-Democrat group led by Ruiz Giménez

JOC (Juventud Obrera Católica) Catholic workers' organisation, very close to HOAC

Junta Democrática A coalition of parties of the illegal anti-Francoist opposition formed July 1974 with the Communists as the leading force. Neither PSOE nor Christian Democrats joined in

LCR (Liga Comunista Revolucionaria) Trotskyists

Movimiento Nacional Amalgam of all the different groups which supported Franco in 1936. It played the part of the single party in totalitarian regimes

MPAIAC (Movimiento para la Autodeterminación y la Independencia del Archipiélago Canario) Terrorist movement for the independence of the Canary Islands based in Algiers

Opus Dei A lay brotherhood of committed Catholics, aimed at influencing university and political life. Nursery of the 'technocrats' of the 1960s. Fell from influence in 1973

OS (Organización Sindical) The 'vertical' Francoist syndicates

PCE (Partido Comunista de España) The Spanish Communist party; Santiago Carrillo its secretary-general 1960

PDC (Partido Demócrata Cristiano) The fusion of PPDC and UDE, later merged in UCD

PNV (Partido Nacionalista Vasco) The Basque Catholic nationalist party, described by its leader, José Antonio de Aguirre, as a party of 'virile and integral Catholicism' with its ultimate aim full autonomy for the Basque provinces. Accepted the lay Republic and joined the Popular Front government because that Republic granted the Basque provinces of Vizcaya and Guipúzcoa autonomy in October 1936 as Euzkadi. Aguirre became President of Euzkadi.

Partido Popular A small but influential party formed in 1976 by liberal Christian-Democrat and Social-Democrat politicians. Later fused with UCD

PPDC (Partido Popular Demócrata Cristiano) A small Christian Democrat party led by Álvarez de Miranda

Plataforma de Convergencia Democrática A coalition of various parties of the anti-Francoist opposition created in 1975

POUM (Partido Obrero de Unificación Marxista) A revolutionary Marxist party founded September 1935 from the former Trotskyist Left Communist party of Andrés Nin and Joaquin Maurin's bloc of workers and peasants. As opposed to the CNT, the POUM held that the workers must seize *political* power

PSOE (Partido Socialista Obrero Español) The Socialist party of Spain, founded 1879

PSP An independent Socialist group launched in 1968 by Professor Tierno Galván. In 1978 united with PSOE

PSUC (Partido Socialista Unificado de Cataluña) Formed in July 1936 by the fusion of the Catalan Communist party and the Catalan branch of the PSOE. Affiliated to 3rd International; Communist influence in the party grew steadily

RSE (Reforma Social Española) A political association of Social Democratic ideology led by the Falangist Manuel Cantarero del Castillo

STV (Solidaridad de Trabajadores Vascos) The Basque nationalist trade union; successful in the 1978 syndical elections

SU (Sindicato Unitario) A left-wing Marxist trade union; split from CC OO in 1976

Tácitos A collective pen-name for group of young members of ACNP formed in 1973. *Tácitos* were Christian Democrats favouring reform from within. Prominent in Partido Popular, in UCD and in Suárez governments

UCD (Unión Centro Democrático) An electoral coalition formed in 1977 under the leadership of Prime Minister Adolfo Suárez. It included the PDC, a number of miniscule Social Democrat and Liberal parties, and several independent politicians, most of them, like Suárez, former Francoists. After its success in the 1977 election it became a unified political party

UDC (Unión Democrática de Catalunya) Catalan anti-Francoist Christian Democrat party led by Anton Canyellas

UDE (Unión Democrática Española) A Christian Democrat political association created in 1974; close to ACNP. Split in 1976: a faction led by Silva Muñoz joined AP; another joined PDC and eventually UCD

UDPE (Unión del Pueblo Español)   A Gaullist-type political association created in 1975 by prominent Francoists. Faded out in 1976

UGT (Unión General de Trabajadores)   The Socialist trade union; main strengths in Madrid, and the Asturias mining and the Basque industrial zones

USDE. A Social Democrat party led in clandestinity by Dionisio Ridruejo until his death in 1975. Later most members joined UCD

USO (Unión Sindical Obrera)   A Socialist-Catholic illegal trade union federation which emerged in 1960 out of HOAC and JOC

MAIN ACTORS

ALONSO VEGA, Camilo (1899–1971) General   Close friend of Franco. Director-General of Military Instruction (1939); Under-Secretary for Defence (1940); Director-General of the Civil Guard (1943); Minister of the Interior (1957–69)

AREILZA, José Ma., Count of Motrico (1909)   Lawyer and engineer. A right-wing Monarchist in the 1930s. Joined the Falange to become Mayor of Bilbao (1937–8) and Director-General of Industry (1938–40). Later, Franco's ambassador to Argentina (1947–57), USA (1954–60) and France (1960–4). After 1964 gradually left the Francoist regime to become the symbol of the liberal right; head of the secretariat of Don Juan (1966–9). Minister of Foreign Affairs after Franco's death (December 1975–July 1976)

ARIAS NAVARRO, Carlos (b. 1908)   Lawyer. Military attorney of Franco's army in Malaga (1937–9); Civil Governor of León, Tenerife and Navarre (1944–57); Director-General of Public Security (the police) 1957–65; Mayor of Madrid (1965–73); Minister of the Interior (1973–4). Prime Minister in the last Franco governments (1974–5) and in the first government of Juan Carlos (1975 to July 1976)

ARIAS SALGADO, Gabriel (1904–62)   Civil Governor of Salamanca during the Civil War; Under-Secretary for Education and National Delegate for the Press and Propaganda in the 1940s, a key post which controlled the media through censorship; Minister of Information and Tourism (1951–62)

ARRESE y MAGRA, José Luis (b. 1905)   A Falangist since 1933; Civil Governor of Malaga (1939); Secretary-General of the Movement (1941–5 and 1956–7); Minister of Housing (1957–60). A member of the Council of the Realm

CAMACHO, Marcelino (b. 1918)   Metalworker, member of the Socialist trade union (UGT) and of the Communist party since 1935. In exile 1935–57. Returned to Spain to become one of the organisers of the Communist-led Workers' Commissions. Imprisoned 1967–72 and again between June 1972 and December 1975

CARRILLO, Santiago (b. 1915)   Son of a metalworker. Leader of the Socialist Youth in the 1930s; joined the Communist party November 1936. In exile after 1939; Secretary of the International Communist Youth (1939). After the 1960s resided in Paris. Member of the Executive Committee of the Spanish Communist party; Secretary-General 1960 and re-elected 1974 and 1978. Returned to Spain in 1977.

FERNANDEZ CUESTA, Raimundo (b. 1897)   Lawyer. One of the founders of Falange. Minister of Agriculture (1939), Justice (1945–51); Secretary-General of the Movement (1939 and 1951–7)

FERNANDEZ MIRANDA, Torcuato (b. 1915) Lawyer and university teacher. Director-General of Secondary Education (1954–5), of University Education (1956–62) and of Social Promotion (1962–6); Secretary-General of the Movement (1969–73); Vice-President of the government (July–December 1973); President of the Cortes (December 1975–June 1977)

FERNANDEZ DE LA MORA, Gonzalo (b. 1924) Diplomat and writer. Minister of Public Works (1970–3). Author of *Twilight of Ideology*, a defence of technocracy

FRAGA IRIBARNE, Manuel (b. 1922) Lawyer and university teacher. Director of *Revista de Estudios Políticos* (1961–2); Minister of Information and Tourism (1962–9); Professor of Theory of the State at Madrid University (1969–73); ambassador to London (1973–5); Minister of the Interior in the first government of Juan Carlos (December 1975–July 1976)

GIL ROBLES, José Ma. (b. 1898) Lawyer and leader of the right-wing Catholic party of the 1930s, CEDA. Minister of War (1935). After supporting Franco in the Civil war, remained in Portugal working for Don Juan till 1962. Returned to Spain; reorganised one of the Christian Democratic groups.

GIRON DE VELASCO, José Antonio (b. 1911) Member of the pseudo-Fascist JONS which merged with Falange in 1934. Minister of Labour (1941–57); member of the Council of the Realm 1971. Returned to active politics in 1974 as the champion of the Francoist *ultras*, the bunker

GONZALEZ, Felipe (b. 1942) A workers' lawyer, member of left-wing Catholic movements (HOAC). Joined the clandestine Socialist Youth in 1962 and the Socialist party in 1964. In 1970 became a member of the party's executive; Secretary-General 1974; re-elected 1976

IBANEZ MARTIN, José (1896–1969) University professor and a member of the ACNP. Minister of Education (1939–51); President of the Council of the State (1951–8); President of the Higher Council of Scientific Research (CSIC) (1939–69). Ambassador to Lisbon (1958)

LOPEZ BRAVO, Gregorio (b. 1923) Marine engineer and a member of the Opus Dei. Minister of Industry (1962–9), of Foreign Affairs (1969–73)

LOPEZ RODO, Laureano (b. 1920) Professor of Administrative Law. Secretary-General of the Presidency of the Government and Commissioner of the Plan for Development (1957–65); Minister of Foreign Affairs (July–December 1973). A prominent member of the Opus Dei

MARTIN ARTAJO, Alberto (b. 1905) Lawyer. Leader of ACNP in the 1930s. Secretary of the Council of the State (1940). Minister of Foreign Affairs (1945–57)

RIDRUEJO, Dionisio (1912–75) Poet and Falangist. National Delegate for Propaganda (1939–41). Fought in Second World War as a volunteer in the pro-Axis Blue Division. Broke with the regime in 1942 to become leader of small Social Democratic groups

RUIZ GIMENEZ, Joaquín (b. 1913 Lawyer and professor. Prominent member of the ACNP. Minister of Education (1951–7). Founded the left-wing magazine *Cuadernos para el Diálogo* (1963). Since then, one of the leaders of Spanish Christian Democracy

SERRANO SUNER, Ramón (b. 1901)   Lawyer, Franco's brother-in-law. Member of the Catholic CEDA in the 1930s. Minister of the Interior (1938–41), Foreign Affairs (1940–2) and Secretary-General of the Movement (1940–1). After 1942, broke with Franco and withdrew from politics

SILVA MUNOZ, Federico (b. 1923)   A member of ACNP. Minister of Public Works (1966–70)

SOLIS RUIZ, José (b. 1913)   Lawyer and Falangist. National Delegate for Syndicates after 1951. Minister of the Movement (1957–69); Minister of Labour (1975–6)

SUAREZ, Adolfo (b. 1932)   Lawyer, member of the Movement bureaucracy. Civil Governor of Segovia (1968); Director-General of Radio and Television (1969); Minister of the Movement (December 1975 – July 1976); Prime Minister (1976—)

TIERNO GALVAN, Enrique (b. 1918)   Lawyer and professor until expelled in 1965 because of his political activities. Founder of what was to become the Popular Socialist Party (PSP)

Introduction

On 20 November 1975, General Franco died. Wired and plugged into a battery of medical machines, beside him the arm of St Teresa and on his bed the mantle of the Virgin of Pilar, in his death-bed agony he was a symbol of the Spain he ruled: a modern industrial state, a consumer society haunted by the relics of a Catholic, traditional state erected during and after the Civil War of 1936–9.

Franco had survived for nearly forty years as Caudillo of Spain – one of the longest terms of one-man rule in modern European history. If his image in his controlled press had been changed over the years – the stern and vigorous general of 1939 had become by 1970 the grandfather in civilian clothes surrounded by his grandchildren – if his direct hold over political life had weakened with age, no one could dispute that he was still the final arbiter of the destiny of Spain. 'All the cards are in his hands,' wrote a critic in 1967, 'he does not *make* politics, he *is* politics.'[1]

Franco's title to this personal dictatorship was based on victory in the Civil War. The memory of that victory and the sacrifice of blood it had cost was the constant theme alike of his speeches and his private thoughts. The grandiose and tasteless basilica of the Valley of the Fallen (Valle de los Caídos) that he built in the mountains near Madrid was a vast monument to the Crusade, his holy war against anti-Spain. Spain must never be allowed to relapse into the political system and social *mores* which had forced a group of military conspirators to rise on 18 July 1936 in order to save the country from disintegration at the hands of a government inspired by foreign ideologies, and run by a gang of incompetent politicians who put party above *patria*.

I

In April 1931 the conservative interests that had ruled Spain since 1875, first by manipulating the electoral machinery of the constitutional monarchy, then under the shield of the relatively benign dictatorship of General Primo de Rivera (1923–30), suddenly found themselves bereft of institutional protection. With monarchist candidates defeated in the great cities of Spain in the municipal elections of that month, King Alfonso XIII left Spain and overnight it became a democratic republic. 'We are,' the King admitted, 'out of fashion.' Engulfed by a wave of republican optimism, conservatives watched the fall of the monarchy as they 'might have watched a bad film'. The Republic was born painlessly out of the withdrawal of the right.

How did it come about that the conservative interests, apparently so soundly trounced in 1931, felt strong enough to back a military rising to overthrow the government of the Republic in 1936? Why did the right win the Civil War this rising unleashed? Why had the Republic failed to rally enough support to make a military coup an unthinkable risk for its perpetrators and why did it lack the strength to defeat them in the war?

For the first time, under the Republic, a democratic system functioned; elections were genuine elections fought by mass parties. This process of politicisation penetrated even rural Spain, challenging the hold of the 'powerful ones' over local life. The fundamental reason for the failure of the democratic experiment of 1931 – 6 was that politicisation raised, among the working class, expectations, a thirst for social justice, which the Republic did not – indeed could not – satisfy; while, on the other hand, conservatives regarded the mere existence of these expectations as inadmissible, a dangerous threat to their way of life.

Maurín, a Marxist commentator of great intelligence, insisted the Republic was a bourgeois republic which lacked a bourgeoisie prepared to carry through the bourgeois revolution that would demolish 'feudalism'. The middle classes were, for the most part, conservatives who put the preservation of order above all else. Those sectors of the middle class committed to the modernisation of Spanish society – the left Republican parties – therefore needed the alliance of the proletarian parties. The result of this coalition was a defiant, Jacobin radicalism in politics combined with a cautious reformism in the social and economic sphere. Thus Azaña's military reforms, inspired by French anti-militarism, alienated many officers; and yet there was no serious attempt by the government, of which he was Prime Minister in 1932–3, to weaken the economic power of those classes which were to support the officers who rose, on 18 July 1936, against a republic of which Azaña was by then President. The classes occupying the heights of the economy in 1931 remained *in situ* in 1936, convinced, nevertheless, that they were faced by an imminent Socialist revolution.

At first the Socialist party (the PSOE) and its trade union (the UGT) were prepared to support a democratic reformist republic in alliance with the left Republicans. The rival anarcho-syndicalist union (the CNT) rejected bourgeois democracy root and branch.* In competition with these more resolute revolutionaries and disappointed at the meagre social reforms of 1931–2, the Socialists abandoned their alliance with the bourgeois left. The key issue was agrarian reform. Urban radicals for the most part, the Republicans lacked the resolution to push through a reform without which the Socialists could not keep their newly won support in rural Spain. Fighting the elections of 1932 separately, the bourgeois radicals and Socialists went down to defeat.

The hard monarchist right had never accepted the democratic republic and ceaselessly plotted its violent overthrow. The 'moderate' Catholic right were 'accidentalists', that is, they accepted a democracy as long as they could dominate it and turn it into a corporatist state. Under José Maria Gil Robles the CEDA, the party of the 'moderate' right, emerged as the largest party in the 1932 elections. When, in October 1934, the CEDA entered the government, the Socialists proved that they, too, were accidentalists, accepting democracy on condition. They staged an armed revolt in the mining province of Asturias. The October Revolution was a watershed. Socialists, alarmed at the advance of Fascism in Europe, believed that there would be no place for them in a state run by Catholic conservatives. To the right, a republic dominated by Socialists was unacceptable.

Such a republic seemed to be imminent in the spring and summer of 1936. Chastened by their defeat in 1933, Socialists, Communists and left-wing Republicans, united in the Popular Front, fought and won – by a narrow majority – the elections of February 1936. However, the Socialists did not join the government. The maximalist wing of the party, under Largo Caballero, without any revolutionary intent or plan, used the rhetoric of the proletarian revolution and the mobilisation of its masses to force an advanced social policy on a government manned by bourgeois Republicans. With the government under pressure from the streets, with peasants invading the great estates, with church burnings and bomb outrages, with what they considered a collapse of the political and social order (which the right were themselves both provoking and using as a proof of the generalised collapse), the Catholic right increasingly deserted legalism for the counter-revolution long preached by hard-core monarchists and authoritarians. Half of

*For a discussion of the nature of working-class parties see below, p.12.*ff.*

Spain had voted for the right in February; by July most of them were prepared, with greater or lesser degrees of enthusiasm, to support a military coup. Gil Robles had already allowed his party funds to be used by the conspirators. Calvo Sotelo, leader of the authoritarian counter-revolutionary right, had consistently appealed to the army to 'save' Spain from democratic disaster. His assassination on 13 July 1936 removed all restraints.

With hindsight we can see that it was the bourgeois Republicans' attack on the church which gave outraged conservative interests the banner of a persecuted church. The attack was natural. The integrist (i.e. reactionary) tradition of Spanish Catholicism which still gloried in the Inquisition was inflexibly opposed to liberal ideas and institutions. The church was a symbol of *ancien régime*. No democrat could permit such an institution to control secondary education. When, in the first days of the Civil War, priests were massacred in their thousands, in spite of the government's efforts, the Republic gave to the conservative right the ideological and emotional unity it needed: the 'spirit of the Crusade'. .

The Civil War was the last of the European religious wars. It was also, *grosso modo*, a class war. In Nationalist propaganda it was presented not only as a war against freemasons, the historic protagonists of anti-clericalism, but also as a war against Marxists, out to bolshevise Spain. Threatened less by the legislation of the Republic than by the rhetoric and the revolutionary atmosphere of the spring and summer of 1936, the Spanish upper classes were enthusiastic supporters of the rising. The middle sectors of society were less consistent. Young intellectuals and professionals supported the Republic; the older generation, alarmed at what Julián Marías called the proletarisation of life styles, often withdrew their allegiance. By 1936 the two best-known intellectuals among the older generation of Spaniards, the Catholic existentialist Unamuno and the liberal philosopher Ortega y Gasset, had become critics of the Republic they had welcomed in 1931. To Ortega, events seemed to fulfil the prophecies of his *Rebellion of the Masses*: the barbarian masses were acting on a stage once the domain of the civilised elite. To Unamuno the lay Republic was 'vulgar'.

Part class war, it was also a war against 'separatism'. Separatists were the third element in the triad which together with masons and Marxists — with Jews thrown in by the more fanatic National-ists — was responsible for the destruction of Spain. In 1932 the Republic had granted limited home rule to Catalonia by a Statute of Autonomy; just after the war broke out it granted a similar statute to the Basque provinces of Guipúzcoa and Vizcaya.[2] To the right this was to betray the unity that was the proudest creation of Spanish history. A unity for which the army was the safeguard.

II

When the military conspirators − and they were the young officer *enragés* of the right rather than the senior officers − rose they saw themselves as fighting for the defence of Spanish values, true interpreters of the national will betrayed by the politicians of the Popular Front government. General Mola, the organiser of the military rising, thought that merely to obey a legal civilian government was to behave like a bureaucratic lackey, subject to a mere 'mechanical' obedience that betrayed a higher and more honourable discipline.* They had hoped to stage a classical *pronunciamiento*, a relatively bloodless officers' coup such as General Primo de Rivera had brought off in 1923. They unleashed a civil war and, on 18 July, their chances of winning it seemed remote.

With the odds stacked against them − the industrial resources, the gold reserves, the skeleton of the administration, the best part of the navy and the air force, even the military maps needed to plan a campaign were in Republican hands − why did the Nationalists win? The answer is, as in all wars, superior equipment and superior discipline in the army and, to back up the military effort, a unified wartime government.

The Nationalists were better served than the Republic by their foreign sympathisers in terms of arms supplies: the German Condor Legion, and Italian troops and equipment more than balanced Soviet aid to the Popular Front, vital though this was in the early phases of the war. As important was the disciplined African army (24,000 troops) under Franco and the superior training of the Nationalist armies. Franco was not a brilliant strategist − his 'slowness' infuriated his German and Italian advisers − but he was competent and determined. The Nationalist cause carried within it conventional military values. The Republican effort to create an effective, disciplined Popular Army was one long struggle with the voluntarism of the militia system −

---

*The peculiar language of military journalism in the late nineteenth century reveals the officer corps' outrage at the politicians' betrayal of the army and nation. 'In this new Capua of verbal diarrhoea we run after the Byzantium of the trivial until one day our country (*patria*, an emotive term) will recede into the abyss.' The claim of the army to interpret and safeguard the 'essence' of the *patria* has a strange affinity with Rousseau's 'general will', with the inhabitants of the officers' mess as the legislator.

militiamen with clenched fists and dungarees flashed across the cinema screens of Europe, the image of a people in arms. In Burgos, the Nationalist capital, or Salamanca where Franco established his headquarters, a uniform was a passage to privilege and respect; in Barcelona 'revolutionary discipline' regarded a salute as a sign of servitude.

The military discipline of the Nationalists was a reflection of political unity: the military weakness of the Popular Front a concomitant of its political feuding. 'In the political field,' lamented the Republican general Rojo, 'Franco won.'

The first result of the officers' rising was to release a workers' rising which galvanised the European left, depressed at the advances of Fascism. The divisions in the Republican camp were a result of this 'spontaneous revolution' backed by the workers' militia. The workers took over factories, especially in Catalonia, and the great landed estates through the various forms of workers' and union control called 'collectivisation'. This was the great social experiment. It was 'the first time' foreign sympathisers like George Orwell had been 'in a town[Barcelona] where the working class was in the saddle'. The problem was, in André Malraux's words, 'to organise the apocalypse', to create a government capable of winning the war.

There were two competing views as to how this should be done. The revolutionary left — above all the CNT and the Marxist revolutionaries of George Orwell's POUM — believed that only a workers' republic could create the necessary enthusiasm to sustain the war by maintaining and expanding the 'revolutionary conquests' of the summer. The bourgeois Republicans and the Communists believed that the spontaneous revolution of collectivisation paralysed the war effort and alienated the middle classes without whose support the war could not be won. By May 1937 Communists and the revolutionary elements in the CNT and the POUM were shooting it out in the streets of Barcelona: a civil war within the Civil War.

With the Republic torn by faction, the supreme political achievement of Franco was to impose political unity from above on the factions in his own camp. Whereas the Republicans never achieved a unified command, Franco's fellow generals, aware of the necessity for central planning of scarce military resources, chose him as commander-in-chief and head of state and of the government.

Like the parties of the Popular Front, the Nationalists were originally a collection of heterogeneous clans, their political diversity reflected in a variety of uniforms in the streets of

Salamanca and Burgos. The Carlists were romantic counter-revolutionaries, the Falangists modern authoritarians whose vision was to incorporate the working classes in a nationalist, corporate state based on the Italian Fascist model. There were old-fashioned conservative monarchists and the disillusioned remnants of Gil Robles' CEDA. In April 1937 all parties disappeared when Franco forced union 'from above' on the Falangists and Carlists, creating a single Movement of which he was head. After 1937 Franco exercised a political and military supremacy enjoyed before him only by Napoleon.

Under Franco, Nationalist Spain emerged from the war in 1939 as a political monolith. This unity was supported by two pillars. As Serrano Suñer, Franco's brother-in-law and the architect of the unification of 1937 was to observe, Nationalist Spain had become a Spain of soldiers. The second pillar was the Catholic church. Far more than the Falange, whose ideology the generals had adopted because they had no political philosophy of their own beyond a barren brand of military authoritarianism, the church of the Crusade supplied the ideological and emotional cement which bound together the Nationalist clans.

That the church was restored to power and privilege − one of the first acts of the Nationalists was to restore the crucifix in schools and bring back the Jesuits expelled under the Republic − reveals the true significance of the Civil War. It had been fought to save the conservative interests threatened by the reformism of the Second Republic and a conservative class scared stiff by the advance of the proletarian parties after February 1936 and by the social revolution of the summer of 1936. The Italian ambassador noticed the traditional ceremony of Franco's court. Franco's first government, appointed in January 1938, reflected the balance of forces in the new regime. It was dominated by conservative monarchists and soldiers.

III

With the conservative reaction of 1939 the society which the middle-class progressives and their Socialist allies had tried, ineffectively, to modernise, and which had experienced the 'spontaneous' social revolution of the summer of 1936, was restored to the *status quo* of 1930.

This society was still a society vastly different from other Western European societies. Whereas in England the vast majority of the population had long left the countryside for the towns, over half of the population of Spain still got its living from the soil, housed in small rural towns and villages. Yet the agrarian sector was inefficient (wheat was the main crop, with yields the lowest in Europe), and behind a complex variety of land tenures lay great social injustices. In the north-west the peasants of Galicia struggled for a living on minute 'handkerchief' plots; the great estates of the south-west were worked by gangs of landless labourers, hired by the day. The labourers of Andalusia were the most wretched class in Europe; unemployed for months on end, they rotted in the small towns of the south. Above these extremes of misery were the peasants of Old Castile – conservative but hard put to scratch a living from the poor, thin soils of their scattered plots.

'Poverty,' remarks Trollope, 'to be picturesque should be rural.' Most travellers in the Spain of the nineteen-thirties, like Gautier a century before, were fascinated by the picturesque, noticing neither the poverty nor the injustices in the countryside. Rural society was sharply divided between rich and poor, between regions of stability and regions of unrest. Outside the regions of genuine peasant proprietorship, property was concentrated in the hands of a land-owning class, and this was especially so in the *latifundia*, (great estates) of La Mancha, Extremadura and Andalusia, where the owners were often absentees. The great estates had been expropriated and, in some regions, collectivised in the Republican zone; after the war this social experiment ended with the restoration of the old landowners. Out of a total agricultural population of something over two million who worked the land, 10,000 families owned roughly half the cultivable land; 150 families owned 32 per cent of the province of Badajoz; in the province of Malaga 1.8 per cent of the landowners controlled 55 per cent of the land. Spain was divided between rich proprietors (a conglomerate of upper-middle-class *arrivistes*, who had often bought their estates when the church and common lands were sold by the Liberals in the nineteenth century, and nobles who had held their lands for centuries), 'middle' peasants who could make a decent living out of their farms, and beneath them a semi-proletariat of struggling micro-proprietors a million strong.

Besides glaring inequalities in income there was an acute regional imbalance between a relatively rich peripheral commercialised agriculture and a primitive impoverished centre: between areas of development and areas of backwardness. The Catalan peasant, in spite of a severe crisis in the thirties, was a prosperous entrepreneur compared with a Castilian farmer on his arid, small farm; the Basque family farmer had not yet encountered the crisis of the nineteen-sixties when his sons would leave the farm, attracted by higher wages in industry. The orange-growers of Valencia who supplied much of Spain's foreign exchange were well-to-do by Spanish standards, though they had suffered a setback when their markets were imperilled by the world depression.

In no country of Europe are the changes in the agricultural landscape so abrupt and violent. 'The north-western provinces,' observed a nineteenth-century traveller 'are more rainy than Devonshire, while the centre plains are more calcined than those of the deserts of Arabia.' The traveller to Madrid from the tourist-infested beaches of the Costa del Sol may pass from the intensively cultivated irrigated plots of Murcia, where a couple of acres or so are a rich farm producing highly profitable garden products, through the great olive and wine monocultures to the bleak, desert-like wheatlands of Castile, where a hundred acres may be a disaster for a family. Even Andalusia, which, to those who do not know it may appear a homogeneous region of the great, extensively cultivated *latifundia* of absentee aristocratic landowners, includes both the rich soils of the Campiña de Córdoba, with its profit-minded agricultural entrepreneurs and industrial crops, and the tragically poor farms of eastern Andalusia where only seasonal emigration to France can provide a living wage. 'Every night,' wrote Costa, himself the son of an Aragonese peasant farmer and whose whole life was a bitter struggle to educate himself, 'over half of Spain goes to bed hungry.' The richly varied but somewhat rebarbative Spanish regional cuisine is based on the necessity of making poor food palatable.

IV

This imbalance in agriculture was paralleled by the imbalance in industrial development so characteristic of developing economies. Spain affords a classic case in Europe of a latecomer to industrialisation and not until the years before and during the First World War did it begin to catch up. Even then its industrial structure was weak, uncompetitive and dependent on imports of foreign capital and technology.[3]

Economic development in such cases tends to concentrate increasingly in favoured areas – for instance, where a skilled labour force and access to transport and credit facilities already exist – leaving the rest of the country impoverished and untouched by the wealth generated by industrial growth. Thus in Italy the north became industrialised while the south stagnated; and so it was in Spain.

Many philosophic historians have developed, since the

eighteenth century, the concept of the 'two Spains' as the key to her
history: the Spain of blind, rigid Catholic conservatism, inward-
looking and nationalistic, in permanent conflict with the open,
tolerant, forward-looking, cosmopolitan Spain of intellectuals and
progressives. That this conflict existed, no one can deny; but to the
economist or sociologist the 'two Spains' are the Spain of development — however slow — and the Spain of poverty and
stagnation. The cities, where the workers lived in shanty-town
suburbs and the wealthy built French-style mansions, stood in
contrast to the rural *pueblos*, the grim, austere Castilian towns
where life had stagnated for centuries and the decaying houses of a
once rich nobility testified to a lost prosperity. The urban Spain of
the dynamic periphery drained the villages in the decaying centre of
a surplus population that could find no gainful occupation.

Thus Spain's late industrial revolution was confined largely to
two regions: Catalonia and the Basque provinces. Already in the
eighteenth century Barcelona, capital of Catalonia, was the most
important centre of the cotton industry outside Lancashire. By
1930, besides cotton and wool, Catalonia had developed light
industry, machine-shops (the first railway engine was built in
Barcelona) and shipping. The Basque metallurgical and shipping
industry had grown round the iron mines near Bilbao and had been
financed by the sale of ore to England. Much of this industry was
controlled by the few members of a powerful local industrial and
banking oligarchy which had prospered exceedingly from the huge
profits made during the First World War.

Both the Basque country and Catalonia saw themselves as
progressive, forward-looking communities tied to a backward
agrarian Castile, symbolised by the 'parasitic' capital, Madrid,
where politicians and civil servants, out of touch with the economic
realities of the country, controlled its destiny. These politicians —
especially the liberals — were often mild free traders; the Catalan
businessmen, the Basque ironmasters and shipowners, scared of
British competition, were fanatic protectionists. In the Tariff Laws
of 1891 and 1906 they got their way when the conservatives erected
around Spain the highest tariff barriers in Europe, barriers which
protected not only the 'infant industries' of the periphery but also
the high-cost wheat farmers of Castile.*

*This enabled Basque and Catalan protectionists to argue that protection was
not a regional and sectoral demand but a *national* interest: protection by 'saving'
industry provided a market for surplus Castilian wheat in the periphery and
maintained high levels of employment generally. Nevertheless, in spite of the
protectionist alliance of wheat-growers and industrialists, the demands of

Consciousness of separate economic interests helped the development, in the later nineteenth century, of a demand for regional self-government for Catalonia and the Basque provinces. There is no surer recipe for the mutation of regional tensions into full-blown nationalism than the political dependence of a prosperous region with independent cultural traditions on a capital located in a poor, backward region.

The Catalans had a separate language, a distinct popular and literary culture, the proud memory of a great mediaeval trading empire and a tradition of political independence dating back to the Middle Ages and which had ended only in 1715, when Catalonia was 'conquered' by Philip V and incorporated into the Spanish monarchy. 'Catalanism' was a term which embraced everything from a passion for Catalan literature and history to full-blown nationalism; no party in Catalonia could neglect it. When the moderate regionalism of the Catalan business community with its demand for home rule could not find a place 'within Spain', the 'nationalist' left, ready to employ the language of separatism, increased in influence. This Catalan nationalism came to appeal less to big business than to the middle class in general.

It was the bogey of 'separatism' that allowed the monarchist politicians of Castile to play on 'Spanish' nationalism and to oppose any concession of home rule to Catalonia. Autonomy would lead to the destruction of 'the unity of Spain created by history'. The Catalan view of Spanish history was distinct: Spain was a plural society of different peoples artificially hammered into the straitjacket of unity by Castilians − what Unamuno, the philosopher of Salamanca, called 'hollow unity, unity without content, unity for the sake of unity'. If the strident tones of Castilian nationalism were abhorrent to Catalans, the language of Catalanism was alarming to Castilians with their claim to the monopoly of Spanish patriotism. Prat de la Riba, the theoretician of Catalanism, called Spain 'a geographical expression' to denote a collection of 'nations': 'Every nationality should have its state.'

Catalan discontents and the Catalan demand for self-government

Catalan industrialists were presented by anti-Catalans as a 'selfish' imposition on the Spanish consumer: cf. the reaction of the left to the campaign orchestrated by Basque and Catalan business interests in 1916 to defeat the very modest tax on the booming war profits of the 1915−19 bonanza. These war profits consolidated Spanish capitalism and the protection afforded by war fostered import substitution. When the 'artificial' protection lapsed in 1920 Catalans and Basques clamoured for higher protection to save this mushroom growth. When the Liberal government in 1923 threatened to lower tariffs, the Catalan business community supported the coup of Primo de Rivera.

had dominated Spanish politics since 1900. The limited home rule granted by the Autonomy Statute of 1932 was anathema to the nationalists. It was abolished and the Catalan language officially suppressed in favour of Castilian, 'the language of Empire'.

In the Basque country the national issue took a different course and a more acrid tone. The majority of big businessmen got what they wanted from Madrid and indeed dominated its financial life. Basque nationalism was not middle-class and progressive. It was in origin a Catholic, peasant nationalism, bitterly opposed by the Socialists as reactionary, as a campaign against the non-Basque immigrant workers who 'defiled' the purity of the race. By the thirties this racism was muted and the Basque national party (the PNV) was becoming − at least as far as its more farsighted leaders were concerned − a Christian Democratic party with support outside the rural areas; but it remained determined to win for the Basque provinces an autonomy as wide as that granted to the Catalans in 1932.

The Basques were granted their Autonomy Statute on the outbreak of the Civil War. The Basque nationalists (except in Navarre which became the recruiting ground of the *requetés* − a Nationalist, fiercely Catholic militia) put their nationalism above their Catholicism and the PNV allied with the Socialists to defend a lay republic. This, to the Nationalists, was the most unholy alliance. While Navarre retained a form of autonomy, the Basque Statute was, like the Catalan, abolished.

V

The victory of Franco brought not only the suppression of 'separatism'. It meant the destruction of organised labour. Its leaders were in exile; those who struggled to maintain the semblance of a clandestine organisation in Spain imprisoned, tortured or executed; its masses cowed by the threat of dismissal, by poverty and despair. Yet by the 1970s the working-class organisations were once again a force; and a force in vastly different conditions. In the 1930s the industrial proletariat, concentrated in two regions − Catalonia and the industrial and mining areas of the Cantabrian coast − were a minority. The largest socialist union was that of the agricultural labourers. In 1970 the balance had changed; the SEAT factory in Barcelona employed 20,000 workers. Marxists could no longer argue, as they had in the thirties, that Spain was, in economic terms, a feudal society.

When the workers' movement revived, it grew up around the organisations that Francoism had failed to burn out of the collective memory: the Socialists, the Communists and the anarcho-syndicalists. To understand their relative strengths, we must examine their traditions and history. This immediately exposes their great weakness: the lack of a unified working-class movement, of a single trade union. It is to the creation of such a movement that all working-class leaders now pay lip-service as the chant 'Unity, Unity' sounds out at every mass meeting.

When the Civil War broke out, the two mass proletarian organisations were the anarcho-syndicalist CNT, and the Socialist party (the PSOE) and its union the UGT, the heirs, respectively, of Bakunin and Marx. Their philosophies were irreconcilable: while Socialists aimed at the capture of the state by the working classes, anarcho-syndicalists sought its destruction.

The anarcho-syndicalists rejected 'bourgeois' politics and hence the bourgeois democracy of the Second Republic. The CNT was a revolutionary union; there was no CNT party and CNT militants either did not vote at all (as in 1933) or voted for other parties (as in 1936). Its organisation was loose, capable of sudden mushroom growth and equally sudden collapses. It contained both 'action groups' who believed in propaganda by deed, i.e. terrorism, and 'pure' syndicalists, proponents of a revolution through a strong, militant union. The violent men appealed to the 'new proletarians', recent immigrants into industrial Catalonia, illiterates wrenched from a rural background, and what Victor Serge called 'the vast world of irregulars, outcasts, paupers and criminals. The 'pure' syndicalists' strength lay in towns where immigrants did not swamp skilled native workers.

It was the anarcho-syndicalists who were responsible for the revolution of collectivisation in areas the CNT controlled: the workers' takeover of the factories of Catalonia and the great estates of Aragon. Their utopian economics dissolved with the shortages of a war economy and by 1939 their organisation was weakened by internal splits and the onslaughts of their enemies — the Communists and the bourgeois Republicans. Nevertheless they left an abiding legacy: the memory of workers' control from the factory floor which, under the name of *autogestión*, was to become a common platform of the workers' movement of the 1970s.

While to the anarcho-syndicalists, Socialists appeared faceless bureaucrats 'smelling of German beer' and concerned only with petty economic gains, to most Socialists the CNT appeared a collection of gun-toting vegetarians, bred on Nietzsche rather than Marx. In 1936 the Socialist party and the UGT were distinguished from their European counterparts only by indulgence in revolutionary rhetoric, which alarmed English comrades like Hugh

Dalton. They were divided between reformist Social Democrats who were willing to co-operate with bourgeois parties and 'maximalists' prepared to use the language of social revolution, if unprepared to implement it. By the end of the Civil War, after a bitter struggle, it was the Social Democrat tradition which triumphed. The 'maximalist' of 1936, the autodidact plasterer Largo Caballero, was relegated to official obscurity, replaced by the respectable physiologist Negrín. Largo Caballero had been ousted by Prieto, his bitter enemy in the party, in alliance with the bourgeois Republicans and the Communists.

The sudden rise to power and influence of the Communist party during the Civil War changed the political landscape of Republican Spain. In 1931 the party was a minute, ill-led faction; by 1939 it appeared to its enemies to be controlling the military and political destinies of the Republic. This was seen not as the reward of superior organisation and dedication, but as the consequence of a subtle tactic of infiltration combined with the activities of Soviet-dominated secret police, ruthless in the elimination of the party's political enemies and creating, in Orwell's words, a 'horrible atmosphere of suspicion and hatred'.

These activities, added to the assassinations in the Republican zone in the early days of the war, were used by the Nationalist propaganda machine not merely to counter accusations of a Nationalist White Terror, but to paint a picture of Spanish democracy as a tyranny of godless 'red' energumens. Communist influence handed to Franco a philosophy of history that he was to exploit until he died. The democratic Republic, by an inevitable and irreversible process, had fallen into the hands of a party dominated by a foreign power, the Soviet Union. After 1939 anti-Communism became the *raison d'être* of Francoism, the staple diet handed out by a controlled press and educational system to a battered Spain.

Nor was it only the Nationalists who beat the anti-Communist drum. In exile the politicians whom the party had destroyed did not forgive or forget. It was the problem of co-operation with men tainted morally by their actions in the Civil War and by their unrepentant Stalinism after it that bedevilled all attempts at forming a united anti-Francoist front. Yet it was, as we shall see, the Communist party that was the most effective organisation in building up a clandestine opposition in Spain itself.[4] Moreover, by the 1970s the party had become something it never was in the Civil War when the characteristic recruit was the middle class professional attracted by the party's disciplined dedication and its anti-revolutionary stance. It had a solid working-class base and controlled the major trade union in Spain.

Chapter 1

Franco and the Legacy of the Civil War

On a sunny April day in 1939 the Nationalist troops entered Madrid. They found a city gaunt and semi-starving after nearly three years of civil war. From then until he died in November 1975, their commander-in-chief, who had been appointed Chief of the Government of the Spanish State by his fellow generals in September 1936, ruled Spain as Caudillo by the grace of God, as his coins announced, and as chief of state and head of government, prime minister and president all in one. What was an emergency wartime government became the foundation of the Spanish state. By two decrees (30 January 1938 and 8 August 1939) Franco gave himself the power to pass any law or decree he chose. He was a Hobbesian sovereign. As his constitutional lawyers defined his powers, he was a 'constituent dictator' the limits of whose powers were self-imposed; as he himself defined his responsibilities in the exercise of this dictatorship, these were to God and History.

What sort of man was General Franco? Like many authoritarian characters he was short, becoming rather podgy in his old age. He was born in 1892 in a modest home in the poor north-western province of Galicia, and his whole career had been spent in the infantry. He had made his name as a brave and exceptionally competent officer in the tough, guerrilla-like campaigns in Morocco where he served, with few breaks, between 1912 and 1925. A professional soldier, his promotions, won on the battlefield, made him at 33 the youngest general in Europe since Bonaparte. He was accustomed to command and his model of society was military. Soldiers, well commanded, obey; subjects well ruled do likewise. Civil disobedience was mutiny. In 1934 he organised the suppression of the miners of the Asturias as if they had been Berber hill tribesmen.

His view of Spanish society and its history can be summed up in one sentence. Great Spain, the Spain of the Catholic kings and their

vast American empire, had been destroyed by democratic parliamentarianism based on universal suffrage.[1] It was classic
nineteenth-century liberalism, in its Spanish.form, run, he held, by
freemasons (to the end of his life Franco remained obsessed by
freemasonry and could rage against it in 1974 as an all-powerful
worldwide conspiracy) and manipulated by selfish party politicians
that had presided over the 'disaster' of 1898. In that year the
United States overwhelmed Spain on land and sea and seized the
remnants of her colonial empire – Cuba, Puerto Rico and the
Philippines. It was this disaster that robbed Franco of his chosen
career: he wanted to enter the navy, but the cuts after 1898 robbed
him of the chance. Political parties had degraded Spain; they must
be destroyed for ever. In 1952 he declared, 'We hate political
parties'. The 'inorganic democracy' of universal suffrage and
political parties must be replaced by organic democracy based on a
corporative suffrage that would represent the 'true' interests of the
nation, neglected by party politicians who appealed to selfish
individual or class interests. He never changed his views. When in
1967 there was a discussion of 'political associations' as innocuous
means of expressing 'contrasts of opinion' within the regime,
Franco warned that 'if on the excuse of the contrast of opinions
what is being sought are political parties, let those who wish this
know clearly that they will *never* come'.[2] And within his lifetime
they did not. 'Liberal decadence' he repeated monotonously
throughout his life, must degenerate into Marxism.

The democratic Second Republic of 1931–6 represented the
culmination of this process of disintegration. Run by masons and
Marxists, it threatened in the summer of 1936 to hand over Spain to
Communists, and by failing to maintain public order it allowed the
government to be cowed by 'the street'. Hesitating and cautious –
the bolder spirits called him 'Miss Canary Island of
1936' – Franco finally committed himself to an armed rising
against the government of the Popular Front in the summer of
1936.

Here General Franco's views linked up with those of the
nineteenth-century officer corps and with the example of General
Primo de Rivera who had overthrown the parliamentary system by
a *pronunciamiento* in September 1923 and ruled Spain as an 'iron
surgeon' until 1930. The officer corps believed it owed allegiance to
the nation, not to any government. It was the duty of the officer
corps to interpret the national will, corrupted by the selfishness of
politicians. If a government betrayed the nation, if government
'fell into the gutter', then the army must save the nation. Passive
obedience to *any* government made military discipline mechanical

and degrading.³ The officer corps obeyed this higher duty to the nation when it rose against the Popular Front government on 18 July 1936, and let loose a civil war that lasted for thirty-two months until 1939.

'We did not win the regime we have today hypocritically with some votes,' Franco reminded Spaniards in 1962. 'We won it at the point of the bayonet and with the blood of our best people.' The political scientists and constitutional lawyers who decorated his regime subsequently added other legitimisations to that of victory in the Civil War. There was the legitimacy of performance – the maintenance of a 'social peace' which, it was held, brought unparalleled prosperity: the 'constituent dictatorship' of the forties became the 'dictatorship of development' in the Spain of the booming sixties. Already in a speech in December 1955 Franco asserted that his political system had presided over the 'rebirth of the nation'. There was endorsement by the sovereign nation of the power of Franco in the two referenda of 1947 and 1966 with their massive 'Yes' votes. Not least, Franco himself shared with Primo de Rivera and Fidel Castro what has been called 'the democracy of the public square' – the endorsement of the mass audiences felt directly by the dictator. He consistently claimed that the 'spontaneous' acclaim of organised crowds legitimised his rule. 'Valencia has said "yes" to my policies,' he confided to his cousin, 'and has given a true approbation of my leadership' (June 1962).⁴ Behind all lay the mystical powers of the charismatic leader, the providential saviour of Spain. This was a role Franco repeatedly claimed for himself. When he asked the country to ratify the Organic Law (radio speech 12 December 1966) he claimed sufficient title from 'the right of him who has saved a society': the precise role of the Weberian charismatic saviour.

Though this charismatic unction weakened with time, sustained by public adulation it never vanished. It was a curious charisma. Franco was an unimpressive public speaker with a squeaky voice. His private personality seemed ordinary; his court formal and boring. His recreations were shooting and fishing, to which he would devote weeks on end to the neglect of his official duties – Spain, he once said, was easy to govern. His habits were bourgeois – he was very much a family man – and traditionally pious.

Apart from the police apparatus he controlled, what then, was the secret of this ordinary man's extraordinary powers? He had that quality which Louis XIV possessed: those who came into his presence were frightened of him and subdued.

Power – and Franco could dismiss any of his political servants at will, unrestrained by feelings of gratitude for devoted service — breeds power. He was (until 1973) head of state and prime minister, carrying out formal duties like the reception of ambassadors and presiding over important cabinet meetings. He was *Jefe del Movimiento* — chief of the only political organisation in Spain — and *Generalisimo* — Supreme Commander of the Armed Forces. As he grew older he exercised his powers less directly and had no particular interest in the details of policy except when they concerned foreign affairs, public order and the army. He let his ministers formulate policy. When they became 'exhausted' he dismissed them. On 28 July 1966 General Muñoz Grandes, veteran of the Civil War and commander of the Blue Division in Russia, a grandee of the regime regarded by many as a possible successor to Franco, read that he had been relieved of his office as Vice-President of the Government in the morning issue of the Official Gazette.

This ruthlessness was a reflection of two qualities that to his adulators — and the personality cult of Franco in a subservient press was as excessive as that of Stalin — constituted his political genius: prudence and pragmatism. These qualities the Caudillo undoubtedly possessed. However, pragmatism and prudence can disguise political obstinacy and a penchant for procrastination, a refusal to face up to the solution of difficult problems by denying their existence. Political myopia was intensified by Franco's belief that domestic difficulties — student revolts and labour strikes in particular — were the work of minority groups inspired from abroad, a revival of the anti-Spain of masons and Marxists, supported by the Soviet Union, defeated in 1939. Like the stereotype of the 'anarchic' Spaniard, which he consistently used as the justification for authoritarianism and the denial of democratic rights, he manipulated another stereotype: that of a hostile world that obstinately refused to understand his regime and its achievements. Combined with an iron political nerve — when the United Nations was sending Spain to an international Coventry, Franco spent the day painting — this constant reference to the machinations of foreign devils was a recipe for political immobilism.

Franco's vision of himself as the saviour of Spain in a Crusade to rescue 'true' Spain from 'anti'-Spain and its foreign allies was to set its mark on the history of Spain for four decades. The most important legacy of the Civil War was the subsequent division of Spanish society into two camps: the victors (*vencedores*) and the vanquished (*vencidos*). The *vencedores* would rule and enjoy the fruits of power, the *vencidos* never. They had represented for the victors absolute evil. Serrano Suñer was the most intelligent politician in wartime Nationalist Spain. Dionisio Ridruejo, a close collaborator, tells us that 'his image of the two sides in the war was that of good against evil'. Hardly surprisingly, since his two brothers had been murdered in the early days of the war, a traumatic personal grief from which he never recovered, and which, since he himself escaped, seems to have left a sense of guilt.[5]

All this was emphasised by the terrible repressions of the 1940s when those who had sided with the Republic of the Popular Front were persecuted, tortured, killed or driven into exile. How could those in power after 1939 contemplate national reconciliation? Since they could only expect vengeance at the hands of the vanquished, the vanquished must be placed in perpetual ostracism. This was what in the 1940s was called 'el pacto de la sangre' ('the blood contract'), and it implied the exclusion of half of Spain from political life. If repentant Republicans were later welcomed as lost sheep, to the end of the regime no one who did not profess to share 'the ideals that gave birth to the Crusade' could serve the state.*

Obviously this Manichaean, absolutist division became weaker with time and was always softened by personal connection. But why did it persist so long? Firstly because Franco was determined that no one should forget the Civil War because it was his victory over 'anti-Spain' that legitimised his rule. For him the Manichaean vision never faded. When, in 1968, it was proposed that the ex-combatants of the Republic should get pensions as did the Nationalists, to Franco the mere suggestion was an outrage ('You can't combine a glorious army [i.e. his own] with the scum of the Spanish population.')

Not only Franco himself, but the right in general, was determined to keep the divisions of the Civil War alive in Spanish society. Victory in 1939 was their passport to power and influence; more than that, its enthusiasms remained the essential centre of their emotional being. Western historians have given particular emphasis to the mobilisation of political enthusiasm on the Republican side in the Civil War because they sympathise with it. Yet Nationalist Spain had its own all-pervading wartime mystique that spilled over into the 1940s and was kept alive by organisations of Civil War combatants. To take away the memory of this

---

*Agustín de Foxá, whose most famous novel was a description of the prison practices of the Communists, wrote. 'It is logical that we hate them (the defeated Reds), it is instinctive, it is telluric; our desire for reprisals is part of the drama of the planet'. *Telúrico* was typical of the inflated prose of the victors.

emotional experience from the veterans of the Civil War was to
make their lives meaningless. Girón, a veteran Falangist and for
many years Minister of Labour, declared that the memory of the
dead of the Civil War was not to be 'devoured with impunity by
pigs'.[6]

Chapter 2

Francoism

Francoism was more than the personal rule of a dictator. He gave his name to a political and social system much more complex and adaptable than his opponents would admit.[1] If the negative element was the exclusion of those who did not share the ideals of the Crusade, the positive side was the articulation in changing forms within the system of the conservative interests which the monarchy had protected and which the Republic of 1931–6 had threatened. While to the outside world and to the opposition Francoism appeared a simple monolith resting on police repression it was, like most authoritarian systems, a Byzantine structure composed of the political groups – they have been called 'clans' or 'families' – that accepted the legitimacy of the dictator's rule.

We must now attempt to sketch the complex political map of Francoism, the structure of the political families, their feuds and cross-alliances, a map made even more complex by the possibility of allegiance to two families. We must then briefly examine the political chemistry by which Franco balanced the families against one another in his governments.

(a)
The institutionalised families

Western journalists in the 1940s and 1950s were fond of referring to the 'three pillars of the Regime': the Nationalist army, the Falange and the church. These were the institutionalised families of the regime, the victors of the Civil War.

(i) The army

In political terms the Spanish army is its officer corps, particularly its senior officers. Only a *minority* of senior officers joined the military rising of 18 July against the Republic' of the Popular Front.[2] But most of those officers who joined the Nationalists and 'provisional lieutenants' who were recruited during the war were to be the most consistent bearers of the mystique of the Crusade. Until the late 1970s senior officers were Civil War veterans or those recruited in the immediate postwar years. The younger the officer, the less likely he is to be moulded by the experiences of the Civil War. Whereas the officers of 1939 were civilian volunteers recruited in an atmosphere of political enthusiasm for the Crusade and its ideals, the younger officers are professionals recruited largely from army families, particularly the sons of non-commissioned officers.[3]

The historic problem of the Spanish army has been an overmanned officer corps. Franco professed the desire to create a small professional army; but he could not return the volunteers of the war to civilian life at a time when there was little possibility of finding them jobs. Given this burden of superfluous officers in a poor economy, promotion prospects were dim, pay was low and the sheer expenditure on officers' pay (80 per cent of the army budget) prevented proper investment in the modernisation of equipment.* Officers were a prestigious rather than an exceptionally privileged class, with the generals as the grandees of the regime often moving into lucrative posts in the public sector. With new openings in civilian life in the 1960s the army lost much of the attractiveness it once possessed as a career in an impoverished country: between 1964 and 1970 the entrants as cadets in the Sandhurst of Spain (the Academia General) dropped by two-thirds. After five years of hard training a lieutenant earns, with recent pay increases, £170 a month.

To a historian it is somewhat of a paradox that those conditions (bad pay and promotion prospects) which in the nineteenth century generated a series of military revolts, have had only the most feeble of reverberations since 1939. In the 1970s a small, clandestine group of young officers organised the *Unión Democrática Militar* (UDM). They wished to detach the army from its alliance with Francoism, and in their propaganda played on what might be called trade union issues – bad pay, poor promotion, 'neglect' and lack of 'respect' in civilian society. But their influence was minimal.[4] Franco kept the generals loyal, not least by well paid posts in the state agencies and private companies; he was troubled by monarchist military frondeurs and occasionally irritated by the

---

*The relatively low expenditure on the army belies the notion of a privileged sector: in 1966 a British soldier cost $12,763 per annum; a Spanish soldier $1,783. Equipment improved dramatically with the Base Agreement of 1953 and US loans; but it remained below European standards. Contacts between US and Spanish officers brought home the shortcomings of the Spanish army's modern weapons etc.

ambitious; they were summarily sacked or won over by emotional appeals to common memories of the Civil War. But most generals and senior officers needed neither punishment nor blandishments; they simply shared Franco's vision of Spanish society. A recent opinion survey shows that cadets − and most of those who do not come from army homes come from the conservative country-side − feel strongly about the 'unity of Spain', and that words like *patria* are not for them mere rhetorical creations; they dislike 'irreligion' and 'pornography'.

The army remained to the end the ultimate guarantor of the regime's fulfilling its task as set out in the Organic Law of the State − 'the defence of the institutional order'. The services were permanently represented by at least three generals or admirals in the government, and the combined voice of the service ministers could be decisive in a divided cabinet on issues of public order.[5] Jurisdiction over political offences, especially when states of emergency were declared, was extensive; military courts tried terrorists (e.g. the Burgos Trials of 1970). Its ideological purity was carefully watched over by security agencies up to 1975. Periodicals like the extreme right-wing *Fuerza Nueva* appeared in officers' messes; to subscribe to a left-wing periodical meant a court martial. In 1973 a colonel was dismissed for a favourable review of Gironella's book on the Civil War, and so were four cadets for possessing 'seditious books' − all of which had been published in Spain![6]

The army, in these conditions, could scarcely be a supporter of any progressive 'opening' of the regime; even less could it share the belief of the UDM that the only way to save the army in the eyes of the 'people' was to detach it from the regime. Some few senior officers disliked its police functions under Francoism, 'which might estrange it from the people'.[7] But the vast majority shared their commander-in-chief's hatred of Communists, masons and separatists and were tougher than their Commander-in-Chief himself on questions of public order. During Franco's lifetime the army on occasion brought pressure on the government to take a firmer line against student rebels and Basque terrorists.[8] After his death, prominent generals opposed what they regarded as 'unconstitutional' steps towards democracy; if it were necessary they declared their readiness to fight another civil war to ensure that 'Francoism continues after Franco, that it lasts for centuries'.[9] But the 'blue generals', the hard-liners like Iniesta and García Rebull, were increasingly isolated; like reactionary bishops they were, in any case, doomed to disappear through age. Generals like Díez Alegría and Gutiérrez Mellado did not see their function as that of bolstering up Francoism at all costs. If not liberals, they were neutral professionals.

The best brains in the army, the professional elite of the General Staff, wanted not counter-revolution, but the modernisation of a poorly equipped army. One such reformer, Díez Alegría, declared in 1974, 'I'm not much of a politician and don't understand much about politics and don't want to understand about politics'. This was, perhaps, the protective covering of a suspect liberal; but under Franco *direct* intervention of generals in politics meant the end of a career. The monarchist and Falangist frondeurs of the forties found this out to their cost, and as late as 1971 the Captain-General of Granada was summarily dismissed for criticising governmental corruption, just as the 'radio general' of the Civil War, Queipo de Llano, had been thrust into promotional oblivion for a criticism of a political appointment.[10] For any soldier the best course of action is to be on the side of the government − as most generals were in 1936. More important, in the years after Franco's death it was clear that the King, its new commander-in-chief, was set on dismantling Francoism. To resist was, in these conditions, to rebel.

(ii) The Falange

In the political iconography of the 1940s and 1950s, beside the army appeared the uniformed Falangists. The founder and first leader of the Falange was José Antonio Primo de Rivera, son of the dictator. Executed by the Republicans in November 1936 he became the 'absent one' of the movement, the quasi-sanctified proto-martyr whose memory was preserved by inscriptions on every church wall of postwar Spain.

In its origins a youth movement, the Falange preached a blend of traditional patriotism and modern authoritarianism. Its aim was to create a national Socialist state, avoiding the pitfalls of bourgeois capitalism and Marxist socialism, the first of which created the class struggle which the other exploited. 'Our state,' wrote José Antonio 'will make the class struggle impossible in that all those who co-operate in the processes of production constitute in it an organic whole.' The 'vertical unions' of national syndicalism would 'harmonise' the conflicts between workers and employers endemic to liberal, capitalist democracy. Falangism constantly harped on 'national revolution' in the regenerationist tradition: it would nationalise the banks and embark on land reform. It was the rhetoric of this national revolution which attracted youthful spirits like the poet Dionisio Ridruejo, academics like Tovar and Laín Entralgo, all of whom were to reject an illiberal dictatorship based on the restoration to power and influence of conservative Spain.

Finally, the Falange held out to Spaniards an imperialist dream: the restoration of Spanish greatness by territorial expansion in North Africa and, above all, the recovery of Gibraltar.

If the Falange is defined as a party owing some allegiance to the ideas of its founder, then it certainly was not the exclusive victor in the post-Civil War state. Even in the years of its greatest influence, when photographs of its notables and rallies filled the press and the cinema screens, it was, in Ricardo de la Cierva's phrase, a 'paper tiger'.

In Germany the head of the party took over the state; in Spain the head of the state, Franco, took over the party. This he did by imposing 'from above' the Decree of Unification of April 1937. By enlarging the party to include Carlists, all army officers and civil servants, he destroyed its identity by diffusion and watered down its social radicalism. Unification left him in undisputed control of what was now known as the Movement. The leader of the 'old shirts', the radical populist wing of Falangism, Manuel Hedilla, was imprisoned. He became the forgotten man of Francoist Spain. 'Franco,' he used to say, 'killed the Falange in 1937. One can't revive a corpse.' Shortly afterwards Dionisio Ridruejo made a brave but forlorn attempt to restore the primacy of the party over the government. He was opposed by the conservatives, supported by Franco and defeated after what must have been one of the most violent scenes in modern Spanish political history.[11] With the appointment of Arrese as Secretary-General of the Movement (May 1941) the process of domestication and subordination was completed with the creation of the 'Francoist Falange'.

In June 1936 José Antonio had prophesied the defeat of the Falange ideals by 'a mediocre conservative bourgeoisie'. In the very first months of the war the Italian ambassador to Franco's court at Salamanca realised that Falangist dreams of a Nationalist social revolution would not be easily accommodated in the coalition of bourgeois interests which supported the Nationalist cause. 'All the parties [other than the Falange] that supported Franco have a bourgeois base'; they had no desire to win over the working class for the Nationalist state — the ambition of José Antonio and his follower Hedilla — but to use the state and the Falangist-sponsored vertical unions to keep the workers in their place. In 1958 Franco's cousin remarked that with the Falange in power, social injustice could have been remedied more energetically. 'That has not been possible,' replied Franco, 'because governments must contain a representation of the forces that contributed to victory', and of these forces the Falange was but a part.[12] Twenty years later Girón could lament the betrayal of the revolution 'by the hidden forces of an unpatriotic and selfish oligarchy'.

Spain never became the totalitarian imperial state of Falangist dreams: such a state depended on the triumph of Hitler's New Order in Europe, an order doomed by 1943. Spain never became a one-party state and all attempts by Falangists to create such a state failed. In 1940 Merino saw that to dominate the state the Falange must become a genuine mass party; once it was (which it never became), it could claim 'all power in our hands'.[13] Serrano Suñer's attempt in the forties to turn the Junta Política of the Falangist movement into the central directing council of the state was beaten out of court by his conservative monarchist enemies. So were Arrese's more modest plans in 1956.[14]

Thus the Falange neither triumphed as a mass party nor became the axis of a one-party state. With the Treasury in the hands of its political enemies it could not even raise the money from a poor economy to finance the attenuated version of the Falangist 'revolution' — an authoritarian welfare state. It did not, as the German party succeeded in doing, create a powerful party administration parallel to that of the state. This was because neither Franco nor the conservative groups that had supported him in the Civil War wanted such a party. They preferred the rule of one man to the rule of a party. It was this combination of personal dictatorship and obscurantist conservatism that led Dionisio Ridruejo to resign all his posts in July 1942; in his letter to Franco he declared the 'authentic' Falange to be dead, victim of the 'conservative clans', its corpse surviving as 'a label for a monstrous deception that deceives no one'.[15]

'Domesticated' by Arrese the Falange did not die a sudden death; Franco still attributed to it an important political role.[16] But as a *party* increasingly it faded away into the wider, vaguer Movement. Up to the sixties the Movement was still identifiable with residual Falangism: with Solís as Secretary-General after 1957 the Movement became a 'communion' of all Spaniards who accepted, or feigned acceptance of, its Principles. These Principles were still Falangist but the party of 'the national syndicalist state' lost its identity in what was now declared to be 'a Catholic, social and representative monarchy'. The Falange was but one family, one limb in the communion, if at times a protrusile one; its blue shirt vanished, replaced by the white uniform of the Movement.

The elements which entered the Movement in the sixties with Solís were Falangists of a new type: bureaucrats and career civil servants who had made their 'oppositions',[17] vastly removed from the old thunderer Girón. They saw the necessity of what Solís called 'political development' through political associations which, within the limits of the spirit and laws of Francoism, might, by giving some outlet to public opinion, save the regime and its personnel. Whereas old Falangists and the radical Falangist youth had been hostile to the monarchy, this new generation accepted it provided it accepted inorganic democracy and preserved the syndical organisation that was the last bastion of Falangism. Solís was even ready to reform the syndicates, conceding a separation of workers' and employers' unions and the right to strike. Solís and his allies were men of the Movement, modernisers after their fashion. Girón and Arrese remained unreconstructed Falangists who were to find their ultimate resting-place in the bunker of the 1970s; members of an old-fashioned family whose cries of rage were useful to those who wished to excuse a failure to 'open' the political system by political reform. If the Falange had vanished, individual Falangists were still respected members of the political establishment, powerful enough to bring about the fall of a reformist minister.[18]

Throughout the last years of Francoism the Movement and its Principles acted in a negative rather than a positive sense. All ministers and public officials had to accept its Principles, with greater or lesser degrees of enthusiasm. Not many of Franco's ministers were 'authentic' Falangists. 'Fraga,' wrote Romero, 'is as much a Falangist as I am Bishop of Constantinople.' 'We have seen for years,' wrote one embittered enthusiast, 'how the merits of the Falange have served to hoist to power men who have nothing in common with Falangism but the shirt with which they cover their lack of security and convictions; the same Falangist shirt that they abandon later when it is the slightest impediment to their ambitions.'[19] Nevertheless, no competing ideology or organisation, except for the Catholic church, could enjoy official favour. When political associations were debated in the sixties, the 'contrast of opinions', which the Fundamental Laws allowed, had to be contained within and disciplined by the Movement: it was the 'box office' of its National Council which vetted the entrance of even anodyne pressure groups into the political arena.

The consolation prize, given to the Falange for the loss of its 'revolution', was the control of the official trade unions. But this was a useless gift (except to the 34,000 bureaucrats it employed), given the failure to create a parallel Falangist corporatist state.

Without a Falangist state Falangist syndicates became bureaucratic shells, in the long run useless to the workers. 'In so far as there is no possibility of a syndicalist state with all its consequences,' admitted the Falangist lawyer Roberto Reyes, 'you must admit syndicalist pluralism [i.e. the end of the monopoly of the official syndicates] because there is no alternative but to admit it.'[20] But this admission was reluctant and late. The official syndicates had frowned on the Catholic syndicalism of the late fifties. But by the sixties *de facto* syndical pluralism came with the Communist-dominated Comisiones Obreras to be followed by USO, which incorporated some of the more radical elements from the Catholic Unionism of the fifties, and the revival of the old Socialist UGT. If a single official union was intended to be one of the permanent legacies of the victory of 1939, after a long death agony, it perished.

By the time Franco died there was little left of the Falange of the Civil War. Its organisation, like its signs at the entry to every village, was rusty. Its original radical ideology had faded, like the inscriptions commemorating its founder on church walls. There was no longer one Falange. For many, membership was merely the formal requirement for entry into the political elite. The Falange of Solís was composed of young, ambitious syndical bureaucrats. Some, like Cantarero del Castillo, tried to revive the social ideals which had appealed to him as a young man in a 'Social Democratic' party within the regime. The young Falangist idealists of the seventies sought to rescue the revolution that had been 'pending' for forty years and which would never take place in the framework of Francoism by reviving the memory and programme of José Antonio: in the elections of 1977 they appeared strumming guitars to songs about agrarian reform. Their meetings were broken up by the followers of the ageing militants who had retired into the bleak authoritarianism of the 'bunker'. None of those who claimed direct descent from the founder gained a seat in the first general election of the new democracy.

(iii) The Catholic church

The Catholic church was much more representative of the coalition of groups in the Nationalist cause than the Falange. Apart from some Basque priests the church, with its priests and nuns slaughtered, had no alternative but to support Franco. It was the blessing of the church, confirmed in the Concordat of 1953, not the ideology of the Falange, that sanctioned – almost sancti- fied – Franco's rule to the average Spaniard in the 1940s and after. These were the years of so-called 'national Catholicism'.

Franco gave something very important in return for this blessing: the control over the intellectual life of Spain, above all control over the secondary education of the middle and upper classes lost during the Second Republic.[21] It was a tragedy that at the very time the church captured the control of education it was going through a period of 'integrist' reaction and was almost completely cut off

from the main currents in Catholic Europe.[22] Just as Falangists like
Dionisio Ridruejo, who had written the words of the Falangist
anthem, turned against the fossilised and bureaucratised Falangism
of Francoism, so Catholic thinkers like the philosopher-sociologist
Aranguren and others deplored the return of the Spanish church to
the philosophy of Menéndez y Pelayo, defender of Spain as the
'hammer of heretics' during the Counter-Reformation. Menéndez
y Pelayo was the intellectual giant of Nationalist Spain.[23]

The church was part of the state. Bishops sat in the Cortes and
the Council of the Realm. Laws must conform to Catholic
dogma – an embarrassment once the Vatican favoured the rights
of national minorities and free trade unionism. Divorce was
impossible, adultery a crime. The church was not only integrated in
the regime: two organisations, the ACNP and the Opus Dei, were
concerned in penetrating and influencing it.

The ACNP (*Asociación Católica Nacional de Propagandistas*)
was a lay Catholic association founded in 1909, with the
encouragement of the Vatican and the financial support of the
Basque industrialists. To the Jesuit Father Ayala, who inspired the
movement, its aims were clear: 'to endow Spain with an elite
(*valores selectos*) . . . to train men for public life.'[24] Wherever
power lay in society, it was the duty of *propagandistas* to master it:
politics, education, the press, the world of business, the elite of the
working class. It claimed it was not a party, in that its members
acted individually; but it had a clear sense of political mission. If
Catholics did not enter politics, Father Ayala maintained, then
politics would enter and destroy the church.

Its support of Franco in the early years was absolute: he was
'homo missu a Deo cui nomen erat Franciscus'; it was the *duty* of
Catholics to support a regime that had saved the church from
destruction. After 1945 the men of ACNP and their ideas began to
replace Falangism as the main coherent force in the government,
dominating foreign affairs and education. It was the
propagandistas, with their contacts with European Catholicism,
who gave Franco the beginnings of international respectability; it
was the *propagandistas* who negotiated the Concordat of 1953.

The direct influence of *propagandistas* in government in its turn
was replaced by that of the Opus Dei. To most Spaniards the Opus
Dei was a more sinister body than the ACNP; secretive about its
operations (what it called 'discretion'), its members sworn to obedience, it could be presented as a form of 'white' free masonry, a
holy mafia of civilian monks.[25] This lay order (it was recognised by
the Vatican as a secular institute in 1947) was the brainchild of
an energetic Aragonese priest, José Maria Escrivá (b. 1902). No

intellectual himself, he was determined to fight liberal 'atheist' intellectuals and, by destroying their influence, rechristianise Spain.

Escrivá's writings reveal an elitism which reached Nietzschean proportions and combine traditional Catholicism with a banal and Americanised version of success,[26] and it is exceedingly hard to imagine how this Samuel Smiles of the Catholic world had such great influence over intelligent men. The lay members of the order *must* use their individual talents to reach positions of influence. Its attraction for new recruits was that those who had reached such positions could give a helping hand. Between 1939 and 1947 it set out to 'conquer' the universities, an over-ambitious project which promoted dubious professors and met with resistance.[27] It was a sign of its failure to 'conquer' the state universities that it was forced to found a university of its own in Navarre.

It was the subsequent advance of the Opus in the world of business, in the professions and in government that was, in the sixties and seventies, to attract most attention, because it was more successful. From 1951 its share of cabinet posts increased steadily. This 'politicisation' of the institution was not to the liking of the Vatican. Calvo Serer, as energetic a man as Escrivá himself, became the ideologue of the Opus. For Calvo Serer, Spain under Franco had returned to its true intellectual moorings, lost in the eighteenth-century Enlightenment and the individualistic liberalism of the nineteenth century. But Calvo Serer's 'third force' monarchism had no attractions for Franco. Serer was in touch with the Caudillo's *bête noire*, Don Juan, even if his vision of a traditional, Catholic anti-parliamentary monarchy was unaccept- able to the Pretender; his attacks on Falangists as a gang of, opportunists were unpalatable to Franco.[28] The men of the Opus Dei were increasingly 'technocrats' like López Rodó, proponents of rapid – capitalist – growth and of the 'neutralisation' of politics through prosperity.

The ACNP and the Opus were rivals with common characteristics. Both rejected the accusation that they were political parties or pressure groups engaged in a concerted, planned operation to gain influence in high places. 'I belong to Opus Dei,' López Rodó was apt to repeat, 'as I belong to the Royal Madrid Tennis Club, which has nothing to do with my political actions.'[29] Both are involved in the periodical press and publishing: the ACNP has a daily, *Ya*; the Opus, magazines and a publishing house. Both distrusted and were distrusted by Falangists whose hold on power they weakened. Both started as enthusiastic supporters of Franco and both developed an 'oppositional' wing more or less tolerated by the regime. By the 1960s Ruiz Giménez, the *propagandista* whom Franco had considered his most docile minister, was calling himself 'more of a Social Democrat than a Christian Democrat' and had become the leading spirit of the only critical magazine of the time, *Cuadernos para el Diálogo*. Calvo Serer likewise moved from qualified disgrace into open opposition and exile; but he was considered an eccentric. The Opus Dei never established genuine contacts with the opposition.

Thus by the 1970s both the ACNP and to a markedly lesser degree the Opus were divided between reformists who wanted to 'open' the regime and rigid conservatives, a development which cynical critics attributed to a desire to be on the winning side should Francoism disintegrate. Both professed concern for the working classes but both were essentially 'parties' of the grand bourgeoisie – the Opus more than the ACNP which kept a wing influenced by advanced Christian Democrat thought and attractive to the young. The ACNP carried on the Catholic corporatist tradition which could be, somewhat uneasily, incorporated into the syndical organisation of the regime where 'vertical unions' were intended to end the 'sterile' war between capital and labour by harmonious co-operation in the interests of higher production. The labour economics of the Opus appeared more modern and have been castigated as a defence of neo-capitalism. Employers must accept collective bargaining in return for productivity agreements; workers must accept that higher production meant, in the end, a larger national cake to be cut up.

When the influence of the ACNP weakened in 1956, and with the economic boom of the sixties, it was the Opus which emerged as the 'organised' Catholic support of Francoism, backed, as its members were, by the most trusted of Franco's ministers – Admiral Carrero Blanco. The Opus was more 'dynamic' than the ACNP and its attractions for the ambitious more obvious; but in the end, in politics, as in the campaign to conquer the university, it overplayed its hand. Its fall from political grace in 1974 was resounding, and much of its former influence was inherited by the *propagandistas*. They reappeared in influential posts in the cabinet of Adolfo Suárez in 1976.

(b)
The political families

We have studied briefly what might be called the original institutional families of the regime – the army, the Falange and the church. If the remaining families of the political jigsaw of

Francoism are less clearly defined, their influence was, at times, as great. All were conservative.

(i) The integral Francoists

The purest ingredient of the regime was what have been called the 'integral Francoists'. Of all the families, the loyalty of the integral Francoists was unconditional and absolute: they were the purest authoritarians of the system and their representative was Admiral Carrero Blanco, Franco's *alter ego*, his confidant and ultimately his first Prime Minister. 'I am a man totally identified with the political achievements of General Franco . . . my loyalty to his person and work is absolute.'[30] For him the political system was immutable and eternal and he professed readiness to use the army to ensure its permanence.

Two other military companions of Franco were totally committed to his leadership. In 1957 General Alonso Vega became Minister of the Interior; now in his seventies, he had been a fellow pupil of Franco at the Military Academy of Toledo, and in command of the Civil Guard. The only person, outside his family, to address his *Generalisimo* with the familiar 'tu', he shared his master's bleak conception of public order; political opposition was the civilian equivalent of mutiny. From 1951 to 1962 Arias Salgado was, as Minister of Information, the ultimate censor of Spanish intellectual life; no man bears a greater responsibility for the stultification of Spanish culture. A distant relative of Franco who had been an electrical goods salesman on the outbreak of the Civil War, he personified that uncritical loyalty which his master valued in his servants. 'He was,' in the words of a newspaperman who suffered under him, 'a perfect doormat . . . He was certain that God had chosen Franco (and Franco had chosen him) to safeguard Spain from Communism, Republicans, Socialism, Protestantism, Masonry, pornography and "liberalism".'[31] For him the Civil War never ended; the enemies were at the gate in 1962 as they had been in 1936.

It was undoubtedly this conception of the necessity of the continuing Crusade against anti-Spain that provided the emotional anchor in the political theory of the integral Francoists. The hard core of integral Francoism was recruited from wartime officers organised in the Brotherhood of Ex-Soldiers. They were reinforced by civilians who served the regime in its early years, filling the posts of those who had been purged. By 1975 many of them were elderly, but still powerful, the defenders of a vanished epoch.

(ii) The monarchists

The monarchists had, since the 1830s, been divided between

supporters of the constitutional monarchy, the last representative of which was Alfonso XIII (who left Spain when the Republic was declared in April 1931), and the Carlists to whom the 'liberal' parliamentary monarchy of Alfonso's line was anathema, the invention of atheists and masons, a mechanistic 'inorganic' contrivance at the mercy of party politics, the government of 'a half plus one' in the Chamber. Both Carlists and Alfonsists wanted a restoration and had supported Franco in the Civil War as a prospective Spanish General Monck for their respective candidates to the throne. Some Carlists – like the aristocratic Conde de Rodezno who had brought Navarre and its *requetés* into the Crusade, and who had been instrumental, in 1937, in forcing unification from above on the movement's *enragés* – were ready to co-operate with the supporters of Don Juan, Count of Barcelona, the son of Alfonso XIII; others remained faithful to the true dynasty represented by the heirs of Don Carlos, the original Carlist pretender of the 1830s.

Although they were conservative and strongly represented in the army, the loyalty of the monarchist clans was not absolute. General Kindelán, head of the Nationalist air force, was a committed monarchist who had engineered Franco's rise to supreme power. Once it became clear that Franco had no intention of restoring the monarchy he became a monarchist frondeur. General Aranda, hero of the Nationalist defence of Oviedo in the early days of the Civil War, became involved in a complicated series of anti-Franco conspiracies which entailed co-operation between the monarchists and the left-wing opposition. None of these plots came to anything. Both Aranda and Kindelán became forgotten men. Both spoke to R.C. in critical terms of Franco and his governments.

Though Franco declared Spain a kingdom in 1947, he showed no signs of restoring the monarchy in the person of a king. As a consequence the monarchists split. They were split both ideologically and tactically. The more liberal wished to return to a constitutional, parliamentary monarchy incompatible with the Principles of the Movement and 'organic' democracy. The more reactionary monarchists in the integrist tradition wanted a monarchy based on the preservation of the political structure of Francoism. The political theorist of this solution was the Opus Dei intellectual, Calvo Serer.*

---

*There were subdivisions in these two main groups reflected in the political mosaic of Don Juan's private council. Don Juan found great difficulty in making up his mind. For a good illustration of how his court and advisers worked see the diary of General Martínez Campos in *Nueva Historia*, no. 1 (February 1977), pp. 17-23.

This division was reflected in political tactics. There were the 'collaborationists' who believed that the only chance of a restoration was to seek it at Franco's hands whenever he chose to step down as Head of State; the 'liberal' intransigents saw that a restoration at the hands of Franco would sully the monarchy and, by making it a mere inheritor of Francoism, compromise its future as a 'monarchy of reconciliation' which would end the divisions inherited from the Civil War.

The monarchist collaborationists (their daily paper *ABC* was uncompromisingly monarchist and Francoist) became one of the main social props of the regime. Most of them favoured the replacement of Don Juan by his son, Juan Carlos, whom the *Juanistas* considered a mere creature and creation of Franco. Those monarchists who wished to turn Don Juan into the 'king of all Spaniards', an alternative to and not a continuator of Francoism, became a centre of the internal democratic opposition to Franco. Don Juan veered unsteadily between his collaborationist advisers and the 'democratic' monarchists; in the end he made a muddled compromise with the Caudillo, to the 'democratic' monarchists a tremendous and irredeemable error.[32]

The Carlists received little in the way of political reward; the Ministry of Justice until the sixties seemed a small return for the Carlist blood shed in the Civil War. The forced fusion of the Carlists and Falangists of 1937, as the intransigent Carlist leader Fal Conde bitterly remarked, left the movement 'damn all'. The old Carlists retired to their tents in Navarre where they nursed a profound sense of betrayal; more than ever before Carlism, which had begun in the 1830s as the revolt of a traditional rural society against the 'liberal' cities, seemed out of place in the industrialised Spain of the sixties. Franco never regarded the old pretender, Don Javier, as a serious candidate for a future throne. The new pretender, Carlos Hugo, moved unexpectedly and rapidly to the left and declared himself a socialist.[33] The Carlists, like the Alfonsists, had early developed a collaborationist wing, including influential figures like Esteban Bilbao and the Oriol family.* The Carlist annual rally at Montejurra became a ritual clash with the police and the Carlists who had flung in their lot with Franco.

The main function of the monarchists in the system was to resist the political preponderance of the Falange. It was the Carlist Esteban Bilbao who broke the ambitious plans of Serrano Suñer for a 'totalitarian' state; as President of the Cortes, the 'old fox'

---

*While Don Juan was still a possible contender, the Oriols attempted co-operation with the Alfonsists: the attempt at common action failed as it so often had in the past.

remained a pillar of the establishment. For the Alfonsist Pedro Saínz Rodriguéz, 'the totalitarian state with its single party is the worst of all political formulas', arbitrary and immoral.[34] Whereas the monarchists wanted a restoration, committed Falangists preferred a regency or even a republic to a conservative monarchy. Clashes between monarchists and Falangists were one of the few visible signs of political vitality in the early years: in 1942 a Falangist enthusiast threw a bomb at the monarchist General Varela. Much as Franco disliked these clashes he could play off the mutual hatred of Falangists and monarchists against each other, thus weakening both.

Given that the monarchists commanded the sort of social influence that impressed Franco, his dealings with them inspire one with a respect for his qualities as a politician. He appeared to have achieved everything he wanted: the restoration of a monarchy faithful to the Principles of the Movement. Juan Carlos swore fidelity to Franco and to the Principles of the Movement when he was declared heir to the throne in 1969.[35] With *revanchistes* like Gil Robles and liberals like Satrústegui without influence, and Calvo Serer, who had deserted the integrist tradition for a democratic monarchy, left to his tireless intrigues in exile, the monarchy looked safely in the hands of men whom the Caudillo could trust: Carrero Blanco and his *éminence grise* López Rodó who had been the political engineers of the 'Juan Carlos solution'. Franco remained in place: Head of State of a monarchy without a king.

(iii) The technocrats and the professionals

'Francoist' monarchists shaded off into a group that has been called the 'technocrats'. They came to the fore in the 1960s and many of them were associated with the Opus Dei. Their central creed was that the prosperity that economic development could bring would be a sufficient surrogate for ideological politics and that development could be best fostered within a modernised authoritarian system. For López Rodó, the technocrat *par excellence*, 'politics [was] the art of solving one problem without creating another' and the state 'the promoter of *bienestar*' (well-being), not the liberal 'gamekeeper state' of the nineteenth century.[36] But the most blatant advocate of prosperity as a substitute for politics was Fernández de la Mora, prophet of the end of ideology: for him the apathy of a prosperous consumer society was a sign of political health.[37]

The last family was that of the professionals, above all the higher civil servants. To understand their importance we must go back to the presuppositions of Franco's political theory. His aim − his obsession – was to 'destroy the nineteenth century'; that is, parliamentary liberalism based on 'inorganic suffrage' and a party system. Destroy the liberal political heritage he did; but he did not destroy the proudest *administrative* creation of nineteenth-century liberalism – a civil service and professional class based on *oposiciones*, the competitive entrance examinations that dominated the life of any ambitious young man. This does not mean that the civil service was a strong, unified structure: it was split up into *cuerpos*, each with its particular and competitive interests and pay structure.[38] It was the preserve of the 'traditional' middle class, and it was rather as a social group that instinctively understood its common interests than as an institution that it was influential.

With the parties and political responsibility destroyed, the regime was increasingly dominated by civil servants, especially university professors who were a part of the civil service. The most typical representative of this class was Fraga Iribarne, the best examinee in Spanish history. Coming from a relatively modest background in the poor province of Galicia, he made a brilliant career as a professor. Immensely industrious, he acquired the tough pragmatism of the self-made man. The grip of the civil service clan on political life was twofold. They advised ministers who had no independent political base and whose tenure of office was temporary. The civil service – apart from the directors-general who were 'political' appointees – was permanent and tenacious of its privileges. Civil servants themselves could serve as ministers. The regime's capacity to absorb ambitious professionals was one of the secrets of its political survival.[39]

This assemblage of disparate and divergent families constituted a highly successful ruling class. What common factors kept them together in the ministerial business for forty years? A shared vision of the necessity for the rising of 1936, a distrust of political systems based on ideologies – and by this was meant ideologies of the left – an authoritarian temperament, loyalty to Franco, Catholicism in both public and private life; all these created a shared mentality, a style that, for those who professed a profound distaste for ideologues, would seem to constitute an ideology *sui generis*.

There was, ambition apart, in the end a stronger bond: a common social origin, a common intellectual apprenticeship in the university. Once the survivors of the 'Blue Epoch' – the early years of militarism, Falangism and national Catholicism – had been thinned out, Franco's ministers came increasingly from the preserves of the 'traditional' middle class: the civil service, the university and the professions, especially the law. The traditional middle class was strengthened by the representatives of the burgeoning capitalism of the 1960s. Bright young men, trained as lawyers, went from business into government and from government back into business. It is an indication of the essential conservatism of the regime that it was this social and intellectual elite that had governed Spain under the monarchy.[40]

(c)
The system in operation: governments 1938–73

The secret of Franco's power lay in his manipulation of the political families (and for this purpose we must include the Falange, the army and the representatives of the church). No one family was given a monopoly of power; no one clan was permanently excluded from office. He chose his ministers as head of state and presided over cabinet meetings as prime minister. Although, as he grew more addicted to hunting and fishing, he took little part in the detailed formulation of policy – public order and foreign policy apart – he was the final arbiter.

'Hour after hour the sessions roll on; while some ministers step outside to stretch their legs, Franco himself has never been known to quit a Cabinet session. This is how he rules Spain. From start to finish he remains imperturbably in his place, attentive, seldom interrupting, unruffled even when his ministers break into angry quarrels.'

One minister described his cabinets as the 'domination of the continent over the incontinent'. A minister who overstepped the mark was slapped down; when policies seemed ineffectual or unpopular, when ministers were 'exhausted', the cabinet was reshuffled by the Caudillo. Even when he had given up his position as prime minister he never abandoned his right, as chief of state, to preside over Friday cabinet meetings. On 17 October 1975, already a dying man, wired up to his doctors' instruments by cables attached to his body, he presided over his government for the last time. For the first time he left before the business was concluded.

Power in Franco's Spain came from above. Ministers did not fight for power in the political market, in elections or in parliament. Power was given and taken away by the charismatic Caudillo. Nor were they, once in power, responsible *publicly* for their acts as ministers; they were educated neither in compromise (except with competing ministers) nor in 'feeling' public opinion. 'To be a Minister of Franco,' Lequerica commented 'is to be a little king.' The elite was bureaucratic, not political, and protected – like all bureaucracies – by secrecy, by the necessity to reveal what it was only convenient to reveal. This explains some characteristic features of Franco's Spain: the prevalence of political rumour.[41] The 'decoding' of guarded press statements about ministerial changes and a perpetual process of speculation became the stuff of political life.

As is so often the case in authoritarian regimes, Franco's ministries were weakened, as governments, by the chemistry of compromise and the need to balance rival groups competing for power. The assembling of the various families by Franco in ministries meant that there could be no 'homogeneous' ministry, no collective responsibility; 'governments of all ideas and none at all'.[42] Each minister pushed his own policy; the only co-ordinator was Franco himself and he interfered little in details of policy, nor did he take action on complaints of ministerial malfeasance – he merely revealed to the minister concerned the identity of the accuser. His early governments were, on occasion, almost paralysed by the mutual mistrust of soldiers and civilians who wanted a more durable and presentable institutional structure than the bleak militarism of a wartime government. In Franco's later governments Catholic conservatives and monarchists sat beside Falangists; military hard-liners beside 'pragmatic' civil servants. His last government, the future prime minister Adolfo Suárez confessed, was 'not a team, everybody went his own separate way'.

This lack of co-ordination and ministerial feuding became a main concern to the technocrats interested in economic planning. Navarro Rubio, one of the first technocrats to enter the cabinet, wrote later against the 'politicians' in the government. 'In internal affairs the lack of ministerial co-ordination became more marked every day. In the Council of Ministers conflicting and disparate lines of policy crossed each other.'[43] It was to get a minimum of co-ordinated governmental action for the Development Plans that the Opus Dei technocrats – their best brain, López Rodó, was a professor of Administrative Law – perforce became administrative reformers. They aimed to achieve in committees better interdepartmental co-operation than could be achieved at ministerial level. They did not altogether succeed.[44]

This inherent weakness was, paradoxically, heightened by the central feature of Franco's political theory: its rejection of the party system of the 'false' and 'degenerate' democracies of the West.[45] It was the lack of the backing of a party that weakened a minister against Franco or his own civil servants. Interventionist by tradition, Spanish governments had always been weak in execution and the governments of Franco were weak in all areas other than public order and labour relations. The lack of any serious attempt at a fiscal reform which might have given the government muscle and the money to implement its social programme and to satisfy the army's constant demands for better equipment, may be seen as a reflection of the social basis of the regime and the poverty of the country; it was also a consequence of administrative debility. On the other hand, it was the lack of a party structure and the consequent necessity of appealing to an electorate with a programme to be honoured – more or less – in subsequent legislation that gave Franco's government a degree of flexibility denied to democratic governments. Ministers gave the vaguest definitions of their intentions; they feared the reactions of public opinion less than they feared the veto of a colleague from a different family. They did not have to win over public opinion; they had to square pressure groups.[46]

Chapter 3

The Institutions of Francoism, 1938–1973: The constitutional cosmetics of authoritarianism

I

However entrenched and permanent the Caudillo's powers – the law-making powers of 1938 and 1939 were never abandoned – the regime did not remain static. The Francoism of 1970 was no longer the undisguised, naked personal rule of 1940. The regime prided itself on its evolution, its capacity to adapt to circumstances: as the constitutional texts put it, 'to perfect itself'. The purpose of perfection was perpetuation, to institutionalise the survival of the Francoist elite. 'After Franco the institutions' was the cry of the committed Francoists. In Weberian language they wished to routinise his charisma, to institutionalise his personal rule in their own interests. With the promulgation on 10 January 1967 of the Organic law,[1] the regime could consider itself perfected. It had a Constitution, consisting of those laws which the organic law recognised as fundamental laws. It had shown its capacity to evolve.

The lawyers of the regime – and they provided the regime with many of its servants – saw this process as the creation of an *estado de derecho*. The German notion of the *Rechstaat* (*Estado de Derecho* in Spanish, that is, a state bound to act according to its own laws) was deeply ingrained in the legal mind. As far back as 1937 Serrano Suñer, the Caudillo's brother-in-law, his Minister of the Interior and a lawyer, wished to convert what he called a state of force into a state of law; a properly organised 'totalitarian' state must be replaced by a military dictatorship acceptable only in wartime. López Rodó in the sixties considered that the permanent concern of the regime was 'the construction and development of the *Estado de Derecho*', dedicated to social progress.[2]

Franco showed little inclination to be institutionalised. Apart from any personal liking of power as such – and though authoritarian by nature Franco was no megalomaniac dictator – the Caudillo believed that only an unchallengeable sovereign could burn out the evils of the democratic heritage and restore a society shattered by the Civil War. This he called 'prudence' and he constantly warned of the dangers of institutionalisation in the 'emotional' atmosphere of the forties. Society must settle down before it could be given political shape. This was the paternal ruler admonishing his wayward subjects. Prudence meant that the process of constitution making, 'opened' in 1937 and debated fiercely in the fifties, was not completed until 1967.

The main internal drive towards institutional evolution was the problem of the succession: *the* problem of all dictatorships. It was all very well to recognise Franco as 'an unrepeatable historical phenomenon' with unique powers.[3] But what if he should die? A shooting accident in 1961 alarmed the political world; and by 1970, in spite of his successive denials and his continued public exhibitions of his prowess as a hunter and golfer, it was public property that he was a sick man. What institutions could replace his exceptional powers and give his political elite an institutional framework, by manning which they could hope to survive for ever? 'After Franco, what?' was the catch-phrase of the time.

By 1947, Franco had definitely decided on a monarchy as the form of government best suited to Spain, once he chose to give up his supreme powers. His problem now became to find a monarch who would swear loyalty to the Caudillo and the Principles of the Movement he represented, and who could be relied on to oppose any return to a liberal parliamentary monarchy. The choice of such a monarch obsessed Franco and his entourage.

Since Franco regarded a Carlist monarch as out of the question – the Pretender was a foreigner and the creed he represented noble but archaic – the choice must fall on a descendant of Alfonso XIII, the king who had left the throne in 1931. In his private conversations Franco showed an uncharacteristic, sentimental loyalty to the memory of Alfonso XIII: he was one of Spain's 'good kings'. His eldest son, Don Juan had, however, bitterly attacked Franco in a manifesto published in 1945. He was a supporter of a liberal monarchy and surrounded by a gang of unsuitable advisers. For years Franco bored his courtiers and his family with outbursts against Don Juan and his evil counsellors.[4]

He therefore opted for his son, Juan Carlos, whom he educated in Spain and clearly held in affection. But he was not declared Franco's heir as Prince of Spain until 1969. Juan Carlos, Franco believed – and time was to prove that this was to be his most serious miscalculation – could be relied on to perpetuate the Principles of the Movement to which, as Prince of Spain, he had declared his allegiance. He had sworn personal loyalty to the Caudillo. A huge man beside his stumpy creator, he stood discreetly beside Franco on all public occasions.

Franco had been less concerned about the succession question than were his advisers. For a long time he staved off awkward inquiries with the reply that if no king was forthcoming, then the Succession Law of 1947 would take care of the problem by appointing a regent. Nor did he show any haste to hand over his powers to his heir once declared. This caution struck his advisers as an excessive display of his vaunted prudence. They pressed him, by outrageous flattery of his 'unique' characteristics, to install Juan Carlos as monarch. His personality 'obscured' the institutions. If the Fundamental Laws did not come into full operation in his lifetime – and they could only do so when the 'provisions for the succession' were completed – they might well never come into force at all. Without the 'constitution' the phrase 'After Franco the institutions' could have no meaning. He must complete his 'high Providential mission' by one supreme act of Patriotism.[5] He must abdicate his powers.

He was unmoved. When seriously ill in the summer of 1975 he handed over his powers to Juan Carlos; the moment he recovered he took them back. Not until he was on his deathbed did he finally hand over his powers to his successor and 'complete the provisions for succession'.

II

With the Organic Law of 1967 the lengthy process of constitution making was completed and 'the culminating step in the institutionalisation of the National State' at last taken. The Organic Law recognised, and in some places modified, the six Fundamental Laws issued over the years after 1938.[6]

Spain was now endowed with what the regime's apologists called its constitution. But this constitution would not be fully operative until Franco handed over his powers to his successor. Spain therefore became a curious constitutional animal: a country that would have a constitution at some undefined future date when the Caudillo stepped down. Political scientists and constitutional lawyers were harmlessly employed in contradicting each other for two decades devising an anticipatory constitutional law (Derecho Constitucional de Anticipacion) which elaborated on the nature of this future constitution.[7] Was the future head of state a limited monarch who could only act in certain prescribed ways? Or were his powers, as the 'monarchical thesis' maintained, unlimited?[8]

The lawyers of the regime repeatedly claimed that the Fundamental Laws had created a constitution truly representative of the sovereign people, superior to the democracies of the degenerate West. The deficiencies of the 'demo liberal' inorganic democracy of one-man-one-vote were a constant theme of government propaganda. In the Law of the Principles of the Movement (17 May 1958) Spain was defined as a 'traditional, Catholic, social and *representative* Monarchy'.

The Spanish parliament, the Cortes, satisfied the representative principle as 'the superior organ of participation of the Spanish people in the tasks of the State'. It was set up in 1942 as a purely advisory body, a controlled legislative chamber. Apart from deputies selected by the Head of State himself, its members were elected according to the principles of corporate organic democracy by the 'natural' organs of society: the syndicates, the municipalities and, after 1969, the 'heads of families'. Other organs, represented by indirect 'fancy franchises', were the National Council of the Movement, the universities and other professional bodies.*

The weakness of the Cortes lay in its lack of any true representative character coupled with its lack of any *effective* control over the government. In the constitutional texts the Cortes could put questions to ministers and amend government bills; but parliamentary questions were formal exercises (mostly in written form) and the texts of laws were worked out in the various committees. Full debates were anodyne public shows.

Judged by the standards of Western parliamentary institutions the central feature was the absence of any doctrine of political responsibility and of any means of enforcing it. The government was both independent of the Chamber (the Prime Minister could not be removed by an adverse vote nor could he dissolve the Chamber) *and* strongly represented in it, both directly and indirectly. In 1967 41.7 per cent of the deputies or *procuradores* – a mediaeval term which exhibited the regime's determination to present itself as continuing a representative tradition that derived

*Of the 561 *procuradores*, 100 were national councillors; 150 syndical representatives; 111 municipal representatives; 104 family representatives; 5 presidents of supreme tribunals etc.; 18 university rectors; 6 representatives of cultural institutions; 23 representatives of professional bodies (Lawyers' College, Chambers of Commerce etc.); 25 representatives selected by the Chief of State plus ministers.

from the more glorious period of Spanish history before the disasters of nineteenth-century liberalism – belonged to the administration in one way or another, a quarter coming from the central administration.[9] It was a Chamber with a working majority of former or present civil servants, hardly a class calculated to challenge the government that paid its salaries.

Many well-meaning constitutional lawyers,[10] by exercising 'anticipatory constitutional law', were optimistic enough to believe that the system would be liberalised from within and that the Cortes could develop into a real centre of power. This was wishful thinking. These optimists could not get round the principles of organic representation and the processes of indirect election. The only feeble concession to a wider representation was the direct election of family representatives on a family franchise. But for a candidate to be put up without government nomination, 0.5 per cent of the electorate had to sign the nomination – and this would mean 50,000 people in Barcelona. Nor could that candidate collect funds for his campaign; only a rich man could stand. After a flurry of enthusiasm and activity the family representatives subsided into relative inactivity. In 1971 the monarchist daily *ABC* described the family representative: 'An organic candidate, bald and chubby with shell-rimmed glasses and a small moustache, rehearsing his speech in the Cortes by repeating, "Yes . . . I agree . . . You are absolutely right".'

We need not examine in detail the other organs of this bizarre constitutional creation, whose true nature was concealed by the ambiguity and generality of its laws. None of the provisions of the constitution were an effective limit on Franco's power. The Council of the Realm – another mediaeval revival – advised the Head of State on important matters and presented him with a *terna* (a list of three names) of candidates for important offices, above all that of prime minister. If in theory Franco was bound to listen, he was not bound to obey, nor was the Council likely to make any suggestion it knew to be unacceptable to the Caudillo.

The National Council of the Movement was another idiosyncratic constitutional invention characteristic of Francoist constitution making.[11] A remnant of the old conception of the Movement as a party, it was by 1970 the ideological watch-dog of the regime, guarding the Principles of the Movement as the communion of all Spaniards who shared in the ideals of the Crusade, that is, the negation of liberalism and all its implications. It must further 'perfect' the political institutions of the country in concordance with these Principles. It was in fact a sort of Upper Chamber of 113 members, some elected indirectly by the local councillors of the Movement and forty appointed by Franco. Thus there would always be a core devoted to the 'spirit of the Movement'.

III

Organic democracy challenged not merely representative government based on universal suffrage but the division of powers as a safeguard for the rule of law. Complicated and confusing as it appeared, the Franco constitution was highly centralised according to the concept of the 'unity of power'. The mechanisms for challenging administrative persecution were imperfect and controlled by the government itself. The Organic Law set up the process of *contrafuero* by which decrees could be challenged as unconstitutional; but the procedure was clumsy and the government was represented on the bodies that processed the petition. Perhaps too much has been made of the lack of independence of a judiciary dependent on a minister for its promotion prospects. A more serious breach of the rule of law was the existence of special jurisdictions: the Military Tribunals with extensive powers over civilians, which could define their own sphere of jurisdiction (13 November 1971); the Labour Tribunal under the Minister of Labour; above all the Tribunal of Public Order of 1963.* The characteristic feature of the constitution was the declaration of rights – often limited in the text – which were whittled away by ordinary legislation and discretional procedures such as the declaration of states of emergency. The *Fuero de los Españoles*, which set out the 'rights' of Spaniards, remained a piece of window dressing originally intended, in 1945, to hoodwink the victorious allies into a belief that Spain was a liberal state.

It was not only that the ordinary Spaniard did not enjoy the right to vote as a simple citizen. The basic democratic freedoms of association and expression were severely circumscribed. The right of public meeting was closely controlled by the Ministry of the Interior and its agent in the provinces, the Civil Governor. Public meetings of more than twenty people had to have governmental permission, while an agent of the government could attend the meeting and could dissolve it if he saw fit.

---

*Military courts dealt by summary procedures with serious political crimes involving violence (e.g. the trial of Grimau and the Burgos Trials of 1970). Since 1963 the Tribunal of Public Order (TOP) has dealt with non-violent political offences. ETA terrorism stopped any 'evolution' towards ordinary jurisdictions. In one month the TOP might deal with 98 cases, from belonging to a terrorist organisation to belonging to an illegal party or union. (For a sample see E. de Blaye, *Franco and the Politics of Spain* (1976), pp. 472–3.)

Illegal propaganda remained as severely and arbitrarily punished as illegal association by the Penal Code (Articles 251 and 252); such propaganda was loosely defined, running from attacking the unity of the state or the prestige of its governors to the circulation of rumours.

In 1966 the censorship which had emasculated Spanish intellectual life and the strict government control of newspapers were abandoned. The Press Law of that year substituted a process of 'publish and be damned'; damnation was a fine or suspension of the periodical concerned by the government if it attacked the Principles of the Movement, and did not 'show due respect' to political institutions and those who manned them, or to the vague concept of 'truth and morals'. These provisions were set out in Article 2 of the Press Law which proved to be a Damoclean sword held over editors and journalists. Señor Fraga, author of the law, became very unpopular when he enforced it.[12]

Under these conditions the organisation of an opposition that publicly challenged either Franco's personal power or the principles of organic democracy was impossible. This was partly a function of police repression and the wide exceptional jurisdictions, of both the military courts and the Supreme Tribunal of Order. But authoritarian regimes have in their hands less drastic methods than imprisonment, torture and the beating up of demonstrators. Administrative persecutions, from denial of a professional career to withdrawal of driving licences and passports, can have wide and intimidating social effects which those who have never lived under arbitrary regimes rarely comprehend.* Moreover, control of all media – radio, television and the press – can blanket an opposition either by denying the public all knowledge of its activities or by presenting those activities as treason to the nation rather than as criticisms of the regime. A classic example of these mixed methods was the regime's reaction to the Munich Congress of the European Movement of 1962 when the internal and external opposition met together to demand a democratic Spain. Those who returned were subject to police persecution and the whole nature of Congress was distorted in the press as a 'dirty' conspiracy of Spaniards 'without faith' in collusion (the Spanish word is *contubernio*) with the foreign enemies of Spain.[13] Time and time again critics of the regime were attacked in the government-controlled press and denied any right of reply.

*Professor Tierno Galván is a well-known case of administrative persecution. A typical case is that of Catalan politician Joan Raventós y Carner (b. 1927), grandson of a Republican minister and leader of Convergencia Socialista de Catalunya. He was dismissed from his professorship and denied a passport for eighteen years.

IV

The problem of defining the essential nature of the Francoist state was not merely made a puzzle for Spaniards by the constitutional rhetoric of the regime. Its classification presented a problem to political scientists. Where could the Francoist state be 'located' in the taxonomy of dictatorial states?

Though it clearly shared some features of totalitarian states, it did not share them all. Particularly there was no mass party and, after the first few years, attempts at mass mobilisation and a complete control of culture withered away. As we have seen, Serrano Suñer's 'totalitarian' state proved a non-starter. This failure to measure up to a totalitarian model led Juan Linz to a definition of the Francoist state as a 'stabilised authoritarian regime', that is, a political system 'with limited, non-responsible political pluralism; without elaborate and guiding ideology (but with distinctive mentality); without intensive or extensive political mobilisation (except for some points in their development) and in which a leader (or occasionally a small group) exercises power within formally ill-defined limits, but actually quite predictable ones'.[14]

One of the distinguishing features of such a regime, Linz argues, is that, rather than seeking 'enthusiasm or support, it expects 'passive acceptance'. And this was what it successfully contrived to obtain. If the Second Republic had seen a process of mass politicisation, the Franco regime survived on the opposite condition: massive depoliticisation. Every survey − and it must be remembered that all such surveys in an authoritarian regime must distort the degree, not merely of political dissidence, but of political interest as such − revealed a profound political apathy.[15] Indeed, to the apologists of the regime this apathy was the supreme tribute to Franco's rule, an acceptance based on the maintenance of social peace. 'Political apathy,' wrote Fernández de la Mora in the booming sixties, 'is not a symptom of social disease but of health . . . The health of free states [*sic*] can be measured by the degree of political apathy. It is not a disturbing factor but a hopeful one.'[16] In the sixties this political apathy looked like an immutable natural phenomenon as far as the majority of the Spanish nation was concerned, a reflection of its acceptance of 'Franco's peace'. 'Time and time again,' Emilio Romero reminded the opposition in 1962, 'those who want to demolish the present system forget the *ultima ratio* of the Spanish people − their refusal to sacrifice the peace they now enjoy.'[17] In 1974 Aranguren denounced the 'apolitical consumerism' that afflicted the majority of Spaniards.[18]

The concept of 'stabilised authoritarianism' based on a combination of limited pluralism, political apathy afforced by the materialism of a consumer society, and repression, has been considered inadequate by those who see Francoism as a typical 'Fascist' compromise between different groups of a capitalist ruling class. This compromise was not ideal but it was a rearrangement of their claims and interests and their insertion in the power structure in such a way as to exclude the working class from political power.

This was something that bourgeois democracies like the Second Republic of 1931 could not promise but which a paternalistic authoritarianism – rooted in the Spanish political tradition and Catholic political and social thought as well as imported in foreign models of the 1930s – could hope to achieve. When the regime talked of the evils of party it was thinking of working-class parties; the joys of pluralism were confined to the political and economic elite. Certainly until the regime suffered a decay of legitimacy in the late sixties, its 'mentality' looked very much like an ideology. What the concept of 'authoritarianism' run by a bureaucracy does not explain is the shifts in the 'mentality' (e.g. from corporativism where the interests of classes are considered harmonious to a neo-capitalism that recognised collective bargaining) and the 'evolution' of the regime.[19]

The *Marxisant* critics of Linz explain the stability of authoritarianism in terms of brutal police repression and the processes of *embourgeoisement* in a media-dominated consumer society. Yet even in these favourable conditions the ideology/mentality of the regime was accepted, they argue, only by the men of the regime: there was a concealed 'potential mobilisation' *against* the regime which no opinion survey before 1975 could bring to light. The decisive rejection of Francoism in the first free elections of June 1977 did indeed prove that the vast majority of Spaniards rejected organic democracy and all it stood for.

Chapter 4

From Autarky to the Consumer Society

'Spain is different' was a slogan much used in the sixties to attract tourists and to justify the continuing existence of a government that stood in stark contrast to the democracies of Western Europe. In 1939 Spain *was* different; it was an agricultural economy with industrial appendages concentrated in the Basque provinces and Catalonia. By 1977 the gap was closing and Spain was ceasing to be very different from her neighbours. An austere pre-industrial society had become an industrial society. Spain had experienced an industrial revolution and the poor of the countryside had moved in their masses to the great industrial cities. In 1939 nearly half the active population of Spain was engaged in agriculture: by 1977 less than a quarter remained.[1] In the sixties the growth rate of the economy was exceeded in the capitalist world only by that of Japan.

(a)
Nationalism and autarky − the economics of self-sufficiency

'In 1940,' wrote París Eguilaz, one of the foremost economists of the new regime, 'the national income, at constant prices, had fallen back to that of 1914, but since the population had increased the per capita income fell to nineteenth-century levels; that is, the Civil War had provoked an unprecedented economic recession.'[2]

How was the economy to be rebuilt? How, above all, was Franco to feed the Spaniards he had, in his own terminology, liberated, and to give them jobs?

The difficulties were forbidding. The physical destruction of war can be exaggerated: the Republicans burnt churches rather than destroyed factories. The Spanish economy was not in ruins as was the Russian economy after the Civil War of 1919−21; rather, it was run down. Roads had degenerated. Nearly half the railway rolling-stock had been lost in the war and transport, according to the American ambassador, was 'indescribably bad'. Industrial equipment was old-fashioned or worn out. Skilled labour was scarce. By the late forties electrical power was in short supply: factories and homes suffered frequent cuts. Above all, agricultural production stagnated; stricken by persistent drought and with no imported fertilisers, cereals, which occupied 40 per cent of all culti-vated land, stuck at a level 13 per cent below the yields of 1931–5. Hence the massive wheat imports of the early forties. Since Argentina supplied the Spaniards with food, Evita Perón became a national heroine. The first bumper harvest came only in 1951.

Until the 1950s Nationalist Spain pursued recovery and reconstruc-tion with the tools of a war economy forged in the years 1937–9 under the influence of Fascist models. The two key concepts were autarky and interventionism. A self-sufficient, self-capitalising economy protected from outside competition by tariffs and administrative controls would be created and regulated by state intervention.

It must be emphasised that, while autarky and protectionism are not one and the same thing, the notion of Spain cut off and surrounded by high tariff walls was already the familiar philosophy of civil servants, opposed only by a few liberal economists. Industrialists and wheat farmers had long clamoured for high protection. Sector after sector, pressure group after pressure group had forced protection and state subsidies for 'nationally' important economic activities on successive governments after the 1890s. Such privileges were regarded as a kind of natural right to be enjoyed by high-cost, competitively weak, national producers.[3] There was the more recent model of Primo de Rivera, the dictator of the twenties, with his pained disapprobation of the preference shown by the upper classes for French wine and by doctors for imported scalpels, and his attempts to regulate all aspects of the economy from wheat to rabbit-skins by regulatory commissions. Autarky was now clothed in the rhetoric of the new Falangist economic nationalism. As the Industrial Law of 24 October 1939 put it, Spain must be 'redeemed [the word is significant] from the importation of exotic products'. Spain must be forced to produce *everything* it needed, regardless of cost; it must be cut off from the outside world by a massive programme of import substitution.

All the customary instruments of interventionism and of direct controls flourished in the forties. Prices and wages were controlled; foreign trade and exchange rates were closely regulated; the National Wheat Service fixed the production of wheat and marketed it; the Institute of Industry (INI), a state holding company, based on an Italian model and run by an admiral and intimate of the Caudillo, was to direct the establishment of basic industries and supplement private investment.

The penalties of interventionism and direct controls, of the consequent 'fear of the market' as a regulator of the economy were the same in Spain as elsewhere in the capitalist economies of postwar Western Europe. Bottlenecks created by bureaucratic decisions encouraged corruption – for instance in the grant of import licences and currency permits. There was a flourishing black market – in the early years particularly in food – that supported a host of minor pedlars and enriched fewer speculators, though it might be argued that such a corrupt system offered at least an indirect approach to the flexibility of a market economy. Thus the availability of scarce industrial raw materials on the black market allowed a 'redistribution' of the official quotes.

Critics attributed the administrative excesses and economic failures of autarky and interventionism to the ideological idiosyncrasies of the new state born of the Civil War.[4] The 'official' excuse in after years was that interventionism and self-sufficiency were less the imposition of a quasi-Fascist ideology than of necessity. In the scarcities of war and the postwar years other Western European states were forced to use direct controls; Spain therefore does not constitute a special case. To plunge the country into a market economy – domestically and internationally – might have invited disaster, and certainly the free market was an ideal, the risks of which few European economies could afford in the forties. What was unique about the Spanish economy was not that scarce supplies were rationed and prices controlled, but the degree of control, the clumsiness of the apparatus that administered it, and the strange-sounding nationalist jargon with which economic decisions were presented to the public.* What distinguished Spanish economic policy from that of other Western European states was that state *dirigisme* and autarky were seen as an ideal and *permanent* solution, not only as a response to the postwar crisis. The economists of the regime did not seek to justify autarky in economic terms, as had the protectionists in the nineteenth century. It was presented and defended as a political ideal; the recipe for a stable society and a suitable policy for an 'imperial military state'.

If there was no alternative to autarky during the Second World

---

*For instance, see the Decree of 20 August 1938: 'It is the function of the state to *discipline* production.' Suppose for the word 'discipline' the word 'plan' had been substituted, would any postwar economist of the left have quarrelled with the statement?

War and if, after the war, the possibilities of rapid recovery were limited by international shortages, the price Spain paid in economic terms for the victory of the right was heavy. It desperately needed imports of capital goods to re-equip its industry, to import fertilisers and food; and to do this it needed foreign exchange that could not be generated by its exports. The rest of Western Europe was set on its feet by the Marshall Plan; Spain could not raise loans from the democracies that ostracised it as a Fascist state. Ostracism, isolation from the international money market, meant that autarky was a political choice: only a liberalisation of the regime, which Franco was utterly determined to resist, and which the Allies would or could not impose by overthrowing him, might have widened the economic options by making Spain respectable in the eyes of potential creditors.

Throughout the 1940s Spain was poor, an economy, in the words of Professor Sardá, in which there was neither consumption nor production. These were the 'years of hunger'. There were years of shortages throughout postwar Europe; the era of 'Fish and Cripps' in Britain. It was the *absolute* level of hardship that distinguished Spain. Per capita income had been cut by nearly one-fifth compared with 1936. In the Spain of the forties where prices were rising faster than wages, where meat and leather shoes were luxuries to the lower paid and underemployed, poverty was made more painful by the conspicuous waste of the fortunate few.

It was not that the regime was indifferent to industrial recovery, however much it retained an agrarian rhetoric; nor that its achievements were altogether negligible.*

By 1948 industrial production had just passed 1929 levels; by 1951 the national income had climbed back to the levels obtaining before the Civil War. Yet it was the relative success of this painfully achieved take-off that forced the abandonment of autarky. Once industry had grown up under the paternalistic shell of autarky, it must burst that shell or stagnate. Surrounded by high tariff walls, enclosed in a domestic market with limited power to consume industrial goods, and incapable of importing the raw materials and capital goods to supply and modernise its industry, the economy was starved. Physical controls and rigid price regulation from above distorted the market, favouring traditional entrenched

---

*cf. the view of one economist: 'This country industrialised between 1939 and 1959 and what is called an industrial take-off happened in Spain after, not before, the Civil War.' Quoted in S. Pániker, *Conversaciones en Madrid* (1969), p. 159. Such statements irritate the economic critics of Francoism and would be contested by those who see industrialisation as a process beginning at the turn of the century but halted in the thirties.

sectors as opposed to the dynamic sectors of the economy. Further growth demanded imports and the abandonment of controls; imports meant foreign loans, since there was no other way to finance them. To cut Spain off from the international market would inhibit further recovery. By 1956 the limitations of autarky, combined as it was with a monetary policy − or lack of it − that encouraged inflation, were shown up by a severe crisis.* inflation was running at 16 per cent and Spain's supply of foreign exchange was exhausted.

(b)
The new economic policy

'A moment arrived in which the desire for industrialisation must be reconciled with the conditions industrialisation demanded'.[5] Already in the fifties there had been timid moves towards the abandonment of a controlled and regulated 'national economy'.[6] The ministerial reshuffle of February 1957 brought into government the team of technocrats who were, over the next four years, to introduce, piecemeal and imperfectly, a new economic policy to reconcile rapid industrial growth and its 'conditions': the creation of a market economy in Spain where prices could control the allocation of resources and the integration of that market in the capitalist economy of the West.

The new team were the technocrats of the Opus Dei: Alberto Ullastres, a former professor of economic history, at the Ministry of Commerce; Mariano Navarro Rubio at the Ministry of Finance; and Laureano López Rodó, another professor, in the key post as head of the Technical Secretariat of the Presidency of the Government.

These men not only forged the new policies; they also created the administrative machinery to implement them, a necessity given the incoherence of the administration. By the Decree of 25 February 1957 the ministries concerned with economic policy were brought together in one committee and the Office of Economic Co-ordination and Planning was set up. This meant that the government could contemplate a coherent, global economic policy; it marked the beginning of an attempt to plan the economy of which the First Development Plan of 1964 was a culmination, a decorative facade to an edifice already built.[7] As López Rodó later claimed, the National Programme for Regulating Investment (March 1959) was the first step that led to the later Development

---

*The main motor of inflation was the increase in the money supply via the rediscounting of short-term government paper by the private banks: this created an enormous breach in any regulation of the money supply by the Bank of Spain.

Plans, the first use of the new administrative machinery to act on the economy as a whole, 'a vast programme that would affect all sectors of national life'.[8] It marked, Franco told the nation in his New Year message, 'a new era'. The new era was reflected in a new style, a semantic revolution with the language of international business (López Rodó was fond of comparing government with an efficient firm) replacing that of economic nationalism *à outrance*; rationalisation was to take precedence over tradition − though they must be reconciled if possible.

Ullastres repeatedly asserted that the aim of the new economic policy was to 'integrate' Spain in the booming world of advanced Western capitalism, particularly into the European market (these were the optimistic years of Europe − the Treaty of Rome was signed in 1957). Spanish thinkers had harped on the 'lag' (the *atraso*) between Spain and Europe. Now the gap must be closed and it was the obsession with the European and American model that made the new planners turn to the expertise of the West. The reports of the OECD and the World Bank all emphasised that if Spain were to prosper she must end the 'fear of the market', dismantle the orthopaedic apparatus of autarky and open up the country to foreign investment and foreign trade.

The first step was forced by the acute crisis in Spain's balance of payments. In the Plan of Stabilisation of 1959 the remedy was taken from the recipe book of orthodox capitalism; an emergency measure to meet the crisis, the plan contained the philosophy that was to underpin the drive to development, the new slogan of the triumphalist propaganda.* It removed some of the physical controls, opened the country to foreign investment, froze wages and limited credit, and by a drastic devaluation hoped to force Spain into greater reliance on export earnings. The immediate result was recession and unemployment. Once the economy had been cleansed of the inherited impurities it would function as a modern capitalist economy in which rapid growth would take care of all problems.

In 1962 the Commissariat of Planning was set up under López Rodó, the last step in a process of institutional change which started in 1959. Decree by decree Spain was to be turned into a capitalist, market economy by a government in close contact with the major Spanish economic and financial interests. Foreign investment was encouraged by allowing the repatriation of profits, and the importation of advanced technology by permitting royalty payments. Spain became part of the world capitalist economy. By

---

*There is no exact translation of the Spanish word *triunfalismo*. It means boasting over present achievements, with the conviction that they will be even greater in the future.

the 1970s the danger of domination by multinational companies was repeatedly denounced by the opposition; the result of 'planning' the economy had been, it was argued, to deny Spain the capacity to control its economic destiny, making it a tributary of international capitalism, paying heavily for technological imports and denying it the capacity for autonomous progress based on native technology.*

(c)

'The economic miracle'

The foundations of the 'economic miracle' of the sixties were laid in the forties when private capitalism was weak. The aim of the National Institute of Industry (set up in 1941 and staffed with a heavy contingent of military administrators) was to create the infrastructure for industrial development. It would invest public funds in those areas where private capital was unwilling to risk a low return (such as the declining coal industry) or in enterprises which needed state aid to get off the ground (for instance, the small beginnings of the car industry); it would invest to expand existing industries (electrical energy) or to break monopoly practices by effective competition in basic industries like steel. (Given the structure of the steel industry this latter was a hopeless enterprise; but the philosophy of autarky demands that if domestic industry is highly protected from international prices, then at least domestic competition should put some constraint on monopoly practices.) The Spanish steel industry remained a poor performer by international standards; but without integrated plants planned in the forties the private sector could not have begun to satisfy the rocketing demands of industrialisation.[9] INI founded and still owns Iberia, the Spanish airline. In the forties it bought up the old Hispano-Suiza factory which had made the finest prewar luxury cars in Europe: the new concern, Pegaso, embarked on the production of an expensive sports car, superbly engineered and presumably meant to 'fit' a domestic market dominated by the few rich. That this car was a commercial failure is less important than that Pegaso became a mass producer of commercial vehicles. Much criticised for the spread of its investments, the inflationary

*cf. F. Maravall, *Crecimiento, dimensión y concentración de las empresas industriales españolas 1964–73* (1976). Multinationals move in when they have 'tested' the domestic market; they are not concerned with exports when tariffs keep up domestic prices (pp. 64*ff*). While it is true that the level of investment in research is very low and royalty payments high, it is hard to see how Spain could have competed with the huge investment in research of the great multinationals.

consequences of its activities, and its propensity to rescue lame ducks rather than finance new enterprise, INI played an important part in the early stages of the industrial take-off, especially in the fifties.[10]

The most spectacular subsequent growth took place in new industry – metallurgy, the chemical industry, food processing; but there was expansion in older industries like shipbuilding which, before orders fell off, could compete successfully with Japan. As in all modern economies the car industry provides a test case. When the SEAT factory was set up in Barcelona in 1952 its managers were concerned that the market might not absorb a hundred cars a month; by 1975 Ford (which makes Fiesta bodies for Britain), Chrysler, Citroen, Renault and SEAT were producing three-quarters of a million cars a year. There were comparable expansions in all consumer durables: washing machines, refrigerators, television sets. Finally, this growth meant an enormous expansion of the building industry, a heavy employer of labour; between 1945 and 1960 the production of cement quadrupled; between 1960 and 1970 it increased four times again.[11]

These dramatic figures are in part a mere reflection of the abysmal point of departure in 1940 and the restrictive policies of the years that followed. In the sixties, as emigration abroad proves, industrial growth could not absorb all the new workers seeking employment. There were sectors that lagged behind – textiles, for instance, and bad performers like the steel industry; once high protection was removed in 1961, it slumped into an acute financial crisis from which rescue was only possible by massive injections of public funds.* It was the stagnation of the coal industry that intensified the militancy of the Asturian miners faced with closures and dismissals. Heavy dependence on imported fuels was a weakness, exposed in 1974. Conglomerations of semi-artisan enterprises persist beside modern large-scale enterprises. Most of the advanced industries depend on foreign licences which in turn entail a heavy drain on foreign reserves in terms of royalty payments. Imports exceed exports.

It was the change in the pattern of these exports which indicated the revolution in the economy: exports of industrial goods became by the seventies more valuable than Spain's traditional exports of agricultural products and minerals. In the early years the

---

*Public investment under the process known as *Acción Concertada* (1964) was supposed to be conditional on the amalgamation of small plants and increased production. For a leftist criticism of the steel industry, where money that should have been invested in the state-integrated factories went to save feeble private enterprises, see Arturo López Muñoz, *Capitalismo español: una etapa decisiva* (1970), pp. 73–94.

agricultural exports of the Mediterranean supplied the foreign exchange at 'subsidised' rates to industry. By the 1970s industry was generating its own exports: the diversified exports of industrial Catalonia and the Basque provinces were worth four times the 'traditional' agricultural exports of Valencia.[12] Valencia itself industrialised; by the seventies half of its exports were manufactured goods. As we shall see, tourism – another 'Mediterranean' product – played a larger part in financing the industrial take-off than oranges, lemons and tomatoes.

Perhaps the most striking proof of the modernisation of the economy was the growth in the sixties and seventies of the service sector, the last entrant in an advanced economy.[13] This expansion was multiplied by tourism, a heavy employer of seasonal labour. It was the services that absorbed some of the surplus work force, extruded from a contracting agricultural sector, that could find no place in a slower-growing industrial sector. It was the expansion of the service sector, as we shall see, that was to modify profoundly the society of the seventies.

(d)

The foreign contribution: tourism, emigrants' earnings and foreign loans

Spain's visible exports could not have financed the imports of capital goods, fuel and raw materials that the economic miracle demanded. The economy was refuelled from abroad: by tourist earnings, by the remittances of émigrés working abroad and by foreign loans. Only these invisible earnings and loans made it possible to realise the technocrats' plans for rapid growth without running up against the balance of payments problems that bring growth to a grinding halt in most poor economies.

Tourism, the early evidence of which in the form of two-piece bathing costumes and bare arms had been frowned on by the bishops, began as a trickle in the fifties. By 1973 it had become an annual flood of over 30 million tourists bringing with them 3,000 million dollars. It was for Spain a new form of tourism: in the 1930s the artistic monuments of Spain were the magnet; now it was the beaches of the Mediterranean coast (a more valuable capital asset – with 300 days of sun a year on the Costa del Sol – than coal or iron) that drew the middle classes of northern Europe to Spain. It was a low-cost tourism which soon saturated the coast, creating the architectural horrors of Benidorm and Torremolinos.*

---

*When R.C. went to Torremolinos in 1950 it had two modest hotels and was still essentially a large village. Benidorm now has 200,000 tourist beds and in July and August takes in 350,000 tourists. This invasion threatens to outrun the water supply.

Spain perhaps wasted a vast capital asset on package tourism which will move on to Morocco and elsewhere. José Meliá, who has made a fortune out of the hotel business, pleads not for more tourists but for better tourists who can pay high prices.* Those who have settled on retirement or have second holiday houses have created foreign colonies originally attracted by low living costs. (Except for wine and cigarettes – the staple diet of many of the English refugees – prices have now risen to English levels; now only the German, French and Dutch find living in Spain 'cheap'.) All this meant building booms (the number of hotel rooms went up seven times between 1950 and 1975) and seasonal employment for 600,000 people.† It has also meant the ravaging of a coast, which gave rise to a protest movement by a growing environmentalist lobby. **

If Spain had become the sun playground of northern Europe, it had also become its service area, supplying workers to the farms and factories of France and Germany. At first the government resisted this loss (emigration is often considered, in biological metaphor, as a loss of 'blood'), but in the sixties it fostered it as a deliberate policy for curing unemployment and providing foreign exchange.‡ By 1973 there were half a million Spaniards working in France and a quarter of a million in Germany.

Loans were the last foreign contribution to the industrial take-off. The American loans after 1953 were, in the words of the distinguished economist Sardá, water that fertilised a desert. This represented an ideological and economic turnabout: the early Francoist legislation had strictly controlled foreign investment on nationalist principles. In the 1960s this was reversed: foreign investment was welcomed. By 1973 one out of every five jobs was financed by foreign investment.

(e)
The development plans

History would judge the performance of Spanish governments,

---

*Hotel prices are government controlled. Meliá wants a free market for expensive tourism.

†Angel Palomino, in his praise of Spanish tourism, *El Milagro turístico* (1972), includes the salvaging of craft industries through visitors' purchases of 'typical' traditional objects as one of the benefits of tourism. These artefacts are no longer made by village craftsmen but in small factories.

**See below, p. 93.

‡Government-assisted 'permanent' emigration reached its peak in 1972; by 1975 it had dropped off drastically.

López Rodó explained, not by the superficial events chronicled in the newspapers (i.e. by their political records) but 'by the volume of goods we have been able to produce'. Nothing annoyed the critics of the regime more than the statistical 'triumphalism' of the regime as Spain approached the ideal of its foreign advisers – a flourishing neo-capitalist economy integrated in the world market. Between 1960 and 1970, the triumphalists could claim a GNP increase of 7.5 per cent a year, outpacing the rest of Europe; the per capita income leapt from $300 to $1,500.

The economic miracle was ceaselessly attacked by the opponents of the regime – not least because economics was a fashionable novelty (young economists, the novelist-journalist Francisco Umbral observed, replaced cadets as sex symbols) and the one area where criticism was more or less tolerated. The achievements of the regime, the critics held, had nothing to do with much publicised governmental initiatives of the three development plans; growth from a low base was inevitable and all government policy did was to distort its processes. Its triumphs were fictitious and fragile, a mere bonus handed to Franco and his technocrats by the European boom of the sixties, a bonus which they were incapable of managing in the interests of sound development. Dependent on these windfall gains it would wither with a European recession as tourist revenues, emigrants' remittances and foreign loans dropped off. Finally, growth had been achieved at the cost of 'those of always': the workers and the poor regions of Spain. Spain, in short, had ceased to be underdeveloped; it was, in the phrase of Julián Marías, 'badly developed'. And this was the fault of the government.

It was the claim of the regime that the three much publicised development plans (1964–7; 1968–71; 1972–5) were responsible for a relatively steady and certainly spectacular growth. The techniques for fostering this rapid growth were, like so much in Spanish history, lifted straight from French example. The Spanish planners 'simply borrowed French planning procedure wholesale and in detail. The basic institutions and processes were imported intact. Even the titles of institutions and offices were retained, merely being translated from French into Spanish.'[14] The basic philosophy of the planners was clearest in the first plan: by indicative planning to stimulate productive private investment whatever the social costs. To worry about the redistribution of personal income or to attempt to even out regional imbalances would merely slow up the processes of growth. Nor could there be any dramatic increase in investment by the government in the public sector. This would entail a high level of taxation which would not merely discourage investment by the private sector but would alienate the support of the one class whose support the regime was determined to retain. The growth model of the technocrats implied an unequal distribution of income and unbalanced growth. It was a bet on the strong: the rich private investor and the prosperous regions.

The two subsequent plans attempted to correct some of the imbalances created by concentration on aggregate growth: they put more emphasis on social objectives, the redistribution of personal income and regional planning to help the poorer provinces. But the main thrust remained reliance on the private sector. López Rodó had been forced by the pressure of the syndicates (the official trade unions) to give regional planning an appearance in the first plan. But both he and Ullastres were unrepentant believers in unbalanced growth: to spend public money in poor regions where there was neither the infrastructure nor the skilled labour for an industrial take-off was to fling good money after bad. Poor regions would benefit more effectively from the spill-over effects of investment in areas where returns were high.

In the first plan one of the main instruments was the 'pole of development' where the government would establish the infrastructure of industrial estates and give tax concessions to industries that moved to them. This was a recipe taken from France: Perroux's *pôles de croissance*. It is clear that the planners were aiming at sectoral growth not overall regional prosperity. The poles were not conceived to give employment in backward regions: they attracted capital-intensive industries and gave 7,000 jobs a year at a time when 100,000 people were leaving the land. Poles were a trendy and cheap instrument of propaganda rather than an effective solution of the economic problems of the poorer regions.[15]

To their critics the plans were at best mere formal pronouncements of good intentions with little practical effect; at worst they were mere market studies, the protective camouflage behind which the agents of monopoly capitalism and multinational companies came to dominate the economic life of Spain.

At least in psychological terms the triumphalism of the technocrats may have infused confidence in entrepreneurs; the plans may, as their French model had done, have acted as 'reducers of uncertainty'. But whether they did much else must be in doubt; the most spectacular increases in the GNP came before the plan came into operation. The plans underestimated certain factors (the rural exodus and the demand for steel, for instance) and failed to direct others (the levels of public investment). Once Spain was exposed to the currents of world trade and the erratic consequences of a freer market at home, planning had to be dropped for simple 'stop-go' policies to get the economy out of inflation and balance of payments deficits.[16]

The main criticism of the economic policies pursued after 1957 and of the development plans after 1964 was less connected with their efficiency in promoting economic growth than with their neglect of the social consequences of such growth and their failure to lift their perspective above the narrow goal of increased production to the wider view of the needs and the wellbeing of society as a whole.[17]

Some of this criticism was unfair. When the development plan of 1964–73 stated that the condition of fulfilling social aims was an increase in the rate of growth it was stating an obvious truth.[18] More seriously, the plans did not solve the housing problems created by the influx of immigrants to the industrial centres: the targets for low-cost, subsidised housing were not achieved whereas 'free' housing rocketed in a burst of speculative building – a 'distortion' recognised by the third plan but which it did not remedy.[19] This failure to provide services for the new cities was to give rise to new types of conflict.*

All the plans insisted that one of their aims was to create a juster society by redistributing income. This remained a pious platitude rather than a guide to policy. The planners believed that any significant redistribution of income would halt growth by halting investment. While the wages and living standards of the working class in general rose dramatically, its share of the enlarged national cake rose less dramatically, at least until the 1970s.† Taxation remained regressive, falling more heavily on the poorer man at a time when profits were rising. It was not until the first budget of the new democracy in 1977 that direct taxes, which penalise those with higher incomes, brought in the same revenue as indirect taxes on everyone's consumption. The government had encouraged investment and domestic capital formation by allowing profits to rise, keeping wages low until pressure from below became irresistible. Ullastres argued that wage increases meant inflation and that inflation was 'the Communist agent' for destroying the economies of the West. 'The only thing that has not developed as might have been hoped,' observed Cardinal Herrera in 1968, 'is social justice.'[20] Workers in steady employment, who could rely on favourable wage settlements were doing relatively well; but as we

---

*See below, p. 93*ff*.

†The share of wages in the national income is a subject of great controversy. For a critical view see Jordi Estivill *et al.*, *Apuntes sobre el trabajo en España* (1973), ch. 5.

shall see, it was the marginal man who continued to suffer from a lack of social justice.[21]

The conclusion of one fierce critic is that the development plans reinforced economic growth, neglected social change and 'braked' political change.[22] This was precisely what the planners wanted: growth would automatically solve what the nineteenth century had called 'the social question' and prosperity would make people forget about politics. As the crisis of the seventies was to prove, their expectations were doomed to disappointment

(f)
The economy and its critics

The Spanish capitalism of the sixties and seventies was criticised by both Marxist critics and the radical exponents of neo-capitalism. To the latter there was no true market economy: it was not only that the traditions of state intervention died hard, but that intervention was haphazard and, in spite of the legislatión directed against monopolies, there was no effective competition; privileged circuits and special interest rates destroyed the mechanisms of the market. The economy was not controlled; it was subject to a maze of controls, symbolised by the 156 autonomous government agencies.

Marxist critics − Professor Tamames, a leading light in the Communist party, is the most prominent − criticised the system precisely because it *was* a capitalist system with the defects of that system exaggerated by the peculiar and intimate relationship of the Spanish state with the great financial and industrial interests.* The economy, he argued, was at the mercy of an oligarchy: the financial and industrial interests, allied with foreign capital. This oligarchy used the apparatus of the state in its own interests, for instance to pump public funds into that classic lame duck, the steel industry, in order to avoid 'that ugly word nationalisation'.[23]

These oligarchs − a hundred or so families − were not a collection of individual entrepreneurs but formed an interconnected network of company directors and bankers.† Ensconced in the private banking system, the financial oligarchy 'possesses almost complete

---

*Perhaps it is not fanciful to see in the National Health Service a model of economic power in Spain. The medical profession and the pharmaceutical industry control policy via their influence in the social services bureaucracy.

†For a classic exposition of the Marxist viewpoint see R. Tamames, *Los Monopolios en España* (1967). Tamames repeats the criticism of Marxist critics of the thirties, e.g. the POUM leader Maurín. It was the 'mediocrity of our great industrial bourgeoisie' that made it so dependent on state aid.

control of the Spanish economic system' and managed, in its own interests, the increasing concentration of Spanish industry. 'The fundamental nucleus of economic power' was the 'big seven' banks.

The private banks were the most conspicuous feature of the economic landscape of Francoism. Given the weakness of the Stock Exchange and the low level of self-financing, it was the private mixed banks which supplied the credit without which industrial growth would have been a complete impossibility.* This monopoly, it was argued, allowed the banks, through their directors sitting on the boards of the companies they supported, to control their clients' activities. Like so many Marxist criticisms this was a criticism of capitalism as such – industrial concentration is a universal phenomenon – rather than of the Spanish form of capitalism. The Spanish private banks were no more influential than the German banks, nor were they markedly less efficient except in one respect: it was harder for a small businessman to raise a loan and the absorption of small local banks (again a process that has gone on everywhere in the capitalist world) by the big seven worsened the situation.

The criticisms of the left are, paradoxically, similar to those of extreme adherents of a free market economy. The consequence of a process of industrial concentration, dominated by the 'oligarchy', is a non-competitive industry within a protected domestic market – what Tamames calls 'neo-autarky'. Protection of domestic producers is held to encourage low productivity, expensive, non-competitive exports and a heavy dependence on imports financed only by invisible exports. It engenders a lopsided economy, slow to modernise. All these imperfections are seen as part of an economy where the state puts its bet on the strong entrenched interests. Yet the representatives of the strong – the big banks – profess to see this mixed economy as a thing of bits and pieces, held together by sticking plaster (*parches*), fabricated by a paternalistic bureaucracy bred in the interventionism of the forties and incapable of understanding modern business conditions.[24]

It was the 'small and medium' entrepreneurs who felt left out in

---

*Under the 1962 Banking Law the commercial banks were to be separated from the industrial or merchant banks. This separation was achieved on paper rather than in reality as the industrial banks were connected with the 'big seven'. The relative importance of the private banks in Spain is illustrated by the fact that, in 1967, seven banks figured among the twenty most profitable and important enterprises. In the USA the most important private bank occupied the thirty-ninth place. Ramón Trías in *Las Fuentes de financión de la empresa en España* (Editorial Moneda y Crédito, 1972) defends the private banking system but suggests some form of control by consumers as a limit on the power of the new bureaucrats (pp. 14*ff.*).

the cold in the new Spain of the 1970s. They protested against the banks' propensity to favour 'their' companies with credit in times of financial stringency when it was denied to the small business-man; they struck out against the planners with their triumphalist conception of development which bred industrial 'gigantism'. These small concerns were very numerous; of the million or so enterprises in Spain, 99 per cent employed under 500 employees but they constituted nearly 80 per cent of the work force. By 1976 small businessmen had begun to organise themselves to press the government for better treatment, above all better access to credit. The concept of 'the small and medium employers' – the *P y ME* – took institutional, corporate form in a body with nearly half a million members.* It was a pressure group that no politician could neglect in 1977 and whose grievances some sought to exploit.

(g)
The two Spains

By the 1970s car-borne Spaniards from the cities were visiting the remote, poverty-stricken hamlets of Galicia as tourists in search of the picturesque remnants of some self-sufficient pre-capitalist society. That these hamlets should have roads at all would have astounded their inhabitants in 1940; but that their lot was still one of relentless labour on land which yielded miserable rewards and that, apart from butane stoves and tractors, the advance of the consumer society had meant little to their lives, showed that the 'two Spains' of poverty and relative prosperity persisted.

If the homogeneity of misery had been the hallmark of the forties, the gap between the 'two Spains' had widened with industrialisation and population movements. The rural areas with a high birth-rate were drained to fill the cities where birth-rates were low; from the 'desert' centre and the poor south emigrants flooded to the pros-perous periphery and the 'industrial triangle' of the north-east.†

*There were two organisations. One believed in a common interest between the large employers and the small businessman; the rival organisation held that their interests conflicted. *El País* (25 January 1977).

†The exception to the centrifugal movement is Madrid. The other historic centres of attraction were Barcelona and the Basque provinces together with the coastal fringe of Catalonia and Valencia. The two latter areas of population growth are connected via Saragossa and Navarre, also areas of attraction. For the earlier popu-lation trends see J. Nadal, *La población española* (1971). The first economist to emphasise these movements and the increasing concentration of population in cer-tain 'core' areas was Román Perpiná (see his 'La problemática de la dilimitación espacial o regional', in *Boletín de Estudios económicos*, no. 83 (1971) pp. 675*ff*. For a specialised view see J. Díez Nicolás, 'Tamaño, densidad y crecimiento de la pobla-ción espanola', in *Revista Internacional de Sociologia,* no. 109 (1970), pp. 87–123.

Rapid, uncontrolled growth has always and everywhere produced such a polarisation of wealth: the south of Italy, for instance, stagnates as Turin and Milan prosper. Wealth is increasingly concentrated in the industrial regions of Catalonia and the Basque provinces, in Madrid and Saragossa; it is to these centres that the rural poor migrate. Madrid is a case of urbanisation unique in Europe, a metropolis that has drained the surrounding provinces, creating a demographic desert.

Certainly the planners showed increasing concern – especially in the Third Development Plan – with these regional imbalances. With less confidence in the 'spill-over' effects of investment in prosperous regions, they showed a greater inclination than in 1964 to invest directly in the poorer regions, to subordinate efficiency and aggregate growth to regional equity. The planners were faced with the social costs of rapid growth once it brought severe congestion in Barcelona and Madrid. But the fundamental contradiction remains: sectoral growth as a target cuts across considerations of regional equity; capital flows to regions where it will find highest returns.

Regional disparities in per capita income remain severe. In the 1970s the disposable income of a family from the poor rural provinces was a third of that of the rich industrialised regions; a family in Jaén, Segovia or Cuenca existed on a fraction of the income of a family in Bilbao or Madrid.[25] Every survey revealed a lower standard of living and a diminished participation in the benefits of the consumer society in the poor regions; in 1970, 70 per cent of Madrid homes possessed a television set; but only 11 per cent in the province of Soria.* The low level of social services in the poorer provinces reinforces regional imbalances: there are fewer hospital beds and the greatest weakness of the health service is its failure to serve rural areas. Seventy per cent of hospital services in Catalonia are concentrated in the Barcelona metropolitan area.

It is not only a continued faith in private investment as the motor of growth that inhibits regional planning. Spain under Franco had the most highly centralised government in Western Europe and the planners could not create, out of fifty disparate provinces, suitable regions for planning purposes, or equip them with regional planning boards that would concentrate the miscellaneous collection of government agencies and ministry 'field services' in the localities. To create 'natural' regions for planning purposes

*For a detailed survey see *Encuesta de equipamiento y nivel cultural de las familias*, published by the Presidencia del Gobierno in 1975, vol. 1. The lower cost of living in the rural provinces favours the bureaucrat on a standard wage: a civil servant who could keep a mistress in Granada can scarcely keep a family in Bilbao.

might imply a back-handed recognition of the underlying political claims of Catalonia and the Basque provinces which the regime could not admit.[26] Least of all could the government allow local participation in planning decisions where 'top down' planning could meet 'bottom up' demands. The Territorial Planning Commissions of the Third Plan constituted 'a typical method of developing pseudo-representative institutions in an authoritarian society'.[27]

(h)
The rural exodus

We must now turn to the rural world, the poor relation of industrial Spain.

In 1940 the levels of agricultural productivity were lower than those of the years before the Civil War. Techniques were still primitive. The mule-drawn 'Roman' plough, the earthen threshing floor, the *noria* with its earthenware jars tied to a primitive wheel irrigating the fields, could be seen by any traveller. There were regions of malnutrition verging on starvation during what became known as the 'years of hunger'. In the fifties it was the pockets of rural poverty that drove field labourers, farmers – and above all their sons – to seek a better life in the cities. Later, when changes in agricultural techniques and management helped to release rural labour for industry, it was the backward areas where the proportion of the active population in agriculture was still high – around half in Extremadura and Andalusia – that supplied the flood of migrants.

In the nineteenth and early twentieth centuries Spaniards had escaped rural misery by emigration to Latin America. They had come mainly from Galicia and the northern provinces. In the late 1950s and throughout the 1960s this pattern changed dramatically. It was the south and centre that became reservoirs of labour and the flood went not to America, but to Barcelona, Madrid and Saragossa or to the farms of southern France. Finally they went to swell the 'Mediterranean reserve army of labour' – Greeks, Algerians, Italians and Turks as well as Spaniards – in the factories of France and Germany. The exodus began in the 1950s and by 1960 Andalusia had lost well over half a million workers; by 1970, 1,600,000 Andalusians were living outside their native provinces – 712,000 in Barcelona alone.[28]

Without this transfer of human resources from rural under-employment to the factories and building sites of the cities there could have been no industrial take-off. That emigration abroad took place at all shows that the growth of industry and services, dramatic though this was, was insufficient to absorb the surplus population. Emigration to France and Germany was the safety valve of the economy when the Stabilisation Plan of 1959 produced a sharp and cruel recession; without it there would have been massive unemployment. Ullastres, author of the Stabilisation Plan, claimed that emigration was less a necessity than a great national project: 'Europe and the world call us and if we go to them it is not to escape a possible deficit in the balance of payments (a reference to emigrants' remittances) but because it is our universal mission.'[29] This was typical of the defensive rhetoric of the regime.

Its nationalistic tone was reflected in the *canción española* – the best-known example of this excruciating genre is 'Viva España' – which presented the emigrant as a king ot hero, an adventurer seeking his living abroad but keeping alive in his heart the Spain he had left. Yet emigration in the fifties, for the emigrant, was not a choice but a harsh necessity. Protest songs reflected this reality.

> I left my land
> I went with pain
> If there is one who deals out justice
> He forgot me.

It was the realisation of the necessity of emigration – both internal and abroad – that caused a sharp shift in the practices and ultimately in the ideology of the regime. It tacitly dropped talk of the peasant as the 'moral reserve' of the nation, to be kept on the land by ambitious programmes of internal colonisation. It abandoned its struggle to keep the rural poor out of the great cities. In 1955 Arrese, then Minister of Housing, regarded 'every house built in the city' as 'a new temptation to the peasant', and as late as 1957 the government was trying to stop immigrants coming to the shanty towns round Madrid. By the sixties the government admitted the necessity of emigration. Instead of seeking to stop the flow to France and Germany the government assisted it. This was a dramatic change in the official vision of the ideal Spanish society.

While those who went to the factories of France and Germany left to return home with their savings, those who emigrated to Barcelona or Madrid intended to settle there. To the Andalusians and Murcians Catalonia was a foreign world speaking a foreign language. In the fifties they complained of Catalan 'racism', of contemptuous treatment by native Catalans. 'What I want is that people should respect me' is ths anguished cry of the 'Murcian' anti-hero of Juan Marsé's novel on the life of an immigrant suburb.[30] As the uncomprehending horror of his upper middle-class girlfriend's mother shows, he did not get it: the 'Murcians' were, to her, illiterate delinquents.

With migration from the rural *pueblos* only the ageing – and they were the illiterates – remained. After the small farmers and labourers had left, the small shopkeepers and artisans deserted a poor market. All this increased the attraction of urban Spain; surveys show that only a fraction of small peasant farmers want their sons to stay at home: they save to educate them for brighter prospects of a world revealed to them by the television set in the village bar. Hence the Spain of deserted villages – one of the favourite themes of the Castilian novelist Miguel Delibes. 'Cortiguera is a dying village, in agony. Its winding streets, invaded by weeds and nettles, without a dog's bark or a child's laugh to break the silence, enclose a pathetic gravity, the lugubrious air of the cemetery.'[31]

The absorption of these quasi-literate village and small-town immigrants, arriving in Barcelona in crowded trains with wooden suitcases and settling in drab suburbs where few native Catalans live, into Catalan society must remain a serious concern for Catalan nationalists. 'Murcians' and other immigrants, rootless and incapable of collective action as a class, remain on the margin of society, rarely rising above the working class, often – apart from large concerns like SEAT – doing the kind of work coloured immigrants do in Britain: tram driving, for instance, is a quasi-monopoly of Galician immigrants and large numbers of Murcians are builders' labourers.[32] The realisation of the size of the problem and its importance for the future of Catalonia has changed initial contempt into an eagerness to argue that the children of immigrants are accepting Catalan values – at least the immigrants are imitating the natives by extensive use of contraception – and learning the Catalan language. In 1934 the Catalan demographer Vandellós, conscious of the low native birth-rate, prophesied that, in a Catalonia where half the population would be of immigrant origin, Catalan culture would be destroyed. The fears that Catalan culture will never be assimilated by Castilian immigrants with only a barbarous 'kitchen' Catalan at their disposal, persist. Hence the insistence on education in Catalan; yet it is precisely in the immigrant suburbs that schools, like adequate sanitation and well-paved streets, are in short supply.

The patterns and motives of the emigrants have changed. Those of the fifties saw themselves as pushed by *intolerable* poverty; those of the sixties were younger and saw emigration in terms of increased opportunities, as an escape from villages and 'agro-towns' where casual labour gave precarious rewards.[33] Emigration – abroad in particular – was a means of social mobility. The chance to educate the children, to save up to buy a bar, a tractor or a lorry for contract work, made tolerable the desertion of families and familiar surroundings for the harsh spartan life in Germany or France where the television was incomprehensible and the choice was between living in factory dormitories or overcrowded, expensive lodgings.[34] Sometimes the emigrant who left as a labourer bought up land and became a proprietor and, often soon in trouble, was forced to emigrate once more.

In 1975 the doors of Germany and France were shut to Spanish workers; the golden age of emigration ended with the recession and unemployment in Germany, Switzerland and France. Moreover, the patterns of internal migration were changing more slowly: Barcelona and Madrid showed signs of an anti-economic saturation and migrants found more opportunities in the towns where growth had been less spectacular.

If emigration abroad was a long-term safety valve and if migration to the cities gave the new industry its labour force, seasonal emigration is the short-term relief for the rural poor. In buses which empty whole villages of all but the old and the children, the active population leaves after the harvest to work in the vineyards and sugar-beet fields of France. The conditions are hard, the contracts uncertain. Others leave to work as waiters and chambermaids in the seaside hotels of the Spanish Mediterranean; still others leave for the olive harvest in Jaén. Such seasonal earnings help the poor peasant to balance his budget, producing as much as 70 per cent of his cash income.

Two case studies from Andalusia illustrate the changing patterns of the rural exodus. The dramatic landscape of eastern Andalusia includes olive *latifundia*, poor cereal farms and the wretched plots in the semi-desert lands towards Almería.[35] The first emigrants were the underemployed casual landless labourers of the large estates; they went in the 1950s to the industrial areas of Catalonia. They were followed by small proprietors who could not make ends meet – three bad harvests mean bankruptcy. These were the emigrants of desperation. Now the emigrants are the young, looking for higher wages and a better life in the city: they are no longer objects of compassion. Emigration, therefore, has *improved* conditions: it has tended to force up the wages of those who remain behind and given the labouring classes a new independence.

The classic latifundia are also under new pressures in the rich *campiña* of Cordoba.[36] The old aristocratic absentee landowner,

his estate run by a bailiff hiring gangs of labourers, is being
replaced by a 'bourgeois' entrepreneur; the palace of the local absentee marquis, where royal hunting parties had lodged, was of
no use to the new purchaser interested only in profits. In the 1950s
the *campiña* was revolutionised by artificial fertilisers,
mechanisation and new market crops like sunflowers which require
less labour. Mechanisation and modern techniques have reduced
the demand for hired hands; the proprietors keep the minimum
labour force needed by mixed labour/rent contracts. Surplus
labour began to leave the land in the fifties. The labourers whom
one saw hanging about, waiting like cattle to be hired, in the plazas
of Andalusia in the fifties, have almost vanished.

Andalusia is still a depressed area; but it is no longer the scene of
the violent social conflicts of the thirties and the extreme misery of
the years of hunger of the forties. The problem then was the
pressure of population on land monopolised by the few. Hence the
demand for a *reparto* − the distribution of the great estates among
the landless poor − or radical agrarian reform. The landed
monopoly of the few rich persists; but to a greater or lesser extent
the landless poor have 'solved' the agrarian problem with their feet
by leaving the land for the cities. Those who remain want decent
wages and the landowners no longer have the social and political
power to resist these demands.

(i)
New patterns in agriculture

The Franco regime was a landlord's regime but it was not a
landlord's paradise. Though it denied the labourer a union to
improve his wretched conditions and resolutely resisted, in its plans
for internal colonisation, any project which involved the
expropriation of private estates, it was committed to the protection
of the small farmer, 'the moral reserve of the nation'. Thus its
legislation gave the tenant farmer security of tenure, a measure
which was universally unpopular with landowners. 'I get 7,100
pesetas a year in rent,' a minor Andalusian landowner complained.

> That's what I was getting in 1947 and that's what I get today
> when 7,100 pesetas isn't worth a tenth of what it was in 1947.
> The law forbids me to raise the rent. If I wanted to get the
> tenant out he'd ask for 200,000 pesetas compensation or more.
> This is why so much building is going on in Spain. No one wants
> to invest in farming because you can't get a decent return,
> especially on land as poor as this is here. On an apartment

building you can make 12 per cent or 14 per cent, whereas the land doesn't make you even 2 per cent.*

For the agrarian reformers of the Second Republic, the obvious targets were the latifundia of the absentee 'aristocratic' land-owners: these vast estates, extensively and poorly farmed, could without modernisation supply a rentier class with the incomes necessary for a life of conspicuous consumption in Biarritz or Madrid. They still exist. But with the emigration of much of the labour force that once worked them, with tractor drivers and mechanics replacing gangs of day labourers, with more modern methods of farming, even the landscape of Andalusia is changing. The whitewashed *cortijo* (the buildings which housed the labourers and mules) is redundant. It no longer dominates the vast tawny fields like a fortress. It is replaced by tractor sheds, Dutch barns and silos.

Latifundia are, in the eyes of a new generation of agricultural entrepreneurs, modern productive enterprises. They no longer see themselves as aristocratic rentiers; they justify their ownership of large estates by their new, 'useful' social function as efficient managers.†

The Franco regime, unwilling to make a frontal attack on private property or revive 'utopian' schemes of confiscating the latifundia and distributing the land to the rural poor, chose to concentrate on what it regarded, with some justification, as the curse of rural Spain: the minute farms of minifundia. These dwarf farms — nearly half of Spanish farms are under 3 hectares — are split into minute fields. There are 22 million fields of less than 2 hectares.** Time is wasted in going from field to field; such units cannot be mechanised. Their owners can scrape only a bare subsistence.

*Ronald Fraser, *The Pueblo. A Mountain Village on the Costa del Sol* (1973), p. 42. However, local landlords failed, on the whole, to cash in on the tourist boom. The Costa del Sol is the creation of Madrid and Basque capitalism, allied with foreign investment.

†For this new self-image see J. Martínez Alier, *La estabilidad del latifundio en España* (1968). He points out how, in general, Cordoban landowners in the 1960s acted rationally, maximising profits. However, even when renting out land would have been more profitable than direct cultivation (owing to high labour costs), landlords were reluctant to act as rational economic men and become rentiers as this would have destroyed their social legitimisation as 'useful' producers. Martínez Alier argues that this legitimisation is neces-sary to resist demands for a *reparto* or radical agrarian reform (op.cit., p. 336).

**The imbalance in landownership is shown by the fact that three-quarters of proprietors (i.e. peasant farmers) occupy only 17.6 per cent of the culti-vable land while 2 per cent of proprietors own 26.9 per cent. See the INE *Censo Agrario de España* published in 1972.

The regime has made a serious effort to meet this problem by *concentración parcelaria* – the concentration of small scattered fields into more reasonable units. Concentration is mandatory when 60 per cent of the local inhabitants (or those owning 60 per cent of the land) request it, and it has been carried out on 4 million hectares. However, concentration has not always cured the evils of small property in spite of its aim to create economically viable peasant farms; normally 10 per cent of the inhabitants of a *pueblo* own 50 per cent of the land. Concentration, therefore, still leaves a rural proletariat of owners of a hectare or so.*

It is only the substantial farmer who can mechanise and survive. The most obvious index of investment is the number of tractors which have replaced oxen, mules and men. In 1962 there was one tractor for every 228 hectares; in 1970, 45. The introduction of the motor cultivator – an advance more dramatic than that of the tractor – was a minor revolution in the small, terraced fields of the Levante.† It was only the prosperous farmer with easy access to credit who could afford long-term investments.** It was the smallholders in the richer regions who did relatively well: with only 3 per cent of the cultivated land they produced 13 per cent of the total output. On the dry lands of Castile and the poor fields of Galicia the peasant's life on a small farm was one of unremitting labour to gain a bare subsistence. Many have sold out to their more prosperous neighbours and emigrated; those who remained are often living at standards below those of an agricultural labourer.‡ The regime had hoped to reinforce its sociological base and fulfil its ideological commitments by fostering a numerous race of

*See R. Tamames, *Introducción a la economía espanola* (1973), p. 84. Some idea of what has been achieved and what still remains to be done is shown by the figures for the number of fields (*parcelas*) per farm and the number of farms under 1 hectare in 1962 and 1972.
1962: Burgos, 41.2 *parcelas*, 2.3 million units under 1 hectare; Corunna, 21.3, 2.7 million; Segovia, 37.5, 1 million; Soria, 56.8, 1.7; Zamora, 37.6, 1.9 million.
1972: Burgos, 39.4, 1.3 million; Corunna, 16.4, 1.8 million; Segovia, 25.4, 531,251; Soria, 39.8, 732,840; Zamora, 33.6, 1.2 million.
†Between 1968 and 1975 the number of small motor cultivators tripled.
**This differential rate may have allowed large landowners to borrow at below market rates for investment, the profits of which, placed in industrial securities, might constitute a transfer from agriculture to industry. cf. J. L. Leal *et al. La agricultura en el desarrollo capitalista español* (*1940–70*) (1975), p. 12.
‡‡cf. José Felix Tezanos, 'Las clases sociales en el campo español', *Sistema*, no. 19 (July 1977). In 1968 peasants who employed no labour owned more television sets, refrigerators and washing-machines than agricultural labourers. By 1975 the positions were reversed.

comfortably-off peasant proprietors. Economic development has created a race of kulaks and a proletariat of subsistence farmers in the poor regions. To economists this process was not merely inevitable, but desirable in terms of efficient production. They argued for the abandonment of excessive price support for wheat which allowed the small farmer to avoid bankruptcy. But even without any ideological enthusiasm for the peasant farmer of the Castilian heartland, could any government, committed to full employment, face a wholesale clearance of smallholders?[37]

All these changes — emigration, mechanisation, the increasingly hard plight of the small farmer — have altered the balance of Spanish society. 'Nostalgia for country life,' writes Amando de Miguel, 'is completely utopian' — indeed, in arid Spain, there is little feeling for the land except as a hard taskmaster.* With emigration an urban life style is perceived as 'superior' to the values of the agrarian *pueblo*.† Folklore, so fostered by the regime in its early stages, now appears to the rural population as embarrassing, a sign of backwardness. Tastes and fashions are becoming the tastes and fashions of urban society. This is not to be seen solely as a loss. The strict social control of the face-to-face society in the rural *pueblo* vanishes and there is an increase in individual choice. Outside the poor regions, the farmer is no longer a peasant bent over the plough; he sees himself as a professional agriculturalist. There is a new middle class of agricultural contractors, agents for artificial fertilisers.

Even the Andalusian day labourer is no longer a pariah in a small *pueblo*; with his shigher wages he can patronise the café formerly reserved for 'the powerful ones' though he would be summarily ejected from a landowners' club in Seville. The society of deference, of grinding poverty and unemployment, the basis of the power of the old electoral managers of the nineteenth-century parliamentary system, is slowly vanishing. The labourer of Andalusia will not engage in a savage jacquerie or invade the local big estates; he will join a trade union. In the tourist-infested province of Alicante the small farmer sells his house and land to a

---

*Amando de Miguel, *Manual de estructura social de España* (1974), p. 102. The lack of feeling for the land in the Mediterranean was noticed by Doreen Warrender. The contrast with England is complete: a Spanish Wordsworth is inconceivable.

†Though its moral coherence has been exaggerated, the inward-looking *pueblo* did foster a sense of community and the loss of this sense of belonging could make emigration a psychological wrench. For the values of the traditional *pueblo* see J. Pitt-Rivers, *People of the Sierra* (1951), a study of a mountain *pueblo* in western Andalusia. The wrench of emigration was most acute in the case of foreign emigration; in the case of domestic emigration there was usually a friend or a relation to help the emigrant to adjust.

foreigner to be turned into a holiday home or a tax refuge. With the proceeds he leaves a primitive but aesthetically attractive house and buys a bleak, colourless apartment in the nearest town.

(j)
Agriculture and industry

We must now examine the role of the agricultural sector in the economy as a whole. Radical critics take the ossified 'traditional agricultural' system, with its abysmally low production, as a 'brake' on industrial growth; their favourite descriptive term of abuse is 'ankylosis'. These critics take a Western model, arguing that a 'healthy' industrial take-off into self-sustained growth is only possible given a previous, or at least contemporary, agricultural revolution such as occurred in eighteenth-century England. This pushes surplus population off the land, increases the food supply for the industrial towns and provides a richer domestic market for industrial products. Yet Spain began its industrial revolution – lopsided and fragile though it may have been – after 1939 *without* an agricultural revolution. How could this have happened? However low the levels of production, agriculture made an important financial contribution to the limited growth up to 1960.

The limited industrialisation, within the structure of autarky in the forties and fifties, was made possible by a transfer of resources from agriculture to industry in the form of savings generated in agriculture. Low wages – the 'wages of hunger' which could not even give a labourer's family decent food, combined with a low level of monetary outlays (the only outside input was fertilisers), allowed savings. These were transferred from the countryside to the towns by the banking system. The relationship between agricultural and industrial prices was favourable to the latter.[38] In addition to this, only agricultural exports – especially from the Mediterranean provinces of the Levante – gave the foreign exchange through which industrialists, at favourable rates of exchange which penalised the agricultural exporters, could import a limited amount of capital goods and raw materials.*

In the later fifties and sixties the capacity to finance industrial growth by agricultural savings declined as costs rose and profits fell. Rural wages doubled between 1951 and 1971. Investment was necessary in machinery and other inputs such as fertilisers. The

---

*The industrialists were favoured because the prices of agricultural exports (e.g. of citrus fruits) were fixed by the international market while the industrialists enjoyed protection from international competition and the monopoly of the domestic market.

relative prices of industrial goods and agricultural products levelled off. Agriculture continued to supply surplus labour to the building sites and factories; but its role as a supplier of capital was replaced by tourist and emigrant revenues and foreign loans.

(k)
The crisis of traditional agriculture

In 1900 Joaquín Costa wrote: 'Every night half of Spain goes to bed hungry . . . The illness that afflicts her is a stomach ailment and the cure must come, not through the ears, but through the mouth.' How far does agriculture fill the Spanish stomach?

In the 'years of hunger' in the forties the whole concentration of the new regime was to produce enough bread – the basic food. Self-sufficiency was achieved by protecting wheat at all costs by state purchase at guaranteed prices and by prohibitive tariffs. This was in part an ideological and political choice: the Castilian peasant, whose only secure cash crop was wheat, was seen as the 'foundation of the race', insulated against the subversive influence of the city with its proletariat mobilised by the workers' parties in the Civil War.* As long as bread remained the basic foodstuff of a poor population the 'battle for wheat' could be justified.

By the sixties, with growing prosperity, dietary habits changed. Demand for bread fell while demand for other products, particularly meat, eggs and dairy products, rose. The traditional agriculture could not respond adequately to these changes. This was partly because subsidised prices for wheat kept land in wheat which might have produced other crops; partly because small farmers resisted changes from the traditional Mediterranean triad of wheat, vines and olives; partly because large landowners, distrusting labour as increasingly 'difficult' to manage and increasingly expensive, preferred a crop that could be easily mechanised.†

The failure to respond to the market demands of the urban

---

*Burgos, the Nationalist capital in the Civil War, was the centre of a region of small cereal farmers.

†Irrigated land that could produce fodder crops like maize remains in wheat. Though the cultivation of maize has increased dramatically on irrigated land and the area devoted to wheat has declined by one-third, wheat is still grown on irrigated land. Wheat is increasing as an irrigated crop in the Campiña de Córdoba simply because it is easily mechanisable on large estates. This is one strong argument against large estates on irrigated land. In Murcia, a province of smallholdings on irrigated land, much more valuable horticultural crops are grown; in other regions, with a wine surplus, irrigated land is 'wasted' on vines.

population had important consequences. By the seventies what the traditional agriculture could not supply — meat and animal food-stuffs for domestic cattle — had to be imported, and this weighed heavily on the balance of payments.

At the same time as 'traditional' agriculture was failing to meet new demands it was generating surpluses. There was increasing talk of the 'crisis of traditional agriculture'. By the spring of 1977 farmers were imitating their French colleagues and bringing traffic to a halt by parades of tractors. They demanded, as farmers did elsewhere, higher guaranteed prices. Yet it was precisely guaranteed prices that had encouraged them to cultivate crops that could not be sold. It was guaranteed prices that sustained the great monocultures: the traveller from Granada to Madrid passes huge areas devoted to olives — the province of Jaén is the single greatest olive-producing area in the world — and then through vast vineyards. By 1953 the surplus wine had to be bought up by state agencies. High guaranteed prices may just save the struggling family farm; the real benefits go to the large operator and are clearly inflationary and a burden on the rest of the population.[39] There is really no way out for the small farmer except co-operation or emigration. Improved credit for long-term improvements may save the enterprising, larger peasant farmers and there is a strong case for encouraging them to use it; but loans to bail out the small farmer on the dry farming lands of the *secano* will only prolong his agony.[40]

By the seventies Spanish agriculture was playing a similar part in the economy and going through the same crisis as in the industrialised economies of the West. In the forties the fortunes of agriculture were decisive for industrial Spain. 'A year of good harvests,' ran the report of the Bank of Bilbao in 1948, 'is a year of prosperity for trade and industry.' The contribution of agriculture to the GNP exceeded that of industry; agriculture dominated exports and it was the fruits of the Mediterranean that gave industry its meagre supply of foreign exchange. By the mid-sixties this situation was reversed. As in France or England, farmers are claiming that they have become the Cinderellas of the economy, a pressure group that was losing out to industrialists and urban workers.[41] Spain had ceased to be different.

(l)
The economy in the seventies

If we examine the Spanish economy in the year 1976 we can see more clearly the degree of its approximation to Western Europe, some of the imperfections of the process of approximation, and the costs to be paid for the particular way in which the economic miracle of the sixties had been achieved.[42]

1975 and 1976 were the worst years for the economy since the crisis of 1959. Why did Spain suffer so badly from the oil crisis and why was the process of recovery in 1976 markedly slower and more precarious than that of the rest of Europe? There was nothing unique about the symptoms of the crisis itself: a slowing down of the growth rate (negative in 1975 and only 2 per cent in 1976), inflation, rising unemployment, a severe deficit in the balance of payments and a punishing drop in investment.

The falling off in investment was in part due to what the researchers of the Banco de Bilbao called 'a profound transformation'; a sharp rise in wages that ate into the profit margins of the employers, a change that presaged a new economic balance in Spanish society and the end of cheap labour. Between 1974 and 1976 the share of wages and salaries in the national income rose from 61.8 per cent to 66.7 per cent.* If the proportion of wages and salaries had dramatically increased this did not mean that wealth was equitably distributed. The richest 10 per cent were nearly twice as rich as their opposite numbers in the United Kingdom.[43]

For the entrepreneur the golden age had become an age of iron. Profits fell from 9.5 per cent to 5.8 per cent of the national income and with them investment. The middle class had, in the sixties, begun to buy shares. In the euphoria of the early seventies they had seen their investments rise in value by 60 per cent; in 1975 they lost more than they had gained in the previous five years. Employers had no profits to re-invest and the new 'investing class' had burnt its fingers: to make up the deficit the government pumped more money into industrial lame ducks, a distortion of the discipline of the market process which shocked a generation of bankers brought up to admire the self-regulatory mechanisms of capitalism.

*Labour costs per hour rose by 30 per cent in 1977. These rises have been so sharp that foreign firms have switched planned investment elsewhere, e.g. Ford which went to Wales instead of expanding in Valencia. See *The New Spain: Business Problems and Opportunities*, prepared by Business International SA (1977), p. 77.

Proportion of wages and salaries in the National Income

	1960	1963	1970	1974
France	58.3	62.4	62.9	69.3
Italy	51.5	56.6	59.8	67.9
USA	71.1	70.0	76.8	76.7
Spain	53.0	53.9	56.9	61.8

The sixties had seen a consumer boom as Spain's patterns of consumption, its way of life, became year by year nearer to the European pattern.[44] It is now argued that the expansion of the sixties had been achieved 'somewhat frivolously' by the boosting of domestic consumption at all costs.[45]

In spite of the gloom of the economic situation, opinion surveys in 1977 revealed an optimism about the future that cannot be explained in economic terms. This optimism was absent among the well-to-do; employers and investors had suffered too sharply. It was the workers who were optimistic – in spite of the fact that their wage increases, which temporarily boosted consumption, were eroded by inflation and that there was scarcely a working-class family in Spain that did not have a relative out of work.

This casts a retrospective light on the social and economic dynamics of Francoism and poses a serious problem for democratic successor governments. 'Social demand is a composite product of private goods, public services and political goods, each of which, within certain limits, can be substituted for the other. For years[i.e. in the sixties] supply has tended to favour the first to the detriment of the other two; but the situation has changed radically. In the last two years [1975 and 1976] the public has been more sensitised to politics and this has created new expectations which, logically, are more optimistic on the part of those who have had fewer political goods and therefore have more to gain by political change which implicitly transmits the notion of other social transformations'.[46] Translated, this jargon means that a sense of political participation, except for the Francoist elite, was a scarce commodity under Francoism. In its place the regime supplied a relatively abundant supply of satisfactions for *all* individual consumers. The problem for the future is whether democracy can supply both 'private goods', that is, maintain the material satisfaction of a consumer society *and* the political satisfactions which are supposed to be inherent in a democratic system, without 'transmitting' social transformations so radical that they will unhinge a precarious economy.

Chapter 5

Society 1939–1977

Critics of the economic performance of Francoism stressed its shortcomings, writing off the undisputed new levels of prosperity as a reflection – and a mismanaged, distorted reflection at that – of the European boom. It was left to the triumphalist propaganda of the government to highlight the successes and to claim that growth was the product of a wise combination of social peace and direction from above. By 1980, it claimed, Spain would be the ninth industrial power in the Western world. Indeed by 1970 the economy seemed more promising than that of the United Kingdom.

The new economy changed the social structure and, less dramatically, the social *mores* of Spain. With rapid industrialisation, with the increase in the numbers of skilled workers and the growth of the service sector where 'human capital' was more important than manual labour, the occupational structure of Spain changed more in two decades than it had in the previous hundred years. A process which had taken half a century in France or Britain was telescoped into two decades. The very suddenness of the onset of modernisation meant that the older values of a pre-industrial society persisted in the era of capitalist growth, a phenomenon that Gino Germani calls 'superficial modernisation', where, say, traditional attitudes to the status of women can exist side by side with the 'rational' values of modern capitalism. By the 1970s Spain had become a curious mixture of traditional – largely Catholic – values and the behaviour thought proper for a consumer society.[1]

(a)
The establishment

In the years immediately after the Civil War nothing appeared to have changed. The conservative society of 1931 seemed restored by victory over bourgeois reformists and their Socialist allies. The dominant class appeared still to be that amalgam of landowners, financiers and entrepreneurs that had grown up during the nineteenth century. Its values were conservative and aristocratic, its mode of operation familial nepotism.[2] In 1944 a *Who's Who* of the thirty-eight most prestigious figures of the banking world of Madrid included sixteen financiers with titles and another six connected with the aristocracy.[3] This establishment world functioned in the protected, closed world of the autarkic economy; it enjoyed the favours of the regime and its members were the familiars of Franco on his three-day shooting expeditions – his sole contact with the world outside his officials and his fellow officers. In the early years, Franco was given to outbursts against the 'aristocracy of blood' and like many modern military authoritarians he expressed admiration for technocrats and engineers, 'doers' as opposed to 'thinkers'.* Yet his own stuffy and tedious court, his grants of titles of nobility, reinforced aristocratic values. There was one uncomfortable accretion to this exclusive world: the new rich who had made their money out of the war and the black market. It was the Catalan new wartime rich who began in the later forties to buy up property in the fishing villages along the Costa Brava.[4]

In this comfortable society of the forties personal favour oiled the machine. 'Everything in Spain,' wrote Ridruejo, 'a telephone, a business concession, a flat, the most insignificant bureaucratic favour, is obtained because you have a friend.'[5] This traffic in influence was the inevitable consequence of a world of scarcities. Franco was fully aware of the corruption and trade in favours. He staffed the INI with officers because he thought of them as the technicians, disciplined by a strict code of honour. But he turned a blind eye to corruption as he did to all awkward situations.[6]

Just as the successes of industrialisation doomed autarky, so the later expansion modified the economic and social establishment that had flourished after the war. The new slogans of the sixties were rationality, efficiency, the maxims of the world of the impersonal, competitive business corporation rather than of the comfortable world of family connection and personal favour. Juan Linz and Amando de Miguel described the new race of business executives in a study published in 1966.[7] They went to business schools; qualifications became as important as connection; competence counted, in the business world, more than enthusiastic acceptance of the ideology of the regime. Emilio Romero deplored

---

Conversaciones, pp. 54, 67. Most of Franco's outbursts were directed against the clique of courtiers that surrounded Don Juan. Franco told Don Juan that the true aristocracy was that of the generals, the leading scientists and businessmen.

the subordination of the old ideologues to the new technocrats. 'Dogmas have gone out of the window. Now we have the solvers (*solucionadores*), the managers, the boys who have been to university in the last few years, especially in the Faculties of Economics.'

The change was not as dramatic as Romero imagined. If Falangist attacks on the rich became unfashionable, if the new gospel of business efficiency struck some blows at the old establishment,[8] the aim of economic modernisers like Ullastres and López Rodó was to foster some new symbiosis between traditional Catholic values, an authoritarian political system and the American way of life. This was the philosophy of the Opus Dei reflected in the language of the Development Plans. Thus the new economic policy did not challenge traditional Catholicism, nor did the bureaucratisation and rationalisation of business life produce a social revolution in the elite. It absorbed the new managerial class or survived by sending its sons to Harvard or the new business schools of the Opus Dei. The new compound of technocracy and Catholicism may be, in the long run, unstable; but it served its purpose in the sixties.

The establishment we have described forms the upper ranges of what is termed in Spain 'the traditional middle classes'.* At its core were the professionals: doctors, engineers, professors, lawyers. Their hallmark was a university education and success in examinations. The successful candidates in the entrance examinations to the civil service and the professions – the 'número unos' – were the core of the political elite and this continuous process of absorption of the ablest of the middle classes is an important factor explaining the political success of the regime. The successful professionals – civil servants and university professors above all – manned the ministries as under secretaries; increasingly they dominated Franco's ministries. Once in power the rewards were splendid. Whereas a British minister must work a month to buy a small car, his Spanish equivalent has only to stay in the job for twenty-two days.[9]

Education was the key to entry into the privileged elite of Francoism; hence the investment in it by the more modest members of the traditional middle class and the passion of the educational

---

*Certainly, as the Marxist Maurín pointed out in the thirties and every historian has emphasised since, Spain developed no self-confident bourgeoisie on a national level; the Catalan industrialists and Basque magnates were effective pressure groups without a national political party to represent their interests. The attempt of the Catalan financier, Francisco Cambó, to create such a party was a failure.

debate of the seventies. An educational system at the service of the middle classes ensured their permanence in positions of power and influence. Only by a democratic educational system, it seemed, could the hold of the middle classes be challenged within the framework of Francoism.

For it was the values of the traditional middle classes that became the social orthodoxy of Franco's Spain in its early years. A majority, probably, of these classes had sympathised with a mildly reformist republic in 1931; with the increasing threat of working-class power and what Senator Marías described as the proletarisation of life styles, they returned, scared, to their conservative moorings. Catholicism, whether sincerely felt or superficially observed, was the hallmark of postwar middle-class life. No non-Catholic could have survived as a minister or civil servant; an abundance of children was almost a promotional necessity for the ambitious servant of a state that made the 'numerous family' the centre of its demographic policy. The sexual hypocrisies, the personal tortures for the adolescent of this rigid ethic – for Spanish Catholicism emphasised its puritanism in the struggle against the 'permissive', lay Republic – have been brilliantly described in Francisco Umbral's novels and the memoirs of Carlos Barral.* Membership of a congregation – a sort of Catholic church Boys' Brigade – was mandatory for children in the forties just as attendance at spiritual exercises was a sign of social acceptability for parents. The bourgeoisie played safe: their social life was one of ritualised, conventional boredom.

(b)
The new middle classes

A dignified austerity, closely allied with Catholicism, had been one of the central values of the middle class – and it no doubt helped to make life tolerable in the hungry forties. A change in the composition of the middle classes together with increased prosperity was to erode the old scheme of things.

The sector of the active population that grew most rapidly in the late sixties was the service sector. This brought new blood into an expanded middle class – top executives, technicians – as prosperity brought new values. These highly paid new recruits were vastly different from the 'suffering middle classes', struggling to keep up appearances, that people the nineteenth-century novels of

*The words 'squalid', 'sordid' and 'ugly' appear repeatedly in Barral's *Años de Penitencia.*

Galdós. Austerity was replaced by conspicuous consumption: colour television instead of black and white; freezers as well as refrigerators; the purchase of second homes – either on the Mediterranean coast or in the Sierras.

This enlarged upper middle class is sometimes referred to as 'the new middle class'. This term is more properly used to describe the rapidly expanding army of white-collar workers: bank clerks, typists, secretaries, laboratory technicians, schoolteachers. Whereas the lower ranges of the 'traditional' middle class were conservative, the 'new middle class' is increasingly radical, its members prospective recruits for the Socialist party. Well paid though many of them are, they see their economic rewards declining as the wages of skilled workers rise. They see themselves as the 'suffering middle classes' of today. Their economic struggles (many are in double employment) have radicalised their attitudes. Bank employees strike like workers or deliberately defy the management by arriving unshaven, without ties, and by opening accounts of 5 pesetas.[10]

Bank clerks were a relatively new accretion to the middle class. Its traditional occupation was government service – the novels of Galdós are full of the middle class civil servants of Madrid.[11] Government employment, if insecure, was prestigious. It still, in the early years of the regime, gave a man a recognised place in society and a decent wage – the Spanish word *decente* has overtones of Victorian middle class respectability. In the sixties the lower ranges of the civil service suffered a decline in status and income; they were no longer 'better off' than employees in the private sector. By the late sixties they began to protest and organise to recapture lost ground. By the seventies a section of them had become radicalised and since employees in central and local government composed 5 per cent of the active population their tide of discontent was of some concern to the government.

To understand their grievances we must examine the jungle of the Spanish civil service. Based on Napoleonic models, it was hierarchical and authoritarian yet a complex, irrational collection of *cuerpos* or corporations of groups of civil servants. There might be 250 such *cuerpos*, several in each ministry. This corporative structure sharply divided the privileged *cuerpos* of the higher civil servants from the lower grades. The privileged *cuerpos* looked after themselves with 'complementary payments' and consultancy fees in double employment – a Treasury official might help a big firm with its tax problems. Their pay kept up with inflation; they had organised their own medical care. The underprivileged of the *cuerpos* with little pull in the service saw their real wages decline after 1964, and their social security benefits did not compare either with those of workers in industry or with those of the privileged *cuerpos*.[12] They felt 'proletarianised'.

The lower grades of the civil service therefore began to consider themselves as workers: they demanded the right to unionise and in the process became politicised; they staged sit-down strikes; they gathered in illegal assemblies and issued communiqués to the press.[13] The Association of Public Employees (AEAP), formed in 1969 as a study group, had by 1974 become an open forum demanding better conditions and the right to form unions. Their illegal unions had branches in ministries.

The quasi-organised discontents of civil servants presented a double challenge to Franco's governments: it was not merely that civil servants were considered the docile executants of policies; they also came from that middle class which had constituted the basic social support of the regime in its early days. Successive governments until 1976 evaded the problem. Civil service reform, to Carrero Blanco and the men of the Opus, meant 'modernisation . . . in accordance with modern techniques'; 'efficiency', not consultation and negotiation. Surely the civil service was a 'family', better off under a stable regime which did not change with elections than dependent on 'fleeting collections of politicians'.[14]

If bank clerks and modest civil servants increasingly act as workers, they cannot entirely throw off white-collar workers' 'middle-class' values. Rather than resolute radicals they are muddled victims of what sociologists term 'status inconsistency'. In the mid-seventies 41 per cent of bank employees favoured 'Socialism' but at the same time supported compulsory religious education. The same confusions and conflicts are evident in the civil service. The movement for unionisation was rejected by the higher civil service, apart from a few political radicals, as unnecessary and socially degrading: 'I am a civil servant, not a worker.' Half of the entire service enjoyed working-class wages and increasingly acted as a working class in labour struggles.* Yet the language they used reflected their ambivalence. Time and time again they used the word *decente* — they wanted the lost dignity of the old *funcionario*, a respected, well-paid member of society. Conflict and confusion penetrate into the intimacies of family life. Thus while a majority of bank clerks favour the nationalisation of

---

*cf. the differing attitude of the lower and higher civil service to 'double employment', to a British civil servant the most eccentric feature of the Spanish civil service. To the lower paid, double employment was a necessity; for the upper ranges, a supplement to a comfortable wage.

the private banks, only a minority favour birth control. Yet since the birth-rate of their class is the lowest in Spain, they must practise in private what they condemn in public. This is typical of the process of change and resistance to change in modern Spanish society.

It is the upper middle class and the rural population that maintain the old family patterns. They alone give some substance to traditional Catholic values and do something to contribute to the campaign for the 'Spain of 40 millions' that it was the government's policy to encourage in the 1940s. The overall birth-rate, however, is declining with family planning and the discreet use of the pill.[15] The same fate has overtaken the regime's campaign for the 'numerous family' as has overtaken its policy of 're-ruralisation'. The ideology of the Crusade could not be combined with the social consequences of economic growth.

The status of women – an important indicator of development – shows similar contradictions between the official ideology of the early years and the ineluctable demands of industrial society. It is a sign of the relative 'backwardness' of Spain that the proportion of women in the active work force is half that of its more developed neighbour, France.

Once women marry, in general, they cease to work outside the home unless driven to it by necessity. The increased employment of women is still resisted; in those villages where a large proportion of women work outside the home, such work is still regarded as 'ugly' (*feo*).[16] Values are in conflict with the facts of economic life. For most Catholic priests – and for most men – the place of women is still in the home, and in spite of the fact that middle-class girls now are increasingly university-educated, the number of women in the work force drops off sharply after the age of 24.* The Falange, which recruited women for auxiliary work in wartime, trained them after the war as Catholic *amas de casa* – housewives.† Attitudes remain 'traditional'. A curious example can be seen in the streets of any provincial town: if two middle-aged married couples sit in a car, the men sit together in the front and the women behind.

Here the behaviour of the young is in strong contrast with that of their parents. The demands of a growing service sector and the changed attitudes of the young will bring about one of the most dramatic of social revolutions: the massive incorporation of

---

*According to M. Rico, 'El trabajo de los mujeres', *España Económica* (April/May 1970), there is no relation between education and 'propensity to work'.

†Pilar Primo de Rivera, sister of José Antonio and leader of the Women's Section of the Falange, maintained that 'in matters of morals the Women's Section has always upheld the position of the Church' (*El País Semanal*, 21 August 1977).

women into all levels of the work force. Indeed the rapid decline in household servants, in the forties a decisive force in the service sector when a village girl could only hope to become a maid, is one of the most obvious changes in traditional society. She would now aim at becoming a waitress, a typist or a cashier.*

These shifts have mainly affected the new urban population. Rural society and rural values were changing more slowly. With emigration the rural population was ageing; the number of agricultural labourers and small farmers fell. Particularly in those areas where concentration of farms had been promoted, a more stable class of prosperous (and conservative) peasant proprietors was forming. One much quoted example of rural change is Zúñiga, a municipality of some 2,300 inhabitants.[17] A crisis hit Zúñiga when charcoal burning collapsed as a subsidiary occupation for the smaller farmers. The land was concentrated under a co-operative scheme which reduced the number of farmers by two-thirds, tripling the size of the average holding: the poorer farmers and labourers found industrial employment. This was typical of Castile where the number of proprietors fell by 30 per cent; small farmers went to the wall. Profit minded and market oriented,† the kulaks of Spain felt increasingly cut off from the subsistence farmers and labourers. They were a rural bourgeoisie, conservative, with much to lose, one of the last reservoirs of traditional Catholic values.[18]

(c)
The workers

If the higher estimates of the middle sectors are reliable, then the working class must constitute around half of the total active population.[19] How did they fare in the new society?

Their living standards rose, and the level of wages and salaries, after remaining stable, was to rise until in the 1970s there was little difference between French and Spanish wage earners' share in the national product. But the gap between rich and poor did not narrow. The 'fan' of wages, the difference between the higher paid workers — especially in the service sector — and those at the bottom, was still large. The gap was most dramatic in the poorer

*For women's place in the work force see Maria Angeles Durán, *El trabajo de la mujer en España* (1972). It is in the poorer provinces, where alternatives are scarce, that domestic service is still a significant employment.

†They were not well served, however, by agricultural extension services; nor did they themselves keep up with the latest improvements. R.C. has visited many peasant farmers' homes without ever seeing the Spanish equivalent of the *Farmer and Stockbreeder*, without which no farmhouse in Britain is complete.

provinces, where the working class remained large and the middle class small.[20] In a rural province like Extremadura social mobility is very limited: with increasing costs the poor peasant cannot survive and the labourer has no hope of buying a smallholding: for this rural proletariat the only chance of improvement is emigration.[21] The peasant farmer and the labourer become building workers (as do 50 per cent of the Extremaduran emigrants); or they latch on, in Andalusia and the Levante, to the tourist trade in a seasonal army of half a million hotel workers.

With the decline in importance of the agricultural sector the urban working class is now the most numerous and potentially powerful class in Spain; but it is no longer the traditional manual working class sharply cut off by dress and behaviour patterns from the *clases acomodadas* – the well-to-do. Nearly half the working class is composed of skilled and service sector workers who enjoy a lower middle-class standard of living* though they have to work harder and longer than their European counterparts to attain it. (Thus a Spanish skilled worker can buy a small car with a year's wages; his British counterpart with seven months'.) Even in a working-class suburb like Comellá near Barcelona manual workers are only 30 per cent of the population and the overwhelming, universal concern is to educate one's children *out* of the working class. 'Everyone knows that studies are the basis of success.'[22]

The Marxist prophecy that industrialisation would produce a homogeneous working class has been falsified. Linz sees the guarantee of future social stability in the upper reaches of the new working class 'with ties', a class that apes middle-class life styles. The assimilation of middle-class habits and values has been easier in Spain than in England. The Spanish worker prided himself on being 'formal' – a word that echoes the middle-class concept of 'decency'. These new recruits have a great deal to lose. Their great grievance under Francoism was the lack of representative unions – which, as we shall see, politicised and radicalised the skilled workers. With free trade unions, radicalism will probably be replaced by pressure for higher wages on the normal European pattern.

All this is not to say that the lot of the working class in the final years of Francoism was universally a happy one. Probably 11 per cent of that class is really poor; there is the traditional poverty of the backward rural areas and the new poverty of the industrial suburbs, in neither case compensated by adequate social services,

*A Madrid taxi driver (who voted Communist in 1977) told R.C. he would soon have a flat in Madrid and 'a cottage in the country' for the holidays. The possession of two houses is the mark of the middle class.

particularly in the countryside. Double employment and long hours of overtime are a necessity for many. In 1970 56 per cent of Barcelona workers spent over eight hours a day at work, and a fifth of those in Madrid had more than one job.* A minority of the work force were given short contracts to enable employers to escape the legal bars to dismissing an employee. They were – and are – the insecure marginal men of Spanish society. It is they who suffer when orders are dwindling; it is they who were the first to go when the economy slumped in 1959 and 1975. It is they who are concentrated in the poorer suburban fringes of Madrid and Barcelona and Seville. Over half a million Spaniards survive on legal minimum wages that cannot support a family – half of their earnings must go on food.[23] Without unions to push for wage settlements they are the odd men out.

On the flood of Marxist and *Marxisant* literature floats the problem of whether or not the Spanish workers have developed a class consciousness.[24]

It seems to us that the working-class consciousness has evolved in three stages. In the forties manual workers were cowed. The worker's life was an agonising struggle to keep his job or to find a new one. The Socialist experiments of the Republic were remembered as glorious, unrepeatable episodes. 'At times,' an old CNT member told Francisco Candel, 'it seems as if it all did not even exist.'[25] It was best to forget and keep one's head down, taking no risk of being sacked as a 'red' by causing trouble over low pay. Fear of losing a job dominated the worker's life when unemployment benefits and sickness benefits were derisory – hence the extraordinary value Spanish workers put on good health.[26] The sackings that came as a result of the recession of 1959–60 repeated the traumas of the forties. Ullastres drank mineral water instead of champagne at a Barcelona banquet to illustrate the need for austerity and belt tightening if the economy was to become healthy. This was little consolation to the worker who found the overtime which made his salary up to a living wage cut back or who was thrown out on the streets and forced to emigrate to France.

Class consciousness could not flourish in this atmosphere of fear, indifference and insecurity. With the boom of the sixties, scarcely surprisingly, most workers thought less about collective action and more of individual satisfactions: the flat – expensive, badly built and with few services, standing in some bleak cultural desert, the television set, the car, the necessity to educate the son,

---

*The unions have been pressing for the abolition of overtime and a higher basic wage in order to increase employment.

the annual holiday. There is nothing like the instalment system to weaken the striker's resolution, nothing like relative wellbeing after struggle to weaken 'solidarity' as a working-class value.* Marxists were alarmed at the growing *embourgeoisement*, the successes of a consumer society in integrating the worker into the capitalist society he should hate. There was no working-class culture as in the 1930s; the soulless suburbs were replete with bars and cinemas, not reading rooms. If the average worker read, he read the sporting press (*Marca* above all), *revistas de consumo* (i.e. magazines like our *Reveille*) or comics. Workers used the unions and the Labour Tribunals to settle *individual* grievances – sickness pay, compensation for injuries – or for guidance on the incredibly complicated wage regulations. In these difficulties they often found redress. 'Ir a Magistratura' ('I am going to the Labour Tribunal') was a proletarian incantation.

The late sixties and seventies saw a change in working-class attitudes. As we shall see, this was the result of the introduction of collective bargaining.† Individual benefit was seen as a consequence of collective action. The official syndicates had been regarded with indifference, workers either did not vote at all or voted for Sophia Loren or Fidel Castro; the syndicates were the useless appendages of a state at the service of the boss – an employer had only to pick up the telephone to get the police into the factory. Changes in electoral procedures, in the machinery for negotiating wage agreements which affected an ever-increasing number of workers, and the Communist policy of 'entrism' (i.e. that the opposition should put up candidates for election to the official unions) led the workers to take the election of shop stewards and the *jurados de empresa* (factory committees) seriously. Solís, Secretary-General of the Movement, professed to want real working-class representatives to revivify the decaying official syndicates so that the poster in union offices – 'Worker, your voice will be heard' – would have some meaning.

The union elections of the summer of 1975 showed the process had gone far beyond any rejuvenation of the official syndicates. Those organisations that supported 'entrism' – it was opposed by the historic unions – had won a striking success in the elections of shop stewards and works' committees in 1966 only to see their

*cf. the letter of a Burgos worker in 1977 when the economic record of Francoism was coming under attack by the left. Of the 59 workers in his firm, 40 had bought a car and most their flats. They ate 'ham sandwiches' and lived in harmony. Now there were trade union disputes and no overtime. (*El País*, 6 December 1977.)

†See below, ch. 7 section (b).

militants sacked and imprisoned *en masse*. In 1975 they were determined to recover this lost ground. Factory assemblies drew up programmes and nominated candidates for 'democratic' unions to 'fill the space', in the jargon of the time, occupied by unrepresentative bureaucrats. In Catalonia, the 'vanguard' which ran the campaign got a turnout of 80 per cent. The bureaucrats were swept aside and, as one of the outraged officials put it, this meant the 'officialisation of reds'. The elections were sensed by militants as a real breakthrough, not merely as a defeat for the 'bosses' who had sacked shop stewards, whose reinstatement was the issue in big concerns like SEAT; not merely as a preliminary 'democratic occupation of the unions' which would be the first stage in the creation of horizontal class unions as opposed to the multi-class vertical unions; but as the dawn of a new era of mass politics with the election of 'authentic' representatives directly responsible to the workers in their assemblies.[27]

It is improbable that working-class consciousness, in the sense the strict Marxists employ the term, was developing. Working-class unity was always weakened by the persistence of a large number of small concerns in which the old face-to-face relationship persisted – for instance, in the small workshops set up by skilled workers returning from Germany or France with their savings. It was in the large factories that the unions were strong. But there was a new militancy, especially among young workers who had not lived through the traumas of 1940 and 1959–60. In 1966 a CNT militant remarked that he would dissuade his son from the kind of actions that were the glory of his own youth. 'Don't think of those things. The first thing is to study. To get mixed up in political squabbles could cost you your career'.[28] By 1972 the son might be telling his father it was time that he did get mixed up in political squabbles.

(d)
The consumer society and its critics

The first tourists on the rough road to Madrid in the early fifties passed through Vitoria; it seemed to them 'typically Spanish', a sleepy provincial town with mediocre hotels and shops offering poor quality goods. Now it is a bustling industrial city of 137,000 inhabitants. Its shops display a wealth of household appliances and processed foods. In 1977 it was the scene of a violent strike by factory workers. When asked what this strike implied for the housewife, one woman replied, 'I have had to give up using sprays and powders for cleaning and have had to go back to soap and water'. This was the response of a working-class wife in an urban consumer society.

Rapid urbanisation is a mark of industrial growth.* In Spain growth has tended to reinforce the dominance of those regions that had already become industrialised by 1936: Catalonia and the Basque provinces. The great exception is Madrid. In the early twentieth century Madrid was still what it was in the days of its founder Philip II: an administrative, financial and social capital. But by the sixties the few modest enterprises of the thirties were swamped by large, modern metallurgical and electrical factories.[29]

Industrialisation brought a flood of rural immigrants. At first they built *chabolas* or *barracas*, shacks which they had built themselves on the outskirts of towns, growing up 'like mushrooms after rain' without proper water supplies and sewerage, without schools or doctors.[30] These shacks still exist around rapidly growing cities like Seville. But in Barcelona the *barracas* characteristic of the mid-sixties are replaced by high-rise apartments. With a high rate of unemployment they breed juvenile delinquency and all the problems that beset high-rise flats in Britain – the police maintain that drug addiction is rising rapidly in the working-class suburbs of Seville. These satellite settlements of bleak tower blocks give Spanish cities the depressing fringe of any great European industrial town.

Though the old shabby working-class districts remain – Vallecas, Cuatro Caminos in Madrid – they no longer contain the bulk of the working-class population. Low-rent working-class housing is still in short supply. Speculative builders find middle-class housing more profitable. In Madrid the 'Costa Fleming' with its luxury flats, pet boutiques, beauty salons and expensive restaurants contrasts strongly with the new, stark working-class suburbs.† This has had an effect on social life in general, on the relationships between classes. A certain paternalism, a familiar relationship between classes could exist in the densely inhabited old city centres with their narrow streets, where the same house might contain artisans, workers and professionals on different storeys. It cannot survive when classes are spatially segregated and live in totally distinct urban environments. In Barcelona the 'Murcians' settled in their own semi-slum districts. Already separated by

*It can, of course, take place without industrial growth; this was typical of Spain in the later nineteenth century.

†In the big cities – as opposed to the small rural towns – the basic infrastructure of power, light and water is satisfactory; it is schools that are lacking and this is critical in Barcelona where immigrant children have to be educated in a strange culture.

language from their fellow native-born workers, they were completely cut off geographically from middle-class Catalans.

The problems of city life are common to all industrialised countries. It is the *rapidity* or urbanisation combined with the feebleness of the instruments of urban planning created in the sixties, the confusion of competing agencies, and the poverty of municipal budgets in a highly centralised system, which inspires only apathy or hostility in citizens, that make these problems particularly acute in Spain.* Take cars and parking: most European cities have been able to adjust gradually to the growing number of cars in their streets; the increase of motor transport in Spain was dramatic and sudden, overwhelming municipal planners and budgets and producing parking problems made more intractable by the indifference of the new car owners to any attempt at regulation. The streets are jammed with double-parked cars, the new underground garages crammed.

There is now a growing environmentalist lobby, a new concern to control and limit the ravages of unrestrained growth. In its origins this must be seen as a quasi-political reaction to the paternalism of latter-day Francoism. In the towns, neighbourhood associations press for better housing and protest against the powers of mayors as mere agents for the central government. There is an increasing protest against 'urbanisation' of unspoilt countryside near the big cities, itself a consequence of the desire of a newly affluent middle class to escape from the polluted cities — Madrid papers carry daily indices of pollution. Publicity for apartments in the country praises fresh air; families 'can live in direct contact with NATURE'. One advertisement carries the picture of a gas-mask: 'In El Roquedal you'll never need this.' Local mayors combined with ecologists to object to development in the Gredos mountains near Madrid. 'Gredos for the goats' ran a popular Metro graffito. The commonest accusation was corruption: the 'official' tolerance of builders who deliberately flouted building and planning regulations and got away with it. The opposition saw local corruption as symptomatic of the regime. It is not that there was one Poulson affair; scandals cropped up in every big city. Recently there have been protests against the destruction of the old quarters of towns like Seville to make way for anonymous office blocks.

---

*For a criticism of urban planning see H. W. Richardson, *Regional Development Policy and Planning in Spain*, pp. 199–213. Urban planning only got under way with the Local Government Act of 1950 and the Urban Planning Act of 1956. For the various attempts to deal with congestion in Barcelona see *Bárcelona. Génesis y problemática del area metropolitana* (1972).

The environmentalists do not object only to unplanned urban sprawl and the destruction of churches and historic buildings, such as the ornate nineteenth-century palaces of the aristocracy that once lined the Castellana, the most imposing avenue in Madrid. They object to the anti-social consequences of tourist-financed growth and the encouragement of foreign investment – two of the pillars of the economic miracle. They protest against pollution from the new Ford factory at Valencia and the rape of the coast by speculative builders. A sociologist, investigating 'the colonial exploitation of beaches' and the purchase by foreigners of second homes in Alicante province, quotes with approval Gerald Brenan's remark that, if there is another Spanish War, it must be against tourists.[31] It is a sign of the increased leisure and mobility of the consumer society that this war will have to be waged not merely against foreign tourists. The car-borne trippers who, during the season, leave 10 tons of rubbish every week in the National Park of Covadonga, are mostly Spaniards.

Protests against the less acceptable faces of industrialisation and the consumer society, in Spain as elsewhere in Europe, are a common plank of left-wing and regionalist opposition.* For the left, to attack the consumer society for which television is the chosen propaganda instrument and the car the 'sacred cow', is to attack the achievements and the 'growth at all costs' ideology of the regime.[32] Hence the criticism of the motorway programme (started in 1972, financed by private capital and following existing, profitable traffic flows) as corresponding 'to an economic social and political strategy that opts for the car as the symbol of Western industrial society'.[33] Motorways, it is argued, symbolise a mindless concentration on growth, an attempt to 'Japanise' Spanish society.

The environmentalist lobby sometimes represents the selfish pursuit of intellectuals who resent the erosion of their picturesque preserves by the masses. Benidorm is ghastly; but it is the money of package tourists that has brought butane gas cookers and cars to the most backward villages of southern Spain. Some new behaviour patterns, near regions saturated with tourists, have disrupted village life and resulted in an incongruous and repulsive mixture of the Western and the traditional: mini-skirted drum majorettes parading in what were originally religious fiestas. But mimetism can have a liberating function – particularly in the sexual freedom

---

*In the case of regionalism these are contradictory. At the same time as Galicia objects to nuclear programmes, it demands capital investment from the richer regions that have 'robbed' Galicia of its natural resources. Cf. 'El fenómeno del regionalismo: una visión gallega del problema *Sistema*, no. 13 (April 1976), pp. 77–98.

of the young. The long, formalised courtship or *noviazgo*, with its constricting effects, is vanishing more rapidly in areas exposed to tourist influences and in the big cities.*

We can only understand the impact of these new living styles if we compare them with the 'years of hunger' in the forties, years made worse by drought and postwar shortages in Europe and the closing of the French frontier until 1948. Without imported petrol, the private car disappeared except for official cars (whose registration mark PMM gave rise to the classic joke *Para mi mujer* — for my wife). Strange contraptions impelled by wood or gas appeared on the streets. There were savage electricity cuts; toothbrushes were reconditioned, fountain pens sold on the instalment system. Francisco Umbral has described these postwar years as 'one long winter' for the less fortunate; a Spain of queues, the passing on of patched clothes, the appalling food, a collective misery from which the cinema was the only escape. Rationing (until 1952) made black marketeering 'a national sport'[34] with food parcels flung out of train windows before the train pulled into the station where the police were waiting. In the backward rural areas these years of hunger were terrible. Here are some descriptions of the privations of the forties given to Ronald Fraser:

> The people ate anything they could find: thistles and weeds . . . Our skin burst open with ulcers from not having enough to eat, from not washing. There wasn't any soap . . . When they saw me giving the food to my dogs they began to cry . . . A lot of others died like that, not directly of starvation but from eating only cabbage leaves and things.[35]

This struggle for survival in the early years of the regime, followed by the 'boom' of the sixties, explains two important and contrasting social and political phenomena.

In the forties the struggle was so fierce that, combined with repression, political activity was inconceivable. When the struggle for existence, for sheer physical survival, was so intense, there was little energy left for public life, even had such a public life existed. These were the years of the culture of evasion.† Conchita Piquer, the star of the revues, set the tone.

> I don't want to know
> Don't tell me neighbour

*See below, p. 98.
†See below, ch. 6 section (e).

I prefer to go on dreaming
To knowing the truth.

(Que no me quiero enterar
No me lo cuentes vecino
Prefiero seguir soñando
A conocer la verdad.)

After the struggles of the forties, the relative wellbeing of the sixties was so welcome that few wished to challenge a regime which took credit for its creation. The apathy of satisfaction replaced the apathy of privation.

It was precisely on the contentments of a consumer society that the technocrats of the Opus Dei rested their political and social philosophy. The Development Plan of 1971 made a confident prediction: 'In 1980 Spain will have passed the barrier of $2,000 per capita income, which will mean that life will be more pleasant and the degree of social cohesion greater'.[36] As we shall see, social conflict did not diminish. Indeed, Spain was to experience a unique combination of social stresses which in Western Europe took place successively and not simultaneously. There were the classic conflicts and personal tragedies of rapid industrialisation similar to those that had accompanied Great Britain's industrial revolution in the nineteenth century: overcrowded cities, the break-up of families, the rural migrant plunged into an impersonal society after the face-to-face society of the *pueblo*. But there were, too, the contradictory conflicts and stresses which develop in advanced industrial consumer cultures. A modern industrial society needs mass higher education, but the School of Economics and Politics at Madrid University bred not docile servants of a capitalist state but student radicals. Prosperity brings with it the revolution of rising expectations.

(e)
The seeds of conflict

We shall deal with the growth of conflict in Chapter 7. Here we seek to deal with the more general sources of deviance and discontent, with the emergence of life styles incongruous with the principles and practices, the values and institutions on which the system was founded.

That these contradictions first emerged among the young is not surprising. 'A sclerotic bureaucracy,' observes Professor Trevor-Roper, 'even a single personal despot, can prolong obsolete ideas beyond their natural term; but the change of generations must eliminate them.' This generational shift, so dear to followers of Ortega y Gasset, was strengthened by the development of Spanish society. With rapid, dramatic economic change the socialising function of the family and the role of the father become less important. A modern industrial society gives youth an autonomy that the elder generation finds uncomfortable, and it is not surprising that the rejection of the values of the older generation was overwhelming among well-to-do university students, significant amongst skilled workers, and minimal in the sons of peasant families. It was students and young industrial workers who rejected the familial authoritarianism which was perceived as a reflection, in their parents' attitudes, of an authoritarian political system. Without direct experience of the Civil War (the majority of the voters in June 1977 belonged to a postwar generation) they rejected as illegitimate a regime founded on the victory of 1939; critics of the social injustices and ecological disasters of rapid industrialisation, they could not accept the mystique of developmental triumphalism. Opinion surveys revealed, in the late sixties, a widespread lack of interest in politics among the young.[37] But for the educated it was the indifference and apathy of scorn, a feeling of impotence in a system run by their elders and in which they could not influence 'those who command' – *los que mandan*.

The consumer society certainly fostered political apathy; but, inevitably, it produced patterns of behaviour incompatible with a rigid authoritarianism. The emergence of new patterns and life styles can be seen as part of a general process of 'Europeanisation' brought about first by the arrival of tourists and later by the steady increase in the number of Spaniards who went abroad in the fifties as *au pairs* and students, as workers in the great emigration of the sixties, and finally as 'ordinary' tourists.

This process affected the young above all. It was the young, as students, who first discovered Paris and London. A visit to Maspero's bookshop in Paris was a traumatic experience to a student fed on a diet of Spanish official culture when access to any intellectual alternative was denied.

I went to Paris with a friend. I was sixteen. I remember that I bought *The Communist Manifesto*. Catholicism had cracked up and there was a great attraction towards sin . . . One entered Maspero, Le Globe, every Paris bookshop, full of enthusiasm . . . This shattered the blissful ignorance of your adolescence.[38]

By the seventies foreign travel was no longer a monopoly of the rich or the young, nor, with the paperback revolution and the greater freedom of the press, was its importance in opening the mind to alternative cultures so significant. In 1977 8 million Spaniards took a holiday abroad, most to absorb the products of the consumer societies rather than their ideologies: cheap clothes in London or pornographic films in France in the days when *Last Tango in Paris* was banned at home.

Except for a minority of middle-class families where the parents nourished the liberal tradition of the Second Republic and the children were the first student militants, the classic family of Francoism was traditional and authoritarian with a careful control of the children's social and sexual activities, a control reinforced by attendance at religious colleges. By the seventies parents had become permissive – not, as a survey in 1977 revealed, because they were 'convinced' but 'because they had no alternative'.[39] Nevertheless the persistence of traditional attitudes engendered severe frustrations and misunderstandings between parents and children. Successful middle-class parents accepted 'modern' ethics in their business life and as consumers; but in the family the old bourgeois values vanished slowly while authoritarianism remained rooted in working-class families. It was working-class fathers who continued to think that a woman's place is in the home.

Amongst the young, the shift in values was first noticeable in clothes and musical tastes. Already in the late forties the *chicas topolinas* with their high-heeled toeless shoes, painted toenails and Camel cigarettes were a pale intimation of liberty, 'the frontierswomen', in Francisco Umbral's phrase, 'of a new morality'. The late fifties and early sixties were the era of competitions for the best mini-skirt, of 'yé, yé', of the quaint imitations of Elvis and rock and roll, of 'Los Beatles de Albacete'. Later came blue jeans and long hair; now Spain has its punk rockers.[40]

In all rapidly changing societies, sexual behaviour is an indicator of the rate and profundity of change. Sexual relations had traditionally been controlled, especially in rural districts, by the institution of *noviazgo*. In the *noviazgo* the *novio* courts his selected *novia* (sweetheart) under strictly controlled family and community supervision which prohibits full sexual intercourse. The result of the masculine desire for sexual satisfaction and the impossibility of finding it with one's *novia* is severe conflict: daily masturbation, petting of cousins, an orgasm while dancing with the *novia*. Nothing is more noticeable in the literary descriptions of urban life in the forties than the regular resort to prostitution by the young. This was a direct consequence of the barriers put between the sexes; once these had gone down in the sixties, so did resort to prostitutes by middle-class youths. By 1977 the estimated half a million prostitutes were feeling the competition of amateurs.*

The *noviazgo* was underpinned by the Catholic attitudes to sex and the Catholic stereotype of the woman as the mainstay of family life. The church consistently frowned on co-education until 1970 when, in the changed atmosphere, a progressive priest could attribute homosexuality to the separation of boys and girls in adolescence. To Catholic apologists woman's place remained in the home. 'Marriage is slavery [to the husband] . . . to love is to endure.'[41] This 'negative valuation' of women means that they are not persons with whom an individual relationship is possible; they are objects, 'boxes to put children in'.

This moral structure − it once seemed immutable − has now collapsed in urban Spain. The *progre* student of the sixties tried to regard his or her companion as a friend (*amigo*) rather than as a destined spouse. What were once the 'progressive' attitudes of a self-conscious minority are now supported by a flood of magazines. Handbooks on lesbianism can be picked up in newspaper kiosks. A plea for the woman's right to satisfaction in orgasm appeared in the summer of 1976 beside a quasi-satirical article on religious relics;[42] women's lib and the right to the 'free use of the body', as opposed to Catholic morality which linked sexuality and procreation, are the publicly proclaimed platform of left-wing youth.[43]

How this new rash of journalistic sexuality has really affected relationships is another question − and an unanswerable one; that going to bed is assumed to be the natural consequence of friendship does not mean that the young have shed all the relics of traditional Catholicism. A recent (1977) survey has revealed that Spanish adolescents are as 'advanced' as any of their European counterparts over matters like abortion, divorce and contraception; but how far this shift is a consequence of the sudden gift of liberty and how far the young act up to the replies they give in opinion surveys is another matter. What is certain is that the generation gap is vast; half Spanish youth favour legalised abortion as opposed to only 15 per cent of their elders.[44] In spite of these differences most Spanish adolescents prefer to live at home and family ties remain stronger than in Britain.

In spite of such contradictions so characteristic of the processes of rapid change, the progressive rejection by the young of traditional

---

*A relatively ordinary prostitute costs 1,500−5,000 pesetas a time. They are cheapest in Bilbao; high-class ones in Madrid are more than 5,000 pesetas.

Catholic values and those of the official culture is a salient characteristic of modern Spain. The student revolt is its paradigm. It was
part of a process which began as an *aesthetic* rejection, by a minority
of bourgeois youth, of the society, and above all the culture, of the
regime; its boring films, its tedious religious formalities, its empty
rhetoric. The words 'squalid', 'hypocritical' and 'vulgar' recur time
and time again in the poet Carlos Barral's account of his youth in the
forties, the years of 'intellectual and moral slavery', and of 'his
blind aesthetic rebellion against that frighteningly ugly and vulgar
world of the postwar years . . . mediocre and dirty . . . a world of
forced smiles'.[45] This was the period when to read Sartre or Gide
was an act of defiance, a symbol of alienation.

In the sixties this process of moral and aesthetic rejection became
politicised, spreading down from an elite of middle-class students
to the student body at large, and from students to urban youth in
general.* The regime, its social *mores* and culture, appeared as a
whole that must be rejected *in toto*; only the indifference of apathy,
alienation or revolt were possible.[46] The process of politicisation
within a Marxist subculture reached odd extremes exacerbated by
repression and then exaggerated by sudden release in 1975† It is
not surprising that Catalan political protest songs reached a wide
audience; it is even more of a sign of the current obsession with
politics when a dancer announces that she returns to the stage in
order to give flamenco style 'a socio-politico content'.[47]

The same processes were at work, more slowly, in the workers'
movement. The older militant unionists, bred in the traditions of
'historic' unionism, who had struggled to rebuild the workers'
movement against fierce repression in the forties and fifties, were
leaving the work force. 'The fears were no longer there,' a UGT
organiser reported of the 1970s. 'Our membership was now
dominated by young people, who did not have the inhibitions that
repression had produced.'[48] Many of the new generation of union
leaders are young men. In the union elections of 1975, union
offices were flooded with 'long-haired beardies'.[49] They were the

---

*For a classic case of aesthetic and moral revolt merging into political commit-
ment cf. the career of Jesús Aguirre (b. 1934), husband of the Duchess of Alba.
His rejection of the regime's tasteless triumphalism led him via a rediscovery
of the poets of the generation of 1927, and conversations with Aranguren and
German theologians, to friendship with the radical student movement of the
1950s and finally to abandonment of the priesthood.

†The domination of Marxists and *Marxisants* left old-fashioned oppositional
liberals stunned and stranded. cf. Julián Marías who complained that in the
forties he was criticised for giving equal treatment to Marx and the Catholic
apologist Balmes, while in 1977 he was criticised for merely mentioning Balmes.
(*El País Semanal*, 2 August 1977.)

self-proclaimed 'vanguard', the standard-bearers of a new militant proletariat.

All the processes we have been describing depended on the rejection of the intellectual, moral and political straitjacket of 'National Catholicism'. 'National Catholicism' in the forties had been dependent on the concept of the Civil War, in Cardinal Gomá's words, as a crusade against the godless (*los sin Diós*), and of Spain as a bulwark against the political and religious heresies of the West and the Communism of the East. In the sixties, while the technocrats of the regime took French planners as their model and entry into the EEC as their aim, the opposition, especially its youth, saw the secular societies of Western Europe as a model when they did not see those of Socialist Europe as an ideal.

To the young, the social life of the forties was soaked in religiosity rather than religion − obsequious piety, formal participation in the observances of their elders. To Carlos Barral the most noticeable feature of Barcelona life after the war was the return of the *curas*;[50] it was the priest who controlled secondary education and who fixed up jobs for school leavers. By the seventies − the age *par excellence* of the amateur social survey in a society almost morbidly concerned with the changes within it − the young were rapidly losing their Catholic faith: 60 per cent of the under-twenty-fives professed no religion. Again this estimate underlines the generation gap: in 1975 over 80 per cent of Spaniards declared themselves Catholics, though the figure of practising Catholics was much lower, as low as 5 per cent in cities.* But the *kind* of Catholicism professed was very different from the puritanical, hell-fire religion of the penitent Spain of the forties. By 1977 26 per cent of married couples used the pill. Most now reject the interference of the church in politics: religion is increasingly 'privatised' as society is secularised.

Secularisation marched hand in hand with the life style of a car-owning, holiday-taking society.[51] Public lectures, attended by audiences inconceivable in Britain, became a surrogate for sermons. The 'Sunday best' was replaced by casual clothes.[52] Sunday became less a day for mass than a day for mass excursions to the countryside; Holy Week was an opportunity for a weekend sunbathing on the Mediterranean, the swimming-pool of Europe − all this in a society where, in the fifties, R.C.'s wife was arrested for wearing a bikini. As with everything else in modern Spain, it was the *rate* of change that is important.

*See *Europeo* (15 February 1975). The inroads of serious semi-secret religious ₃ects ('Bible Groups') has not, as far as we know, been investigated.

Secularisation and modernisation left a Catholic society deeply divided. While 'progressive' priests could defend homosexual love, or become militant Socialists professing Christian Marxism, more conservative priests – usually older – thundered against the ravages of the permissive society and the heresies of the West, especially its films, and Marxism. In the 'years of hunger' priests were easily recruited and the surplus exported; now Spain shares the crisis of vocations common to the Catholic world.[53] The 8,201 seminarists of 1963 had become 2,701 by 1973. It is often the prospect of active social work among the working classes that makes the priesthood attractive to young priests: but their elders are 'disoriented' when worker priests 'enrol in the revolution' with Marxists.[54]

Yet we must be wary of overestimating the rate of real change which may not be reflected in the products on display in newspaper kiosks or in the replies to often badly framed opinion surveys. Nor must be judge the lasting effects of a sudden burst of liberty by an outcrop of politically committed and sexually explicit films. Above all we must remember that the processes of penetration and adaptation are unevenly distributed geographically. Attendance at mass differs strikingly between, say, Tarrasa and Vitoria, both industrial towns but with very different historical traditions. The religious map of Spain is complex and differs from that of Western Europe where religious practices are more rooted in the countryside. Industrialisation has not secularised northern cities, and rural Andalusia remains the most irreligious region of Spain simply because the Catholic church there has seemed, to the mass of the population, so much a part of the local economic and social establishment.[55]

The economic chasm between the two Spains of development and stagnation is still reflected in contrasting life styles though the contrast becomes less glaring. In at least one respect country dwellers are beginning to imitate city dwellers: they have smaller families and in private practise contraceptive methods which they reject in public.* An Andalusian day labourer, who sees the world divided between the rich who do not toil and the poor who are condemned to unremitting, permanent drudgery in a village where the labour market is controlled by the 'powerful ones', still retains the values of a society with no social mobility; a bi-polar society where a man cannot rise by his own efforts, where he cannot defeat

---

*cf. Manuel García Ferrando, *Mujer y sociedad rural* (1977), p. 102. The author's survey reveals a high level both of knowledge of modern contraceptive methods and of disapproval of their use. He argues that there is no separate 'rural subculture' where family planning is concerned.

a fate that has placed him for ever on the bottom rung of the social ladder.* Even so, he is no longer the semi-slave of the fifties. Seasonal earnings allow him to refuse derisory local wages.[56]

The picture of rural brutality drawn by the 'social novelists' of the fifties was exaggerated. J. López Pacheco could describe a village where the inhabitants stoned the first car they saw as some strange monster, where they were too frightened to turn on a light switch, preferring to work by candlelight. Although relatively recent sociological investigations reveal, in rural Castile and Andalusia, a degree of rural isolation impossible to imagine in, say, Devon or Cumberland,† such attitudes are now inconceivable.[57] The car and the lorry may have shattered rural tranquillity and vulgarised village life by the importation of plastic tableware and by the omnipresent boom of pop music; but they have also allowed the young to meet a wider range of partners. The same is true of the formerly backward hinterland of the Costa del Sol, swept into the tourist revolution in the 1960s. New attitudes – the easily beddable Swede is now part of folklore – came with new riches. A taxi licence, bought in the forties for 400 pesetas, now sells for a quarter of a million; a peasant might sell his holding to a foreigner for a hundred times its value as an agricultural enterprise. A village with no cars in 1957 had ninety fourteen years later.[58]

If Spain has contracted physically with the car it has been culturally homogenised not by the propaganda of Spain 'One Great and Unified' but by television. In a country where newspaper readership was low – a result of the boringness of the papers rather than of a functional illiteracy – television was exceptionally important.[59] Television, vapid as it was, had become by the 1970s 'the Spanish vice'.[60] It was not merely that television integrated the working class into the consumer culture; its late programmes, by keeping workers glued to the box after ten o'clock, are held to be responsible for a decline in industrial production. This, to its opponents, was the ultimate contradiction of a consumer society dedicated to ever-increasing production. Nor was this the only contradiction. Tele Clubs for communal viewing were fostered, in

---

*The fatalistic attitudes of the working class in the early sixties, especially their belief that any improvement in their condition is due to 'luck' and not work, are described in *Estudio Socioeconómico de Andalucía*, pp. 128–35.

†See Víctor Pérez Díaz, *Pueblos*, chs 5 and 6. His observations were made with the help of a small group of adolescents in New Castile. R. C. on a tour of Cuenca (1977) noted a radical change in the public behaviour of *novias* and *novios*. This was very marked in the capital itself, where a good deal of public breast-fondling that would be frowned on even in Barnstaple was apparent.

the mid- and late sixties, by a Ministry of Information that controlled all programmes. Some of these clubs became not the social gatherings where passive viewers absorbed the propaganda of the regime but, like the neighbourhood associations which also originally enjoyed official patronage, vehicles for a nascent political opposition.[61] Once again, modernisation did not bring the results its proponents envisaged.

Chapter 6
Culture 1939–1977

We cannot understand the cultural history of Francoism without
the realisation that the Second Republic of 1931–6 which vanished
with the victory of 1939 was, at least in its beginnings, a republic
of intellectuals, even if some intellectuals – the Catholic authoritarian Maeztu, for example – opposed it, and if others became
disabused with its 'proletarian' style. The thirties saw the culmination of a cultural renaissance, in both Castile and Catalonia,
which gave Spanish intellectuals a European reputation for the
first time since the sixteenth century. Ortega y Gasset contributed
little to professional philosophy, but works like *The Rebellion
of the Masses* struck an original note and were widely translated; the same is true of Unamuno, the Catholic existentialist,
and his *Tragic Sense of Life*; and of the poetry of García Lorca.
These were only the best-known figures: García Lorca's
contemporaries, the generation of 1927, Alberti, Cernuda, Jorge
Guillén, Salinas, were considerable poets.[1]

(a)
A Francoist culture?

From the first days of the Civil War it was evident that the
Nationalist new state would find it difficult to attain intellectual
respectability. The majority of the European and Spanish
intelligentsia sided with the Republic. That Maeztu was executed by
Republican militiamen could not wipe out the memory of the
assassination of García Lorca which was to provide the European
liberal conscience with a permanent accusation against the Franco
regime, a symbol of the fate of culture at its hands.

Almost all the poets of Lorca's generation, to their admirers the
architects of a new Golden Age, went into exile. Miguel
Hernández, the self-taught peasant poet of the Republic at war,
died in prison in 1942. Almost all the intellectuals and artists with a
European reputation joined the 'other Spain', the Spain of the

exiles who saw themselves as the true bearers of Spanish civilisation while their homeland lay in the darkness of despotism:[2] Gaos and Ortega, the leading philosophers; the cellist Casals; the film director Buñuel; the rival historians Sánchez Albornoz and Américo Castro; the surgeon Trueta; Madariaga the essayist. Two of them, the poet Juan Ramón Jiménez and the biochemist Severo Ochoa, received the only Nobel prizes awarded to Spaniards in Franco's lifetime.

Franco, therefore, could not number among his supporters intellectuals whose prestige matched those who had supported the Republic. No doubt this did not give him much cause for concern. There is little that intellectuals can do against modern totalitarian regimes apart from exerting a marginal influence on their image abroad. In Spain, the blessing of the church compensated for the hostility of the intellectuals; it legitimised the regime and gave it the basis for the cultural unity it needed.

If the lack of intellectual support had little influence on the regime, the interruption of the intellectual renaissance that had begun with the generation of 1898 – 'Europeanisers' and liberals for the most part – and was continued by the generations of Ortega and García Lorca, has obsessed the liberal critics of Francoism. Many consider the forty years of Francoism a 'cultural desert' Julián Marías, the disciple of Ortega, rejects this image and praises the cultural achievements of independent-minded liberals who like himself or the poet Vicente Aleixandre stayed in Spain or returned from exile.[3] Others, like José Luis Aranguren, a liberal, Catholic opponent of the regime, distinguish between the culture of Francoism and culture during the Francoist period. The first was a nullity and the mediocrity of the second the responsibility of the regime.[4]

The reasons for the collapse of the efforts by a new cultural establishment, which had occupied the educational system and the mass media as a conquering army might occupy enemy territory, to create an official culture, were twofold. Up to 1943 Spaniards could believe that the curious blend of totalitarianism and Catholicism of their new state might find a place in a new European order created by Hitler; with the defeat of the Axis the Spanish edition of Fascism was left isolated and alone, a monstrous survival in a hostile world of democracies and socialist states. The political theorists of the regime could pride themselves on the European dimension of their thought when, in 1940, they wrote on the 'Doctrine of Caudillaje' (i.e. a Spanish version of the *Führerprinzip*), or pose as the ideologues of imperialism while they hoped to snatch a small portion of Africa and recover Gibraltar from the hands of a victorious Hitler. In 1945 this was an absurdity.[5] The regime's favoured psychologists might argue that Marxism and psychoanalysis were the creation of Jews, that the natural sciences were 'a manifestation of aggression', that all democrats were degenerates;[6] but the idiosyncratic cultural constructs of the forties could not fail to be infected by the culture of Western Europe in which they were encapsulated like some specimen from a vanished past. The hold of the regime's ideologues on post and patronage and the *cordon sanitaire* of a fierce censorship delayed the exposure of the trivialities and anachronisms of Francoist culture; but in the end there could be no such thing as a Spanish sociology or psychology unique to the regime. In 1949 Freud was permitted reading: by the mid-fifties bright young Spanish sociologists were studying in America.

The second difficulty was inherent in the nature of Francoism itself. In spite of obvious common elements in all the forces that supported the rising of 18 July – Falangists, traditionalists, monarchists, Catholics – Francoism lacked a common cultural ideological base. The Nationalists were united, as one of them observed during the Civil War, 'by negatives', by what they hated rather than what they loved. The cultural policy of the regime became more concerned with control by censorship of possible alternative cultures than with the creation of an original culture of its own. Beneath this unity in rejection there was a difference of emphasis and personal style: for instance, between the 'virile' and 'poetic' exaltation of enthusiastic Falangists and the pious clericalism of the ACNP. Moreover there was no single agency to co-ordinate the cultural policy of the regime. Finally, Francoism was short of money to control and patronise culture yet rich in supporters who distrusted intellectual activity as such.[7]

Nevertheless, in spite of these limitations, it is possible to identify a Francoist culture, or at least to identify cultural manifestations which expressed the aesthetic, intellectual and artistic principles of the groups who supported Franco. In spite of their heterogeneity, there was a common style, a common language, in 1939: exalted nationalism, the glorification of the military spirit and the military virtues, a fervent Catholicism, a preference for classical and traditional styles. Informing this language was a principle common to *all* groups of the regime. This was the idea, derived from the Catholic polymath Menéndez Pelayo* and revivified by Maeztu in

---

*1856–1912. His main work was the *Historia de los heterodoxos españoles*. His *La ciencia española* is an attempt to prove the superiority of Catholic culture over secular science. Maeztu (1874–1936), who had started his career in philosophic journalism as a 'Europeaniser', became a counter-revolutionary defender of the Hispanic tradition.

his later years, that Catholicism constituted the essence of Spanish nationality and of national unity and that the defence of Tridentine Catholicism was the foundation of the imperial greatness of Spain in the sixteenth century. It was the splendours of this imperial past that the new regime wished to inherit and continue: the artistic achievements of the Golden Age; the architecture of Philip II's monastery-palace, the Escorial; the plastic tradition of the Castilian religious sculptors of the sixteenth century; the neo-classical poetry of the Renaissance and the passionate spirituality of the Spanish mystics.

(b)
National Catholicism and the imperial dream

The style and content of the culture which the new state wished to impose on Spain found their first representative in Eugenio D'Ors (1881–1954). He was *the* intellectual of Nationalist Spain; this was hardly surprising since he was the only writer with an established reputation who had supported Franco. He was a man of wide culture, unsystematic as a thinker and given to windy, unintelligible prose, loaded with pretentious neologisms. He attracted young Falangists by his enthusiasm for the *eones* (permanent cultural values) to be found in Mediterranean culture, by his love of ceremony and symbols. He joined the Falange in 1937 after a ceremony that had all the pomp of an initiation into a mediaeval order of chivalry; his reward, in the following year, was the secretaryship of the Spanish Institute.[8]

Falangists, influenced by D'Ors, were active in the early cultural initiatives of the regime: their reviews *Jerarquía* (1936–8) and *Vértice* (1937–46) combined the exaltation of empire and Catholic apologetics so characteristic of early Francoism. It was members of this group who founded the review *Escorial* in 1940.[9]

Escorial was the brainchild of the poet Dionisio Ridruejo, a friend of José Antonio and admirer of Hedilla. In 1938 he was made National Delegate of Propaganda at the age of 25. Passionate, honest, a brilliant orator (he was called 'the Spanish Goebbels'), he was soon convinced that the conservative clericalism of the regime was a betrayal of the national revolution of the Falange. His closest collaborator was another disillusioned Falangist, Pedro Laín Entralgo. Laín was professor of the history of medicine, a liberal Catholic rather than a Falangist, influenced by Ortega, Unamuno and above all by the philosopher Zubiri, a Catholic whose liberalism kept him apart from 'official' Spain.

As its title showed, *Escorial* rendered homage to the glorification of empire and it included among its contributors writers wholly identified with the regime. But its guiding spirits were young Falangists conscious of the intellectual heritage lost in 1939. For them the purpose of the magazine was to 're-establish the intellectual community'; that is, to renew contact with the prewar writers, a contact which the elitism of Ortega's thought, always attractive to young Falangists, made a possibility. If Ortega did not collaborate, those associated with his open-minded rejection of the harsh, integrist tradition did: Marías, his philosophical disciple; the historian Luis Díez del Corral, the ethnographer Julio Caro Baroja; Zubiri and established prewar writers like Menéndez Pidal and Marañón.

Clearly this was not at all pleasing to 'official' Spain and once Ridruejo left *Escorial* in 1942 it relapsed into orthodoxy. Ridruejo's resignation was more than a personal matter: it meant the collapse of the attempt to create a Falangist culture with a minimum of intellectual respectability. Those who had collaborated closely with Ridruejo discreetly drew apart from the regime. The poets Rosales and Vivanco had dedicated their sonnets to José Antonio. Panero had published *Poesía heroica del Imperio* in 1940. Disillusioned, they now withdrew into religious, personal poetry. Laín was to figure in attempts to liberalise the regime from within – an endeavour of which he was later to realise the futility and for which he was to do penance in public.[10]

These 'desertions' were evidence of the difficulties confronting the regime if it was to forge an 'alternative culture' to the pre-1939 liberal tradition. The regime was now more and more dependent on traditional Catholicism for its cultural content.

Catholicism, apart from being an essential ingredient of Francoism, was from the outset well organised to exploit the cultural vacuum of the postwar years. Apart from Catholic influence in the universities, Catholics controlled the Superior Council of Scientific Investigations (CSIC), founded in 1939. The 'sections' (*patronatos*) of the CSIC were active in every sphere from archaeology to physics, though it could achieve little in experimental science since its funds did not allow acquisition of the necessary apparatus. Its founding charter declared its aim to be 'the re-establishment of the fundamental unity of Christianity and the sciences, a unity destroyed in the eighteenth century'. 'The CSIC,' said Ibáñez Martín as Minister of Education, 'was born, above all to serve God . . . to inject theology into all our cultural activities.'[11] Its periodical, *Arbor*, was above all the platform of the intellectuals of the Opus Dei. The rigid orthodoxy of the Counter-Reformation was to be, according to Calvo Serer, who was to

Arbor what Ridruejo had been to *Escorial*, the 'backbone' of the new state. It was to restore the sense of nationhood lost with the corrosive influences of the protestantism of the Reformation, the rationalism of the eighteenth-century Enlightenment and the liberalism of the nineteenth. The task of the CSIC was, according to Calvo, to 'rechristianise culture'.[12]

The ACNP created no such belligerent propagandist journals as *Arbor* and was less organised. But the success of its publishing ventures reflected the postwar popularity of religious works. The ACNP's Bible, Thomas à Kempis, devotional manuals, 'Christian' novels like *Ben Hur* and *Quo Vadis*, enjoyed unprecedented sales.

The same Catholic tide swept over university life, particularly in the faculties of art and literature.[13] Modern philosophy, the German philosophy imported by Ortega, was rejected by university professors, second-rate theologians who lectured on St Augustine, Thomas Aquinas and Suárez.*

If the nineteenth century was treated as non-existent by the philosophers, by historians it was either passed over or dismissed as the breeding ground of that liberal decadence which culminated in the Marxist, masonic Republic of 1931–6.[14] Here historians reflected the vision of the Caudillo: 'The nineteenth century, which we would have liked to eliminate from our history, is the negation of the Spanish Spirit.' The Enlightenment of the eighteenth century was likewise anti-Spanish; only the War of Independence of 1808, a war against the foreign atheist French, received some attention. The task of the historian was to glorify Castile as the 'hammer of heretics', as the austere architect of a national unity based on religious uniformity. This was combined with the new regime's vision of itself as the heir to the imperial tradition. The result was a proliferation of works on the Catholic kings, the discovery of America and the soldier-saint Loyola, founder of the Jesuit order.[15] In poetry the *garcilasista* movement represented a similar return to empire for it sought to revive the style of the soldier-poet Garcilaso de la Vega (1501–36) who had imported Petrarch's verse into Spain. Garcilaso's pastoral verse was acceptable for its form rather than its content; his colourless imitators did not detect what a modern scholar has called 'his lack of serious Christian concern'.

To underline the imperial heritage official architecture took as its

---

*Neo-scholasticism rejected or ignored not merely all modern philosophy – except for the works of Catholic apologists like Balmes (1810–45) and Donoso Cortés (1809–53); French liberal Catholics like Maritain were considered too heteredox for teaching purposes. They had taken a critical attitude during the Civil War.

model Herrera's Escorial, symbol of the great Spain of the Hapsburgs. The influence of the 'Escorial style', utterly opposed to the functionalism that had been fashionable under the Republic, was reflected in government buildings: the most explicit example is the Air Ministry (1943–51). The more pretentious monumental style produced the Arch of Triumph that dominates the western road into Madrid, the Labour University at Gijón, and culminated in the colossal Valley of the Fallen (Valle de los Caídos). This gigantic mausoleum of the Civil War dead, set in the mountains some forty miles from Madrid, was the grandiose, tasteless reply of Franco to the nearby austere Escorial of Philip II. The Caudillo supervised the plans and frequently visited the site. It cost 1,000 million pesetas. Twenty thousand men (many of them political prisoners) took twenty years to hew out the huge basilica from solid rock and top it with a cross 150 metres high. No other building better symbolised the combination of the Nationalists' wartime military-religious ideal – the 'spirit of the Crusade' – and the grandiloquent evocation of the imperial past. In it Franco, like José Antonio before him, was buried.[16]

The plastics arts reflected either the fashionable religiosity (Segrelles' St Francis was bought by Franco) or constituted, as did poetry, a return to 'safe' established academic traditions in landscape painting and portraiture.[17] Zuloaga (1870–1945), whose reputation was made before 1936, painted Franco and Millán Astray – the general who had provoked Unamuno by his cry of 'Death to Intelligence' – as Castilian *hidalgos*, hieratic figures set against a sombre Castilian background. Such academic art received official patronage while 'modern' art was regarded as tainted with liberal vices. Solana (1886–1945), the painter of 'sordid' Spain, was posthumously awarded a gold medal; less because his pictures corresponded with the regime's vision of Castile than as an attempt to incorporate an established reputation into the artistic patrimony of a regime singularly short of celebrities, most of whom were denizens of the 'other Spain'.

(c)

Liberalisation from within?

Attempts to pick up the threads broken in 1939 began soon after the war. In the first place there were the intellectuals and writers of the prewar generation who continued working in Spain independent of official patronage and mostly indifferent to the ideology of the regime. Since public criticism of the regime's present performance was impossible, the interpretation of the past by historians could be a mild surrogate for such criticism, indirect and the concern of a minority though it must be. The historian and philologist Menéndez Pidal continued working until 1970 as if the official version of Spanish history did not exist. Manuel Giménez Fernández (b. 1896), a former Minister of the Republic and professor of canon law and history at Seville, showed in all his works that the much celebrated enforced Catholic unity of the sixteenth century, the Spain of the Inquisition, was consistently opposed by the best spirits in Spain; this was to praise dissidence. Ramón Carande published in 1942 the first volume of his work on Charles V and his bankers, a work of economic history far removed from the exaltation of empire, since it showed the terrible cost of that empire to Spain.* All this could be regarded as symbolic of contact with the 'other Spain', the intellectuals in exile, and with the liberal tradition in Spanish intellectual life.

The living link with that tradition was Ortega. It is hard now to realise his importance for the university youth of the postwar years. To accept Ortega's methods 'was to accept implicitly the liberal principles of the European intellectual he represented'.[18] It was to reject the philosophy of the regime. For Aranguren, 'to defend Ortega and Unamuno was to defend the intellectual future of Spain'.

Ortega himself returned to Spain in 1945 and in his first public lecture – his characteristic mode of expression – made clear his contemptuous indifference to Francoism. Expected to make some statement of his political views, he acted as if the regime did not exist by lecturing on the theatre. He refused to teach in the university and if his efforts to create an alternative, private university in collaboration with Julián Marías came to nothing, they were a token of his rejection of official Spain. Marías wrote a history of philosophy (1947) which, if it grossly exaggerated the philosophical importance of his master Ortega, nevertheless was a spring of pure water in the marsh of neo-scholasticism.

The intransigent Catholicism of the regime's intellectuals, the 'National Catholicism' of the official church, could not satisfy those who wanted an 'authentic', 'vital' Catholicism, intellectually respectable and socially active. The concern of a minority of liberal Catholics like Marías and his fellow philosopher Zubiri was to find some synthesis between modern thought and Catholicism, to end the intellectual isolation of Spanish Catholics, cut off from Europe. Such endeavours could only prosper on the margin of

*Since the mid-1940s the ethno-historian Julio Caro Baroja (b. 1914) has been consistently studying the marginal cultures of the Spanish past: the Jews, *moriscos*, Basques, agrarian traditions, witches.

official life. The 'Catholic Conversations' of San Sebastián and Gredos (1951) brought a small group of Catholics, for the first time, in touch with liberal Catholics like Maritain and, less happily, Teilhard de Chardin. Laín Entralgo was such a liberal-minded Catholic. 'My God. What is Spain?' he asked. In his *Spain as a Problem* (1948) the answer he gave was, by implication, a minor assault on the ideological foundations of the regime. In an earlier work he had written admiringly of the writers of the 'generation of 1898' at a time when they were considered anti-Spanish and tainted with liberal heresies. Now he moved to reject the notion of Spain as the monolithic bulwark of an intransigent Catholicism.

The mild modernism of Laín brought on his head the counter-blast of Rafael Calvo Serer's *España sin problema* (1949), a work inferior in every way. For Calvo Serer the Civil War had solved *the* problem of Spain since the victorious Movement had restored the Catholic conception of life, consubstantial with the history of Spain. There was no need for any national regeneration through a renewal of contact with the liberal tradition: the Catholic tradition and the national tradition were one and the same thing.

The intellectual autarky displayed in the hermetic vision of Calvo Serer vanished more slowly than economic autarky. The opening of the mind was to be a more painful process than the opening of the market. José Luis Aranguren, professor of ethics and sociology (the conjunction is a telling indication of the status of sociology in Franco's Spain) was a Catholic who rejected the dominant neo-scholasticism and felt uncomfortable in a university that seemed haunted by the ghost of Menéndez Pelayo. Like the poets Vivanco and Rosales he felt himself 'totally alien' to the 'public life' of the forties; but he could not, like them, withdraw from it. The intellectual must choose.

Aranguren's insatiable intellectual curiosity was to drive him beyond liberal Catholicism to the 'discovery' of Marx and an invitation to Mary MacCarthy to lecture in Madrid. He revived the traditional function of the intellectual as the ethical conscience of society — a society, he held, that had been literally 'demoralised' by Francoism and where the defeated found refuge in their own impotence, the victors in the lust for power at all cost, and the neutral in the pursuit of wealth and sensual pleasures. By the sixties he was one of the most important intellectuals in the democratic opposition.[19]

With Ruiz Giménez as Minister of Education in 1951 the recovery of the liberal tradition in Catholicism was favoured, for the first time, from above. Ruiz Giménez habitually talked of the 18 July and his 'undeviating loyalty' to Franco; but he quoted Ortega and Unamuno. He appointed Laín and Tovar, a fellow liberal Catholic of Falangist origins, as Rectors of Madrid and Salamanca. It was a timid opening, 'a modest effort', as Laín put it, but one too bold for its time. Ruiz Giménez and his collaborators brought on them selves a furious attack by the Catholic hard-liners of the regime: the hierarchy, the religious orders and the men of the Opus Dei. *Arbor*, the periodical of the CSIC, led the campaign against what Calvo Serer called the 'hand stretched' to heterodox liberals. The works of Ortega and Unamuno were having a pernicious influence on youth. The minister who quoted them and favoured their circulation must go. Ruiz Giménez fell in 1956.

(d)
Censorship and the nonconformists

While the 'official' culture still dominated the rhetoric of the regime, its failure to capture the public mind — much less the imagination of creative artists — was increasingly evident. It had not killed off the liberal tradition. It could not prevent a revival in creative literature which, if it did not explicitly reject the regime, shared none of its presuppositions and was an implicit criticism of its values.

The censorship struggled against this emergence of an alternative culture and the spread of 'foreign' ideas. A censorship set up under wartime directives (1938) continued functioning for nearly thirty years of peace. Its positive function — the control of all information — produced a press of inconceivable boredom, full of flat accounts of official functions, just as weeklies like *Hola* were devoted to the goings-on of European royalties, Madrid society and the minutiae of the family life of the *generalisimo*. The only 'hard' political information was the foreign news and that was consistently slanted to emphasise the contrast between the turbulent democracies and the social peace enjoyed by Spaniards.

The negative function of pre-publication censorship became more important when there was more to censor. In the early days there were few attempts to challenge the regime; all authors realised that overt political criticism was impossible. Church influence on the censor's office made any attack on Catholic morals or any touch of eroticism unpublishable. Ecclesiastical censorship reached levels of comic absurdity in its puritanical aversion to bare flesh. Boxers' torsos were concealed in painted vests and film stars' busts reduced; the word 'thigh' was struck out from one of

Pemán's plays — and Pemán was hardly an *avant-garde* writer.*

Sometimes questionable passages unexpectedly slipped past; sometimes an innocuous word was struck out. Authors learned to live with this arbitrary machine by avoiding certain subjects — for instance, any justification of strikes — by oblique reference or *in extremis* by publishing abroad.† When asked whether he had been bothered by the censor the novelist Miguel Delibes replied, 'By roundabout methods I managed to say more or less what I wanted to say'. And what he wanted to say was far from conforming to the regime's image of Spain.[20] The censorship could not prevent authors — especially novelists — drawing a picture of Franco's Spain that exposed its blemishes for all who could read.

Already in the 1940s the flat, conformist literary landscape of Spain was shaken by books which would scarcely have raised a tremor elsewhere in Europe. All these books had one thing in common: they were indifferent to politics as such, but their return to realism was a 'tremendous' (hence the term *tremendismo*) criticism of the *society* of postwar Spain, the Spain, after all, that had emerged from General Franco's victory. For these authors its cities were peopled by profiteers, by hypocritical, materialistic, formally Catholic bourgeois families and their aimless, alienated children; its countryside was desolate, crushed by a poverty that turned its inhabitants into violent brutes.

The sensation created by Camilo José Cela's *La familia de Pascual Duarte* will be forgotten by no one who visited Spain in the 1940s. The book took the form of the confessions of a condemned murderer; its violence — including matricide and the gratuitous slaughter of a mule — shocked; its picture of sordid misery stood in sharp contrast to the official version of rural life. The murderer is a wretched peasant from Extremadura, one of the poorest provinces of Spain. His crimes could be explained by his violent, unbalanced, psychotic character — he shoots his favourite dog because its eyes remind him of his dead son — yet they are also the result of a violent, unjust social situation; the last of his victims is the local landlord. Cela's later novel, *La Colmena* (1951), was 'a

---

*For some amusing examples see F. Vizcaíno Casas, *La España de Posguerra* (1975). Clerical censors sometimes disapproved of works acceptable to the regime; they banned García Serrano's *La fiel infantería* which had won the National Literary Prize.

†For instance, Camilo José Cela *Pascual Duarte* was published abroad and held up for five years by the Spanish censors; however, it was widely read before it was published in Spain. Cela says he had 'endless difficulties' over the publication of his next novel, *La Colmena*. The supreme irony is that Cela had himself been a censor.

slice of life drawn without charity' – the portrait not of an abnormal individual but of a rotten society, that of postwar Madrid dominated by money and sex. This was not the protest of a radical – Cela had been close to the Falange and served a period as a censor himself – but of a cross-grained man who could not stomach the society he lived in.

Three years after *Pascual Duarte* came Carmen Laforet's *Nothing* (*Nada*). It was a best-selling, fictionalised autobiography of an 18 year-old girl who came to Barcelona (*c.* 1940–1) to stay with her broken-down family while studying at the university. The house is full of old furniture, cockcroaches and moral decay. Uncle Juan is an unsuccessful artist and wife beater; his brother – a minor black marketeer – seduces the heroine's best friend's mother and then attacks her daughter; the aunt is an insensitive, puritanical bigot. All is dominated by pretension and hunger: the family can afford no meat but keeps a maid; the heroine is caught drinking the water the cabbages have been boiled in. A 'tremendously' depressing book in spite of a contrived happy ending, it is a portrait of the moral bankruptcy of a parasitic bourgeoisie 'saved' by Franco in 1939.

There was nothing in the background of Miguel Delibes (b. 1920) to mark him out as an artistic rebel – indeed he did not consider himself as such. A Castilian from Valladolid, from an impeccably bourgeois family of eight brothers, a sincere Catholic, a passionate hunter, he had fought in the Nationalist navy; yet his mild social realism and his passion for truth and his search for justice made him incapable of writing anything flattering to the Spain he lived in. Castile was not a cradle of national glories but a land of wretched villages, deserted by their inhabitants for the anonymous life of the cities; his guidebook to Castile was rejected by the Ministry of Tourism, and his journalistic descriptions of deserted villages got him into trouble with the censors.

The 'objective' novel found its masterpiece in Sánchez Ferlosio's *Jarama* (1956), a finely conceived work based on the superficially boring conversation of a group of young working class *Madrileños* on a picnic and bathing expedition to the Jarama river, scene of one of the bloodiest battles of the Civil War. His work exposes the vacuity, the tedium of life in post-Civil War Spain, the political anomie of the period:

'To think that this was the front and that
so many men died here!'
'That's right. And we go and swim in it.'
'As though nothing had happened: and there was

very likely some dead body just where you
decide to dive in.'

or

'Well, no. Politics for me . . . I only read
cinema posters.'
'But you ought to be more aware of what's going
on, Mely.'
'More aware? Go on! Why?'[21]

The aesthetic and social revolt of a younger generation was
represented in the cinema by Luís García Berlanga and Juan
Bardem. In 1955 Bardem launched in Salamanca his famous attack
on the Spanish cinema: it was politically and socially false, finan-
cially 'rachitic'. To remedy this he and other young directors
introduced into Spain the neo-realism of the Italian cinema – an
indication of renovation through importation which had been, and
was to remain, a characteristic of Spanish culture. Their most
notable success was *Welcome Mr. Marshall* (1952), a corrosive
satire on the arrival of Spain's new American allies in a rural
pueblo. Bardem openly criticised the corruption and hypocrisy of
the Francoist bourgeoisie – his *Death of a Cyclist* (1955) was an
international success; but Bardem fell a victim to the censorship,
the 'rachitic' economic foundations of the industry and his own
artistic crisis. Berlanga continued in a vein of black humour, a
characteristic reaction in the underdeveloped Spain of the forties
and fifties that can be sensed in such magazines as *Codorniz*. There
could be no direct criticism of the regime; only mankind in general
could be pilloried. Today Berlanga's *The Executioner* is considered
to be one of the best Spanish films.[22]
Poetry is a subtle indicator of shifts in the moral climate and is
less susceptible to censorship, though poets were censored. The
personal poetry of Dámaso Alonso broke out from the retreat into
religious mysticism which had marked the disillusion of poets like
Rosales, Panero and Vivanco and rejected the innocuous, formal
neo-classicism of the Garcilaso school. His admirer, the poet
Bousoño, wrote: 'I have repeatedly said that *Hijos de la ira* (1944)
is a work of protest written when nobody in Spain protested.'*
'Compromise' was never accepted by the greatest poet of modern

---

*Quoted in V. Gz. de la Concha, *La poesía española de posguerra* (1973), p. 295.
cf. the comment of H. St Martin in *Roots and Wings* (1977), p. 9: 'He brought
into the open things that millions of Spaniards spend a great deal of time trying
not to say out loud.'

Spain, Vicente Aleixandre, faithful to his symbolist roots and alien to the society that surrounded him.

The artistic canons of official art were simply neglected and no artist worth his salt could work within them. It was artists who first established a direct connection with the lost world of the thirties.* Miró came back to Spain in 1940. His Civil War poster *Aidez L'Espagne* was a frontal attack on 'obsolete and decaying' Francoism. The most famous living Spanish painter after Picasso, who remained in exile, his work was totally neglected by the regime; as for Picasso, he was dismissed as 'an enemy of the soul, of good and of every divine and human value'.

Modern art the regime could tolerate; indeed its elite began to recognise that purchase of the works of Tapies represented a good investment. Those who sought to inject new life into the theatre and cinema received harsher treatment. Apart from a few university fringe groups, the theatre of ideas was revived by Buero Vallejo (b. 1916), imprisoned as a supporter of the Republic until 1946. His *History of a Staircase* (1949), with its direct criticism of Spanish society, was as shocking in its impact as Cela's novels. He was a prolific and gifted writer; his works, heavy with symbolic rejection of contemporary society and its values – for instance, many of his characters are blind – were consistently mauled by the censor.[23]

The processes of renewal and renovation in historiography were the work of established professors, above all of a Catalan historian, Jaime Vicens Vives (1910–60). The rhetorical historians of the regime had sought in the empire the moral and political origins and inspiration of the new state. For them the nineteenth century was an age of decadence, dominated by 'foreign' liberalism and French ideas. It was, paradoxically, the influence of the French *Annales* school which turned Vicens from the study of the Middle Ages to the study of the nineteenth century. Vicens' studies of Catalan history, in particular of the bourgeoisie in the nineteenth century, were significant for two reasons. Firstly he was an unrepentant Catalan (when lecturing at Oxford he talked of Catalonia importing 'foreign' coal; by this he meant coal from the Spanish province of Asturias). Secondly, for traditional erudite narrative he substituted quantitative methods, as did his fellow Catalan historians and successors, Nadal, Reglá and Fontana. Vicens scorned the philosophising – what he called *ideologismo* – and the 'grandiloquent and ineffective baroque style of

---

*This recovery took place first in Barcelona around the review *Dau al Set* (1948). Palencia, Ortega Muñoz and Zabaleta renewed landscape painting. Oteiza and Ferrán and later Chillida introduced abstract sculpture.

the pedagogues of the old school' which were the current stock-in-trade of the regime's historians. For this style, characteristic, he thought, of Castilian historiography, he substituted the 'common sense' of Catalonia, the concern for ordinary people, the subjects of social history.[24]

Two Madrid historians, Artola and Jover, turned to the nineteenth century and its problems as relevant to the understanding of contemporary Spain. Apart from its sympathetic treatment of liberalism, the title of Artola's work, *The Origins of Contemporary Spain*, was a challenge to orthodoxy, since it sought the origins of contemporary Spain not in the glories of the empire and the Golden Age, but in the nineteenth century. All these historians were bringing Spanish historiography up to European levels: something that José A. Maravall and Luis Díez del Corral were doing for political thought, and the economists of Barcelona – they included Sardá and Fuentes Quintana – did for Keynesian and post-Keynesian economics. Like the poets, dramatists and novelists, these social scientists were opening Spain to a world of ideas outside the narrow confines of the rhetorical culture of the regime.

(e)
The culture of evasion

The steady alienation of intellectuals and artists from the ideology of the regime was increasingly evident. Just as Giménez Fernández had argued that in the sixteenth century the 'best spirits' of the age fought its intolerance, so their descendants in the forties and fifties exposed as best they could in their own works the rhetorical rigidities of the regime. But it is important to realise that these renovating currents left the general public untouched. 'Intellectuals,' Ridruejo sadly concluded, 'have never known a time when their social influence has been so restricted.'[25] The mass of Spaniards were immersed in what we call the 'culture of evasion'.

The culture of evasion was an escape from immediate reality. It embraced a far greater audience than the official culture we have examined already or the 'independent' culture that struggled for existence by its side. It was not that other countries did not have their cultures of evasion, equally false and vulgar;* merely that the role of the culture of evasion was particularly important in a Spain of poverty and political repression. Nor was it that the regime

*For instance the US cinema of the 1930s or, even more strikingly, the Indian cinema of today.

deliberately encouraged this culture of evasion as a safety valve or
to encourage political passivity; it merely allowed private interests
to exploit a consumer culture, devoid of political or intellectual
content, and therefore innocuous. Deliberately or not, the regime
benefited from a consumer subculture whose extraordinary
popularity allowed it to create the image of a carefree Spain
basking in the social peace that the Spanish people had attained
under the paternal care of General Franco. The cinema, together
with the radio, spectator sports, on a lesser scale the theatre, and
from the sixties television, were the elements of a mass culture of
great importance.

The regime was fully conscious of the potential propaganda
value of the cinema and its dangers in a country where the cinema
was extremely popular.[26] In 1947 there were over 3,000 cinemas
with an average seating capacity of 500 – only the United States
had a greater number of cinema seats per capita. The new regime
met the problem by rigid censorship: a prior censorship of scripts
until 1976, then of the final version. In addition, the ecclesiastical
censorship classified films 'morally', publishing its verdict in the
press. Censorship operated both at a political level and in defence
of Catholic morality, firmly excluding any suggestion of eroticism.
After 1941 the dubbing of foreign films was made compulsory,
with comic results: mistresses were converted into sisters to avoid
the stigma of adultery at the risk of hints of incest; sinners were
mysteriously devoured by tigers; 'voices off' assured the audience
that, contrary to what it had seen on the screen, the criminals did
not escape punishment.

At the same time the regime used for propaganda purposes a
cinematographic industry sorely in need of government subsidies.
It was these subsidies that created the 'heroic cinema' of Civil War
epics whose star, Alfredo Mayo, as the virile, gallant soldier, was
the incarnation of the self-sacrifice of military life. Beside the
heroic cinema there was the 'costume' cinema with its hyperbolic
treatment of Castilian history and imperial Spain: films like *The
Lion of Castile* (1951), *Dawn of America* (1951), *The Princess of
Ursins* (1953).[27]

With some striking exceptions, the heroic and imperial cinema
was not a great commercial success. Directors sought less ideologically charged themes, which corresponded to a general inclination
to forget the war by a public resistant to the grotesque
grandiloquence of historical drama. Apart from light comedy and
some relatively successful adaptations of the classics (*Quijote* in
1947; *Lazarillo* in 1959) film companies exploited to saturation
point traditional Andalusian folklore, creating a cinema based on

'Spanish song', already a popular genre before 1936. Its immensely popular stars, Imperio Argentina, Conchita Piquer and later Lola Flores and Carmen Sevilla, were the 'missionaries of optimism', in the phrase of Terenci Moix.[28] The genre was expanded beyond Andalusia to include colourful versions of nineteenth-century Madrid − Juan de Orduña's nostalgic music hall melodrama *El Ultimo Cuplé* (1956) and the romantic version of Alfonso XII's court, *A donde vas Alfonso XII?*, were two of the greatest money-spinners of the Spanish cinema. Until at least 1960 these films continued to be commercial successes, reinforcing the image of a generous, happy-go-lucky, temperamental Spain.

Given the limited output of the Spanish cinematographic industry after 1939 − around forty-five films a year in the forties, rising to seventy in the fifties, the culture of evasion was fed on foreign products. Thus between 1939 and 1961, 879 Spanish films were shown in Madrid compared with 4,277 foreign films, of which half were American; on average they ran twice as long as native products. Censorship, therefore, did not deprive Spaniards of Hollywood films and Italian beauties. Here the culture of evasion was double-edged. If foreign films allowed Spaniards to escape into fantasy, at the same time they could point a painful contrast to the poverty of the forties and fifties. 'The cinema,' wrote Francisco Umbral 'gave us the measure of our misery.'[29] In most countries, the culture of evasion reinforces dominant social values. In Spain foreign films, their influence intensified by popular magazines like *Primer Plano*, undermined the official view of life. Esther Williams and Betty Grable could not be ingested into the official culture or the morals of continence and austerity. Enthusiastic Falangists flung ink bottles at Rita Hayworth's *Gilda*; bishops thundered against the film as the agent of the 'collective heresy of the West'.

The history of the theatre is as discouraging as that of the cinema and the contrast with the theatrical revival of the thirties all the more marked. There was no attempt at an 'imperial' or 'heroic' theatre; plays were merely trivial.[30] Imitators of Benavente, who himself churned out thirty plays before 1954, produced domestic dramas, comfortable in their conformity to Catholic morality. The longest-running play in Spanish theatrical history, Torrado's *Chiruca* (1941), was an elementary farce. Apart from the inimitable Jardiel Poncela and Miguel Mihura − both of whom displayed an idiosyncratic humour that has been undeservedly neglected by foreign critics − the Spanish postwar theatre was a poor thing. What popular vitality it had was to be found in another expression of the culture of evasion: the revue.

The *revista* − the lightest of light musical comedy − was the only erotic expression allowed by the censorship; it had been too popular a genre to prohibit altogether, though the expanse of female flesh was severely limited. It was based on folk-songs, mainly from Andalusia and Madrid, and its exponents achieved a popularity similar to that of the pre-1914 music hall stars in England like Marie Lloyd.

Revue audiences came from a social stratum beneath that of the *bien pensant* theatre-goers of Madrid and Barcelona. A similar gulf separated their literary tastes. This was partly a function of price. Most Spaniards could not afford books. The cheap paperbacks of the Austral classics (1,500 titles by 1972) catered for an intellectual minority. It was 'kiosk literature' that provided the Spaniard of modest means with an abundant variety of sub-literary products: light romances, westerns, detective novels. The output of their authors was stupendous. Between 1944 and 1951 José Mallorquí wrote 130 of his 'Coyote' westerns and his hero became almost a mythological figure in postwar Spain. The success of kiosk literature is explicable: it was cheap, simply written, and reflected traditional moral values.[31]

These same characteristics inspired the scripts of the radio soap operas, without doubt the subcultural product with the widest audience in the forties and fifties. The melodramas of Guillermo Sautier Casaseca made half Spain weep; he sold a million copies of a version of *Ama Rosa*, the heart-rending story of an upper middle-class boy who is ignorant of his humble origins. These interminable melodramas, the Sunday 'Match of the Day' and weekend shows and competitions were the principal stuff of postwar radio. Radio was a mixed system with a state section that monopolised all news programmes and a commercial section financed by advertisements. The fifties were the golden era for radio; its stars (announcers like Bobby Deglané), its programmes ('Sports Roundabout', 'Weekend Cavalcade'), were listened to all over Spain. The sentimental songs popularised by the radio – 'typical' Andalusian and Spanish romantic melodies – were part of the culture of evasion: they created, as the writer Carmen Martín Gaite put it, 'an artificial silence' because they avoided all reference to the present or the immediate past.[32]

Only one other spectacle could compete in popularity with the cinema: football. The 'national sport', bullfighting, was in decline. In the postwar years it produced a myth: Manolete, killed in the ring in 1947. His extraordinary popularity obscured more orthodox talents and some of the basic problems of bullfighting: the monopolisation of rings and bullfighters by a small group of entre-preneurs; the effects of mass production on the quality of the bulls;

the promotion of mediocre fighters by modern publicity methods; the filing of bulls' horns to reduce the danger that was the essence of the sport. All this contributed to a crisis from which bullfighting was only rescued by the avalanche of ignorant tourists in the sixties.

Bullfighting sustained the official stereotype of Flamenco Spain; but it was football that drew the crowds. In the pauperised Spain of the postwar years Real Madrid, the powerful team of the capital, built a stadium to hold 100,000; Barcelona followed shortly after. Franco himself never missed 'Match of the Day'.

Football had a dimension far beyond its function as a spectator sport. It was a catalyst of Spanish nationalism. The victories of the Spanish teams in the European Cup after 1956 were seen as *national* victories. Matías Prats thrilled Spain with radio commentaries with almost epic overtones; in 1967 he was made a *procurador* (member) of the Cortes. The victories over 'perfidious Albion' (1950) and the USSR (1964) were propaganda successes of the first magnitude, triumphs over historic enemies. Hence the myth of a 'Spanish style' of football, 'virile', impetuous in attack, an incarnation of those Hispanic values exalted by the propaganda of the regime. It was ironic that 'Hispanic values' were best represented by a Basque team, Atlético de Bilbao.

Yet Spain was in Franco's period a sporting power of the second order. The great international triumphs of 1956–64 were the consequence of massive importations of foreign players and the adoption of modern tactics in place of the renowned 'Spanish fury'. Foreign names (Kubala, Di Stefano, Kopa, Puskas) replaced the great postwar Spanish heroes (Zarra, symbol of 'fury', Panizo, César, Gaínza). The big clubs spent vast sums on transfer fees to acquire foreign players. Sport as a whole suffered. The spectacular successes of the big clubs concealed a feeble infrastructure. Basic sports – athletics, swimming – were forgotten. In the forty years of Francoism Spain won only five Olympic medals.

Football, bullfighting, kiosk literature, radio shows, the cinema, were all part of the culture of evasion, casting its 'artificial silence' around the real problems of a pauperised country. Those struggling to make do on second-hand clothes and scanty rations could escape into a world of illusion in the dazzling career of a Manolete, a Conchita Piquer or a Zarra. In the cowboys of kiosk literature with their rough justice, in radio melodramas where lovers triumphed over misunderstanding and class barriers, the working classes found the literary expression of their unrealisable, intimate hopes. Football, like the state lottery with its much publicised 'fat prize', provided an even more tangible hope of social mobility by magic;

between 1963 and 1973 Spaniards spent 14,000 million pesetas on the pools.[33]

If popular songs, kiosk literature and sport were the principal ingredients of popular subculture, they could not satisfy the tastes of the middle classes whose sense of status demanded a more sophisticated, 'smart' product. These were satisfied by foreign best-sellers and the works of a few native authors who continued traditional narrative forms: Agustí's *Mariona Rebull* – the *Forsyte Saga* of a Catalan family of industrialists; Antonio Zunzunegui's 'realist' novels of Bilbao and Madrid; Gironella's even more realistic trilogy on the Civil War. Like Fernández Florez' *Lola* (the adventures of an exotic prostitute spy – a curious exception in the puritanical atmosphere of the 1950s) all these works lacked any creative originality: they were routine products. Nor was this poverty compensated by the quality of foreign imports.* These made the fortunes of publishing houses, since the mere fact that a book was written by a foreigner was enough to convince middle-class readers that it was profound.

That the foreign cinema, popular foreign books and kiosk literature played so great a part in postwar Spanish culture is significant. It reveals a certain disinclination of wide sectors of Spanish society to absorb and find satisfaction in the official culture of the regime, especially the heroic-imperial culture of the Falange. But it also reveals, in the same sectors of society, a lack of intellectual preoccupations and curiosity which conveniently coincided with the desire of the regime to depoliticise Spain. The result would be a growing divorce between the intellectual and the masses, indifferent not merely to neo-scholasticism and the Catholic kings of official culture, but also to the efforts of those intellectuals who stood apart from the regime.

(f)
Social protest in the arts

To the writers of the mid-fifties this gap was a matter of great concern. They wished to give 'the silent people' a voice which neither liberal philosophers nor 'subjectivist' writers like Carmen Laforet or Cela had succeeded in doing. If newspapers and magazines 'idiotised' the people, then it was the function of the creative writer 'to give the public a vision of reality it could not find

*The popularity of a foreign book was often the result of a successful film version; this accounts for the vogue of Daphne du Maurier and Somerset Maugham. On best-sellers see J. M. Martínez Cachero, *La novela española entre 1939 y 1969. Historia de una aventura* (1973).

in the press'.[34] Literature must protest. This was the self-imposed role of the 'social' poets, novelists and dramatists who appeared around 1955–6.

Until the mid-sixties they sustained a literary movement characterised by overt social criticism and, for many, explicit political commitment. It no longer sufficed to expose the alienated individual's existential anguish; literature must eschew a self-indulgent 'subjectivism' and describe 'the social situation of the collectivity'.

The new road to 'social realism' had already been opened by an older writer who had known García Lorca and the artistic freedom of the Second Republic: Gabriel Celaya, the most gifted of the 'social poets', who was to remain a cultural hero of the left long after he himself had deserted 'social poetry'. Celaya's revolt was both personal and artistic. He left his bourgeois wife to live with a working-class mistress whose father had been a Socialist militant. He saw poetry as an instrument to change society by exposing its injustices: 'Poetry is a weapon loaded with the future.' Like most of the 'realist' writers of the mid-fifties he was a Marxist and joined the Communist party.*

The best known of these writers was the Paris-based Juan Goytisolo (b. 1931), whose first novel, *Juego de Manos* (1954), describes the descent into alcoholism and pseudo-anarchism of a Madrid adolescent who rejects the passive, conformist values of his bourgeois family. This generation conflict was to become a standard theme of fiction, just as it became a fact of life. *Central Eléctrica* (1958), by Jesús López Pacheco (b. 1930), is an archetypal social novel. It describes the construction of a hydro-electric station in one of the most backward regions of Spain. The class struggle is symbolised by the exploitation of the workers, many of whom perish in macabre work accidents, leaving their families without compensation. They are peasants – 'prehistoric' and 'animal' in the eyes of the city-born employees of the company – with no alternative but to work on the dam that submerges their village and who can find no means of livelihood in the new village built by the company on barren soil. They are forced to emigrate. Was this the Spain of official pronouncements where 'a new dawn, a splendid dawn, is rising'?[35]

Alfonso Sastre (b. 1926) was representative, like the social novelists, of a younger generation who saw the theatre – and indeed every form of art – as a revolutionary instrument of social

---

*Besides Celaya, the other great name in the social poetry of the early fifties was Blas de Otero. He was also a Marxist and a member of the Communist party.

and political criticism. His theories, elaborated in essays as obscure as they are abundant, illustrate another aspect of this generation: its eager and at times naive absorption of foreign ideas after a period of intellectual starvation. Sastre, by the 1960s, had absorbed Brecht and become a committed Marxist.[36]

Sastre's plays are difficult; they are violent in their attacks on Spanish society and, for the first time, the political overtones are clear. How could a Spanish audience miss the parody of the triumphalist rhetoric of the regime in *Sad are the Eyes of William Tell*, one of his best plays?

'There is no reason to be sad! None whatsoever! We can confidently look to the future! All is going well! Extremely well! Highways are being built! The living standard of the working class is rising! We have freedom of the press – except for lies and errors. Prior to the administration of Admiral General Gessler this country was choked by chaos, corruption, Barbarism! The proletariat is happy! Everyone is so happy!'[37]

Sastre openly sympathised with the Asturian miners whose brutal treatment at the hands of the police was the subject of his play *The Red Earth*. Scarcely surprisingly, the censors systematically destroyed his dramatic career. In 1960 he was one of 227 Spanish intellectuals to sign a public protest against the censorship; in 1961 he was clapped in prison.

Censorship did not merely crush individual playwrights. It ruined the efforts of nonconformist writers, actors and directors to launch an independent, non-commercial theatre. Its actions exposed the limitations of the cultural liberalisation introduced by Manuel Fraga Iribarne as Minister of Information after 1962.

Fraga's plans included government help in the promotion of cinema and theatrical productions 'of quality'. The latter failed through a combination of censorship, poor acting and the indifference of a middle-class public with no intellectual curiosity.

Nevertheless the modicum of liberalisation doled out in the sixties helped modify the cultural climate of Spain. Thus the producer Querejeta seized the opportunity to launch the 'new Spanish cinema' in 1965; it sought to combine high artistic standards and social protest, although only Carlos Saura and to a lesser extent Patino and Picazo showed outstanding talent.[38] The Official School of Cinematography gained a new impulse: it produced some of the most interesting directors of the seventies. In 1967, the so-called Salas de Arte y Ensayo (experimental art cinemas) were authorised; even with restrictions and delays, a selection of the *avant-garde* European cinema could be seen in Spain.

'Critical realism' also entered the arts. The innovating spirit of the artists of the *avant-garde* fashionable in the late fifties had been directed towards 'informalism'. Its programme reads like a parody of the windy cultural manifestos of the regime. 'Informal painting constitutes in its extreme forms of expression a destructive action as the justification of being.' Nevertheless its products made an international reputation and sold to the prosperous bourgeoisie of the sixties. In the early sixties, artists began to point out the basic contradiction between art for art's sake and social criticism, to underline the failure of 'informal' art to reflect immediate reality. 'Informalism' did not disappear — indeed the newly established commercial art galleries were determined it should not — but groups and individuals who saw art as a chronicle of reality, as a socio-political manifesto, mushroomed in the 1960s.*

Almost all the writers we have mentioned were members of the Communist party or intellectual fellow travellers. Marxism became, for a period, the dominant subculture of the opposition, making its way into every intellectual activity. Carlos Castilla del Pino represented the Spanish version of the attempts made elsewhere to couple Marxism and psychoanalysis.[39] Historians discovered the class conflict. Tuñón de Lara, the historian of the Spanish labour movement, became as influential in the sixties as Vicens had been in the fifties. Marxist sociology became the intellectual fashion among radical students. The philosopher Sacristán began his edition of the complete works of Lukács. The new wave affected Aranguren, the leading liberal Catholic intellectual of the postwar years. Ever ready to capitalise on the intellectual fancies of the young, he imported the Christian-Marxist dialogue from France and Italy in a book on Marxism and Ethics.

Thanks to the flexibility of the Ministry of Information under Fraga Iribarne (1962–9) Marxist literature began to appear in Spanish bookshops. In the 1950s the works of Camus, Sartre or Maritain had been a forbidden fruit; after 1965–6 Marx, Gramsci, Dobb, Sweezy or Marcuse — to quote the fashionable writers in

*The 'informalist' painters Saura, Feito, Canogar, Juana Francés, Suárez, Millares, Rivera and the sculptor Serrano formed the original group of *El Paso* in 1957. The best examples of 'critical realism' are perhaps Genovés, Barjola, Ibarrola and the so-called Equipo Crónica and Equipo Realidad. Canogar also adhered to social realism. See C. Areán, *Treinta años de Arte español* (1972); V. Aguilera Cerni, *Iniciación al arte español de posguerra* (1970); and V. Bozal, *Historia del Arte en España* (1972).

Madrid and Barcelona Universities – could be read without difficulty. Three different editions of Che Guevara's Bolivian diary were printed in 1969.

The Marxism of the new realists was the most evident sign of their militancy in the anti-Francoist opposition. But they rejected not only the official culture, but the liberal Spanish tradition identified with Ortega y Gasset as well. Juan Goytisolo, the theorist and the most prolific of the novelists of the generation, violently attacked Ortega's aesthetic ideas. When in 1964 Ortega's disciple Marías published a second edition of his *Diccionario de literatura española*, a young critic denounced him sharply for the exclusion of a number of writers, 'most of whom held either Marxist or Marxist-influenced positions.'[40]

If imported Marxism was the main philosophy of rebellion, the culture of the exiles was seen as a similar radical alternative to the 'sclerotic' official culture, more intransigent in its rejection of the regime than the domestic liberal tradition. It was the left-wing opposition that, in the sixties, steadily recovered the culture of exile in magazines like *Triunfo*. Buñuel's films, once banned, were shown to full houses in 1970. The luminaries of 'National Catholicism' were neither read nor remembered. What conceivable relevance could they have to the Spain of the nineteen-seventies? Their only legacy to Spanish culture was an inflated prose style.

(g)
Mass culture

The cultural opening which began in the sixties with Fraga was to narrow on occasions: publishers could encounter serious difficulties in printing left-wing books and in 1969 four publishing houses were closed by government action. In April 1970 the Minister of Information told the Cortes, 'Information is an instrument of state policy . . . In my opinion there is too much freedom of expression in Spain'. But Spain was never to return to the claustrophobic atmosphere of the past. Right-wing vandals could not put the clock back; hysterical fears of a Marxist takeover found expression in attacks on left-wing bookshops.

That it should be a novelty for a citizen of a Western society to be able to buy what books he chooses is a startling indication of the price Spain had paid for Franco's peace. The enforced cultural isolation of the regime had for decades made the renewal of contact with the world outside Spain a difficult – even dangerous – undertaking; but in the long run the demands of a modernising society must erode the intellectual straitjacket imposed in the

forties. Fraga believed that the Spain of development and tourism
could not be satisfied with the reactionary policies of his predecessor, Arias Salgado.[41] He also hoped that a degree of cultural
liberalisation would improve the image of the regime abroad. The
financial support of the Ministry of Information to the 'cinema of
quality' after 1964 was part of a prestige campaign to make
political capital out of the possible international success of the
young Spanish artists.

The regime acted as if it believed that greater cultural tolerance
would have only minor social effects. It realised, for instance, that
the influence of Marxism was mainly restricted to university circles
(perhaps it believed in some form of cultural homeopathy – that a
little dose of Marxism would kill the disease), and that the deep
cultural divide between masses and elites deprived 'progressive'
ideologies of much of their potential impact. While this divorce
continued, the regime could ignore the growing ideological radicalisation of the intellectuals.

In the 1960s this divorce was indirectly reinforced. Nineteen-
fifty-six was not only the year of student rebellion and of the emergence of the postwar 'realist generation'; it also saw the birth of
Spanish television, the undisputed instrument of the 'culture of evasion' in the Spain of economic and industrial growth. If only 1 per cent
of Spanish homes had a television set in 1960, 90 per cent of Spaniards
were watching it ten years later. 'Everybody watching the television
serials with open mouths,' the Catalan writer Josep Plá said in 1972,
'such is today's culture.'[42] Its regional and social diffusion was
completed in the space of a few years. This is important, since
although television was the main entertainment of Spanish society
in the last twenty years of Franco's rule, it was also the only cultural
area never to be enlarged by the various 'openings' of the regime.

The programmes on Spanish television offered little variation
through the years, except for a considerable improvement in
technical quality. Television is state-controlled, but financed
through commercial advertising. American telefilms, competitions,
sports, musical shows, remained the basic components of
programmes. After twenty years of Spanish television only one
national telefilm has been produced. Theatrical productions have
been rare and poor; serials based on novels have been usually
deplorable; cultural programmes irrelevant; political information,
grotesque – a glorification of 'Spanish peace' through an exaggeration of conflicts abroad and silence (or distortion) on those at
home; political interviews non-existent until Franco's death, except
for controlled press conferences by ministers.[43] Spanish television
still remains (1978) rooted in mediocrity.

The television explosions explains the decline in cinema attend-ances.* The film market was still very much the same as in the forties and fifties: only one Spanish film was shown for every four foreign films. Hollywood spectaculars continued to make by far the biggest profits. The Spanish cinema still lacked capital resources. The 'new Spanish cinema' had no success with the public (partly because of distribution difficulties), which preferred the vulgar comedies and 'spaghetti westerns' which had replaced the 'folkloric' cinema of the 1950s as the archetypal Spanish film. *No desearás al vecino del 5°* (*Thou shalt not covet thy neighbour on the fifth floor*), an execrable sex comedy, broke all box office records for Spanish-made films between 1965 and 1974.

The Spanish theatre still depended on the routine tastes of its middle-class public. It is true that in the sixties and seventies there were reputable productions of Brecht, Peter Weiss, Molière, Sartre, Genet, Pinter, García Lorca, Valle Inclán, that the Ministry of Information tried to promote an independent theatre, and that serious Spanish playwrights saw their work on stage. Buero Vallejo, for instance, became a 'consecrated' author for both public and critics. But light comedy dominated the commercial theatre. The 1960s were the golden years of Alfonso Paso, epitome of triviality and mediocrity in subject and style. For years he mono-polised the theatres of Madrid with half a dozen or more of his plays running simultaneously. 'Ten years of uninterrupted mediocrity,' a critic wrote in a résumé of theatrical activity between 1956 and 1966.[44]

Live television reinforced the already immense popularity of sport: television — and Manuel Santana's victories — made tennis a popular sport after 1964—5. But the basic structure and the social role of sport remained unchanged. Its attraction continued to be based on professional super-stars. State help remained scarce while the nationalist exploitation of Spanish successes continued unabated. Television and tourism helped to maintain a declining industry — the Spanish sport *par excellence*, the bullfight. It explains the unparalleled success of *El Cordobés*, a mediocre, if charismatic, bullfighter, a social myth of rags to riches for the popular classes.

---

*The growth of television partly explains the decline in cinema attendance after the mid-1960s: 400 million spectators in 1965, 273 million in 1974; 9,029 cinemas in 1966, 5,178 in 1975. In 1968 the cinema still contributed 46.3% to the revenues of the National Entertainments Syndicate; discos and cabarets 26.8%; sports 8.3%; bullfights 7.6%. In 1974 the respective proportions were 35.2%, 37.4%, 10.2% and 4.8%. ['Cine espanol 1975', *Sindicato Nacional del Espectáculo* (1976), p. 5.]

In 1976 less was read in Spain than anywhere else in Western Europe.[45] In the sixties, Spain's paperback revolution was set off by publishers with cultural rather than commercial aims and was responsible for the diffusion of left-wing ideologies amongst students. Most publishers still relied on translations of second-rate foreign best-sellers.[46] What was remarkable was that so few Spanish authors became best-sellers and that the literary quality of these best-sellers was undistinguished.*

'Kiosk literature' was the domestic production that continued to sell well. Love stories gained new life with the proliferation of 'photo-novels', cheap and well-printed picture novelettes which embodied the yearnings of the popular classes: cars, luxury homes, yachts. *Simplemente María* (*Just Mary*) sold 170,000 copies a week for eighty-one weeks. The novelist Benet considered an annual 5,000 copies a success.[47]

(h)
The cultural landscape of the seventies

The regime, Marías claimed in 1962, had not succeeded in creating a single 'false prestige'; for him, incurable optimist that he is, Spain was the scene of 'a flourishing intellectual life'.[48] This life was not confined to the circle of Madrid intellectuals. Barcelona was the capital of a Catalan culture which had survived the winter of repression to blossom in a second Renaissance. The 'school of Barcelona' was the Catalan reply to the 'new Spanish cinema' of the 1960s; Catalan literature was the most *avant-garde*, experimental and Europeanised in Spain. But this 'flourishing intellectual life' existed, not merely on the margin of the regime, but divorced from the preoccupations of most Spaniards.

By 1970 young writers believed that an aesthetic, linguistic revolution rather than social criticism was the way to liberation. It was a break with the Marxist conception of realism which had so influenced the 'postwar realist generation'. Young philosophers also looked beyond Marxism for new philosophical alternatives which they found either in analytical philosophy or in Nietzsche's writings, the two most powerful new influences in the late 1960s and early 1970s.[49]

Whatever their faults and excesses, the 'social' novels and poetry of that generation had given the literary world some sort of recognisable shape and unity of purpose. This now vanished. The novel

---

*The exception was Cela and, in the seventies, Francisco Umbral. See R. Rubio, 'La novela española, a la conquista del "best-seller"', *Ya* (15 December 1976).

Tiempo de Silencio by Luis Martín Santos, the story of a blood feud set in the sordid poverty of postwar Madrid, seems to have killed the genre; it was a sarcastic exercise in language rather than a social chronicle. 'Social poetry', Celaya maintained in the seventies, had suffered a twin blow: a mushroom growth of social poets had turned what had been an exciting discovery into a cliché at the very time when the advent of the consumer society had taken the edge off the protest against primitive poverty.[50] The discovery of Latin American literature reinforced the flight from the cruder forms of social realism. Its descriptive exuberance and the stylistic freedom made experimentalism in forms and styles the main concern of new Spanish writers. 'I believe,' the novelist Juan Benet said in 1969, 'that novels of today, yesterday and the day before yesterday lack imagination.'[51]

In contrast to the realist novel of previous years, Benet created a metaphorical, enclosed world of hallucination peopled by strange, vague characters. It won him the acclaim of the younger generation of writers.[52] The 'destruction of language' – as a means to eliminate the whole Spanish cultural past – was the main purpose of the trilogy published by Juan Goytisolo between 1966 and 1975: the 'revolutionary' assault on syntax and grammar was symbolised in the concluding passage, written in Arabic. Gimferrer, the theorist of the so-called *novísimos* (very new) poets – who appeared in 1970 – denounced the 'fossilisation' of language in all previous poetry. Abandoning social poetry, the *novísimos* sought to recover the purity of aestheticism or the attachment to a personal vision characteristic of Aleixandre. 'Compromised' poetry was rejected. 'I do not believe you can demand any other compromise from a poet than authenticity.'* This creed did not interfere with the political attitudes of the new writers. They were as committed anti-Francoists and as close to left-wing groups as the 'realist' generation.[53]

Far from being a 'cultural desert', in the final years of the Franco era the map of Spanish culture had become a complex pattern of cultures that did not communicate with one another. There was the great divide between liberals and Marxists, between the culture of the masses and that of the sophisticated elite, between the interests

---

*Carlos Sahagún. See José Olivio Jiménez, *Diez años de poesía española* (1972), pp. 15–32. A new generation of playwrights sought to renew the drama via an allegorical, symbolic theatre, likewise abandoning the political, realist theatre of the early 1960s. Fernando Arrabal anticipated this new vanguard theatre. Spanish by birth, he lives in Paris; his reputation rests on a series of literary and political scandals rather than on familiarity with his plays, most of which were forbidden until Franco's death.

of the younger generation and their elders. A cultural establishment still thrived on the elegant essayism in the tradition of Ortega; Marías was still, in 1977, one of the most prolific literary journalists.[54] Although Marxism was challenged or ignored in the arts and although 'critical realism' had been partially or totally abandoned in favour of the philosophies of the new vanguards – Spanish versions of hyper-realism, minimal art, op art, body art, magic realism, it still exercised a preponderant influence on sociologists, historians and economists.

Years of censorship and isolation help to explain not merely the divorce between the culture of the elite and that of the masses, but the mimetism and politicisation which in differing degrees affect cultural movements in Spain. Cultural fashions are rapidly and uncritically accepted. A certain *mystique de gauche* distinguishes the 'new' intelligentsia. Political activism has created some false reputations – a revenge, perhaps, for the false reputations which the now moribund official culture had tried to create in the forties.

Years of censorship and isolation also explain the present-day obsession with politics and sex, those twin demons of Francoism which seem to have possessed Spanish culture since Franco's death. The 1976 publishing boom flooded bookshops with books and pamphlets committed in politics but often poor in quality.[55] Weekly magazines have discovered the market value of a combination of oppositional politics and formerly forbidden sex: full frontal nudes accompany leading articles by prominent politicians. Pornography itself has created a new minor industry: it pontificates on the ideal length of the penis, on ways to excite women, on the 'naturalness' of incest and lesbianism, on the excitements of bestiality – all concealed by spurious appeals to the tolerance necessary for a democratic system. The cinema has exploited to the point of saturation the eroticism that for years was denied it. This does not mean that Madrid and Barcelona have become the Copenhagens of Latin Europe; but 1977 is a far cry even from 1975.

Even if the immediate symptoms of the new liberty have been disappointing – an excess of green (the Spanish adjective to qualify a dirty joke) and red (for politics) – the public will weary of a politicised entertainment industry and the breasts of Susana Estrada, author of *Wet Sex*. The recovery of freedom will have, one hopes, a positive effect on Spanish culture. The decline of the folkloric cinema and the appearance in 1976–7 of a number of excellent films is perhaps an indication. For the first time in many years a remarkable novel by a Spanish author (Juan Marsé) has been the year's best-seller (1977). The daily *El País* has given a new vigour to the press.[56]

For Miró the years of Francoism were a scratch on the skin. His image of Spanish culture − and above all Catalan culture, for he is a committed Catalan nationalist − is of a carob tree, deep-rooted and evergreen.[57] The award of the Novel Prize for literature to Vicente Aleixandre was not merely a reward for an unsullied and outstanding talent. It was a recognition that Spanish culture had survived. Or to put it another way, it had proved impossible to cut Spain off from the modern world.

Chapter 7

From 'Conformism' to Confrontation

(a)
Franco's peace

The regime of General Franco considered its greatest political achievement to be the establishment of an era of peace and order without precedent in the history of Spain. Its apologists constantly harped on the repeated revolutions, the chronic political instability of 'liberal' Spain, and, in contrast, celebrated the silver jubilee of Franco's rule as 'twenty-five years of peace'. In the 1966 referendum on the Organic Law of the State official propaganda appealed to the electorate with the slogan 'Vote Peace'.

Yet as the Minister of the Interior confessed in December 1972, 'subversion' — a favourite word of the regime — had existed since the end of the Civil War: from the guerrilla war of the 1940s, the student riots and strikes of the sixties, to the ETA terrorism of the seventies.[1]

Conflicts in Franco's Spain were much more severe than was apparent in the propaganda of the regime or reflected in a manipulated press, radio and television. It is essential to grasp the extent and importance of these conflicts. They were less intense than was suggested by opposition historians and foreign journalists, eager to pick up any signs of resistance to feed a public hungry for signs of the imminent collapse of the regime. Resistance was heroic but its repercussions in Spain were limited. It revealed the repressive nature of the regime, the inadequacy of its institutions for solving the conflict of a modern society; but Franco died in his bed. If his plans for the succession had not been destroyed by the assassination in December 1973 of the chosen instrument of *continuismo*, Admiral Carrero Blanco, the chances of the political survival of a form of Francoism might have been much more promising. This was the general opinion when Franco finally died.

Before the sixties it is explicable that expression of discontent was isolated, occasional and sporadic. Repression was efficient – between 1939 and 1945 the clandestine Socialist party saw six of its executive committees imprisoned – and until the end of the diplomatic isolation of Spain in the fifties the government was not concerned with the effect of brutal repression on its image abroad; on the contrary, it capitalised on international hostility. Franco presented such hostility as yet another example of the eternal international plot against Spain, the work of those expert manipulators of the Black Legend, the freemasons. This simple technique of creating support lost its efficacy through over-use. By 1970 only committed Francoists felt the 'Numantian' emotions of a nation besieged by its traditional enemies.[2]

Even when international opinion was of some concern to the regime, repression continued. In 1962 Spain applied for entry to the European Community and membership became a permanent aim of foreign policy; yet a year later the Communist militant Julian Grimau was garotted in spite of universal protests from the countries of the Community (and from Cardinal Montini, later Pope Pius VI). In 1974 the 'opening' of Prime Minister Arias[3] gained some interest, even sympathy, in Europe; eighteen months later the European powers withdrew their ambassadors in protest against the execution of five terrorists.

Repression, severe and effective though it was, by itself does not explain the widespread political indifference, the demobilisation of opinion and the lack of serious, *overt* social unrest in the forties and fifties. After all, repression did not stop strikes, student demonstrations and the activities of ETA in the sixties. Other factors were at work in this earlier period.

In the first place, the regime enjoyed more support than its opponents liked to admit. This support was not reflected in the enthusiasms of hired crowds – the officially induced adulation which deceived and delighted the Caudillo – but in the tacit acceptance of the Francoist system by large sections of society. The grandiloquent rhetoric of the Falange did not attract the general run of Spaniards, most of whom regarded the original creations of the regime – organic democracy and the vertical syndicates – with scepticism and total indifference; participation in municipal elections, which would have been a sign of relative enthusiasm for the system, was absurdly low.[4] What was decisive was that the Franco regime represented the restoration of traditional values in education, the family, in religion and the social order, values more deeply rooted in Spanish society than the liberal-democratic reformists of the 1930s had believed. The regime benefited from the sheer exhaustion of that society after three years of civil war which could be regarded as the outcome of the efforts of an unstable liberal democracy to transform traditional Spanish society and its values. As distinguished a member of the opposition as Dionisio Ridruejo recognised sadly what he called 'majority social support' for Francoism.[5]

(b)
Working-class protest

We must now examine the factors that were demolishing the official version of 'Franço's peace': the transition from the Spain of conformity based on repression and the manipulation of apathy to the Spain of *contestación*.[6] Workers, students, sections of the church and the Basques and Catalans had by 1970 all moved towards a rejection of the regime. This evolution escaped a dictator who was the prisoner of his own stereotypes. To him, workers with television sets, cars and football were not a revolutionary force. Students were 'good boys' out to get jobs but led into bad ways by a few addicts to foreign ideologies. The church which he had saved from destruction was, lamentably, showing signs of an incomprehensible ingratitude; but, then, it was a few Communist infiltrators in the priesthood who were causing trouble. As for the regional aspirations of the Catalans, that was simple 'nonsense'.[7]

The Civil War had signified the ruthless destruction of working-class unions and parties; they were prohibited and proscribed (Order of 10 January 1937); those leaders and militants who survived from the war years were, in the 1940s, imprisoned, tortured, and many executed. Nevertheless Franco and his advisers, in spite of conservative prejudices, were fully aware that the working class must, somehow or other, be incorporated in Nationalist Spain if the new state was to appear a modern, legitimate enterprise. This concern is reflected in the fact that the first Fundamental Law (9 March 1938) of the new state was the Labour Charter (*Fuero del Trabajo*). The Charter was a compilation of Fascist corporativist ideas, the native national-syndicalist rhetoric of the Falange and 'social Catholicism' – this last ingredient long familiar to Spanish ideologues of the right. It was a declaration of principles; their implementation would require subsequent decrees and laws.

Its Italian Fascist origins were evident in the assertion that the syndical organisation of the National Syndicalist State was to be founded on the principles of 'unity, totality and hierarchy'. Each branch of the economy was to be organised in a single 'vertical syndicate' or trade union, membership of which was compulsory for employers, technicians and administrative staff and workers. The syndicates were not conceived as organs to defend the workers' interests but as instruments in the service of the state and under its 'hierarchical direction'. The new syndical organisation (OS), created between 1938 and 1940, remained under the control of the relevant minister, always a Falangist, a 'man of the Movement'; the presidents of the various national syndicates and the local officials of the OS were invariably Falangists or Falangist fellow-travellers nominated from above or 'elected' in elections controlled by the ministry.

The functions of the syndicates, as laid down in the law of 1940, did not include collective bargaining. They were conceived as instruments of social discipline at the service of national production. As in their Italian counterparts, the co-operation of worker and employer within the vertical syndicates was supposed to replace the class struggle, characteristic of liberal capitalism, by a class harmony distinct from the dull uniformity of Socialist societies. A new euphemistic rhetoric was coined: workers were producers; employers entrepreneurs (*empresarios*); strikes — when their existence was recognised — labour conflicts; rural unions, brotherhoods of farmers and stockbreeders.

National syndicalism was to be the alternative to liberal capitalism and Marxist materialism, the syndicates the channels (*cauces*) through which the workers participated in the 'tasks of the state'. Thus the syndicates were amply represented in all official bodies from municipalities to the Council of the Realm: for instance the Organic Law of 1967 created 150 syndical deputies in the Cortes. None of the 'syndical' deputies was a worker elected by his fellow workers. They were either appointed or chosen by complicated and controlled indirect elections. Closely connected with the union bureaucracy, they were firmly opposed to any reform of the system. In the seventies they found a refuge in the bunker.[8]

The artificial representation of the syndicates in the Cortes underlined the main weakness of the OS: lack of any true representative character. The OS — social centrepiece of the new state — failed precisely because it did not or could not organise factory unions that were both truly representative of the workers *and* identified with the regime. It hesitated before it allowed the election of shop stewards (*enlaces sindicales*) and the setting up of works committees (*jurados de empresas*). The one early attempt, in 1941, to create representative unions with a real say in the management of the economy was defeated by employers in alliance with anti-Falangists in the government.[9] The OS remained 'a bureaucratic mastodon'.

If employers benefited in the early years from the denial to the workers of the right to strike (strikes were crimes according to the Penal Code until 1975) and of their power to negotiate collective agreements, the workers themselves benefited from the cumbersome and complex paternalism of the regime. Much of the social legislation (family allowances; the all-important Law of Labour Contracts of 1944 which made it difficult to sack a worker once employed) was the work of the Falangist José A. Girón de Velasco, Minister of Labour 1941–56. The system of social security became immensely complex and spawned a bureaucratic monster – and it is characteristic of all such growths in an authoritarian system like Spain that such agencies escape effective budgetary control. The system had many other defects: miserable old age pensions; unemployment benefits which covered perhaps only half of the unemployed; inadequate public medical services which drove 40 per cent of the population to use the private sector and in which overburdened doctors pandered to the Spanish propensity for pills and potions. In spite of all these defects – the chief being that social services did little to redress a badly skewed distribution of income – the social paternalism did confer some tangible benefits. Above all, the 1944 Labour Law, though it was often grossly abused by employers, gave a substantial proportion of the work force complete job security.[10] This security was the compensation prize given to the working class in return for depriving it of its independent unions and the right to strike, and it is clear from surveys in the seventies that the workers continued to value security highly. Employers may, for a decade, have had their way, via the Ministry of Labour awards, over wages; but the decisions of the Labour Courts forced them to abandon all hope of modernising their enterprises by introducing capital-intensive methods. If a compulsory superfluity of hands was no great disadvantage in the years of autarky with starvation wages and when no new machinery could be imported, it became a drawback in the boom of the sixties.

The complicated labour legislation of Francoism had one overall objective: to prevent the labour conflicts characteristic of democratic regimes. Hence the grant of individual rights to workers which were often upheld in the Labour Courts and the systematic denial of collective rights; hence the intervention of the state in labour issues; hence the strict state control of unions. This, together with the dismantling of the historic unions and the limited bargaining power of the workers in a stagnant economy, accounts for the infrequency of labour conflicts until the late fifties. Only the Barcelona transport boycott and strike of March 1951, the strikes in the Basque country in May, protests against the cost of living in 1956, and the Asturian miners' strike of 1958 had any national importance. In general, conflicts were spontaneous protests against, for instance, dangerous working conditions in the mines, or the lack of proper washrooms; isolated and uncoordinated, they were relatively easily dealt with by the regime. It was enough to make a few arrests, a few concessions and sack a few local authorities guilty of lack of foresight and flexibility.*

Harsh repression prevented any effective action by clandestine unions. Such unions, the creation of heroic nuclei of committed militants who risked torture and imprisonment, abounded but their existence was nominal and their influence over the working class was minimal.† In 1960, with little prospect of leadership from the official syndicates, which were neither representative nor militant, and when clandestine unions were ineffective, the workers were demobilised, concerned with the satisfaction of their individual needs rather than with collective action. Ridruejo, in 1961, spoke of 'a loss of working-class consciousness'.

Within a few years this situation changed radically. In 1962 the Asturian miners (45,000 strong) came out for two months, to be followed by 70,000 Catalan and 50,000 Basque workers – all for higher wages. For the first time since the Civil War these strikes were fully – if tendentiously – reported in the press. It was the characteristically tough and rough reply of the Minister of Information, Manuel Fraga Iribarne, to a journalist's question on torture that concentrated national attention on the miners' strike. From now on strikes became a regular feature of Spanish life.** In 1964 there were 484 strikes; during the next decade, when strikes were still punishable under the Penal Code, there were nearly 5,000.[11]

How are we to account for this revival in working-class militancy? Firstly, the government had modified national syndicalism by introducing collective bargaining in 1958. Hitherto wage levels had been set by the Ministry of Labour. Though it still operated within

---

*J. Blanc, 'Las huelgas en el movimiento obrero español', *Horizonte Español 1966* (1966), vol. II, pp. 249*ff*. In May 1947, the clandestine opposition called for a general strike in the Basque provinces. About 50,000 workers stopped work, but the strike was limited to the province of Biscay. (Beltza, *El nacionalismo vasco en el exilio*, 1977.)

†AS (*Alianza Sindical*) was an alliance, formed by exiles, of Socialist, CNT and Basque nationalists; ASO (*Alianza Sindical Obrera*) was formed in 1962 from a splinter group of the AS and a small Catalan union; the Communists had their own union, OSO (*Oposición Sindical Obrera*).

**Official figures of strikes are as follows: 1963, 777; 1964, 484; after a fall in 1967–9 the number returned to around 500, rising in 1970 to 1,500 and in 1974 to 1,926.

the vertical syndicates, wage negotiation in *convenios colectivos* gave the works councils a new importance and the shop stewards a crucial role. While workers wanted representatives who really represented them, so did the more go-ahead employers anxious to modernise and to negotiate productivity deals. Freer collective bargaining was a necessary precondition for a neo-capitalist industrial take-off.*

The natural consequence of collective bargaining was strike action. The first strike over a wage agreement came in 1961; it was followed by the Asturian strike of 1962 in protest against a productivity-linked increase. The peculiarities of the new mechanism of collective bargaining increased the propensity to strike, since until 1973 only factory agreements were legal. If this initially favoured the employers, it also multiplied the occasions for strikes.

The new economic policy of 1957–60 not only modified the machinery of wage negotiation. The propaganda emphasis on 'development' set off a revolution of rising expectations in *all* classes. The workers wished to share the rewards of the consumer society and the economic miracle which industrialisation promised. Moreover this was a relatively new working class; a generation that had emerged after the Civil War, young, and composed largely of immigrants from the poorest rural regions. The million workers who flooded into Madrid and Barcelona between 1951 and 1960 had experienced neither industrial conflict nor repression; their memory of the Civil War was vague and distant.[12]

This new working class found itself in a strong bargaining position after 1962. Expansion allowed the large employers to satisfy wage demands; between 1965 and 1971 average wages doubled and unemployment – thanks largely to the 'export' of the unemployed to the factories of Europe – remained low.[13]

It was this combination of new bargaining methods and a new working class, with unsatisfied expectations in a much publicised economic boom, that explains the revival of the working-class movement after 1962. When the government ended the wage freeze imposed by the Stabilisation Plan of 1959, there was a massive wave of strikes. The harmony of capital and labour, the central theme of national syndicalism, if it had ever existed, was now a thing of the past.

In the 1960s labour troubles were concentrated in the old industrialised areas with a high per capita income and traditions of labour militancy: Barcelona, the Basque country and Asturias, and

---

*It would also prevent dramatic, across-the-board wage hikes by the Ministry of Labour. Girón's increases alarmed employers.

the new factories growing up around Madrid. In the seventies bad strikes took place in what had been predominantly rural regions with little experience of industrial conflict: Galicia, Navarre and Seville.[14] There were also sectoral changes: strikes continued in the building industry, mining and metallurgy, but in the seventies the worst strikes were in the new car factories. Whereas strikes in the declining coal industry of Asturias, the almost mythical centre of working-class militancy, fell off in violence and intensity, they increased in the new industries and services staffed by the traditionally passive middle classes (teachers, doctors, bank and post office employees). Perhaps the most striking indication of the economic and social evolution of Spain was the total absence of rural strikes. Andalusian agrarian anarchism, and the day labourers' strikes of the thirties − to romantic revolutionaries *the* characteristic expression of the Spanish temperament − had given way to industrial conflicts similar to those that troubled the developed industrial economies of the West. Once again, Spain was ceasing to be different.

Such conflicts, in most cases, turned on wage claims. Nevertheless from 1967 to 1969 the official statistics show a steady growth in 'solidarity' strikes, often in support of dismissals of shop stewards; this was a clear indication of the growing radicalisation and politicisation of the workers' movement and its demand for representative unions. There were public demonstrations, especially on 1 May, and confrontations with the police.

The impact of these strikes on the public in general is hard to judge. The system of factory agreements, while it multiplied potential conflicts, made nation-wide strikes an impossibility. In the forty years of Francoism not a single vital sector was paralysed by strike action.[15] Nor were there serious strikes in sectors (e.g. aviation, electricity, transport, hotels) where the impact on the public would have been immediate. The threat of militarisation hung over railway workers and was used to end the 1970 Underground strike in Madrid. Tourism, so important for the image of Spain abroad, remained free from strikes until after Franco's death.

Nevertheless strikes increasingly filled the newspapers and caught public attention after 1967.[16] After 1970 strikes which began in one factory, via the mechanism of repression and sympathetic strikes, ended up as local general strikes.[17] Finally, the Basque provinces witnessed, in 1970 and 1974, purely politically motivated strikes − the one working-class activity the regime had repeatedly and expressly condemned.

This revival of the working-class movement had profound repercussions, for both the regime and the opposition. For the regime it meant the end of the official syndicalist vision of a society rid of class conflict and united in a 'national project'. The leaders of Spanish syndicalism, therefore, sought some new definition of the purpose and functions of the OS. With the appointment of José Solís Ruiz, an enthusiastic Andalusian likened by a journalist to a small-town American demagogue, as Minister of the Movement (1957), a new *aperturista* wind blew through the fossilised bureaucracy of the OS. By a radical reform of its structures that would make it fit to handle labour relations in what had become a modern industrialised society, Solís hoped to capture the newly self-conscious working class for official syndicalism. Most of the union posts were made elective; legislation of the Penal Code classing all strikes as sedition was modified; syndical congresses were summoned to discuss the role of the OS. By the Organic Law of 1967 the central principle of Falangist syndicalism was modified: the term 'vertical syndicates' was dropped and the notions of hierarchy, unity and totality were abandoned. For the future syndicates were defined as public corporations for the defence of the interests of employers, technicians and workers, with the last two combined in a single union, the UTT. The road to some form of democratic unionism within the OS seemed open.

Yet that road was never taken. It proved impossible to remodel Spanish syndicalism on Western, democratic lines. Workers could not organise independent unions free from the tutelage of the state, with elected officials and with the right to strike. The 'opening' of Solís proved a false dawn, darkened in 1967 by the dismissal of hundreds of shop stewards elected in 1966. The Syndical Law of 1971, far from implementing and extending the liberalising measures implicit in the Organic Law of 1967, was restrictive.

The reforming enthusiasms of Solís encountered a cold reception from the conservative bureaucrats of the OS and were finally scotched with the political defeat of Solís and his 'men' by the technocrats of the Opus Dei. In any case the prospect of reform had come too late. It is possible to argue that a serious reform, tried much earlier, making the OS representative of the workers, might have integrated the working class into the Francoist system. When 'reform' finally arrived it was evident that any attempt to democratise the OS would threaten the regime itself. It is characteristic of authoritarian political systems that it is impossible to change one element within them without endangering the whole structure. Even committed Francoists recognised that the official syndicates were ineffective; but the regime could not allow the complex syndical organisation, interwoven and embedded at every level in the social and economic life of the country, to escape government control and come under the control of a new workers' movement. That this was a real possibility was demonstrated in 1966: the Workers' Commissions (*Comisiones Obreras*, CC OO) won a resounding success in the union elections of that year when 83.3 per cent of the workers voted.[18]

The emergence of the CC OO as the most important force of the working-class opposition was of great importance for the future. The culmination of the working-class revival of the sixties, it filled the vacuum between the official syndicates and the old-style, ineffective clandestine unions.

As far back as the 1950s the Catholic workers' organisations, allowed to function under the Concordat of 1953 (HOAC, JOC, VO), had tried to fill this vacuum. They were the first critics tolerated by the regime of the social and economic structure of the country. In the name of Catholic social doctrine their magazines, with the approval of some bishops, denounced harsh working-class conditions and the failure of the official syndicates in a professedly Christian state to ameliorate them. The HOAC and the JOC defended the right to strike and their shop stewards were active in wage bargaining between 1958 and 1961. The review of the Catholic Youth (*Juventud Obrera*), sold at factory gates, contained the only serious exposure of official unionism. These activities irritated the government and the attempt of Solís to limit Catholic unionism earned the harsh criticism of the Cardinal Primate, the conservative Pla y Daniel. As we have seen, the uneasiest bedfellows among the families of the system were conservative Catholics, who while denouncing liberalism professed a social conscience, and the 'reformist' Falangists.

The same circumstances that had seemed to favour 'independent' Catholic unionism explain the emergence of the Workers' Commissions. In their origins (1956–60) they were spontaneous, *ad hoc* committees, elected by workers' assemblies in each factory to negotiate wage agreements directly with the employers. Starting in Asturias and the Basque country they were manned chiefly by Communist militants and Catholic activists; but they included Socialists, independent Marxists – the FLP, for instance – and radical Falangists.

The success of the CC OO was due to their concentration on immediate demands; it was by hard work on the shop floor, particularly the energy expended on the remedy of individual grievances over bonuses, family allowances and safety conditions, that politically committed leaders won the confidence of fellow workers in whom the fears of the forties still survived. While the traditions of the working-class movement were still alive in the older militants, the leadership was often young. An American journalist describes the Asturian leaders as 'in their early twenties at most, wearing tight flared jeans, form-fitting T-shirts or shirts unbuttoned most of the way down their chests . . . They looked like a crowd of young bucks whom on a Saturday afternoon you expected to find at the town square chasing girls'.[19]

Originally the CC OO, as a temporary substitute for the machinery of the OS, dissolved themselves after each round of negotiations. After 1962, given their success in the miners' strike of that year, they assumed more stable forms extending beyond a single enterprise: a provincial committee in Vizcaya; the Madrid metallurgical committee which united a large sector. In 1966, after the first National Assembly of the CC OO, they ceased to be a spontaneous, *ad hoc* device, and became a permanent organisation.

As such, until they were declared illegal in 1968, they acquired a semi-legal, semi-official status, even using OS premises for their meetings. Many CC OO militants were elected as shop stewards and served on works committees. Solís even believed they could be incorporated into the OS, and his supporter, the powerful but cordially disliked journalist Emilio Romero, held inconclusive meetings with the CC OO leaders.

It was the readiness of the CC OO leaders to use the machinery of legal syndicalism in wage negotiations that accounted for the success of the CC OO: they could deliver results and expose the rigidity and resistance of the entrenched OS bureaucrats. With a dynamic and intelligent leadership the CC OO captured the loyalty of sections of the new working class; with no attachments to the UGT or the CNT younger workers saw in the CC OO the embodiment of their developing class consciousness.[20]

It was the 'historic' unions – the anarcho-syndicalist CNT and the Socialist UGT, together with some small local unions – which refused any truck with official syndicalism. To do so, they held, would favour the reformist scheme of Solís. In ostracising the official syndicates the historic unions committed a grave short-term error which lost them a good deal of support: they only retained influence in those regions which had been their traditional strongholds: the UGT in the Basque country and Asturias, the CNT in Catalonia.

The historic unions were profoundly suspicious – even hostile – towards the CC OO. Apart from what seemed like collaborationism with the OS, the old hands, with bitter memories of the Civil War, saw the commissions falling into the hands of Communists, who were the main advocates of 'entrism' or penetration of the official syndicates. This was seen as the resort of a party that had only very feeble union traditions of its own on which to build. Once it ceased to be a strictly local and spontaneous movement, the role of the Communists in an *organised* movement grew rapidly; organisation was always the party's forte.

This Communist leadership became an acknowledged fact only in 1976. The movement then split into three separate unions. The majority remained in the old CC OO, faithful to Communist leaders like Camacho and Sartorius – the latter a typical middle-class intellectual recruit to the party. Of the two 'minority' groups, one (the CSUT) was allied to the Maoist Workers Party (PT) and the other, the Sindicato Unitario (SU), was affiliated to the Revolutionary Workers Organization (ORT), a Marxist-Leninist group with its origins in the Catholic left of the sixties.

From now on the CC OO would constantly be accused by rivals and defectors of being a mere 'transmission belt' (*correa de transmisión*), through which the party would capture the working-class movement for its own ends. This was unfair. The CC OO leaders acted as unionists, independent of any party, their object being to create a strong, single democratic trade union open to all parties. Early on they rejected clandestine unions; they would become secret societies divorced from the masses. It was this rejection of clandestine unions, linked to proscribed parties as the UGT was linked to the PSOE, that was the secret of the success of the CC OO. Using what they could grab of the official union machinery, the CC OO could fight and be seen to be fighting for higher wages and better conditions. 'A clandestine union cannot fight for better wages.' The leaders of the CC OO felt that the regime, economically and socially, was other than it was in 1939, 'and we are not faced with a terrorist dictatorship'.[21] Until they exhausted the regime's tolerance the CC OO were prepared to use every legal loophole, to exploit every opportunity to infiltrate that the *relatively* more favourable conditions of the sixties offered. It took the Communist party leaders, trained in clandestinity, some time to appreciate the originality of the CC OO and the significance of the strike activists of the sixties. At first they saw in the new militancy not the result of the dynamism of the Spanish economy, but the symptom of some final crisis of the regime.

Just as it was to survive student riots, so the regime survived strikes. But it could not tolerate the CC OO once it realised, after the union elections of 1966, that far from being assimilable within the OS, the Commissions threatened its very existence by presenting the workers with a more effective weapon in conflicts with employers. On 17 October 1967 the CC OO mounted a demonstration of 100,000 in Madrid against the high cost of living – the biggest opposition demonstration that Francoist Spain had seen. The government reaction was immediate and drastic. The CC OO were declared illegal, their leaders gaoled and hundreds of shop stewards sacked. In 1973 nine of the CC OO leaders came up for trial (in trial number 1001) and were sentenced to 150 years' imprisonment. The CC OO leaders – especially Camacho – became working-class heroes, and repression did not stop strikes. Even weakened by internal discussion, the CC OO were successful once again in the union elections of 1975.

It was ironical that the legacy of the forty years' monopoly of official syndicalism was a workers' movement dominated by Communists, a domination far more secure than the grip of the Communist party on the workers' movement at the outbreak of the Civil War. The regime had even failed to domesticate the Catholic unionism of the fifties: Catholic unionists had moved towards Socialism (USO) or the extreme left (ORT). Nor had the persistent persecution of the historic unions succeeded in destroying their memory among the working class: after 1974 even the CNT, the most persecuted of all the historic unions, showed signs of life; by 1976 the UGT had made a dramatic come-back into working-class politics.[22]

(c)

The student rebellion

In February 1956 police and students clashed in the streets of Madrid. What in retrospect appears a minor riot appeared to those bred in the 'peace of Franco' to be a major political happening. It was also the beginning of the 'university problem', that sea of troubles which, advancing and retreating over the next twenty years, was to embarrass the regime and erode its legitimacy.

The 'events of February' were the culmination of a longer process of student discontent with the compulsory 'vertical' students' union, the SEU. It was the SEU which opposed a university congress of young writers encouraged by Falangist militants of the SEU who seem to have been responsible for the street dust-up in which a young Falangist was shot. The government reacted with what was to become its standard response: police action, arrests, accusations of Communist infiltration and the dismissal of the rival ministers directly concerned – Fernández Cuesta as Minister of the Movement and responsible for Falangist student rowdyism and Ruiz Giménez as the liberal Catholic Minister of Education.

The February events were magnified out of all proportion by the foreign press and by Madrid rumour-mongers.* Dionisio Ridruejo, arrested for his part in the projected writers' congress, put them in proportion: they were of modest importance, the concern of a minority of students. Yet the 'events' were revealing as evidence of the increasing politicisation of university students; a process which even if it affected only a minority of students from the privileged sectors of society, proved nevertheless to be irreversible, an indication of the failure of the efforts of the regime to attract the postwar generation. All the regime had gained, as the Rector of Madrid University, Laín Entralgo, had observed in 1955, was the 'distracted passivity of the great mass'.[23] Those of the younger generation interested in and capable of participation in political life were already alienated from the system.

The protagonists of the February events were a variety of Marxists and Socialist groups, 'progressive' Christians, orthodox Christian Democrats and Liberals. From 1956 onwards it is possible to talk of a 'new opposition' on the campuses of Spain. The Communist party, prominent in the February troubles, was to have considerable political influence in the universities until the late sixties. Clandestine anti-Francoist groups grew up and disappeared like mushrooms: Socialist groups (independent of the PSOE in exile but nevertheless acting as members of the party); 'revolutionary' Socialists in the Popular Liberation Front (FLP) which played an important role in the student opposition of the late fifties and sixties, combining, as it did, left-wing Christians and independent Marxists. There were small Christian Democrat groups. Their Union of Democratic Students (UED) which, together with the Communists, was responsible for the spectacular demonstrations of 1965–8, demonstrations which preceded the rash of student agitation which spread over Europe in 1968. It was from these groups and mini-groups (groupuscules) that the 'new left' of the seventies was to emerge.

After a period of relative calm, university agitation built up again in 1962–3 and thereafter became endemic. Its processes became stylised in a standard pattern. After a 'free assembly', students would march to the Rector's office; police action, arrests and academic sanctions followed; renewed protest brought new and more violent clashes with the police. The final act was the

---

*R.C. was dining with a former minister of Franco during the crisis. The ex-minister gave the distinct impression that if the Falangist student died – although he believed the shot to have been accidentally fired by a fellow Falangist – the regime would be 'in crisis'. This episode is typical. Apart from a foreign press always ready to position the regime on the edge of catastrophe, even those *inside* the regime – especially if recently removed from power – exaggerated its fragility.

closure of the university or faculty concerned. From 1965 student protest was backed by a handful of prestigious professors – Aranguren and Tierno Galván among them. The student movement was exposing the 'contradictions' of the regime. It was a Falangist professor of economics, Velarde Fuertes, who forbade the police to enter his faculty buildings; it was the faculties of political science and economics, conceived as training schools for the administration of the new state and technicians for the new economy, that produced the richest crop of student rebels.

In 1969, after Barcelona students had broken a bust of Franco and after a wave of unrest in all universities in protest against the death of a Madrid student, the government declared a state of siege. That the government (which had other reasons for wishing for a temporary clampdown) should have singled out student agitation as its motive is an indication of the importance of university unrest – or at least of the importance that the government chose to give it.[24] As always the 'revolutionary' activities of students could be safely relied on to rally the conservative bourgeoisie.

Student protest always centred on two issues: in the short term a demand for the democratisation of the student unions; in the long run for the democratisation of Spanish society. Student protests concerned standard student issues like Vietnam or support for workers' strikes. Underlying them was rejection of a university where there was no academic freedom, where teaching was poor and frequently in the hands of professors distinguished only by their loyalty to the regime. University protest was *political*, as Julián Marías observed, for the simple reason that there was no free political life elsewhere, no alternative channel for the discharge of political energy. For this reason the 'university problem' could only be 'solved' by political concessions which, by definition, the regime could never make.

All the regime could do was to alternate repression and timid attempts at reform. Students were sent down, professors who sympathised with them dismissed; police were in permanent occupation of the universities between 1968 and 1973.

Nor could the government gain anything by reform. The attempt to create a 'democratic' student union by the authorities as a substitute for the SEU was a failure (1965). Students preferred to create their own alternative unions. The official syndicate, once the repository of Falangist hopes for a new generation of student patriots, simply faded away.

The more ambitious reform of 1970 likewise failed.[25] If conflicts were less violent in the seventies, they were more widespread and students were joined by staff without tenure (the so-called PNNs), often former student activists and all underpaid. In 1973 every university in Spain was on strike; in 1974 secondary school children demonstrated against entrance exams.

As the whole educational structure of Francoism reeled in crisis, so the student movement was becoming increasingly ideologically radical. Christian Democrats disappeared; Communists lost influence. The militants of the seventies represented the extremist left that had grown up in Europe after May 1968. Maoists, anarchists and Trotskyites were concerned less with political issues than with a cultural revolution, a rejection of all the moral values of contemporary society. For them the university was less an instrument for the transmission of culture than a student-controlled laboratory for social, sexual and educational experiments. In practice the increased participation of students shattered the traditional, almost Germanic, authority of Spanish professors. Not only were examinations boycotted; students even demanded the abolition of the university. Things did not quite come to such a pass, but the legacy of Francoism was a crisis-ridden mass university, without prestige and with no clear idea of its function.[26]

Judging by what happened in France, Germany and Italy and at Essex University there would have been student troubles, with or without Franco. But the response of the regime deepened the crisis. For Franco, the university question was a question of public order and nothing more. Not that the regime was in danger, as ingenuous critics argued in 1965, casting back to the university troubles which had helped to precipitate the fall of the former dictator, Primo de Rivera, in 1930. Franco survived for ten years; but not one of those years passed without an epidemic outbreak of the 'university problem'. Students, in spite of their Byzantine internal squabbles, more than any other social group familiarised Spanish society, starved of true political discourse since 1939, with the language of democracy. In 1965 student strikes and demonstrations were the concern of an exiguous minority, confronting not merely the police, but a society which did not understand, still less sympathise with, the activists. By 1970 the movement was no longer a secret society, the preserve of a self-selected elite recruited by personal contact from upper middle-class families with a Republican background. The student movement had lost its exclusive, clandestine character and entered on a period of 'mass mobilisation', endowing itself with an extensively shared subculture.[27] Apart from the committed activists, a majority of students were vaguely liberal and indifferent to Francoism. More and more Spaniards — including the parents of the students — were asking themselves whether the time had come for some kind of political reform as the only way to restore peace to the campuses of Spain.

(d)
The church – the decline of national Catholicism

A labour movement dominated by Communists was not the only irony in store for the regime in its later years. In the seventies, in Spain, according to the Caudillo himself a country specially chosen by God, in the Spain of the Crusade, of family prayers, of Eucharistic Congresses and religious processions, the government was fining priests for sermons and had sent up a special prison for seditious priests. Dedicated right-wing Francoists were shouting in the streets that the Cardinal Archbishop of Madrid be sent to the firing squad.

The conflict with the church, which after 1965 could not be concealed, was to Franco himself the most irritating and inexplicable of all conflicts. He was himself a sincere Catholic; his regime was based on the supposition that Catholicism was the essence of Spain; Catholicism was the only ideological link between all the victors of the Civil War and the church had blessed and legitimised the rising of 18 July. To lose the support of the church would, therefore, imperil the legitimacy of the regime itself.

The regime had done all it could to deserve that support by making its laws conform to Catholic dogma. It had prohibited civil marriage where one of the parties was a Catholic; there was no divorce, no sale of contraceptives. The church, under Franco, regained the property confiscated by the Republic, just as it saw its hold over secondary education restored and strengthened with the aid of state subsidies.

In 1953 Spain and the Vatican signed a Concordat which seemed, at the time, to benefit both contracting parties. The state was declared a Catholic confessional state and the church and the regular orders enjoyed extensive economic and legal privileges – for instance, a priest would only be tried on criminal charges with the permission of his bishop. In return the Vatican recognised what amounted to control by Franco over the nomination of bishops. The recognition of his government in the Concordat gave Franco's regime the international respectability it lacked.[28]

The alliance created what was called 'national Catholicism'. Even so, there were frictions as there had been under that most Catholic of monarchs, Philip II. Quite early in the fifties Catholic Action criticised the official syndicates and working-class conditions; since Catholic Action was dependent on the bishops, prominent bishops endorsed this criticism.[29] Apart from concern for what the late nineteenth century called the 'social question', the native Basque and Catalan clergy had traditionally sympathised with Basque and Catalan regional demands. This source of tension re-surfaced in May 1960 when 339 Basque priests denounced the lack of liberty for 'some peninsular peoples'; and in 1963, when the Abbot of Montserrat, the monastery that symbolised Catalan culture, denounced the regime in *Le Monde*. Thus in both Catalonia and the Basque provinces it was the local church that became the first vocal expression of the latent nationalist sentiment, repressed by a fiercely centralist regime after a civil war fought to restore the unity of Spain.

All this was far from being an open confrontation between church and state. This could not come about as long as the hierarchy was dominated by the bishops and cardinals of the Crusade. The memory of 7,000 priests martyred by a lay republic and a detestation of atheistical Communism bound the generation of bishops, who had seen in the rising of 18 July the salvation of their church, to a state that had avenged the slaughtered saints, rebuilt churches and professed as its aim the burning of Communism out of the national soul.

These loyal Francoists did not begin to thin out through death and retirement until the late sixties. To criticise the syndical organisation, to deplore poverty was not a criticism of Francoism; it was simply a call to Christian charity. With the exception of the unruly lower clergy in the Basque provinces and Catalonia, the official alliance of church and state, affirmed in every public ceremony where bishops appeared side by side with civil governors and generals, remained a political reality and the basic emotional foundation of the regime.

Given this essential legitimising role, it was not the state that, in the seventies, sought conflicts with the church. It was changes in the church that made the old alliance of throne and altar uncomfortable for the church, changes that came with the pontificate of John XXIII and the Second Vatican Council.

That these external changes found some response in Spain is explicable only if we realise that there had been a spiritual renewal in the Spanish church. A process of self-criticism by a movement of renovation sought to transform the rich and ritual-laden official church, with its concern for the education of the bourgeoisie and its glorification of temporal power, into a missionary church faithful to the Christian message of evangelical poverty and the brotherhood of man. This process of renewal was the work of a minority of active laymen in Acción Católica and a new generation of priests, influenced – as always – by French Catholic thought. The cultural 'opening' of Ruiz Giménez in the early fifties encouraged Catholic intellectuals to break with the dominating integrist philosophy and end the intellectual isolation of Spanish Catholicism. Some priests chose to live as worker priests in the industrial suburbs, their activities supported by the publications of HOAC and JOC which were not subject to state censorship.

The movement of renewal represented a conflict *within* the church rather than a crisis in the relations of church and state. The bishops remained firmly Francoist and unsympathetic to progressive Catholicism just as their predecessors consistently opposed modernism. It was not that they were rich, proud prelates: they lived modestly in flats rather than in palaces and by the 1970s were driving their own small cars.[30] Nor were they all pliant timeservers. The eccentric and unyielding individualism of Segura, Cardinal Archbishop of Seville, enraged Franco who regarded this austere puritan – he banned dances in his diocese – as a madman.[31] But coming mostly from a family background of rural poverty, they exhibited the rigid conservatism of the postwar middle class.

While Spanish progressive Catholics could rally little support from the hierarchy, from 1958 they could count on a more powerful ally: the Vicar of Christ himself. John XXIII's encyclicals *Mater et Magistra* (1961) and *Pacem in Terris* (1963) were disturbing documents to the Spanish bishops and to Franco himself – though with characteristic aplomb the Caudillo claimed that, as long as twenty years before, he had anticipated their spirit. This was false.

The new Pope defended ideological pluralism, and human rights including freedom of religious expression and association, even supporting dialogue with the Communists. In vain the official propaganda presented John XXIII as a jovial, kindly old man; his ideas were a frontal attack on the principles of Francoism. His encyclicals were, as a result, censored. John XXIII, according to Ruiz Giménez, had given 'a new meaning to our life as Christians', a new social conscience, a new relation with the laity symbolised in the new liturgy.[32]

The religious and political consequences of the winds of change blowing from the Vatican were considerable. Christian Democracy, hitherto restricted to the circle surrounding the former Republican ministers, Gil Robles and Giménez Fernández, was strengthened. In 1962 John XXIII asked Ruiz Giménez to spread the new ideas in Spain. In 1963, together with a group of young Christian Democrats, he founded the monthly review *Cuadernos para el Diálogo*. *Cuadernos* started by treating contemporary problems from a Christian Democrat viewpoint; gradually, with the collaboration of Marxists and opposition intellectuals, it became more democratic and less Christian. In this it followed the evolution of its founder who declared himself 'more of a Social Democrat than a Christian Democrat'. For a period it appeared as if Christian Democrats would become the principal force in the democratic opposition. Ruiz Giménez, supported by the Vatican, became the leader of Izquierda Demócratica (the Democratic Left). Although ID never recruited more than a handful of intellectuals and lawyers, it was a common assumption that post-Franco Spain would see a Christian Democrat party playing a role as important as that of the Christian Democrats in postwar Italy.[33]

John XXIII's successor, Paul VI, was no improvement from Franco's point of view. He was a *bête noire* of national Catholicism − as Archbishop of Milan he had protested against the execution of the Communist leader Grimau. The Second Vatican Council endorsed the policies of John; the separation of church and state, endorsed by the Council, must have immediate consequences for the church of 'national Catholicism'. It became clear that the Vatican was determined to change not merely the character of the episcopacy, but the nature of its own relations with the Spanish state even if this implied a revision of the Concordat of 1953.[34]

The stern, unyielding conservatism of the Spanish hierarchy had been revealed in the Council debates. If it was to weaken the hold of these conservatives then the Vatican must wrest from Franco the right to interfere in the nomination of bishops granted by the Concordat. A renovation and rejuvenation of the hierarchy was accomplished with tact by the Nuncios Riberi and Dadaglio; between 1964 and 1974 they nominated fifty-three bishops. The great names of the church of the Crusade were dying off; when Franco died only half of 'his' bishops, the generation of the Civil War, were still active.[35]

The rejuvenation of the episcopate − in a decade (1964−74) its average age dropped by ten years − corresponded to an increasing radicalisation of the younger clergy. Young theologians discovered Marxism; a few priests became active in the Workers' Commissions; in working-class suburbs many defied the police by allowing opposition syndicates to use their churches; they preached in favour of working-class demands, to the astonishment of their congregations. In the Basque provinces parish priests demanded the nomination of Basque bishops and the use of Basque in services; some even went so far as to protect ETA terrorists. In March 1966 police besieged the Barcelona convent where the constituent assembly of the illegal Democratic Union of Students was taking place and a fortnight later a hundred priests demonstrated in the streets in support of students. In 1969 a similar demonstration in support of striking workers took place in Bilbao while in Andalusia bishops were once more protesting against the harsh conditions of the rural poor in the south.

The reaction of the state was sharp and predictable. Five Basque priests were condemned to ten and fifteen years' imprisonment in 1969; in 1970 two more received similar sentences in the Burgos Trials and Father Gamo, a Madrid worker priest, three years. In 1972 Father García Salve was imprisoned as a leader of the Workers' Commissions. Altogether, between 1972 and 1975 priests were fined 11 million pesetas.

These tensions and conflicts would not have seriously affected the relations between church and state if the regime had been able, as in the past, to count on the massive support of the hierarchy. Profoundly divided since the Vatican Council, the conservative and *franquista* bishops were increasingly isolated. As long as Mgr Morcillo was Archbishop of Madrid and as long as he, together with his auxiliary bishop, Mgr Guerra Campos, controlled the Episcopal Conference (the body that represented the collective voice of the Spanish church), the conservatives appeared in control, immune from the pressure of the lay progressives of Acción Católica. But Paul VI gave no support to Morcillo and expressed his 'concern' for Spain, that is, in Vatican language, his disapproval of the Francoist church.

In 1969 Paul VI imposed Mgr Enrique y Tarancón as Cardinal Archbishop of Toledo and Primate of Spain; on Morcillo's death Cardinal Tarancón became Archbishop of Madrid and President of the Episcopal Conference. A liberal Catholic — a friend of Paul VI convinced that the decrees of Vatican II must be applied in Spain and that the church must separate itself from Francoism in decline — was now the visible head of the Spanish church.

Prayers for Franco were still said in every mass; yet his last years saw nothing but conflict. The worst troubles came in the Basque provinces where the new Bishop of Bilbao, Mgr Cirarda, in sharp contrast to his predecessor, energetically defended his clergy against the government. In April 1969, basing his actions on the Concordat, he refused to authorise the trial of a number of his parish priests and fiercely criticised the local government-controlled press which had censured them. In 1970 he not only refused to say a solemn mass to celebrate Franco's capture of Bilbao in the Civil War, but published a letter, read in all Basque churches, demanding clemency for the accused in the Burgos Trials. He condemned both terrorism *and* repression.

Mgr Cirarda earned the hatred of the extreme right and in the pro-Franco demonstrations after the Burgos Trials there were shouts against 'red bishops'. Mgr Guerra Campos, after Morcillo's death the most conspicuous of episcopal *franquistas*, warned in his apocalyptic television talks that Satan had penetrated even the defences of the Spanish church; but his fierce integrism was an echo of a vanished epoch.

The 'Cirarda affair' was a presage of future troubles. In the seventies the public pronouncements of the hierarchy left no doubt about its progressive alienation from the regime. Individual bishops protested against police violence or asserted that Christian principles demanded political freedom. The Bishop of Bilbao, Mgr Añoveros, was put under house arrest for publishing a pastoral defending the use of the Basque language. In 1975 the Suffragan Bishop of Madrid, Mgr Iniesta, had to leave the capital after publishing a homily condemning the September executions.[36]

The collective publications of the hierarchy confirmed the liberal evolution of the church. It was no longer the church of the Crusade but the church of reconciliation; not with the regime but against it. In 1971 the Assembly of Bishops and Priests voted in favour of a resolution asking pardon of the Spanish people for its partisanship in the Civil War. In 1973 the bishops, in *The Church and the Political Community*, demanded the revision of the 1953 Concordat and the independence of church and state. They would renounce their privileges if the state gave up its intervention in their nomination, thus abandoning the last traces of regalism, the old claim of the Catholic kings to be masters of the church in their own state. By 1975 the bishops had gone beyond a claim to be free of state control; in their peculiar pastoral and evangelical jargon they were making an apologia for liberal democracy.

These developments were very distasteful for the regime and its conservative supporters. For the first time in its history Spain witnessed hysterical and aggressive outbursts of right-wing anticlericalism. 'Progressive' priests and their churches were attacked by an extreme right-wing group, the Guerrillas of Christ the King. Cardinal Tarancón was given police protection. The bishops' declarations were attacked in the right-wing press with frequent allusions to Marxist infiltration.

The regime could not solve the problems posed by the developments in the post-conciliar church. Franco and his government professed acceptance of the decisions of Vatican II; but all negotiations for a revision of the Concordat broke down on Franco's refusal to surrender a veto over Vatican appointments. Until his death Franco governed his Catholic state with the opposition of the Catholic church.

Franco did not understand what had happened. He was justified in thinking that he had done more for the church than any other Spanish ruler, as both he and Carrero Blanco repeatedly recalled. In the reaction of the church he could see only ingratitude. He could not admit that it was he who was acting contrary to Catholic teaching. After all, he was responsible to God, not to His church.[37]

(e)

Regional discontents

'Impose on them unity, unity above all' had been the counsel of the traditionalist leader, Pradera, to the military rebels of 18 July. Franco conceived his mission as the destruction of the 'separatism' encouraged by the Second Republic. He immediately revoked the Statutes of Autonomy granted by the Republic to Catalonia and Euzkadi. The use of Catalan and Basque in schools was prohibited and all manifestations of regional culture – other than harmless folklore – suppressed. Spain 'One Great and Free' was the regime's credo. It had never become free or great and by 1969 even Spanish unity was in question. In the two most prosperous regions of the country the 'peace of Franco' of official propaganda was beginning to look like a euphemism.

In 1970 a military tribunal sitting in Burgos handed down nine death penalties and 518 years' imprisonment for terrorism on sixteen young Basque nationalists. The sentences released the customary anti-Spanish outbursts of the European left. In Spain itself, the severity of the sentences, the youth of the accused and their defiant attitudes during the trial, the appeal to Franco for clemency, the pastorals of the Basque bishops, the siege of 300 Catalan intellectuals in the monastery of Montserrat – all covered extensively in the press and on television – moved opinion as no other political event had done since the Civil War.[38]

The commutation of the death sentences by Franco was only a truce. The newspapers in the following years reported repeated acts of terrorism and violence committed by ETA. Bank robberies, attacks on the police and the Civil Guard, kidnappings, succeeded one another in the Basque country. In December 1973 came the most dramatic terrorist outrage: the assassination of the President of the Government, Admiral Carrero Blanco.

By the end of 1976 20 members of ETA and 60 policemen had been killed; there were 150 Basques in prison, their sentences ranging from 24 to 128 years; another 500 were in exile in France.[39]

The ferment in the Basque provinces on Franco's death proved the limitations of his authoritarianism; he could not, as Stalin had done, simply eliminate peripheral nationalisms by forcibly transplanting nations. He could revoke the 1932 Statute of Autonomy but he failed in his attempt to destroy Catalanism.

Catalan culture, rooted in a living modern language, was too dynamic and rich to disappear. Many of the most important cultural movements of post-Civil War Spain started in Catalonia: writers like Espriú, Pla, Villalonga, Oliver; essayists like Fuster, historians like Vicens Vives and his school; artists like Tapies, architects, doctors and economists testified to the vitality of Catalan intellectual life. The publishing houses of Barcelona were among the best in Spain, its university considered itself the equal of Madrid. The fifties saw a Catalan cultural renaissance. In the sixties, with greater official tolerance – in itself a testimony to the strength of Catalanism which gave governments no alternative but to turn a blind eye – there was a flood of books in Catalan. A popular youth movement crystallised around the 'new song' (*nova cançó*) which revitalised folk music. The intellectual and literary production of Catalonia continued to be impressive, though much influenced by foreign (above all French) models.* Excessive experiment, a penchant for abstract forms and the importation of *avant-garde* modes from abroad were some of the more unfortunate consequences of repression and censorship at home. The 'underground' protest culture of Barcelona intellectuals, according to Terenci Moix, was neither Catalan nor popular. A hybrid of 'Milan and California', it flung up a succession of new names whose 'popularity' was exhibited by the conspicuous wearing of fisherman's *alpargatas* (sandals).[40]

Catalan culture, however much it prided itself on this openness to 'advanced' currents in European art, maintained the national identity of the Catalans. Cultural nationalism became a surrogate for political nationalism when political nationalism was perforce a clandestine affair. It was the bourgeois intelligentsia that was later to furnish political Catalanism with an intelligent and flexible leadership.

The evolution of Basque nationalism was very different. Whereas native Catalans (though not the new immigrants) used Catalan in the family and in their business affairs, only a few Basques could speak their difficult tongue, unrelated to any

---

*The best-known writers were the Goytisolo brothers (in exile), Carlos Barral, Castellet, Ferraté, Marsé, Vázquez Montalbán, Moix and Gimferrer. Barral's *Años de penitencia* is a fine poetic portrait of the life of an adolescent in the 1940s; Marsé's *Ultimas tardes con Teresa* is the story of the doomed liaison of a 'progressive' bourgeois girl student with a poor immigrant. Other writers (e.g. Juan Goytisolo and Juan Benet) are less useful to the social historian since they are too experimental and consciously *avant-garde*.

European language and, unlike Catalan, a refractory instrument for the transmission of modern culture. Though some of the most remarkable modern creative writers and artists have been Basques, there was no true Basque intellectual bourgeoisie. The clergy were the intelligentsia of Basque nationalism, both in the thirties (Franco had executed fourteen Basque nationalist priests in the Civil War) and, as we have seen, again in the sixties.

Without a modern language, with its native intellectuals bound culturally to Castile, Basque nationalism has always seen itself as threatened. After the Civil War industrialisation accelerated immigration until it had reached a demographic saturation point. Between 1950 and 1970 the population had increased by 62 per cent, largely through the immigration of non-Basques. In a chaotic process of urbanisation, the ugliness of an industrial landscape and polluted rivers and towns (Bilbao has one of the highest levels of industrial pollution in Europe) have invaded the Basque country. The *caserio* or family farm, the cradle of Basque culture and language, is in rapid decline as farmers and their sons seek an easier life and higher incomes in industry.[41] By 1970 only 600,000 of the 2,300,000 inhabitants could speak Basque; whereas it is impossible to move a step in Barcelona without hearing Catalan spoken, no one walking in the streets of the Bilbao of the sixties would have suspected that the native language was other than Spanish.

After 1939 Basque nationalism was in crisis. The Basque government in exile was as ineffective as all other skeleton republican institutions. There was no cultural renaissance as in Catalonia; on the contrary, there was a general weakening of the idea of a Basque cultural identity. Basque culture was reduced to the work of a few oral poets, of a handful of enthusiastic philologists and ethnographers – often priests – finding its most vigorous expression in rural sports. In the forties and fifties it is no exaggeration to say that the game of pelota and the 'harmless' folk activities encouraged by the regime, were the most visible of Basque culture.

It is against the background of this patent crisis in Basque nationalist sentiments and the moderation and passivity of the illegal 'historic' party of Basque nationalism (the PNV) that we must see the rise of ETA. Founded in 1959, ETA (*Euzkadi ta Azkatasuna* – the Basque country and liberty) defined itself as a patriotic, democratic and non-confessional party; but under the influence of the wars of liberation in Cuba, Algeria and Vietnam, it moved ideologically towards the Marxist revolutionary left. In 1962 it would call itself 'a revolutionary movement of national liberation', with the revolutionary war as its means. In 1966, after endless ideological polemics and the expulsion or secession of dissident groups, it defined itself as the 'Basque Socialist movement of national liberation'. ETA combined Socialism and nationalism by its interpretations of nineteenth-century history. The oppression of the Basques began with the rise of capitalism; *ergo* 'the solution of the national problem necessarily involves the destruction of bourgeois power'. Class struggle and national problem, then, form a unit. All but the 'military' wing of ETA were obsessed by the fear that terrorism would be interpreted as showing contempt for the class struggle and over-confidence in the individual act.[42]

ETA would continue to suffer from chronic internal divisions. Like previous dissensions these were based on rivalry between pure nationalists and Marxists, between protagonists of the armed struggle and those who wished to combine 'military' activities with the political action of the Basque working class.[43]

The emergence of a movement like ETA in a region with the cultural characteristics of the Basque country is surprising. The Basques were tenacious fighters; but this conservative, religious, prudent and pragmatic people had shown no sympathy for terrorism, least of all terrorism of the Marxist left. Initially ETA violence was rejected as incompatible with the traditional conceptions of Basque life and culture: the Basques had not experienced a workers' revolution – as had Catalonia during the Civil War – or guerrilla action after it, as had Asturias. Nevertheless ETA survived an extraordinary and fierce police repression. And this continuous action fulfilled at least one of its aims: the mobilisation and reactivation of Basque nationalist sentiment.

There is no simple explanation for the appearance of ETA and the astonishing revival of Basque nationalist sentiment. It was not a case of a nationalist reaction in a depressed and deprived region; the Basque provinces, like Catalonia, were prosperous, industrialised and with the highest per capita income in the country. Nor could Basques argue, as could the Catalans with a certain justification, that they were economically plundered by a central government in which they were under-represented and by a financial and banking system centred in Madrid and indifferent to local interests. Basque banks and industry flourished under Francoism; Franco nominated more Basque ministers than any previous regime. A Basque composed the Falangist anthem *Cara al Sol*; a Basque built the Valle de los Caídos; for thirty years the Cortes was presided over by Basques who were strongly represented in the Ministry of Foreign Affairs. Police repression was no more brutal in the Basque country than in Asturias or Madrid. ETA was not a product of repression; rather, repression came as a result of the activities of ETA.

ETA was the creation of a small group of resolute revolutionary terrorists. The governments of Franco reacted to its activities by an indiscriminate campaign of repression which ended by completely alienating Basque opinion, including that originally hostile or indifferent to ETA. Unable to distinguish a political problem from one of public order, the regime pursued the one policy that most benefited ETA; it could not even make a relatively harmless gesture of goodwill such as the concession of some form of economic autonomy proposed by Basques loyal to Franco. The regime was victim of its own strict conception of public order. States of emergency were declared in the Basque provinces on numerous occasions after 1968, during which the police forces acted like an army of occupation, with the impunity and independence that such forces enjoy in regimes that are not responsible to public opinion.

Favoured by mountainous terrain, by the proximity of the French frontier, by a language which made police infiltration difficult, and by the sympathy of the Basque clergy and youth, ETA accomplished most of its purposes. The spiral of action-repression-action earned a terrorist movement widespread local sympathy. It was indiscriminate repression that solved what ETA saw as the main problem of a terrorist movement – the creation of mass support, the water for the fish to swim in. From 1970 the Basque problem was the main problem confronting Francoism and its worst legacy to the democratic monarchy that succeeded it.

ETA left the democratic opposition with no option. Even those who believed that ETA terrorism merely meant more generalised repression, through the strengthening of the position of the hardliners of the bunker, were forced at least not to condemn it in public. ETA was, after all, the most tenacious and active of the groups opposing Franco. With that masterpiece of magnicide, the assassination of Carrero Blanco, the chief prop of *continuismo*, ETA resolved, single-handed, the main problem of the opposition: the problem of 'Francoism after Franco'. As the ideologue of the regime, Fernández de la Mora, confessed, it was a terrible blow 'against the continuity of the state of 18 July'.[44]

The steady deterioration of the situation in the Basque provinces proved that the unitary philosophy of the regime, its doctrinaire centralism, provided no permanent solution for the old problem of Spanish regionalism.

Repression was a short-term solution in the early years but counter-productive in the long run. As Prat de la Riba, the prophet of Catalan nationalism, had predicted of a previous dictatorship, out of the winter of repression comes the spring of national revival. The relative absence of violent activity in Catalonia was deceptive.

Beneath apparent tranquillity nationalist sentiments became more firmly founded in a culture and a language. Indeed it may be that it was this cultural self-confidence that made terrorism superfluous, a terrorism that perhaps suited the more racist nationalism of the Basques and their emphasis on physical prowess and exuberant youth. In contrast to the divisions produced by the appearance of ETA in the Basque provinces, the democratic opposition achieved in Catalonia a degree of unity and co-operation without parallel in Spain. In November 1971 the government could not prevent the meeting of the Catalan Assembly. Three hundred representatives of all the clandestine political groups in Catalonia agreed on a basic programme which included the re-establishment of the autonomous government of the Statute of 1932.[45]

(f)
The politics of opposition

We must now turn to the more complex problem of the political opposition as such. To understand its evolution we must go back to the defeat of the democratic Republic in 1939.[46]

After the defeat of the Republic, the leaders of the 'historic' opposition, composed of the remnants of those parties that had supported the Republic in the war − Socialists, Republicans, Anarchists, Basque and Catalan nationalists − were, for the most part, perforce in exile, cut off from the clandestine struggle within Spain. Only the Communists successfully survived the difficulties created by exile combined with repression at home.

It was the Communists who first grasped the importance of action within Spain itself in the fight against Franco. Even if they committed serious errors in political tactics, their cadres, largely built up in prison where the party ran courses for new recruits, formed the only continuous and significant clandestine organisation. The party supported guerrilla action between 1944 and 1948; but though subsequently romanticised, the armed struggle, for all its heroism, failed. The guerrilla 'war' took the form of minor acts of sabotage and a continual struggle to elude the Civil Guard. Due to strict press censorship no echoes of guerrilla activity reached the average Spaniard outside a few rural districts where, by 1950, guerrilla activities had been incorporated into the tradition of *bandolerismo* (banditry) and were now frowned on as imperilling innocent people.[47] Yet, even if a failure, guerrilla activity represented the conviction of the Communist party that the *internal* struggle was a necessity. The rest of the historic opposition put its faith in salvation from abroad, hoping above all that the victorious

Spain: Dictatorship to Democracy

allies would somehow instal the exiles as a democratic government in Spain, since Franco would not be allowed to survive the defeat of the Fascist powers whom he had aided in the war.

All attempts to set up a republican government for the allies to restore revealed the chronic divisions of the exiles, particularly over the question of Communist participation in any future government. Don Juan and his Liberal Monarchists came out against Franco in 1945 in the hope that they would be a more acceptable democratic alternative than the Republican parties. But hopes of effective action by the allies faded. The symbolic gesture of diplomatic boycott was counter-productive. It merely allowed Franco to sound his favourite appeal for 'Numantian' resistance to intervention by degenerate democracies.

Once the hope placed in allied intervention proved an illusion the opposition – both the Republicans and the Liberal Monarchists – had no answer to the problem of how to overthrow Franco. The Socialists in 1947 attempted an agreement for joint action with the Liberal Monarchists of Don Juan; it collapsed in ruins once Don Juan began to feel his way towards some understanding with Franco. With the signing of the agreement of 1953 with the USA the opposition's international prospects were at their lowest ebb. 'Now,' Franco is reported to have said, 'I have won the Civil War.' The greatest democratic power had accepted Franco at his own valuation as the 'Sentinel of the West', ruling a country that was the spiritual reservoir of anti-Communism in Europe.

By 1953 the historic opposition had ceased to exist as an effective political reality in Spain itself. Discontented monarchist generals ceased to trouble Franco with their conspiracies. That they did so is important. They had plotted, partly because they saw Franco as a vulgar opportunist, partly because he did not seem, with hopes of allied intervention, securely *in situ* as a safeguard for conservative values. Now he was secure and Gil Robles despaired as he saw 'the cowards and the egoists' rallying behind the dictator.[48] Of the Republican opposition there remained only a few Socialist enclaves in the Basque provinces and the mining districts of Asturias, sporadic terrorist action by the CNT, a latent nationalist sentiment in Catalonia and the Basque provinces, and the collective memory of those Spaniards who kept their loyalties secret for forty years to reveal them on Franco's death.

For the older exiles a restored republic remained the only possible regime for a post-Franco world and an indispensable emotional anchor; but for their sons and their relations in Spain the Republic had become, by the 1960s, a moving historical memory that prevented an effective alliance with the non-Republican opposition in Spain itself. The exiles wrote more and more for themselves. Paris and Mexico City were no longer, by 1960, the intellectual and political capitals of the 'other Spain'. The exiles lost any real hope of return and settled down somewhat uneasily in nationalistic Mexico with its deep-rooted suspicion of Spain, more comfortably in Argentina where there was a strong tradition of immigrant absorption. They watched their leaders die off as Franco lived on. 'Emigration,' wrote one of them, 'is showing our bald heads and burying each other's dead.'[49]

At the end of the fifties it was clear that the Communist party, after abandoning the armed struggle, had emerged as the most important focus of opposition in the interior and that the historic opposition was being replaced in Spain by a new opposition born without an umbilical cord attaching it to the exiles' world of shadow governments, and with little or no connection with the Republican tradition. This new opposition formed round a few notables: Christian Democrats around Giménez Fernández and Gil Robles, both ministers under the Republic; Social Democrats around Ridruejo, who by 1956 had abandoned all hope in the regime and the new state ('The victors of yesterday,' he wrote, 'we feel the vanquished of today'); the Liberal Monarchists around Satrústegui. These groups had no influence outside a few intellectuals, lawyers and university students and professors. In spite of signs of radicalisation in the university, the regime, struggling though it was with severe economic problems, had little to fear from the opposition. The Communists, under the leadership of Santiago Carrillo, had abandoned the idea that the regime could be overthrown by the direct action of the guerrillas; yet in spite of this implicit recognition of the strength of Franco's state Carrillo believed that the regime was in crisis and its end imminent. The party's attempt to act on this assumption and to topple it by a 'pacific national strike' in June 1959 was a complete fiasco. As Carrillo's opponents, Claudín and Semprún, argued, the march to power would be a long one: the regime no longer represented a reactionary clique dominating a poor, fragile economy; in its new neo-capitalist form Spanish 'Fascism' could present an altogether tougher resistance. Carrillo's 'subjectivist' optimism hid the 'objective' social and economic changes in the booming Spain of the sixties. His 'triumphalism' about the party and its prospects were based on an illusion. Claudín and Semprún were expelled as heretics in 1964. Yet it was on their 'revisionist' heresies that Carrillo, in the end, was forced to base his policies.[50]

Nevertheless, in spite of quarrels between the leadership abroad under Carrillo and the militants in Spain, the party was the most visible and resolute opponent of the regime: resolute because of the dedication of its cadres; visible because its image as *the* opposition to the regime was created by the regime itself.[51] The Communist peril was largely an invention of Franco. While constant harping on the perils of Communism strengthened the attraction of the party to those whose alienation from the regime was irreversible, at the same time it paid dividends by increasing the attraction of Franco's Spain as an ally of the anti-Soviet West. The importance of the Communist party was enhanced by the incapacity of the Socialists of the PSOE to handle the problems of clandestinity. After repeated arrests of its executive committee the party transferred its organisation to France in 1945. The exile leadership increasingly lost touch with the interior and was accused of 'squandering the gains' made by the heroic sacrifices of the early 1940s.[52]

Yet, as we have seen, by the late sixties the troubles in the Basque country were the most serious evidence of a more general level of conflict. The decisive factor was the emergence of a new generation. Its presence is the constant factor in all the manifestations of protest. This new generation, brought up under authoritarianism and oppression, had no direct experience of the Civil War, no fears of the renewed collapse into anarchy prophesied by the regime as the certain consequence of democratic parliamentarianism. It accepted no other legitimacy but that founded on freedom.

The growth of conflict was not capitalised by a coherent political opposition. Except in Catalonia the democratic opposition was deeply divided until 1976 and, with the exception of the Communist party (PCE), it was weak, badly organised and without any widespread support in opinion.

In the sixties political groups that were to transform themselves into political parties in post-Franco Spain became more clearly defined. The Socialist party (the old PSOE) continued to be an exile organisation rather than a Spanish party. It was to create an independent domestic party that Professor Tierno Galván founded his Socialist Party of the Interior in 1968: but this divided the party rather than solving the underlying problem of the relations of the 'exterior' leadership to the 'interior' struggle. It was not until the 1970s that the 'interior' took over the leadership of the party and set it off on a process of spectacular growth, leaving the 'historic' PSOE of the exiles in the impotence of isolation.[53]

Rather than the growth of a coherent opposition the mid-sixties saw a mushroom growth of 'groupuscules' in the new Marxist left. Of Trotskyite or Maoist inspiration, often bitterly critical of the orthodox Communists as traitors to Marxist-Leninism and allies of an imperialist bourgeoisie, they fell into Byzantine sectarian quarrels which weakened their initial influence in university and working-class circles. The Carlists of the Young Pretender, Carlos Hugo, inheriting the bitter disillusionment of party militants with Francoism, professed to be Socialists. In Catalonia the historic parties of the Republic had all but disappeared, replaced by new groups formed around new personalities and diverse ideologies from Socialism to Christian Democracy. The Catalan branch of the Communist party, the PSUC, had emerged as the only approximation to a mass party, thanks to its role in the CC OO and its considerable influence among university students and progressive intellectuals in general.

The moderate, democratic opposition, unlike the Communists, had no organised cadres, no mass base. It was composed of groups of like-minded notables who engaged in a continuous intellectual and moral confrontation with the regime. Hampered by repression it could find no solution to the growing strength of the Communist party. Without Communist support the moderates would lack real force; with it, they would lack credibility with the Western democracies and would run the risk of compromising the future Spanish democracy – memories of the Communist tactics of infiltration and absorption in the Civil War died hard, particularly among Socialists.

Thus the united opposition, actively pursued by the Communists, once they had abandoned guerrilla activity in 1949, never came about while Franco lived. Deprived of effective political action, the non-Communist opposition was limited to those *actes de présence* possible within the regime's constantly shifting margins of tolerance. Their most notable appearance was the Munich meeting of June 1962 when 118 political figures of the moderate, non-Communist opposition, both internal and in exile, opposed as inadmissible, coming from a non-democratic government, the official Spanish request for accession to the EEC. The meeting was a success and the regime reacted accordingly. But as we have seen, it was distorted in the official press as a Communist plot 'against Spain' and the Spanish participants, after being slandered as traitors and 'rats', were severely sanctioned.

After Munich the activities of the moderate opposition were confined to the preparation of manifestos and the legal defence of political prisoners.[54] It had no direct connection with the proliferation of conflicts in the final phase of Francoism. Reduced to impotence by the regime, far from directing events it was directed by them. After the designation of Don Juan's son, Juan Carlos, as future king and successor to Franco in July 1969, the moderate opposition lacked any convincing reply to the question posed by the

Secretary of the Communist party in 1964: 'After Franco, What?'

Carrillo had posed the question because he was convinced that the strike wave of 1962 presaged the immediate collapse of a regime based on and serving the interests of a narrow oligarchy. This oligarchy could be forced from power by a broadly based democratic coalition − a revival of the Popular Front of the 1930s. The resolute Stalinist now began to appear as a democrat. The PCE committed itself to follow 'the peaceful road to Socialism'. Repudiating the dictatorship of the proletariat, it offered to collaborate with the liberal 'national' bourgeoisie in order to establish a democratic regime. Though time proved false the assumption on which his policy was based, Carrillo supported the collaborationist line consistently throughout the sixties and seventies, though he now based it on an interpretation of recent history which he had denounced as heresy in 1964 and for which he had expelled the heretics from the party. In this reinterpretation the regime was no longer a brutal dictatorship, its syndicates could and should be infiltrated; prosperity was changing Spanish society. The PCE could not prosper as a revolutionary vanguard; it must become a respectable party ready to take its place in a pluralist democracy.[55] He condemned the invasion of Czechoslovakia, drew apart from Moscow and began to flatter the church and the army. The church was no longer the opium of the people but the 'yeast of progress'; the army was courted with the offer of decent pay and living conditions, the navy with the promise of submarines.

But the ideologue of Eurocommunism, though he drew upon himself bitter attacks from the pro-Soviet faithfuls under the Civil War veteran Lister and was repudiated by the extreme left as a revisionist traitor and imperialist lackey, could not win over the moderates for a united opposition. The visceral anti-Communism of the regime combined with memories of the tactical unscrupulousness of the party to create suspicions. The moderates feared that the party's superior organisation and the influence it had won in the CC OO, combined with its financial resources, would allow it to control any united opposition.

The democratic opposition, therefore, continued weak and fragmented, unable to offer a clear democratic alternative to decaying Francoism. Critics even maintained that a 'tolerated opposition', exploiting the varying margins of permissiveness of the regime in its later years, strengthened the regime by giving it a deceptively liberal appearance. At no time did it appear that the regime could be overthrown. Its repressive powers remained intact. It denied absolutely any means by which the opposition groups could organise as effective political parties.

What, then, was the function of the democratic opposition? There is some truth in Carrillo's apologia for his own 'subjective' optimism.[56] No opposition can survive if it constantly predicts in public the longevity of the regime it seeks to overthrow. This was even more the dilemma of the democratic opposition. Even if that opposition consistently underestimated the political nerve of Franco and overestimated its own influence, it accomplished an important task. In periodicals like *Cuadernos para el Diálogo* it educated Spanish opinion in democratic ideas; it kept up a continuous process of criticism of the regime, undermining its moral credibility and denying its legitimacy. The massive rejection of Francoism in the election of 1977 reflects the importance of this contribution.

Although Franco and his regime could continue to live with and contain the growing conflicts produced by economic development and the rise of a new generation, these conflicts tested the institutions of that regime to the limits and found them wanting. Whatever limitations the law of 1966 placed on the freedom of the press, newspapers now increasingly exposed the conflicts of Spanish society. Their language changed: bombs were called bombs; strikes, strikes. The alienation of the progressive Catholics was evident when the weekly of Acción Católica's youth movement rejected the notion of the Civil War as a Crusade and condemned 'white' as well as 'red' assassinations.[57] The dissatisfaction of the conservative monarchists was made public when, after printing a contemptuous parallel between Franco and Haile Selassie in April, in June the monarchist daily *ABC* praised Republicans and Socialists for supporting a constitutional monarchy.[58] Clumsy sequestrations – police, arriving late, had to snatch copies of *ABC* from passers-by in the street – could not put the lid back on Pandora's box. 'We have discovered suddenly, thanks to the Press Law, that Spanish society is a society of conflicts,' wrote a journalist in the Madrid evening paper *Informaciones*; and this a bare two months after the publication of the law.[59]

It was not only conflicts in society as a whole that were being revealed by the press. For the first time the press revealed *in extenso* the internal struggles that were eroding the cohesion of the families of the regime. Falangist journalists attacked monarchists; the Movement's press waged a bitter campaign against the Catholic technocrats of the Opus Dei. The Catholic *El Alcázar* replied in kind by an onslaught on the official syndicates.

It is these family feuds that we must now examine.

Chapter 8

Family Disputes

(a)
The early struggles

That there should be political disagreement within the regime was only natural. Regardless of the political unification imposed 'from above' in 1937 the 'families' of the regime, even if, with the exception of the Carlists, they did not have an autonomous political life, retained or acquired distinct ways of thought.[1] Despite the ideological and emotional affinities between Francoist families, there was always a certain degree of political pluralism *within* Francoism.

As a result, up to 1969 and even afterwards, all Franco's governments were coalition governments where the different families were represented. Their particular influence was always dependent on the immediate political interests of Franco. Up to 1945, he leaned mainly on the Falangists and soldiers. Later, after the defeat of the Axis, he gave key ministerial jobs to a number of prominent Catholics whose presence might help to improve the image of the regime in a world opinion now dominated by the victorious allies. After 1957, when it was evident that only industrialisation and economic growth could legitimise his regime, Franco would lean more and more on the technocrats of the Opus Dei and would relegate the Falangist 'old guard', the Falange of 18 July, to an obscure and secondary political role.

The feuds of the political families, disguised by the euphemisms of official rhetoric and behind appeals to the unitary spirit of 18 July and to loyalty to Franco, were concealed from public opinion by strict press censorship until the new and less restrictive Press Law of 1966. Until then, while the political elite was fed on rumour, the general public had only a vague knowledge of the political struggles within the regime except in the event of some resounding crisis: for instance, the fall in 1942 of Franco's brother-in-law, Serrano Suñer, Minister of Foreign Affairs and the architect of the new state; or the crisis of 1956. In both instances, it was not possible to prevent internal tensions from coming into the open. It might have been thought − and indeed has been since argued − that the fall of Serrano was due to changes in foreign policy, the need to move away from too intimate an alliance with the Axis of which Serrano was cast as the main supporter. But its connection with the domestic tensions within the regime could not be concealed: the conservative monarchists were bitter opponents of Serrano's political plans for a totalitarian state based on the Falange, and only a few days before his fall a Falangist had tossed a bomb at the monarchist general Varela.[2] In 1956 the storming of Madrid University by Falangist hard-line students revealed the mistrust of part of the Francoist political class towards the cultural tolerance of the Minister of Education, Ruiz Giménez.[3] There were speculations and rumours about serious disagreements between 'liberal' Catholics − such as Ruiz Giménez − and Falangists such as the Minister Secretary of the Movement, Fernández Cuesta. Both offending ministers were dismissed. This procedure, repeated in 1969, of summarily sacking both contenders in a family dispute, was called 'Franco's judgements of Solomon'.

Control of both press and radio could not hide these ministerial crises within an authoritarian regime. Throughout its history they were the public manifestation of tensions over the nature of 'Francoism after Franco'. Franco himself made clear his determination to remain Chief of State to the end of his days. 'You can be sure,' he said in 1958, 'that as long as the Lord gives us life, we shall continue to use it in the service of God and for the grandeur of the Fatherland.'[4] Unique historical phenomenon as he was to committed Francoists, he was not immortal. The families of the regime, like the members of a natural family, manoeuvred to get the lion's share of the inheritance.

It was the claim of the monarchists which gave Franco most trouble in the early years. Though he declared Spain a monarchy in 1947 he refused to install a monarch. The head of the royal house, Don Juan de Borbon, was an exile in Portugal. Franco did not dismiss the possibility of a regency and, in any case, proclaimed his right to nominate his successor as Head of State, thus violating the central principle of the hereditary monarch. Moreover, Franco had, on several occasions since 1937, spoken of the 'instauration' rather than of the 'restoration' of the monarchy. This seemed an indication that Franco did not have Don Juan in mind as the future monarch but a new prince, or at least a monarchy altogether different from the liberal monarchy which had ruled Spain between 1876 and 1923 and which Don Juan represented. He detested Don Juan's flirtations with the democratic opposition and professed to believe that his court would be dominated by an ignorant aristocratic clique unfit to be the dominant political class of a modern state. He likewise rejected the Carlist alternative – the Pretender, he repeatedly asserted, was the foreign-born representative of an outworn, if heroic, creed. Unable to find a suitable heir, given Don Juan's liberalism and refusal to abandon his claim in favour of his son Juan Carlos, and unwilling in any case to relinquish his power as head of state, Franco did nothing.

The discontent of the thwarted monarchists came into the open in the forties. In 1943, a number of members of parliament and eight out of the thirteen lieutenant-generals of the army petitioned Franco for the restoration of the monarchy. Don Juan himself published manifestos in 1945 and 1947 urging Franco to relinquish power and give way to a constitutional monarchy. With the Pretender's knowledge, some amateur plots to overthrow Franco were organised over this period. Because of their drawing-room conspiracies or because of their conspicuous monarchism, a number of monarchist politicians were either fined or confined to remote villages. The result was a personal estrangement between Franco and Don Juan and the emergence among his supporters of a liberal, overtly anti-Francoist wing. In 1954, four monarchist candidates contested the local elections in Madrid only to be severely defeated, partly as a result of official pressures.

Three years later, a small group of liberal monarchists led by Joaquín Satrústegui formed an illegal political party, Unión Española, which was prepared to co-operate with the clandestine anti-Francoist opposition, sometimes without Don Juan's approval. This small band of liberal monarchists was one of the *bêtes noires* of Francoism, and particularly of pro-Franco monarchists who believed not only that the only practical hope of a monarchist restoration lay in collaboration with Franco, but who, as resolute conservatives, believed that the future monarchy must not reject the principles of the regime whose founder had saved them from destruction by victory in the Civil War.[5]

In the opposite monarchical camp the discontent of a majority of Carlists with the evolution of the regime and with the exclusion of the Carlist Pretender from the line of succession became more and more evident as time passed. Don Javier, the Carlist Pretender, returned from exile in 1952 to proclaim his rights before the faithful. The expulsion of the Pretender became something of a political ritual until 1968, when the whole family of Don Javier was expelled from Spain. By then, the Carlist movement under the leadership of Don Javier's son, Carlos Hugo, had evolved into a fiercely anti-

Francoist, self-styled Socialist movement, utterly incomprehensible to those who identified Carlism with an ultra-Catholic movement.[6]

If the monarchists were disappointed in their hopes, the mere possibility of a monarchist restoration was anathema to Falangists; the tug-of-war between monarchists and Falangists over the nature of the Francoist state was to be one of the enduring family feuds of the regime. Though the Succession Law of 1947 had proclaimed Spain to be a kingdom, it was well known that Falangists preferred a regency as the formula for solving the succession problem. They made their attitude public by minor acts of insubordination and were snubbed in public by Franco for their outbursts of enthusiasm.[7]

If up to 1953 Catholics and Falangists seemed the most powerful families in the regime, around 1953 there seemed to emerge as an alternative to both what its intellectual progenitor, Rafael Calvo Serer, called a 'third force'. This 'third force' was to include the right-wing intellectuals of the Opus Dei (Calvo was one himself), the 'collaborationist' monarchists who still recognised the claim of Don Juan, and the pro-Franco Carlists. The avowed aim of the 'third force' was the restoration of a traditional, social, popular monarchy, that is, the restoration of Don Juan, whose historic rights the 'third force' acknowledged, but as the king of a monarchy whose content would be the ideals of the National Movement of 18 July 1936. The Falange scented in these schemes a new monarchist revival. It reacted by staging a gigantic mass rally in Madrid on 28 October 1953 where, in the presence of Franco, the Falangist leader Fernández Cuesta openly rejected the aspirations of the 'third force'.[8]

During the 1950s attacks on the monarchy were frequent in the Falangist press. In the next decade, the preferences of the Falange fluctuated between a regency and a one-party presidentialist regime on the lines of the Mexican PRI. Catholics seemed, by and large, indifferent to the form of the state. Martín Artajo and Castiella were monarchists but Cardinal Herrera Oria, always an influential voice for the ACNP, talked privately in favour of a regency under some prestigious general.[9]

Franco, therefore, had to reconcile radically opposed positions if he was to find a formula for the succession which would be acceptable to all the families of the regime. He played with the contradictory possibilities available as a means of maintaining the internal equilibrium of the regime. He had undoubtedly chosen as his heir Prince Juan Carlos, the son of Don Juan, whom he began to incorporate into official life in the 1960s. But he deliberately delayed his final and public decision until 1969, partly because he feared that an early solution might lose him the support of the non-'Juan-Carlist' monarchist groups, partly because uncertainty reinforced his position as the only unifying factor in the political system he had created.

The pretensions of the Falangists were displayed in their rivalry with the monarchists. Given the position of the Movement as the sole legal political force, all the political families realised that their political future would be dependent on the internal structure of the Movement and on the role assigned to it in the constitution. It was by making the Movement into an affair run by Falangists that the Falange saw the prospect of political survival.

In the immediate postwar years, Serrano Suñer had attempted to make the Movement the single party in a totalitarian state, A *Rechstaat* – he saw no contradiction in the combination – which might put some limits on the Caudillo's personal power.[10]

This was the first serious attempt to endow the regime with a constitution and to institutionalise a Falangist Movement as the dominant family in the successor state; the attempt, as we have seen, was sabotaged by the conservative monarchists. There were many other constitutional drafts but none of them would be as well known as the projects of Arrese in 1956. Arrese, a prominent leader of the Falange, was little concerned with preserving any of the social radicalism of the heroic period; he was an 'organisation man' who had 'domesticated' the Movement within Francoism. As early as 1945 he had pointed out the need to give a firmer legal structure to the Movement, to transform it into an institution with constitutional powers.

The main problem was the relationship between the concept of the Movement as embracing all loyal Francoists and the Falange as a distinct organisation. Since the end of the Civil War, men of Falangist origins, the so-called 'blue' sector of the Movement, kept control of the huge bureaucracy of the Movement: syndicates, social security services, the provincial administrations, the National Council. The ideas of Arrese were therefore seen as an attempt to give constitutional powers to the Falange as the main force within the Movement. They were opposed by the non-Falangist sectors of the regime. Franco himself simply ignored Arrese's plans for eleven years (1945–56), refusing even to convene the highest organ of the Movement, its National Council.[11]

In March 1956, only one month after his appointment as minister, Arrese revived his old projects. He saw the institutionalisation of the Movement as *the* essential step for the continuity of the regime. His revived plans included three new fundamental laws:

a Law of Fundamental Principles of the Movement which would define the doctrines of the Spanish state; an Organic Law of the Movement to give it powers within the state; and a law which would reorganise the supreme powers of the state with the separation of powers between the head of state and the president of the government.[12]

Arrese's new plans ran up against the old conservative opposition that had defeated Serrano Suñer. First, they did not even mention the monarchy because Arrese, as a Falangist, had not discarded the idea of a regency. Secondly, his projects still retained a totalitarian flavour in their language and style, and despite the cautious manner in which he introduced the text, they still appeared as a manoeuvre to perpetuate the power of the Falange-Movement after Franco's death.

Franco, however, had already decided in favour of a different political formula: a monarchy based on the Principles of the Movement, but a Movement which was not the Falange but the union of all the forces which had supported the rising of 18 July 1936. In 1957 Franco reshaped his government, making substantial changes which marked the decline of the historic Falange and the rise of the Carrero-López Rodó-Opus Dei group. Carrero, whose antipathy to the Falange enthusiasts was notorious, entertained no doubts on the future of the regime: 'Spain,' he said in the summer of 1957, 'is already a monarchy'; a monarchy which he anticipated would be traditional and Catholic with a monarch fully identified with the preservation of the essence of Francoism.[13] Carrero had obviously opted for Prince Juan Carlos. Arrese was transferred to a politically irrelevant post as Minister for Housing.

Franco tried to solve and define the position of the Movement within the state with the Law of Principles of the Movement of 1958. The law was a synthesis of Franco's ideas about the state he wished to bequeath to Spain: the monarchy of the National Movement. Principle VIII defined Spain as a 'traditional, Catholic, social and representative monarchy'. The Movement was defined as 'the *communion* of Spaniards in the ideals which gave life to the Crusade', and not as the closed 'movement *organisation*' which *FET y de las JONS* had been. The law signalled the triumph of the monarchical principle. The twenty-six original points of the historic Falange were dissolved into twelve vague Principles.

This vagueness, however, would in itself allow different interpretations of the Movement and of its role within the state. These discrepancies, together with the continued uncertainty as to the successor of Franco, were to determine the political dynamics of the regime in the 1960s. They led to what was to become a permanent

crisis of identity in Francoism, a crisis that became public property
with the Press Law of 1966.

(b)
'Political development' in the sixties

Arrese's place as Minister of the Movement was taken by José
Solís, an ebullient and passionate politician whose whole career had
been identified with the syndicates. On 17 March 1957 Solís
solemnly proclaimed that Spain was about to enter a new political
era which would be characterised by what he termed 'the full incorporation of the people in the activities of the Movement'. Arrese
had talked of 'winning the streets' and of 'institutionalising the
Movement'. With Solís the emphasis was different. The Movement, a term which during Solís' years as minister would replace
'Falange', could only be institutionalised in so far as it ceased to be
a Falangist bureaucracy and became an open, dynamic institution.
The Movement could fulfil the role assigned to it in the Law of
Principles of 1958 only if it provided a home for the 'plurality of
opinions' of the different families of the regime; it would only survive if it proved itself capable of attracting the new generations and
of providing a channel and a safety valve for the social discontents
revealed in the 1956–7 crisis.[14]

This was the beginning of what, in 1964, Solís himself called
'political development'; that is, a gradual evolution towards greater
participation which was increasingly seen as the necessary political
complement to the programme of economic development which the
regime launched after 1957. The semantic changes with respect to
the postwar years were remarkable. There was no longer any
question of building a national syndicalist state. Now the problem,
the plan, was to transform Spain into a modern state according to
the principles of 'organic democracy'. The regime's 'channels of
representation' (*cauces*) – syndicate, family, municipality –
would be reinforced. Greater autonomy would be given to both
workers and employers within the syndicates. Syndical elections
were to be democratised. Collective bargaining would be reintro-
duced as the fundamental principle of labour relations. The 'vertical' syndicalism of the postwar period was to give way to the
syndicalism of conciliation and co-operation. Economic liberalisation, a new and more tolerant press law, and a new organic (i.e.
constitutional) law would complete the modernisation of the
regime.[15]

'Liberalisation', 'political development', 'institutionalisation',
these were the concepts which together with the neutral terminology

of the technocrats were to form the new official language in the 1960s. It was not that a coherent, neatly outlined political programme had been agreed upon by all the political families of the regime. The evolution of the Francoist system followed rather from the conviction of the political class – and particularly of the regime's second generation – that some kind of modernisation was needed to match the demands of what was termed 'a new historical reality'. Only some such evolution could save the Francoist political class from gradual extinction.

After 1960 the 'liberalising' trends were reinforced by the exclusion of Spain from the new European Economic Community on account of the nature of its political regime. Spain made an application for membership in February 1962. Its rejection, confirmed later, emphasised the incompatibility of Franco's regime with the principles of liberal democracy which inspired the EEC.

Thereafter the regime was obsessed with the idea of attaining that minimum of democratic credibility which might win it legitimacy in the eyes of Europe. The official rhetoric was to insist again and again that Spain was a true democracy, a *Rechstaat* where the rule of law obtained. The Spanish regime, Franco said in September 1962, was 'the clearest, the firmest and the most loyal example of democracy'; it was, he repeated in 1966, one of 'the many democratic experiences known to history where the phenomenon of political parties was lacking'. The regime had not destroyed democracy, argued Fraga Iribarne, the government spokesman after 1962 and the advocate of 'liberalisation': the regime had attempted 'the revision of democracy in order to guarantee its survival'.[16]

'Political development' as a slogan fitted in with the new image that the regime was trying to build for itself as a political system 'in an open process of creation'; that is, as a regime whose Constitution was open to reform and flexible enough to admit new institutions. 'Political development', that 'grand design' of the 1960s, according to Fraga, aimed at consolidating the regime by a process of institutional and political renewal. The driving force behind 'political development' was the General Secretariat of the Movement under the leadership of Solís. One of his first moves had been to create a National Delegation of Associations. In 1964 the National Council of the Movement approved a proposal to open the door to political associations within the regime: 'The Movement will promote the associative process within its institutional framework . . . pluralising . . . if possible the means for constant fulfilment of the Fundamental Principles.' To the National Council of the Movement would fall the task of channelling 'the contrast of opinions concerning political action'.[17]

The idea of Solís and his close associates was clear. As in the plans of Arrese, the overall purpose was to give recognised, constitutional powers to the Movement. But where Arrese still had in mind a restrictive, totalitarian organisation, Solís and his young men wanted a more open system. 'Political development' was but a more flexible conception of the Movement which would allow the existence of political associations which accepted the legitimacy of Franco's rule and its ideological foundations, as formulated in the Law of Fundamental Principles of 1958.

Three ideas were central to this conception of the Movement. First, that political activity would be legal only 'within' and 'from' the Movement. Second, that political associations would be under the strict control of the National Council of the Movement. Third, that the acceptance of political associations in no sense implied any return to the party system characteristic of liberal democracy. It was an attempt to give the Movement a more 'representative' character, not to dismantle it.

In practice, 'political development' brought neither immediate nor substantial changes in the structure of the political system. Only the legalisation of political associations might have had a dramatic effect in the atmosphere of the sixties. But this was delayed, as we shall see, until 1974.

Moreover, the 'political development' of Solís and the 'liberalisation' of Fraga got off to a poor start. The 'Munich affair' in 1962 showed that the regime was not prepared to allow political activity outside the Movement, while the execution in 1963 of the Communist leader Grimau showed the limits of the so-called liberalisation. The hopes raised by the encouraging speeches of Fraga on taking office as Minister of Information in 1962 vanished the following year with the vehement hostility displayed by the Minister in answering a letter signed by a large number of prominent Spanish intellectuals, demanding an inquiry into the alleged torture of miners during the strikes of Asturias in 1962 and 1963.[18] In 1963 a special court was created to deal with crimes against public order. The TOP, as this court was called, became the symbol of the repressive nature of Francoism. In 1964 came another disappointment with a new Law of Associations in which the right of *political* association was not even mentioned. Someone suggested the creation of a Society of Friends of the Chihuahua.

This timid and hesitant process of liberalisation, however, continued. Franco himself, while retaining his usual ambiguity and 'prudence', seemed at least not entirely opposed to 'liberalisation'. In his Christmas messages in the 1960s he referred to the need to continue the process of 'perfecting' the regime. In March 1963 he asked the National Council of the Movement whether the organisation, functions and administration of the Movement were up to the requirements of the times. This was seen as a formal go-ahead for 'political development'.[19]

'Liberalisation' brought into the official syndicates the changes which we have examined in another chapter. In 1965 a new law was approved to differentiate between political and economic strikes; neither was legal, but at least economic strikes would not be regarded as seditious. In 1966 Fraga saw his Press Law approved; a law which, although still restrictive by Western standards, by modifying the rules of censorship gave newspapers a degree of freedom unimaginable in the early years of the regime. There was greater tolerance in the theatre and cinema. Publishing policy became more liberal. Liberal magazines such as *Cuadernos para el Diálogo* and *Revista de Occidente* were authorised. In Catalonia publishers were allowed to print books and magazines in Catalan and several publishing houses ventured to publish politically committed literature – previously forbidden *auteurs maudits* and Marxist books. Even if this cautious 'opening' reached only a minority of Spaniards (mainly small university circles in Madrid and Barcelona), and even with arbitrary restrictions, the new policy of the Ministry of Information contributed to a renewal of Spanish culture in the 1960s.[20]

As for politics, the disappointment with the 1964 Law of Associations did not mean the end of 'political development'. The political evolution of the regime continued to be defended, particularly by the sector of the Movement closest to Solís. Emilio Romero, the editor of *Pueblo*, the organ of the official syndicates, and as such one of the most influential (and hated) journalists of the regime, published in 1964 a book called *Cartas a un Príncipe*. As its title made clear, it was intended to sketch out a programme for the monarchy of the future; the monarchy should be a political system that would give institutional expression to the plurality of political forces existing within the regime.[21] The book was an instant success – five editions were sold in five months. Later, in March 1965, *Arriba*, the Falangist newspaper, asked for the institutionalisation of a political opposition within the regime.[22] At about that time *Ya*, the Madrid Catholic daily, began to publish editorials and articles which favoured a gradual liberalisation of the regime. All these developments were, of course, to be formally contained within the Principles of the Movement.

In 1964 Calvo Serer, the former champion of reactionary integrism, published from Don Juan's headquarters a book (*Las nuevas democracias*) wherein he studied what he called the positive aspects of democracy and tried to show the compatibility between democracy, Catholicism and the monarchy. Together with the writer Pemán and the historian Pérez Embid, Calvo Serer outlined a new edition of his monarchist 'third way' avoiding both the 'collaboration' of surrender' with Franco and any illegal co-operation with the democratic opposition. Their hope was to maintain the liberal image of Don Juan while keeping their contacts with Franco. The editorial line of *ABC*, the Madrid monarchist paper, continued within the strictest Francoist orthodoxy; but the non-political articles which Pemán published almost every day – he is a facile writer – increasingly acquired liberal overtones. One of the greatest political surprises for many years took place on 21 July 1966 when the government banned *ABC* because of an article by a young and prominent monarchist, Luis Ma. Ansón, in support of the monarchy of Don Juan: 'The European Monarchy, the democratic Monarchy, the popular Monarchy, a Monarchy for all.'[23] Contrary, therefore, to what Fernández de la Mora, the ideologue of technocracy, had argued in 1965, even official Spain was not experiencing the 'twilight' of ideology, but its rebirth.[24]

If the promoters of 'political development' hoped to gain the 'participation' of the tolerated opposition they were sadly deceived. Fraga's 'liberalisation', the so-called 'democratisation' of the system advocated by Romero and others, was totally unacceptable to a democratic opposition. In 1964 Ruiz Giménez resigned from the Cortes and severed all connections with the regime. The democratic opposition regarded the Francoist edition of democracy as a farce. They saw no mitigation whatsoever of the repressive nature of the regime; on the contrary, repression grew even fiercer against growing student and labour unrest.

This display of the old firmness was, however, not sufficient to lull the suspicions with which the Falangist 'old guard' and the right wing of the regime regarded the 'pluralist' conception of the Movement and the increasing permissiveness exhibited in public entertainments and bookshops. They accepted liberalisation only out of loyalty to Franco; even so, their pressures delayed and mutilated the liberalising process. At the same time, new ultra right-wing magazines and groups emerged, expressing in increasingly violent ways their dissatisfaction with the political relegation of the Falange and with the foreign and internal policies pursued by Franco's ministers. Of these groups, the most enduring and influential was *Fuerza Nueva* (New Force) which took its name from the magazine founded in 1967 by the Madrid lawyer Blas Piñar.

As far as Franco himself was concerned, he seemed to have chosen to play the card of 'continuism', an intermediate position between the 'immobilism' of the ultras on the right and the 'opening' of the 'liberal' *aperturistas*. It became gradually evident that Admiral Carrero Blanco was to be the architect of this continuism. In contrast to the truncated political lives of most ministers, his political career had been one of steady success: Under Secretary to the Presidency of the Government since 1940, he became in 1968 Vice-President of the Government. From this privileged position Carrero would be in charge of the delicate task of implementing the innovations contained in the Organic Law of State published on 10 January 1967. In what was regarded by the opposition as a scandalously rigged referendum and by Francoists as a proof of the 'democratic' legitimacy of the regime, the law was approved by 95.86 per cent of the voters.[25]

(c)

Opening and immobilism

From the 1960s the political class was divided by struggle between *aperturistas* – those who believed that the regime must be 'opened' in order to survive by winning a wider support, usually called 'participation' – and *immobilistas*, who resisted any change in what was called the 'essence' of the regime. To the immobilists Francoism was a coherent structure, an indivisible whole. To modify one of its component parts or to revise one of its ideological foundations would engender a continuous process of change that would destroy the political system.

Throughout the Franco regime the word 'party' was politically taboo and the formation of parties remained a crime.* The only form of political organisation permitted was 'association', a characteristic semantic invention of Francoism. Between 1969 and 1973 the nature of associations and their function in the system was the grand debate within the regime, dividing the *aperturistas* from their enemies.

Evolutionists in the regime hoped to turn associations into domesticated parties – though, of course, the word was avoided – which would be not only a recognition of the limited pluralism of the families of the regime, but would even bring in new recruits

---

*Under the decree of 13 September 1936, the Law of 9 November 1939 and the Penal Code (Articles 172–174), which punished any attempt to establish a regime based on the division of Spaniards into political or class groups. In 1968 the revised *Estatuto Orgánico del Movimiento* allowed 'el legítimo contraste de pareceres' in associations in the Movement.

by more effective forms of 'participation'. Hard-liners wanted to keep them as no more than harmless pressure groups of yes-men. It was the hard-liners who won the debate. In their final form political associations, as the Francoists conceived them, did not, as we shall see, create free parties. As Gil Robles, a leader of the democratic monarchists, was to put it, associations in their final form merely 'legalised the several sectors of the single party . . . names changed but the monopoly remained intact'.[26] The fear of the term and concept of party remained embedded in the Francoist mentality through fear, as Franco's official biographer later argued, 'of the unknown people'. This meant that no political association that did not conform to the principles of organic democracy could be legalised. It was a member of Franco's last government who stated the obvious: 'Whilst the protagonist of an epoch in Spanish history still lived it was impossible to think of any real change.'[27]

Franco boasted that the Organic Law of the State of 1967 (LOE) completed the institutionalisation of his regime which had begun thirty years previously. If he believed that the new law could guarantee an orderly and precise functioning of the state, he was mistaken. The culminating constitutional achievement of Francoism was so vague and imprecise on fundamental matters that it opened the way to antagonistic interpretations which accentuated pre-existent differences between the regime's political families. The LOE ratified the monarchy as the form of the Spanish state, but it neither solved the question of the successor nor defined the role of the Movement in the future monarchy. During the Cortes debate on the LOE Professor Fueyo Alvarez had coined a phrase that was to make a political fortune, 'After Franco the Institutions'.[28] But what were the institutions? And who would man them?

As we have seen, it took Franco two years to end the uncertainties about the succession. On 22 July 1969 he nominated Prince Juan Carlos as his heir and future King. The nomination was a political triumph for the Carrero-López Rodó tandem, a reward for ten years of tenacious intrigue. Francoists unanimously accepted the decision of the Caudillo and the Falangist 'regentalists' (supporters of a permanent regent as head of state) themselves proclaimed their loyalty to Juan Carlos with the same rhetorical zeal they had displayed in proclaiming their loyalty to Franco. For the Falangists, provided they could secure a place in the sun under the new monarch, the final defeat of the 'regency' solution was a minor setback;* for the liberal monarchists in Don Juan's camp the nomination of his son ended all their hopes of somehow liberalising the regime from within. The Carlist Pretender, Carlos Hugo, had abandoned all hope of restoration at Franco's hands. His expulsion in 1968 was the final defeat of a claim that went back to the 1830s.

It was not only the succession problem that occupied the political class. Even when it was settled the nature of the regime, embalmed in the LOE, and the role of the Movement within the Francoist state divided the political establishment.

On the one side stood the *políticos*: Fraga, and Solís and his Falangists who continued to emphasise the necessity for enlarging 'participation' via associations. On the other stood Carrero Blanco and the technocrats of the Opus Dei who, if not hostile to all political evolution, were indifferent to 'liberalisation' and hostile to the Falange *políticos*.

It was impossible to conceal these divisions. There were demonstrations with shouts of 'Opus No' by young Falangists; the Falangist press (*Arriba, Pueblo, SP*) never concealed its deep antipathy for the Opus Dei. In 1966 the founder of the Opus Dei himself, Mgr Escrivá, thought it necessary to intervene and in a letter to *Le Monde* asked the Minister of the Movement, Solís, to stop the anti-Opus campaign by the Movement (Falangist) press.† This was a *public* indication of the power struggle that had been going on since 1957 'behind the curtains', to use the Spanish

---

*It was only a minor defeat for the 'regentalists', since they never went beyond discreet insinuations to Franco to postpone the nomination, or embarrassing him with other potential pretenders such as Juan Carlos' cousin, D. Alfonso Borbón-Dampierre, who in 1971 married one of Franco's granddaughters. All this never amounted to a coherent movement against the nomination of Juan Carlos. It seems that D. Alfonso's candidacy was supported by Solís and Admiral Nieto Antúñez, the Minister for the Navy in the 1960s and a close friend of Franco. The restless Solís tried in 1968 to establish contact with Don Juan when he thought that Juan Carlos would rely in the future on his then associates, López Rodó and Carrero. See L. López Rodó, op.cit., pp. 288–90, 411–18.

†The campaign had started because of the increasing liberal tendencies of the newspaper *Madrid* under the inspiration of the mercurial member of the Opus Dei, Calvo Serer, now converted to democracy. Even if *Madrid*'s new-found 'democratic' enthusiasms were equally obnoxious to Falangists and Opus Dei technocrats, the Falangist press took the new line as a pretext to launch its offensive against the whole Opus Dei. Mgr Escrivá's letter is in J. M. Ruiz Gallardón, 'El nuevo Govierno: Un lustro en la política del Regimen', in *España. Perspectiva 1974* (1974), pp. 69–71. For the *Madrid* affair see R. Calvo Serer, *Franco frente al Rey* (1972), pp. 205*ff.*

phrase. It was to explode into notoriety with the Matesa scandal, which, in October 1969, discredited the men of the Opus but ended the ministerial prospects of their opponents.*

In view of the growing power of Carrero Blanco, the main interest of the men around Solís centred on three objectives. First, they would try to make the Movement and the syndicates independent of Carrero's fief, the presidency of the government. Secondly, they would attempt to make the Movement the only channel of political representation; even if this led to the formation of political associations, they would be safely under the umbrella of the Movement's National Council. Finally, they would try to reform the syndicates in order to make them a more representative labour organisation, but under Falangist control. Thus the syndicates would become so embedded in the political and social structure that they could only with difficulty be removed, while the National Council of the Movement would become a new second Chamber, superior to the Cortes and with power to criticise and control the government.

The 'men of Solís' were not a party with a programme. Their plans were a defensive reaction of a group of individuals with similar views about Spain, the Francoist regime and its future. Nevertheless, if all these plans became realities, then Solís and his associates could await the succession to Franco in the certainty that the Movement would be the preponderant force in the new monarchy.[29]

Carrero and López Rodó saw the potential dangers in the plans of Solís. Carrero was a conservative who put 'unity of power', as the constitutional lawyers defined the system, before any other political consideration. He disliked the style and resented any influence of the Falange. López Rodó had based his political career on administrative reform and economic growth. He hoped that economic development would transform Spain into a modern, industrial state. He never made his political options explicit, but he played an important role in the 'de-falangisation' of the regime and in the rise of the technocrats to power throughout the 1960s. Together with Carrero and General Alonso Vega, a close associate of Franco and Minister of the Interior, he was one of the architects of the nomination of Prince Juan Carlos as heir to Franco.[30]

It was the third generation of the regime which was to press for its opening. They were young Falangists, monarchists and Catholics born around 1930–40 who had neither fought in the Civil War nor shared in the nationalist mystique of the 'ideals of the

*For the Matesa scandal and the crisis of 1969 see below, pp. 189, 264.

Crusade'. This third generation was, compared at least with its pre-decessors, a more liberal, tolerant, Europeanised generation, by and large convinced that the new and modernised Spain of the 1960s required a new political system which would bear some credible resemblance to Western democracies. This, however, did not prevent them from acknowledging the legitimacy of the regime by accepting public office. They believed in reform from within, not in revolution from without.[31]

The position of the Solís group, who had led the battle for political development in the early 1960s, was ambivalent. A majority supported the opening of the regime as long as it did not threaten to alter the structure of the Movement. They accepted an opening on the lines of their version of 'political development': associations within the Movement under the control of its National Council. Their view of 'democratisation' of the regime did not imply any acceptance of liberal democracy. On the contrary, even in 1974 and 1975 the politicians, writers and newspapers of the Movement continued to insist on those criticisms of liberal democracy and capitalist society which had inspired the original ideology of the Falange. A socialising, populist rhetoric was always an essential component of the Movement, especially during the years of Solís (1957–69) when the Movement became identified with the syndicates. The men of the Movement saw opening as a step towards what they chose to call Social Democracy, a Social Democracy which bore no relation whatsoever to social democracy as conceived in Western Europe. Their attitude towards *aperturismo* would, therefore, be contradictory and unclear. Most of them were *aperturistas* in the sense that they had evolved the idea of political associations. But when, in the 1970s, the pressures for a true democratic opening of the regime became increasingly persistent, the 'men of Solís' put the defence of the legitimacy of the Movement and the spirit of 18 July before the democratising, reformist thesis.[32] As one of them was to put it in 1976: 'Only we have invented it [the opening via political associations]. Only we will set it up and only with us can it work.'[33]

Fraga went in the opposite direction. He became the leader of the reformists and the founder of *centrismo*, that is, the idea that a great force of the centre was necessary to underpin the gradual evolution of the regime towards democracy.[34]

José Ma. Areilza, a former ambassador to Buenos Aires, Washington and Paris who had left the Spanish diplomatic service in 1964 to become political secretary to Don Juan between 1966 and 1969, went much further. In 1968 he warned that the real question for Spain was not so much the reorganisation of the Movement, then under review, but the foundation of a state 'based on democratic consensus and on harmonious plurality'.[35] Areilza was convinced that Franco's regime would never be accepted by Europe and that its evolution beyond the framework of Francoism was inevitable. His ideas were close to the democratic opposition with which Areilza had maintained contacts when he had acted as secretary to Don Juan. But he would never either abandon legality or close the door to an agreement with those reformists within the regime who were committed to the establishment of a fully democratic system. Perhaps he thought that an understanding between regime reformists and the democratic opposition represented the only way out of Francoism into liberal democracy. Areilza believed it necessary to organise a liberal right (a 'civilised' right, as he put it) which would be the guarantee for his gradualist non-revolutionary evolution.[36]

The militant immobilists were the ultra-right wing of Blas Piñar, the Falangist old guard led by Fernández Cuesta and Girón; the various organisations of former Civil War combatants led by Falangists – Girón himself among them – or by right-wing generals like Iniesta Cano, García Rebull and Pérez Viñeta; and finally the pro-Francoist wing of Carlism. Their power was by no means negligible. The immobilists held many seats in the Cortes, the National Council of the Movement, the Council of the State and the Council of the Realm. They were strongly represented in both local and provincial administrations. They could count on the sympathy of part of the army, especially of senior officers who had fought in the Civil War or in the Blue Division in Russia; and they could equally rely on the support of some prominent prelates. They also had great influence in the circles close to Franco's family. Above all, the immobilists professed to monopolise loyalty to Franco: they were the force behind the mass rallies which were held in Madrid on different occasions after 1970 to rally support for the Caudillo.[37]

Immobilism found its philosopher in Gonzalo Fernández de la Mora, the ideologue of the decline of ideologies and the hammer of liberal heterodoxy throughout the sixties in his book reviews for *ABC*. Appointed Minister of Public Works in 1970, Fernández de la Mora was an anti-liberal and reactionary conservative, a *maurrasien* and admirer of Donoso Cortés and Maeztu.[38] He believed that old-fashioned politics should be replaced by technology and economics. His *Twilight of Ideologies* (1965) was an apologia for technocracy. Ten years later he coined the expression 'State of Works' (*Estado de Obras*), which was an attempt to defend the Francoist system based on the formidable changes in the economic infrastructure – reservoirs, ports, motorways, railways – brought about by the regime. Fernández de la Mora's arguments were simple: these changes increased fivefold the capital Spain had inherited in 1940. Franco's state had Europeanised Spain by transforming it into an industrialised country with a modern and expanding economy. All this was, according to Fernández de la Mora, the fruit of a certain system of government. 'Only madmen,' he concluded, 'could fail to support such an effective and promising political instrument.' Immobilism had founded a new orthodoxy.[39]

The immobilists, in the last resort, could count on the support of Franco. Although he liked to boast that his supporters were 'more Francoist than Franco' he regarded the question of the future of the regime as finally settled. Spain, he asserted, was already a settled post-Francoist state. 'All was tied down, well tied down.' The continuism of his *alter ego*, Carrero Blanco, was closer to immobilism than to the opening of the reformists. The technocrats of the Opus Dei avoided taking sides openly in the debate; but they continued to work closely with Carrero Blanco.

The first bitter polemic between immobilists and *aperturistas* broke out in 1967 when the Cortes began to discuss the drafts of the laws of Religious Freedom and Family Representation and the Organic Law of the Movement and its National Council. After the hopes raised by the Organic Law of the State, the expression 'opening the regime' was on everyone's lips throughout 1967.

There were many who came to think that 1967 was the great lost opportunity of Francoism,[40] for immobilism won almost every political battle fought that year. The three laws mentioned above were approved after amendments which nullified their already scant liberal content. The offensive of the right against the Law of Religious Freedom was so violent that even the editor of the conservative *ABC*, Torcuato Luca de Tena, began his comment in the Cortes debate by saying, 'To the right of the right of the European right sits the Spanish right'. Under the new law Spain remained a Catholic confessional state which tolerated – under the supervision of the Ministry of Justice – the practice of other religions.[41]

With the Organic Law of the Movement in 1969, the Movement was again defined as an 'organisation' and not as a 'communion', as in the LOE. The difference was not merely semantic. The 'Movement-communion' of the reformists meant the possibility of political pluralism within the framework of the regime. The 'Movement-organisation' implied the maintenance of the huge bureaucracy of the original Falangist party. It was the latter thesis which won out after debates of unprecedented passion for a

Francoist parliament. Soon afterwards, in October 1967, the candidates of the Movement-organisation swept the board in the general elections − the first to introduce direct election of deputies (108 out of 564) by the heads of family. The immobilists had enforced many restrictions in the new electoral law. There were to be two deputies per province, thus grossly over-representing rural Spain; with no public meetings and no fund-raising campaigns independents could not hope to compete against official candidates.

It was, therefore, the 'ever-present' ones who won, as the cartoonist Máximo put it. Although some official candidates were defeated, two out of three of the new deputies had been members in previous parliaments. A small number of independent candidates were elected, but none of them was truly opposed to the regime. The regime, however, gave them every opportunity to become so. In September 1968 the Minister of the Interior, Alonso Vega, ordered the cancellation of a series of meetings which the small group of independent family deputies had called to co-ordinate their parliamentary activities. Another promising channel (*cauce* in the jargon of the regime) seemed to have been closed.[42]

The reformists had only two hours, if not of glory then at least of momentary satisfaction. On 4 December 1968 the National Council of the Movement approved, after long and bitter debates, a Statute of the Movement, of which Article 15 contemplated the constitution of associations 'within the Movement' for the 'formulation of opinion' and for the promotion of the 'legitimate contrast' of ideas. Even if some *aperturistas* regretted the moderation of the text, the Statute of the Movement represented the greatest victory so far obtained by the supporters of reform: it seemed to open the way to political association within the regime. This hope was short-lived, like so many hopes in the past. In July 1969 the National Council approved the Statute of Associations which developed Article 15. The Solís Statute − so called since Solís had been its main promoter − was severely restrictive. It referred to 'associations of opinion', not to 'political associations'. Electoral participation was not included among the rights of the new associations. A minimum of 25,000 members were required to register as an association. Most important of all, legalisation of associations rested in the hands of the National Council of the Movement;[43] it became the 'box office' through which associations were permitted to enter the political arena.

Such restrictions reflected the insoluble contradiction which haunted *aperturismo*: the constitution of political associations without the creation of a party system. Indeed, this was the crucial question. Franco had said on a number of occasions that the party system had plunged Spain into civil war; he regarded political parties as 'unfortunate and artificial' and was determined to prevent their rebirth. ' . . . if under the pretext of the contrast of opinions somebody is after political parties,' he warned in 1967, 'let him know that *that* will never return.' The Solís Statute made certain that they would not.

Only men of the regime accepted the Solís Statute. Pío Cabanillas, an associate of Fraga, promoted a group called *Acción Política* (Political Action). Manuel Cantarero del Castillo, an honest high-minded Falangist, revived his old notion of turning the radical remnant of the Falangistas into what he called 'Social Democracy' by founding an association called *Reforma Social Española* (Spanish Social Reform). Ballarín tried to launch a Christian Democrat association. Piñar was prepared to register his ultra right-wing *Fuerza Nueva* (New Force).[44]

When those who took advantage of the Statute were only those who accepted the legitimacy of the regime, the attempt of the reformists to present associations as a third way between a multi-party system and a single-party state lacked any political credibility. The democratic opposition did not show the slightest interest in the process of political association within the regime. Their position was made even clearer in an open letter to Franco sent on 23 December 1969 by 131 prominent politicians and intellectuals, and in a document handed over to the visiting German Foreign Minister in April 1970 by four leaders of the moderate opposition (Tierno Galván, Ruiz Giménez, Satrústegui, Areilza). The opposition would only accept a democracy with free elections, political parties, free unions, rights of assembly and amnesty for all political prisoners. The Catalan Assembly, the illegal body which had united all the Catalan opposition since November 1971, added to these minimum conditions the restoration of the 1932 Statute of Autonomy for Catalonia.[45]

The problem of the democratic opposition was that, except in Catalonia, it was deeply divided except in the negative sense that it rejected Francoist reformism root and branch. It had already committed itself to what it later was to call 'democracy without adjectives'. But efforts for unity could not prosper as long as the democratic opposition continued to regard an alliance with the Communists as damaging to its democratic credibility and as a dangerous manoeuvre which would simply play into the hands of the regime.[46] The opposition was to remain divided until 1976. It remained powerless to overthrow the regime. It had moral strength, and this asset the opposition continued to exploit against Franco until he died in 1975. It managed to create a democratic language and a democratic ethic. It remained as a moral indictment against Franco, preventing his regime from obtaining the democratic legitimacy it sought. These were its abiding contributions to the democratic future of Spain.

The nomination of Juan Carlos took the democrats by surprise and they could do nothing about it. The exiled Socialists were republicans. Tierno Galván had thought since the late 1950s that Don Juan could restore democracy. So did Gil Robles, but his attempt to gather all the moderate opposition around Don Juan failed in 1962 when Don Juan disowned the Munich meeting. From then on, Christian Democrats remained mostly indifferent to the form of government, except for a group under Alvarez de Miranda which remained close to Don Juan. The same could be said of Social Democrats. The Communists were republicans in theory, but in practice they were pragmatic enough not to make the dilemma of republic or monarchy a major political issue.[47] None of them wanted Juan Carlos. His nomination, therefore, in so far as it reinforced the chances of continuity of Francoism after Franco's death, was a blow for the hopes of the opposition.

Chapter 9

The Regime in Crisis: Carrero Blanco and Arias Navarro, 1969–1975

(a)
Carrero Blanco and continuism

The next step in the operation to ensure a gradual transition towards a Francoist monarchy with Juan Carlos as king was the strengthening of Carrero Blanco's power. In fact he was to act as the effective prime minister from October 1969 until his assassination in December 1973, although officially he would be the Vice-President of the Government until July 1973 and its President only in the last six months of his life.

Carrero took control of the government in October 1969 after a manoeuvre of Solís and his men against the technocrats had back-fired, ousting Solís himself. On 10 August 1969 the government admitted that credits of up to 10,000 million pesetas (about £80 million) given to Matesa, a textile firm, to export textile machinery had been used for private investment abroad. The top men of Matesa were arrested; three ministers, all of them members of the Opus Dei, were seriously involved in the affair. This was the greatest financial scandal in Spanish history. It was a political bomb and the Movement ministers, with the support of Fraga, hoped to use it to blow the Opus Dei from power. This manoeuvre of the 'politicians' against the technocrats failed. Franco settled the affair, as in 1956, with one of his notorious judgements of Solomon. He sacked three Opus Dei ministers; but he also sacked Solís and Fraga who had instigated an intense press campaign against the Opus Dei.[1] Since the first woman in a bikini had appeared on the cinema screen in 1962, conservatives – Carrero Blanco and Franco among them – had been alarmed at the results of Fraga's liberalism on public morals.

The press exploits pornography as a commercial venture. The cinemas are plagued with pornography. To foster cheap tourism, playboy clubs and striptease joints are protected. To put an end to this situation I see no other solution than to put in the Ministry [of Tourism and Information] a person who allies moral reliability and proven political loyalty.

These were the opinions of Carrero Blanco. Fraga fell from grace, a victim of the supposed correlation between pornography and 'liberalisation'.[2]

The new government included thirteen new ministers, most of them close associates of López Rodó. For this reason it was described in the jargon of political journalists as 'mono-colour' or 'homogeneous'.

The new Minister of the Movement, Fernández Miranda, apart from being yet another lawyer-professor-politician, was a tepid Falangist, but his political origins were a misleading guide to his actions as minister, the first of which ran directly against the wishes of the Movement. In December 1969 he suppressed the National Delegation of Associations, which meant the death of the Statute of Associations approved only six months earlier. Fernández Miranda was intelligent enough to realise that there was no 'third way', that political associations would sooner or later reproduce the political parties condemned by the ideology and the legislation of the regime. In January 1970 he coined the expression 'pluriform-ism', a first indication of his ability to hide the government's lack of answers to the problems of the country behind elusive, pseudo-political terms.*

In 1971 and 1972 Fernández Miranda was to underline the incompatibility of the presuppositions of a regime based on organic democracy and the principles of liberal democracy. Parties were a 'dialectical trick'. In a celebrated speech to the Cortes in November 1972 he rejected political association. 'To say yes or no to associations is simply a Sadducean trap . . . The question is to see whether in saying yes to political association we also say yes or no, or whether we do not say yes but no, to political parties.' The unanimous conclusion derived from this rhetorical puzzle was that since political associations might become parties, there could be no political associations. And, in fact, that is what happened.[3]

Carrero mistrusted associations. In 1968 he said that Spain had become a modern democracy after the approval of the Organic

---

*After 'pluriformism' came 'nationalisation of power' in 1972, and in 1973 'the institutional offensive'. It was never clear exactly what such concepts meant.

Law of the State. Like Franco, Carrero detested political parties. He believed that the regulation of some form of opposition within the regime was unnecessary and counter-productive. Carrero opposed even the possibility of the disciplined deputies of the Spanish Cortes forming parliamentary groups. This would be 'perjury', he warned. Even less would Carrero tolerate political associations. The regime, he argued, had its own channels of representation in organic democracy.[4]

Carrero's main concern after 1969 was to restore the authority of the executive over all the institutions of the state. This was the meaning of the formula 'unity of power and co-ordination of functions' which appeared in the government's declaration in October 1969. Carrero thought that with a homogeneous cabinet he would be able to fulfil an ambitious programme: the reform of education; a new Syndical Law; the reflation of the economy after the 1967–9 crisis; integration into the EEC; and finally, an improvement in the sadly deteriorated relations between the church and the state.

He was only partially successful. The Spanish economy experienced between 1971 and 1973 a remarkable recovery. López Bravo, the Minister for Foreign Affairs, gave foreign policy a new look. His predecessor, Castiella (1957–69), had been so obsessed with Gibraltar that he had been called the Minister for *the* Foreign Affair. Now, with the suntanned, handsome López Bravo Spain signed a commercial agreement with the EEC and re-established diplomatic relations with China and East Germany. President Nixon visited Madrid in 1970.[5]

With the church, however, relations deteriorated still further, particularly after 1971. It was then that church-state relations reached the level of an open, embittered confrontation highly damaging to the regime.[6] The new Education Law of 1970 conceived of the university, less as a school for the indoctrination of a now discredited ideology, than as a nursery of managers and technicians for the new capitalist, industrial society. But the Law did not solve 'the university problem'; student troubles persisted. Nor did the Syndical Law of 1971 end labour unrest. It came as a severe disappointment after the promises of democratisation held out by Solís throughout the sixties.[7]

It was under the bleak authoritarian rule of Carrero that the 'peace of Franco' came to an end. In July 1970 three workers died in Granada after a clash between police and strikers. Later, in December, came the dramatic trial of ETA militants in Burgos; though it seemed rather that the accused, in a blaze of publicity which set off anti-Spanish demonstrations throughout Europe,

were putting the regime on trial. It was perhaps the gravest crisis
the regime had faced. In 1972 and 1973 spectacular ETA kidnap-
ings, hold-ups and terrorist activities succeeded one another.
Labour unrest in Spain, with severe local general strikes at Vigo,
Ferrol and Pamplona, between 1970 and 1974 reached Italian or
British levels. Universities were closed. A new terrorist group
emerged. FRAP, originally a left-wing split from the Communist
party, killed a policeman in Madrid in May 1973.

Carrero responded to these conflicts and challenges with tougher
police measures. The Public Order Law was 'reformed': those who
refused to pay heavy fines could be imprisoned for up to three
months. *Madrid*, the most liberal of Spanish newspapers, was
closed by government order in 1971 and its editor, Calvo Serer,
went into exile. Liberal magazines (*Cuadernos para el Diálogo,
Triunfo*) were fined or issues banned; left-wing publishers ran into
difficulties with publications. The Minister of Justice vetoed in
1971 an opposition candidacy to the elections for the Lawyers'
Association. Leaders of the Workers' Commissions, arrested in
1972, were given sentences in 1973 of up to twenty years in jail.[8]

The government had no political answer to this increasing level
of conflict. Even the internal evolution of the regime came to a
halt. Fernández Miranda resorted to his best verbal tricks in an
effort to calm the *aperturistas*. But this was no longer possible. In
February 1970, forty-six members of the National Council of the
Movement sent an open letter to the government asking for an
immediate regulation of political associations. In 1971 Fraga
published a book, *El desarrollo político* (*Political Development*),
which was the most coherent exposition of reform from within
written by a Francoist. Fraga's thesis was simple and clear: industrial, developed societies, such as Spain was in the 1970s, required
modern political institutions. Only political and social reform
could restore stability to Spain. 'In politics,' said Fraga in January
1973, 'two aims must be gradually pursued: an opening of alternative choices (liberalisation, associations) and greater participation
at all levels (representation, democratic legitimacy).'[9]

Areilza continued writing in the most widely read journals (*La
Vanguardia, ABC*) in support of evolution towards democracy. His
most celebrated article, written in 1970, in which he recalled that
democracy meant popular sovereignty, responsible government
and political parties, brought an angry reply from Carrero Blanco
himself. Writing under the pen-name Ginés de Buitrago, Carrero
pointed out that democracy had brought to Spain the overthrow of
three monarchs, two chaotic republics, twenty-five revolutions,
more than one hundred governments, the assassination of four

prime ministers – and all this in the space of only one hundred years.[10]

In 1972, *aperturismo* won a new, if extremely cautious, recruit in Silva Muñoz, a former Minister of Public Works and a member of the ACNP. He was one of the main characters in the '1972 political spring', so named in view of the large number of political lectures delivered in Madrid. In October Silva wrote in *ABC* asking for the introduction of a system of representation of 'an ideological-political nature' as a complement to organic democracy; a year later he asked for an extension of direct political representation in the Cortes and for the introduction of universal suffrage in the elections to the National Council of the Movement.[11]

The elimination of *Madrid* did not silence the press. *Ya* and *Informaciones* became mouthpieces of reform. *Cambio 16*, a new magazine, combined an excellent and comprehensive news coverage – if sometimes uncomfortably close to its models *Time* and *L'Express* – with searching and spirited criticisms of the Francoist system. In fact, in the 1970s the press became, and was to remain, a 'paper parliament', a true Fourth Estate, where almost every opinion could find a place. Opposition views (Communists excluded) began to appear in the daily press through articles and interviews with opposition leaders. A number of highly gifted cartoonists satirised the regime, its bureaucracy, its style, its moral values. They were a highly successful vehicle of anti-Francoist opinion. The diffusion of left-wing literature could not be arrested. A history of the Republic and Franco's era written by the Marxist economist Ramón Tamames became one of the best-sellers of 1973. It was a vindication of democracy and a hostile indictment of the regime.[12]

Those who visited Spain during Carrero Blanco's presidency were confronted with a paradoxical and puzzling situation. A degree of public political debate unprecedented in Franco Spain lived side by side with a return to the ice age in politics.

The stiff measures introduced after 1971 did not appease the hard-liners who worked themselves up into a state of near frenzy at the new permissiveness as evidenced in the spread of subversive literature on display. Right-wing commandos began to attack left-wing bookshops and art galleries. The right called mass rallies in support of Franco (1970, 1971) and the police (May 1973).[13] In the Cortes, right-wing deputies protested in disgust against the pro-Eastern foreign policy of López Bravo and such conciliatory gestures as proposals to recognise conscientious objectors and to grant pensions for Republican Civil War veterans. The regime's right detested political associations. They were prepared to accept an interplay of only three 'tendencies', as their leader Girón said in May 1972: a 'progressive and revolutionary' tendency (i.e. the Falange); a 'conservative and traditional' one (the Catholics); and a 'moderate, middle-of-the-road' third tendency possibly identified with López Rodó.[14]

The government was divided. While Carrero (under his pen-name Ginés de Buitrago) charged against Areilza, while Fernández de la Mora excoriated democracy in his articles in *Arriba* under the pen-name Diego Ramírez, other ministers talked of political associations and reform.[15] The Under Secretary of the Interior, Cruylles, resigned in February 1973 to write a resounding article about the internal disputes in the cabinet.[16]

Something deeper than a mere ministerial malaise was afflicting the Francoist state: a crisis of the regime which had begun with debates over political associations in 1967–9, a crisis of contradictions. Spain was officially a Catholic state; yet the church was at odds with the regime. Strikes were illegal but there were hundreds of them every year. Spain was an anti-liberal state yet desperately searching for some form of democratic legitimacy. It was a state whose official ideology was 'an integrating national Socialism',[17] but which nevertheless had transformed Spain into a capitalist society. 'In Spain,' the ultra right-winger Blas Piñar said in October 1972, 'we are suffering from a crisis of identity of our own state.'[18]

If Piñar was right, even Franco was infected. After two years of political stagnation, Franco delivered a surprisingly liberal Christmas speech in 1972. 'We have to depart from any closed and exclusivist criterion . . . The disparity of ideas and tendencies is not only legitimate but necessary.'[19] *Aperturistas* were delighted. A group of thirty-nine, most of them third-generation Falangists, proclaimed their support for Franco's message in view of its 'dynamic and modernising content'.[20]

At the beginning of 1973 it seemed, despite the inevitable scepticism of the opposition, that the regime was at last ready to embark on the democratisation which reformists had been long demanding. Carrero himself addressed the National Council of the Movement on 1 March, pleading for 'definite measures to enlarge the participation of Spanish people in political life'.[21]

That this participation would have been strictly controlled there can be little doubt; but even a modest opening was doomed. In May 1973 a policeman was killed in Madrid by members of FRAP. Soon afterwards, Cardinal Tarancón scandalised the right when he vetoed the entrance into Madrid of a political pilgrimage which had been carrying an image of the Virgin of Fatima all over Spain. The right used both incidents to launch a new offensive against a government presided over by the most loyal of Francoists.[22] Political bully-boys, stridently defending the 'essence' of the regime, their political blackmail was effective: a minister who hinted at reform was a traitor preparing to abandon ship. Only if such political rats were swept from power could the ship remain afloat.

Franco reshuffled the cabinet in June. He nominated Carrero as President of the Government. The new cabinet was to the right of its predecessor. Its programme was summed up by Carrero as 'to continue'. The new government, therefore, was to appease the ultras but without entirely renouncing a timid 'opening' under strict surveillance from above. So it seemed at least from Carrero's speech to the Cortes in July and from the 'institutional offensive' promised in October by Fernández Miranda, Vice-President in the new government.[23] If this implied a modicum of liberalisation, an act of unprecedented violence brought regime reformism once more to a halt. On 20 December 1973 Carrero was assassinated by a commando of ETA, the Basque revolutionary movement. His address was in the public telephone directory; he was unwilling to change his accustomed route to daily mass. His car was blown clean over a church in the most exclusive residential quarter of Madrid.[24]

(b)
Arias Navarro 1974–5[25]

Fernández Miranda as Vice-President of the Government handled the crisis which followed Carrero's assassination with remarkable serenity. Public order was maintained. There was no indiscriminate repression. The army did not intervene. The orders given by the Chief of the Civil Guard, General Iniesta Cano, which might have brought tanks into the streets, were reversed by the government, and the favourite general of the extreme right was reprimanded. With no tanks, there were no demonstrations.

Fernández Miranda did not make personal political capital out of the crisis. Franco appointed as new Premier Carlos Arias Navarro, the Minister of the Interior with Carrero, and responsible, therefore, for the internal security which had so spectacularly failed to preserve Carrero's own life. Why Franco chose Arias is a mystery. Perhaps the fact that Arias had been introduced to Franco by his close friend Alonso Vega, and the fact that Arias, like Carrero, was neither a technocrat nor a Falangist may explain his nomination.

Arias was a relatively obscure member of the political class with a reputation of being both a hard-liner and an efficient administrator, a reputation he had won as public attorney in Málaga during the Civil War, as director of the police in the 1960s and later as mayor of Madrid. He formed his government in January 1974. Arias retained eight ministers from Carrero's cabinet, dismissed López Rodó and the technocrats, appointed some unknown politicians from within his private circle, put one of Fraga's men (Pío Cabanillas) in charge of Information and brought back into government several men of the Movement of Falangist origins. This was a government unanimously regarded as a government for continuity.[26]

Three main questions confronted the new government: public order, the political situation in general and the economic crisis, signs of which were unmistakable in the second half of 1973. The problem of Franco's succession was still a dormant threat, though in a new form. Now the question was whether the ageing Franco should resign as Chief of State — he had already handed over the presidency of the government — and crown Juan Carlos as King.

What Don Juan's reaction to the coronation of his son would be was unknown; the Old Pretender had not abdicated his rights despite the nomination of Juan Carlos in 1969. In January 1974 it was rumoured that Don Juan was to tour Europe to get the support of the EEC for his candidacy. Calvo Serer, one of Don Juan's advisers in Paris, wrote an article in *Le Monde* arguing that Juan Carlos should return his crown to his father immediately on Franco's death, so that true democracy could be restored. The article caused a political scandal in Spain and strengthened the convictions of those who saw in the *immediate* 'instauration' of Juan Carlos the best guarantee for the continuity of Francoism.[27]

These convictions acquired new force in the summer of 1974. Franco fell seriously ill with phlebitis. Juan Carlos was installed as a caretaker Head of State between 19 July and 1 September. The belief that Franco's life was drawing to its close — in spite of his daily one-and-a-half-hour session on the golf course in the summer of 1975 — dominated the political atmosphere during the whole period of Arias' first government. The years of Carrero had shown that immobilism was impossible, that the problems of Spain needed new and imaginative answers; now it was clear that the monarchy could only survive with some sort of democratic consensus.

On 12 February 1974 Arias disclosed to the Cortes a detailed political programme, promising an immediate democratic opening of the regime. The political key of his speech was the idea that the national consensus, so far expressed 'by way of adherence' to Franco, must in future be expressed 'by way of participation' in the regime. The government promised a new Statute of Associations which would allow the immediate formation of political associations. This surprising speech embodied what was called 'the spirit of 12 February'.

The speech of 12 February revitalised Spanish political life. It aroused, inside and outside Spain, an enthusiasm and interest equalled by no other political event of Francoist Spain. Arias won the full support of the *aperturistas*, the unanimous applause of the press, still surprised and gratified by the liberal spirit of the new Minister of Information, Pío Cabanillas. Arias could even count on a sceptical 'wait and see' posture in both the Francoist right and the democratic opposition. The only root-and-branch opponents were the ultra right and the revolutionary left.[28]

The press now enjoyed an unprecedented degree of freedom by Francoist standards and it used its new elbow room with a remarkable sense of responsibility. It played a substantial role in the revival of the democratic consciousness of Spain. The success of *Cambio 16*, with almost half a million copies sold every week, revealed both an astonishing awakening of political curiosity in a society which had been characterised by political apathy, and the desire for substantial political changes. 'My distinguished colleagues,' Emilio Romero ironically wrote later, 'were smoking the hashish of liberalisation and *apertura*.' *Cuadernos para el Diálogo*, the liberal magazine, was, according to Romero, in a 'permanent orgasm'.[29] These excitements were to prove not so permanent after all. Restrictions on press freedom retained by Cabanillas multiplied after his resignation in October 1974 − apparently a secret report on the mild wave of pornography released by Pío Cabanillas had impressed Franco with the moral dangers of liberalism.

With Cabanillas' successor, Herrera, fines and suspensions returned. But the change was irreversible. Spain rediscovered the female nude in films, plays and magazines. The press continued to report in detail strikes and terrorist actions and to comment at length and in depth on the political situation. The views of the opposition leaders appeared with relative frequency in the daily press and in the weeklies. The government banned lectures and conferences by members of the opposition. On 26 November 1974 some of the more prominent among them were arrested, if only for a few hours. But basically, the existence of the moderate opposition (Christian Democrats, Liberals, Social Democrats, Socialists) was tolerated. A liberal journalist, Pedro Calvo Hernando, could write in May 1975 that 'the names of Felipe González, Dionisio Ridruejo,. Joaquín Ruíz Giménez and José Ma. Gil Robles . . . are familiar names to almost every well-informed Spaniard'.[30]

The freedom of the press and the implicit recognition of the right of moderate opposition to existence were the most visible effects of the 'spirit of 12 February'. For the truth was that Arias could not bring about his promised gradual democratisation of the regime. The hopes of February 1974 had turned, by September 1975, into horror at the execution of five young left-wing terrorists.

Arias failed for a number of reasons: the resistance of the bunker – that is, the Francoist right, Franco included; the fears raised by the Portuguese revolution in April 1974; the mounting pressures of terrorism, labour discontent and student unrest to which the government's only response, in order to appease the bunker, was a tough policy, particularly in the Basque country. Finally, Arias failed because he was too much of a conservative and a Francoist at heart to carry out a true democratisation of the regime.

Thus in the twenty months between 12 February 1974 and Franco's death (20 November 1975), Arias fluctuated between encouraging speeches and disappointing reactions, hopeful promises and regressive measures.

The speech of 12 February was followed by two serious crises: the execution of a young Catalan anarchist (Salvador Puig Antich) and the house arrest of the Bishop of Bilbao, Mgr Añoveros, following a moderate homily in support of the use of the Basque language. The execution of Puig Antich brought the usual organised hostile demonstrations against the Spanish regime all over Western Europe and anger and frustration in Spain. The Añoveros affair worsened church-state relations. The Vatican supported the Bishop.[31] Arias had to give in and withdraw any sanctions against the Bishop. But the erosion of confidence suffered by his government was formidable. According to Gabriel Cisneros, a young reformist of Falangist origins who had apparently written the 12 February speech, the Arias government suffered in three months the erosion of three years in normal circumstances.[32]

To restore the government's credibility, ministers tried to relaunch the thesis of the democratic opening. This operation reached its finest expression in a speech by Cabanillas in Barcelona in April 1974. The whole Spanish press published a photograph of the Minister waving a *barretina*, the traditional Catalan cap; such a mild recognition of the 'peculiarity' of Catalonia was regarded as an unprecedented gesture in Franco's Spain. Cabanillas talked of renovation, freedom and tolerance and promised to put an end to state intervention in the media.[33]

The government, however, had no luck. The revolution of 24 April in Portugal gave a pretext for the bunker to launch an offensive against the government in general and against Cabanillas in particular. On 28 April Girón published an apocalyptic manifesto in *Arriba*, the Falangist daily, denouncing the freedom of the press and condemning any liberal interpretation of the Arias programme. The *gironazo*, as the manifesto was called, was directed against the liberal ministers of the cabinet. Girón explicitly excepted from his blast Arias and Utrera, a right-wing Minister of the Movement. He warned that the right would not tolerate treason to Franco, his regime and the memories of the Civil War.[34]

A few days later, Blas Piñar denounced the 'vile press' and the 'dwarfs' who had infiltrated the government in order to subvert the regime.* On 13 June there was a fresh disappointment for the reformists: the Chief of the Army General Staff, the highly prestigious General Manual Díez Alegría, a leading advocate of the political neutrality of the army, was dismissed. He was regarded as a liberal and opponents of the regime began to think of him as the potential Spanish Spinola.†

The change in the political atmosphere was discouraging for liberals. When Arias addressed the country on 15 June 1974 his language seemed to show a dramatic turn to the right. 'First of all,' he said, 'I want to ratify the leading role of the Movement in the present political situation . . . The Movement and the Spanish people are one and the same thing.' The message was transparent. The Movement would continue to be the centre of gravity of political life. There would be no '12 February spirit' opposed to the fundamental principles of the regime.[35] This was the language of 1969, the language then used by Solís and his associates. Not surprisingly, they were alone in welcoming the new Arias. As Emilio Romero put it, the enthusiasts of the '12 February spirit' would need a candle to find it under their rocking chairs.[36] If the large number of left-wing militants arrested since Arias took office was taken into account the 'spirit of February' might be said to have been totally extinguished.**

Yet the Arias of 12 February could still stage a brief comeback in the summer of 1974. Franco's phlebitis encouraged those who believed that no democratisation of the regime was possible with Franco *in situ* as chief of state. Now there was a chance that the

---

*He referred to a group of journalists who had attended a press conference of the Communist leader Carrillo in Paris only a few days before.

†He began to receive anonymous gifts of monocles, since Spinola always wore them. For his view on the army see M. Díez Alegría, *Ejercito y Sociedad* (1972).

**Between 13 January and 8 February 1974, 150 people were arrested. There was serious unrest in Spanish jails throughout 1974; more than 100,000 people signed a petition addressed to the government in support of an amnesty. 'Hemeroteca 74', *Triunfo* (21 December 1974).

Caudillo would retire and hand over to Juan Carlos. Franco, however, like the old dictator in García Marquez' novel *The Autumn of the Patriarch* published soon afterwards, after a short retirement, took back his powers once the doctors declared him fit. 'Arias, I am recovered' was all he said to his Prime Minister in order to communicate to him his dec:sion to return to office. Arias answered a few days later, on 10 September, in a press conference where he ratified his determination to carry out the programme of 12 February, expressed his satisfaction at having served under Juan Carlos during Franco's illness and promised political associations before January 1975.[37]

Arias wished to underline the independence of his government. He wanted to make clear that the return of Franco – which apparently took him by surprise – did not imply a change in the democratising projects of his cabinet.

If Arias believed that he would be able to govern independently of Franco, he was mistaken. On 13 September, only three days after his press conference, a bomb explosion in Madrid which cost eleven lives and was attributed, on doubtful evidence, to ETA and the Communist party, gave ample ammunition to the right-wing opponents of Arias. Blas Piñar opened fire with a violence unusual even for him: 'Mr President, we dissociate ourselves from your policies . . . We want neither to obey you nor to go along with you.'[38] Pío Cabanillas – the most prominent liberal in the cabinet and the *bête noire* of the men of the bunker – was dismissed on 29 October on Franco's insistence. The Minister of Finance resigned and so did many members of the administration, under secretaries who were known for their reformist views: Oreja, Ricardo de la Cierva, Fernández Ordóñez and others. For *Tacito*, a group of young Christian Democrats of the ACNP who had been publishing articles in support of reform in *Ya* since June 1973, the crisis of 29 October meant the end of the political hopes raised by the speech of Arias on 12 February. Such was the opinion, too, of many other reformists of the regime: the 'spirit of February' had evaporated.[39]

They were right. In December Arias at last disclosed a disappointing Statute of Associations. In February 1975 he emphatically rejected any suggestion of a constitutional reform. In April, martial law was declared in the Basque country after a period of terrorist actions, political strikes, demonstrations and police violence. Martial law unleashed a repression whose violence exceeded anything so far seen in the Basque region.[40] In June 1975 Arias brought Solís back into the government – an unexpected decision which liberal opinion saw as the return of a relic of the past, of a political ghost who had long lost any pretensions as a reformer. On 27 August, after a number of policemen and civil guards had been killed by terrorists, the government passed a new Anti-Terrorist Law which made the death penalty mandatory for terrorists, who were to be tried by summary procedures in military courts. One month later, the new law was applied to five militants of ETA and FRAP.[41]

That the October crisis and the resignation of Cabanillas had meant the end of the 'February spirit' was abundantly clear in the text of the new Statute of Associations approved by the National Council of the Movement on 16 December 1974. The new statute was but a minor improvement on the Solís Statute of 1969. The constitution of 'political associations' with the right to take part in elections was authorised. But a minimum of 25,000 members (distributed in at least fifteen provinces — a clear indication that no regionalist groups would be tolerated) was still required for every association. Legalisation was still controlled by the National Council of the Movement.[42]

This latter condition meant that, once again, associations would be 'within the Movement'. Only political associations which accepted the legitimacy of the regime and its ideology would be allowed. By definition this excluded the whole democratic opposition. Without it, the 'democratisation' of the regime would be a farce.

To the democratic opposition, the restrictive nature of the Statute of Associations hardly came as a surprise. On the contrary, it justified the scepticism of the opposition towards all the Arias projects and confirmed the thesis that the opposition had always maintained: 'reformism' was a sham and an acceptable degree of democraticisation could never come from the regime itself.

The defeat of the right in the Italian referendum on divorce, the fall of the Portuguese and Greek dictatorships, the impressive performance of Mitterrand in the French elections, reinforced the views of the opposition. In July 1974, given Franco's illness and the possibility of his death, a unitary body of the opposition, the Democratic Junta, was formed in Paris. The Junta was originally formed by the Communist party, some politicians linked to Don Juan (Calvo Serer, Trevijano) together with a handful of independent political 'notables'. Soon afterwards the Socialists of Tierno Galván, the Carlists of Carlos Hugo, the Workers' Commissions, the Marxist Party of Labour (Partido del Trabajo) and other local groups joined in. The Junta asked for a 'democratic break' (*ruptura*) with the regime as the only way towards democracy in Spain. Its manifesto demanded the formation of a provisional government, amnesty, legalisation of all political parties, the restoration of all democratic freedoms, autonomy for the regions, and a referendum to decide upon the form of the state.[43]

The moderate opposition of Christian Democrats, Social Democrats, Socialists and Liberals did not join the Democratic Junta, mainly because they saw it as a Communist-dominated affair, rather like the various 'Front' organisations of the thirties. But there were other reasons. The Socialists objected to the presence in the Junta of the miniscule Socialist group of Tierno Galván.[44] The moderate opposition disapproved of the prominent role within the Junta's executive of individuals without any party affiliation, with bizarre and erratic political pasts like Calvo Serer and Trevijano, while neither Catalan nor Basque groups were included.

Even more, the moderates feared that the presence in the Junta of representatives of Don Juan might prejudice the future form of the state. The Socialists (PSOE) were republicans. The rest were divided. Prominent Christian Democrat, Social Democrat and Liberal leaders still kept up contacts with Don Juan in 1974–5; they believed that a monarchy under Don Juan would restore democracy, while the monarchy of Juan Carlos was seen as a device to keep Francoism alive after Franco's death. But, as that tremendous event seemed more and more imminent, it became evident that the army would not allow any solution other than that foreseen by Franco's laws: the installation of Juan Carlos. Confronted with this reality, the moderate opposition preferred a cautious and pragmatic approach. The question would be neither the form of the state (republic or monarchy) nor the monarch himself (Don Juan or Juan Carlos) but, rather, the nature of the future monarchy. In this, their position was clear and uncompromising: only the full restoration of democracy could legitimise the monarchy which was to follow Franco. The issue in 1974–5 was, therefore, whether or not the monarchy of Juan Carlos could become a democratic monarchy. The moderate opposition was sceptical, but was not prepared to indulge in the radical 'anti-Juan-Carlism' of the Democratic Junta and, in particular, of the Communist party's General Secretary, Santiago Carrillo.[45]

For all these reasons, Socialists, Christian Democrats, Liberals and Social Democrats decided not to join the Democratic Junta. Instead, they formed their own alternative unitary body: the Platform of Democratic Convergence, officially created in July 1975 by the PSOE, the USDE (the Social Democratic party of Ridruejo), the ID (the Democratic Left of Ruíz Giménez), a selection of Catalan and Basque parties (the Basque nationalist party, PNV, included), two parties of the radical left, the Carlists (who had left the Democratic Junta), together with some small, regional parties of Valencia and Galicia. Neither Gil Robles, as leader of the Christian Democrats to the right of the ID, nor the Liberals signed the founding document; but they kept close to the Platform.[46]

The opposition, therefore, continued to be divided. The Arias government tried to exploit the situation through a policy of tolerance towards the moderate opposition which could isolate the Communists and the Democratic Junta. But Arias miscalculated. The moderates were as firm as the Junta in their rejection of the programme of 12 February. At their XIII Congress held in France in October 1974, the Socialists of the PSOE, under the new and dynamic leadership of Felipe González, committed the party to *ruptura* – the 'democratic break' with the regime. The Congress resolutions went far beyond the extreme limits of Arias' own concept of reformism; full amnesty, democratic freedoms, free elections within one year.[47]

In June 1975, at a meeting held in Valencia, the Christian Democrats asked for a 'democratic change' and immediate elections to a constituent Cortes. The main Catalan leaders had demanded full democracy in a series of public lectures in Barcelona in the spring of 1975. For the Basques there was no question; after the 1975 martial law, Arias became the symbol of repression and systematic violence against the Basque people.[48]

For Arias, therefore, there was not the remotest chance that the opposition would accept his version of 'democratisation'. The crucial question for him was the reaction of the reformists of the regime. It was their rejection of the Statute of Associations of 1974 that decided the final failure of the 'democratic opening' of Arias. The *tácito* group considered the statute as the 'statute of the anti-associationists', an obstacle rather than a reinforcement of that democratic evolution from within which the *tácitos* saw as the only solution for the political crisis of Spain.[49] Several *tácitos* resigned from office with Cabanillas. The 'democratic evolution' of *tácito* as the only alternative both to *continuismo* and to *ruptura democratica* went far beyond the Arias programme. It included free elections to a legislative Chamber, and recognition of the rights of assembly and political association. Soon afterwards, on 24 February 1975, Fernández Ordóñez, a well-known economist who had been president of INI until October 1974, asked for a 'constitutional reform'. This was the language of the opposition.[50]

Equally decisive for the survival of the Statute of Associations of Arias was the reaction of Fraga Iribarne, ambassador to London since 1973 and the most determined advocate of reform. Before the approval of the statute, Fraga had indicated his desire to create 'a great association of the centre' which would unite all the reformists of the regime ('from the evolutionist and modern right to the Social Democrats of Christian origins and liberal spirit') under a programme of social and political reforms in order to transform Spain into a democratic state.

After December 1974 Fraga became the centre of Spanish political life. His energy is enormous; his industry prodigious. The press followed breathlessly his visits to Madrid, his meetings with Arias, his ministers and the leading figures of the political class. The object of these visits was the negotiation of Fraga's conditions for co-operation with Arias' plans by forming his 'great association' under existing legislation. In January 1975 it was rumoured that Areilza, Silva, Cabanillas, the *tácitos*, Fernández Ordoñez and many other prominent *aperturistas* would join Fraga in a political association which was christened the 'Holy Alliance'.[51]

It became clear that Fraga's proposal to establish a Congress elected by universal suffrage was unacceptable to the Francoist right. Fraga had no guarantee that his association would be legalised by the National Council of the Movement. And there was a final difficulty. A group of prominent figures of the Movement (Romero, Fueyo, Herrero Tejedor, Pinilla, Solís) had met on several occasions in early 1975 to study the possibility of launching a political association which could represent the views and interests of those who, since the 1960s, had been advocating political development which would accept as its premise a full identification with Franco and the regime. Their idea was not so much to create a Spanish imitation of the Mexican PRI as to create a Spanish version of the Gaullist UDR. In June 1975 they founded *Unión del Pueblo Español* (UDPE, Union of the Spanish People) under the presidency of Adolfo Suárez, a former director of RTVE and a close associate of Herrero Tejedor, the Minister of the Movement since April 1975. With the support of Herrero Tejedor, with the Movement's press and radio networks (directed since January 1975 by Emilio Romero) and the huge bureaucracy of the Movement behind it, UDPE emerged as the great association of *continuismo*.[52]

To the entire political class, the launching of UDPE was proof that the government would not live up to its promise of political neutrality but was putting all its weight behind a tarted up version of *continuismo* in order to sabotage Fraga's proposed 'great association of the centre'. In these conditions Fraga refused to play the game of political associations. Instead of his 'association of the centre', he formed (together with other reformists like Areilza, Cabanillas, Ordóñez, the *tácitos* and his own associates) a couple of limited companies for political studies (FEDISA, GODSA), making it clear that the kind of reform he envisaged could not be contained within the legal framework of association. In October 1975 Fraga publicised his ideas in a series of articles printed in *ABC*. It was a vast political project which included political as well as social, religious, educational, military, economic and judicial reforms. 'Democratic legitimacy,' he wrote, 'should be attained in elections to a legislative Chamber by universal suffrage.'[53]

Without Fraga, without Areilza, without the *tácitos*, the 'opening' of Arias was doomed. Nine months after the approval of the statute, only eight political associations had registered. Only one, UDPE, had the requisite 25,000 members. Six were Falangist in origin. Five stood clearly for continuity, the powerful UDPE among them; one, the UDE of Silva, was only timidly evolutionist; and only one, the *Reforma Social Española* (Spanish Social Reform) of the eternally pugnacious Cantarero, supported the reform of the regime. All this made clear that only the committed Francoists of the political class had accepted the idea of political associations. 'Outdoors,' (i.e. outside government circles) a Madrid weekly observed, 'the answer has been a resounding *no*.;[54]

Arias had failed. The economic situation had deteriorated seriously in 1975. Labour unrest had increased. Nineteen-seventy-four witnessed the largest number of strikes in Spanish history. The first two months of 1975 saw spectacular waves of strikes: even actors struck and theatres had to close. The Workers' Commissions won a great victory in the syndical elections held in October 1975.[55]

Terrorism continued; 1975 was the most violent year since the days of the guerrilla *maquis* of the forties. Eleven policemen were killed in the first eight months of 1975. Their funerals were occasions for violent right-wing demonstrations, with assaults on ministers' cars and ageing crowds shouting 'Iniesta, Iniesta'. When the executions of September unleashed, not merely the traditional furies of the European left, but the protests of the Vatican and the withdrawal of thirteen ambassadors, the right organised, for the last time, a mass demonstration in support of Franco against an uncomprehending and hostile world. Franco did not disappoint them in his last public appearance before the faithful (1 October). 'All is part of a masonic leftist conspiracy of the political class in collusion with Communist-terrorist subversion in the social sphere.' On the same day four policemen were killed by terrorists.

When the news of Franco's illness broke the prolonged official silence on 22 October, everything seemed to show that the regime was in crisis. The government was floundering in a vain attempt to contain within the political system severe conflicts, knowing that if it failed to do so it was doomed; yet, paralysed by fears of the bunker, it was unable to move.[56] It was this fear of a right wing, strong among the ageing of the political elite, that dominated the thinking and tactics of Arias.

Arias had discredited *aperturismo* just as Carrero had discredited immobilism. From the regime's point of view the situation had even worsened. Carrero's intransigence had so reinforced the arguments of the regime reformists that even an anti-Francoist like Aranguren could observe that they were about to replace the democratic opposition. The tragedy of the opposition, Aranguren noted in 1973, was that the *aperturistas* seemed to have deprived it of its arguments. 'Thus for the bourgeoisie, for the new middle and working classes,' he wrote, 'the opposition will increasingly become, not so much dangerous, as without purpose.'[57]

Arias proved the pessimism of Aranguren to be mistaken. When Pío Cabanillas was dismissed it was the Finance Minister, Barrero de Irima, who might be considered typical of the *haute bourgeoisie* of Francoism, who resigned in sympathy. The Prime Minister's two years of irresolute reformism and lapses into repression had proved the thesis of those who had maintained that any democratic evolution of the regime was impossible. An opening engineered from above had been ruled out of court − not merely by the lack of any genuine conviction on the part of the government and the Prime Minister. What chances it had were also destroyed by the symbiotic relationship of terrorism and the bunker and the undeclared alliance between terrorism and the opposition.* The extraordinary influence of the bunker, composed, as every photograph of its rallies showed, of the ageing worthies of the regime, derived from the argument that any opening of the system would make it incapable of dealing with terrorism. On 1 October the faithful Francoists carried placards proclaiming 'We don't want an opening (*apertura*) only a strong hand' (*mano dura*). The argument of the opposition was that only the immediate institution of a 'democracy without adjectives' and a complete political amnesty would, by meeting the demands of at least some of the terrorists and rallying the population behind a democratic government, isolate terrorism and reduce it to impotence.

When Franco died on 20 November 1975, the alternative was no longer immobilism or 'opening', as when Carrero was assassinated in December 1973. The dilemma now was either 'reform' or 'break' (*ruptura*).

To find a way out of this dilemma was to be the main political problem of the monarchy of Juan Carlos.

---

*A prominent Socialist intellectual deplored to R.C. the fact that it was impossible to condemn terrorism root and branch.

Chapter 10

From Dictatorship to Democracy: The Reign of King Juan Carlos, 1975–1977

(a)
The failure of Arias Navarro's pseudo-reform

Franco died on 20 November 1975 after a long agony which Spaniards followed with a mixture of expectation, malevolence and anxiety. For a month, radio, television and the press flooded the country with continuous clinical reports macabre in their medical detail. Franco's resistance was extraordinary. He survived surgical operations which might have killed even a fit and younger man. But not even hibernation could prolong his life.[1]

When Franco died, the question was whether his regime would die with him, was Franco's death the end of an era, or would Francoism continue without Franco, as Fernández de la Mora and many Francoists had predicted? Would their battle cry 'After Franco, the Institutions of Francoism' become a political reality?

In a famous sentence – 'All is tied up and well tied down' – Franco had expressed his support for continuity. It was believed that the army, whose senior officers had been Franco's loyal comrades-in-arms, would not allow any departure from Francoist legality. The key institutions (the Council of the Realm, the Cortes, the National Council of the Movement) were in the hands of staunch Francoists. According to the law, Arias could continue as Prime Minister until 1979. Above all, the new Head of State, King Juan Carlos, had been appointed by Franco as the best guarantee for the continuity of the institutions and spirit of Francoism. The institutional strength of continuism seemed formidable to the opposition.

It was gradually to become clear that one institution was *the* key to the post-Franco transition: the King. Juan Carlos was a young man of 37, who since 1969 had appeared, conspicuous at Franco's side, on State occasions as his future successor. In 1975 he was a political enigma. So far his statements had been rare and irrelevant. His family life, his sporting prowess were public property. His real political ideas were known only to his more intimate friends. He had confined himself to proclaiming his loyalty to the regime and to hinting at some vague sympathy towards the spirit of the new generations.

The hints proved to be more significant than the professions of loyalty. Juan Carlos could not ignore that Western Europe would accept his monarchy only if it brought a dramatic departure from the previous regime.* He could not ignore the climate of expectation after Franco's death, and the fact that the hopes of all those who wanted a democratic transformation were placed in him. Cardinal Tarancón spoke for them all when, in his passionate homily at the coronation mass, he asked Juan Carlos to become 'the King of all Spaniards' and that 'the juridical and political structures might offer to all the opportunity to participate freely'.

His own coronation message was the first indication that Juan Carlos was to be, in Areilza's words, 'the motor of the change'. His appointment in 1969 had infuriated the democratic opposition and the Communist leader, Santiago Carrillo, had prophesied that his reign, as 'Juan the Brief', would last only twenty-four hours. Vague though his pronouncements were, they seemed to indicate a determination to play the one card that, according to liberal opinion, would save his throne and legitimise a new monarchy, dubious in its origins: the card of a constitutional, democratic and parliamentary monarchy.

Juan Carlos' first appointments were, however, disappointing,† and the greatest of these disappointments was the confirmation of Arias Navarro as President of the Government (Prime Minister), a solution possibly accepted by the King in view of the impossibility of obtaining a liberal president from the Council of the Realm.**

*No head of state had attended Franco's funeral. Only a few days later, President Giscard of France, President Scheel of West Germany, Vice-President Rockefeller of the USA and the Duke of Edinburgh attended Juan Carlos' coronation ceremony.

†He brought Fernández Miranda back to political life as President of the Cortes. Hardly a liberal, he was known for his great capacity for political manoeuvring and his knowledge of constitutional law, and he had been totally identified with Juan Carlos since the early 1960s.

**According to the law, the King had to nominate the President of the Government, choosing one of the three candidates put forward by the Council of the Realm.

It looked as if institutions manned by Francoists could block any change after Franco. Arias, in turn, paid a price. He had to change his government and to accept a policy of political reform that was much more liberal than his programme of 12 February 1974.

The new Arias government nevertheless included a number of prominent Francoists: the evergreen Solís as Minister of Labour, Admiral Pita de Veiga, and the new Vice-President for Defence, General Santiago y Diaz de Mendívil. However, in the endless commentaries and informed gossip that were still the stuff of political life, attention centred on the incorporation into the government of three well-known reformists: Fraga Iribarne, Areilza and Garrigues, as ministers of the Interior, Foreign Affairs and Justice.[2]

From its earliest days, the new cabinet appeared divided on three fundamental issues: first, whether the new government would follow the reformist policies advocated by Fraga and Areilza; secondly, if it did adopt reformism, whether it would come out with a clear programme and a timetable for its implementation; and finally, whether the government would go to the country in a referendum or whether it would submit its reform to a Cortes still dominated by loyal Francoists.

Even supposing the government implemented a reformist programme, would the democratic opposition be prepared to accept a political reform which stopped short of full democracy – democracy, as the phrase went, 'without adjectives'? The public attitude of the opposition was clear enough. They wanted the *rapid* and total liquidation of Francoism in a 'democratic break' (*ruptura democrática*): amnesty for all political prisoners, legalisation of all political parties, dismantlement of the Movement and syndicates, free trade unions, and free elections to a constituent parliament which would decide upon the form of the new state. The Communist party demanded the formation of a provisional government to preside over the transition.

This was something completely different from the 'bestowed democracy' promised by the government. The problem with this 'bestowed democracy' was whether it was going to be a democracy at all. The government had in mind a *gradual* evolution towards a Western-type democracy without a constitutional break; that is, using the Francoist institutions to reform Francoism. The government promised 'the perfection of the institutional system', the extension of freedoms and civil rights and 'the reform of the representative institutions' (i.e. the Cortes). But the government made it clear that this was going to be achieved through a *slow* process of evolution: 'A break (*ruptura*) is unjustified, sterile and disruptive disqualifications,' the government's declaration read, 'are discarded.'

These were the limits which the Arias government set upon itself. Doubtless the government feared that a bolder reform programme would prompt immediate hostile reaction from the bunker.[3] The resistance of the bunker to any political reform, however slight, was evident throughout 1976 and 1977. The Prime Minister himself, according to his Foreign Minister, was perpetually afraid of phantoms, obsessed by the supposed need to avoid a direct confrontation with orthodox Francoism. He tried to secure its neutrality through a policy of conciliation and concession. The experiment failed. The Arias reform proved unacceptable to the bunker and could gain no support from the democratic opposition.

The hopes raised by the King's message and the government's declaration soon vanished. In the first three months of 1976, the Arias cabinet was confronted with a formidable wave of strikes and street demonstrations. Both public services (Madrid underground and buses, Barcelona firemen, the post office, the telephone company) and the main industrial sectors were hit by strikes. Between 10 and 19 January more than 200,000 workers were on strike in Madrid alone. By 26 February strikes had affected 2,377 firms in twenty provinces.*

There was much discussion about the nature of these conflicts. Were they 'economic' strikes or were they politically inspired? Even if most of them were purely industrial strikes, the leading role played in them by the illegal unions and the vast proportions of the strike movement constituted a challenge to the government as the movement acquired political overtones. On 20 January 1976 the opposition called for an amnesty demonstration to be held in the centre of Madrid. On 1 February about 75,000 people demonstrated in Barcelona in support of an amnesty and autonomy for Catalonia. In the Basque country, after a short truce, ETA renewed its terrorist campaign in January.

Unrest and public disorder reinforced the bunker's offensive against the reformism of the government. Paralysed by internal division, lacking the initiative provided by determined leadership, the ministry remained impotent in front of the labour offensive. The right saw this as an indication of weakness and abandonment of the principle of authority.† An air of mistrust and discontent

*Altogether 17,731 strikes were recorded in January, February and March 1976 (*La Vanguardia*, 4 October 1977). 1974 had seen the highest number of strikes since the Civil War: 1,926.

†The way in which the government handled the problem of the Sahara caused discontent among the nationalist right, prominent in the bunker. Neglecting previous pledges of self-determination for the Sahara, Spain agreed to the partition of the territory between Morocco and Mauritania. This spared Spain a colonial war, but its national prestige suffered. See *Cuadernos para el Diálogo* 21–7 January 1978.

entered the employers' ranks as it became evident that the government had no policy to deal with what looked like an overwhelming economic crisis.*

Nor was the opposition satisfied with the government. Its main emotive demand was for the amnesty of political prisoners, a demand not satisfied by the royal pardon of November 1975. In March 1976 there were still 550 political prisoners, most of them Basques. What was novel in the new situation was that the discontents of the opposition were public with the *de facto* recognition of the existence of political parties, even if *de jure* they were to remain illegal until 1977. Already in January 1976 most of the hitherto clandestine parties came into the open, holding congresses or distributing manifestos.

The paradox of and the danger inherent in this situation — 'We are all illegal,' declared *Doblón* — was that a universal atmosphere of political expectation had yet to materialise in substantial, legal reforms. The ambiguity of the government and its hesitations were only too obvious: it had renounced re-establishing democracy by decree; it refused to go to the country in a referendum. Real or fictitious fear of the bunker led the government to attempt a compromise with the old Francoist Cortes. Its mandate was extended for another year and a joint commission for the reform of the Fundamental Laws (i.e. the Francoist 'Constitution') was created with members from both the government and the National Council of the Movement.

On 28 January Arias explained his reform to the Cortes. His 'Spanish democracy', as he called it, contemplated the legalisation of political parties with the exception of Communists and 'separatists', a two-chamber system and the regulation of the rights of assembly. Arias mentioned neither a new electoral law nor whether elections would be held or not. He did not mention such crucial questions as regional autonomy, the repeal of the anti-terrorist law and the dismantlement of the Tribunal for Public Order (both symbols of repression), or the reform of the syndicates. Instead he used the language of the past. Arias spoke once again of the Movement, of the Fundamental Principles, of the enemies of Spain. The Francoist right was satisfied. Its main newspaper, *El Alcázar*, said that Arias had proved his loyalty to Franco and Francoism.[4]

El Alcázar was right. Arias himself would proclaim his Francoist faith before his ministers in a tense meeting of the cabinet.[5] In these

---

*The peseta was devalued in February 1976, but the economy continued to deteriorate through 1976. See above, pp. 75–7.

conditions, the reform was more than difficult: it was impossible. The reformist ministers (Fraga, Areilza) tried to rescue some credibility for the government by defending the idea of reform behind Arias' back. Fraga told *The Times* that a referendum would be held before the end of 1976 and that there would be a general election in the spring of 1977. Areilza toured Europe in February 1976 to reassure Western governments of the reformist will of the monarchy. From then on, the head of the government, an exhausted, suspicious and hesitant Arias, was to be the main obstacle to reform. Arias, lashed by the press, attacked by liberal opinion, proved unable to adapt himself to the new political situation in Spain.

Moreover, the government was the victim of its own ambiguity, particularly as far as public order was concerned. The refusal to modify the laws of assembly and the demonstration in a time of intense mass mobilisation was to court trouble. Under these conditions, confrontations between police and demonstrators were unavoidable. The situation was made even more explosive by the existence of a police force trained under an authoritarian concept of law and order and accustomed to identifying protest and dissent with subversion.

Violent clashes soon occurred. The police used drastic methods to curb street demonstrations. A worker was killed at Elda (Alicante) on 23 February. On 3 March the worst incident took place: five workers died in Vitoria after the police opened fire on the crowd. A general strike in protest was declared in the Basque country. Strikes, violent demonstrations and protest marches erupted everywhere.

The government suffered from an irreversible process of erosion. The events of Vitoria created a wave of bitter disillusion.[6] Many observers saw them as the end of reformism. This was to be only partially true in view of later developments. The events of Vitoria signalled, in fact, the end of the incoherent and wavering reformism of the Arias government, ill devised and unskilfully executed. Confronted with growing mass pressure and with the escalation of conflict, the government reacted as any government of the previous regime would have done: it put the restoration of law and order in the streets before any other political consideration.

The chief victim of this process of erosion was Manuel Fraga Iribarne as Minister of the Interior directly responsible for the maintenance of public order. He had been warned by at least one of his friends that this post would, in the parlance of the time, 'burn him out'. Though abroad at the time, he accepted full responsibility for the Vitoria shootings. The transformation of Fraga after the proliferation of conflicts was remarkable. He saw strikes and demonstrations as a personal challenge. His vehement personality gave him the image of a provocative, aggressive politician. Once the hope of reform, he became now the *bête noire* of the opposition.

Fraga always judged this as an unjustified, unfair reaction. Always conscious of historical parallels, he saw the hostile attitude of the opposition and the liberal press as a repetition of the savage 'Maura, no' campaign in 1909 – the campaign of the left against the return to power of the conservative leader Antonio Maura following the repression of Barcelona's Tragic Week.*

If the opposition was unfair to Fraga, Fraga was incapable of understanding the dilemmas of the opposition. A reform such as that outlined by Arias on 28 January and events like those of Vitoria left the opposition with no option. It was an illusion to expect its co-operation or its neutrality. The answer to Vitoria was the unification of the opposition.

On 26 March the Democratic Junta and the Platform of Convergence joined in the so-called Democratic Co-ordination. Almost the entire opposition joined: Communists, Socialists, Christian Democrats, Carlists, the Communist left, Social Democrats and the illegal unions. Five of the leaders of the new body were promptly arrested. Fraga apparently referred to them as 'his' prisoners, refusing to free them despite pressure from other ministers.[7] The divorce between the government and the opposition seemed now complete, and the chances of success for Arias' political reform so slim that a new government would be needed to give the idea of reform new political credibility.

After the incidents at Vitoria, the government tried to regain the initiative. A new draft for the Political Association Bill was sent to parliament later in March. Under the new law, political associations would be legalised by the Ministry of the Interior rather than by the National Council of the Movement as in the 1974 Law. No minimum membership would be required. The government also agreed to send to the Cortes a law modifying the Penal Code which banned political parties. Only so-called totalitarian parties were to remain banned. The idea was to isolate the Communist party from its new allies. This was something which the opposition, now united in Democratic Co-ordination, simply could not accept.†

The opposition was, in its turn, trapped in a serious dilemma, a

---

*The Tragic Week was a spontaneous uprising in Barcelona against the sending of troops to Morocco in July 1909. See J. Romero Maura, *La Rosa de fuego* (1975).
†For the new impulse to reform see *Actualidad Económica* (16 March 1976). *Cuadernos para el Diálogo* (27 March 1976) printed the opinions of twenty-one parties of the opposition rejecting the new government plans.

fact that the government either failed to grasp or misconstrued. First, the opposition still lacked any real organisation, any real contact with a future electorate. With the exception of both the Communists and the Socialist party (PSOE), which had experienced a spectacular rebirth, the great majority of the parties of the opposition were mere names – 'taxi parties', as they were ironically described, to indicate that all members of the party could cram into a single taxi.

Secondly, by refusing to take part in the political process, the opposition faced the risk of remaining cut off from Spanish political life. Its main strength was the support of Europe. It was highly unlikely that Western Europe would give democratic legitimacy to the Spanish monarchy if there was no place in it for the democratic forces.* But apart from this moral support there was very little that Europe could do. Besides, it was not altogether certain that Western Europe regarded the process of reform as scornfully as did the Spanish opposition. The United States might well prefer the gradual reform of Arias to the 'break' of the opposition. The King, on the other hand, had as much foreign support and general sympathy as the opposition itself.

The opposition, therefore, faced a difficult political choice. It could not ignore the risks implicit in a policy of obstinate refusal to accept the process of reform. If reform as conceived by Arias was unacceptable, the 'democratic break' was impossible. The King had the support of the army. No one had the power to restore democracy from below. In March and April 1976 prominent opposition leaders suggested the idea of a 'negotiated break' (*ruptura pactada*): that is, negotiations with the government to install 'democracy without adjectives'.†

There was, moreover, the additional risk that a totally intransigent opposition might endanger the entire process of democratisation. The Francoist right, the bunker, stubbornly opposed Arias' plans despite the many concessions made by the government. The 'No to change, no to any break, no to reform' proclaimed by Blas Piñar at Cartagena in February 1976 summed up the attitude of the

---

*In February 1976 several leaders of the opposition toured Europe. They were given the sort of treatment usually reserved for official representatives of foreign governments.

†'La oposición democrática y el pacto', *Triunfo*, 3 April 1976; X. Tusell 'La oposición en la encrucijada', *Actualidad Económica*, 2 March 1976. The expression 'negotiated break' was apparently coined by the Communist leader, Santiago Carrillo, in an interview in *Il Corriere della Sera*, 5 March 1976; see J. Vidal Beneyto 'El año político: la clase dominante y la sustitución del franquismo' *Anuario Económico y social de España, 1977* (1977) p. 30.

bunker. The same anti-democratic stance might be detected in Fernández de la Mora's articles in *ABC*, in Girón's speeches, in the leading articles in right-wing newspapers ʿ(*El Alcázar, Fuerza Nueva*), in the manifestos of right-wing organisations: New Force, the Federation of Combatants, the Spanish National Front and others. 'The only political system we accept,' said Girón in Madrid on 18 March, '[is] the Regime of 18 July.'[8] In March the bunker won what in the heated atmosphere of the time seemed a significant victory: the ultra Martín Sanz won the election to fill a vacancy in the Council of the Realm.

Caught between the offensive of the bunker and the rejection of the opposition, Arias ended a victim of his own doubts and ambiguities. He was too loyal to the past and to Franco's memory to carry out a reform which, in the long run, must put an end to Francoism. He did not trust his ministers. He lost the confidence of the King. On 26 April *Newsweek* published an article allegedly based on an interview with the King where it was argued that Juan Carlos regarded Arias as a 'complete disaster', the 'flag-bearer of the bunker', an 'immobilist' who obstructed reform.[9] The Minister of Information denied that the interview had taken place, but the King remained silent: he did not publicly disown the content of the article.

On 28 April Arias gave the King every reason to confirm the *Newsweek* article. His televised address to the country to explain once again the future of his political reform sounded like a provocation to the democratic opposition. He mentioned Franco seven times, calling him 'the veteran captain' and 'the provident legislator'. He resorted to the old clichés of 'international Communism', 'treason to Spain', 'insatiable rancour'. He once again ignored the question of an amnesty and rejected the possibility of opening a constituent period. He promised a bicameral system with a corporative Senate and a Congress for the 'representation of the family', an obvious echo of the past even if the introduction of universal suffrage was promised in the same speech. Without revealing its terms, he announced a new electoral law and a referendum, without mentioning how its fair conduct would be guaranteed.[10]

A few days later, two youngsters died in a clash between right-wing and left-wing Carlist factions in the annual pilgrimage to Montejurra. The opposition saw in this an excessive police tolerance towards the right-wing Carlists.[11] The reformist credibility of the government had reached its lowest level.

Only the King remained. In April Juan Carlos met several Christian Democrat leaders, something Arias had never done. Juan

Carlos seemed determined to give new impetus to reform. He went to Washington in June, accompanied by Areilza. His address to the American Congress was a resounding personal success and a considerable reinforcement for his reformist strategy.

In June the immobilists of the bunker fought their last battle. On 9 June the Cortes passed the new Law of Political Association (which recognised political parties) after an impressive parliamentary performance by the Minister of the Movement, Adolfo Suárez; but the Cortes rejected the reform of the articles of the Penal Code which penalised party activities. The contradiction was a scandal. Reform had suffered a deadly blow. A few days afterwards, the National Council of the Movement decided against the constitutional reform announced by Arias on 28 April.

As usual the pretext for the reaction of the Cortes had been a new terrorist action by ETA: the assassination of the local chief of the Movement at Basauri (Biscay), which followed other recent killings by the same organisation.[12] But the real reason was that the Francoist right was not prepared to accept any reform of the regime of 18 July. Arias made the mistake of believing that he would be able to secure the bunker's support for a reform which respected a substantial part of Franco's legacy. This was the strategy which best suited his personal convictions. The reaction of the Cortes showed, however, that concessions would not satisfy the bunker. His policy bankrupt, Arias resigned on 1 July. The King, only too willing to have a prime minister closer to his views, accepted his resignation.

The 'decomposition of Francoism' (in Ricardo de la Cierva's words) in the six months which followed Franco's death was evident; it seemed as if most Spaniards had thrust him from their memories.[13] Despite the ruthless methods used by the police to maintain public order, despite the arrests of opposition leaders, Spain enjoyed in June 1976 a level of political freedom far greater than anything known between 1939 and 1975. Political parties held open meetings and congresses; demonstrations were authorised; the press had almost total freedom. Yet the opposition felt it was living under some extension of Francoism: suddenly a meeting would be banned by a zealous civil governor, or a newspaper censored. It was a curious situation: no Spanish paper could reprint the 'interview' with the King in *Newsweek*. Yet the review itself was on sale in Spain and its contents known to everyone interested in politics.

This precarious liberty was enjoyed when little progress had been made towards constitutional reform. The Cortes 'elected' in 1971 remained in office. The Movement, the official syndicates, retained their powers intact. The Council of the Realm, the Council of the State, continued to be Francoist strongholds. Constitutional reform had stuck since 9 June. The way to reform through the Cortes seemed blocked. When Arias resigned, there seemed to be no alternative but the democratic rupture which threatened to plunge Spain into an incalculable political future.[14]

(b)
The success of the Suárez reform

Almost the entire Spanish political class thought the King would appoint José Ma. de Areilza, Arias' Minister of Foreign Affairs, as the new Prime Minister. After Fraga's reformist image had crumbled as Minister of the Interior, Areilza appeared as the only politician with enough prestige to carry out a programme of reform with the consent of both the democratic opposition and moderate Francoists. He had experience, an aristocratic demeanour (an engineer, he had married a title) and an international reputation. Areilza seemed the incarnation of the 'civilised right', the man who could restore a constitutional and parliamentary monarchy as Cánovas had done one hundred years earlier.

However, it was Areilza himself who had to inform the journalists, who had gathered in his home waiting for the latest news, that the new President of the Government was Adolfo Suárez, the former Minister of the Movement. The Council of the Realm had apparently sent a *terna* (a list of three names from which the King had to choose one) made up of López Bravo, Silva Muñoz — both, it will be remembered, former ministers under Franco — and Suárez. A young, handsome man of 43, he was a former civil governor and director of the Spanish television, and still the president of UDPE, the Gaullist-inspired political association committed to *continuismo* in its more moderate form.

The nomination of Suárez was both a great surprise and a great disappointment. Some saw it as the return of *carrerismo*, the return of the ideas and the men loyal to Carrero Blanco; others, as a manoeuvre of the ACNP — the fifty children of the ten new ministers seemed to journalists a proof of their Catholicism — and the big banks with which many of Suárez' men were connected. His appointment appeared, in Ricardo de la Cierva's words, 'a mistake, a formidable mistake'. Eleven months later, however, Adolfo Suárez called the first general election held in Spain since 1936.[15] It was this well-groomed member of the Francoist political elite, whose impeccable suits and ties, in an era when to appear in casual clothes seemed an indication of democratic sentiment, who was to restore democracy in Spain.

Seen in perspective, what the first Suárez government achieved seems extraordinary. In November 1976 the Francoist Cortes approved a Law of Political Reform which created a bicameral system based on universal suffrage. On 15 December the reform achieved overwhelming support in a national referendum. On 30 July 1976 the government granted a partial amnesty which freed about 400 political prisoners and the Tribunal of Public Order was suppressed soon afterwards. In September Catalonia was allowed to celebrate her national day and, in January 1977, the Basque flag was legalised. Forty years of rigid centralism seemed buried. In February a new Law of Political Association legalised political parties. On 9 April 1977 the Communist party was legalised by decree. Only a few days before, the government had dismantled the Movement. In March the syndicates, the other great Francoist institution, disappeared after the Cortes had passed new legislation re-establishing the free trade unions destroyed in 1936. On 11 March a new amnesty was granted. In May 1977 the main leaders of ETA, some of them with death sentences for terrorism, were released from prison and expelled from Spain. Finally, in the elections of June 1977 the party Suárez led, the Union for the Democratic Centre (UCD), emerged as the strongest party.

It was a formidable record of success and to his admirers Suárez appeared to have saved Spain from the political chaos that bedevilled her neighbour, Portugal. This success, however, was often as much the result of fortunate circumstance as the outcome of a well-planned strategy. There were problems which the government either did not understand or solved in a way which was counter-productive for the process of reform to which the government and the King were committed. Such was the case in both the Basque question and the problem of public order.

Over the Basque problem the government was led by events, giving in to mass pressure. Thus it yielded to the two most immediate aspirations of the Basques: the legalisation of the Basque flag (invented in 1889 by Sabino Arana, the father of Basque nationalism) and an amnesty. But it yielded after many delays and apparent contradictions; piecemeal concession, far from appeasing the Basques, fuelled popular discontent and maintained an explosive climate where violence could prosper. In the summer of 1976, the Basque country was again the scene of huge demonstrations and violent clashes: two people were killed and a general strike was declared throughout the area in September. Later, in January 1977, the government faced a rebellion of Basque mayors over delays in legalising the Basque flag. In May six people were killed in clashes with the police in a highly tense 'pro-amnesty week'. The government was forced to grant a new amnesty under the threat of boycott of the June elections in the Basque provinces.

Fraga had declared that to fly the Basque flag on public buildings 'they'll have to trample on my dead body': yet to the opposition the government seemed to be pursuing in the Basque case a policy of public order which was not substantially different from that of Fraga himself. This was the rule everywhere. The right of assembly continued to be arbitrarily regulated by civil governors.* There was no substantial reform of the police forces to adapt them to the new political atmosphere. The police, trained in authoritarianism and with no clear orders from the government, continued to use harsh methods, including the beating up of suspects which could no longer be kept out of the press.†

The government argued that the stability of democracy demanded an energetic defence of public order in a country where forty years of partisan propaganda had identified democracy with chaos. It believed this was the only answer to those who made the government weakness responsible for the deterioration of law and order allegedly reflected in street demonstrations, strikes, terrorism and political kidnappings.[16] In this the government miscalculated. Conservative opinion continued to blame 'democracy' for the deterioration of order: they saw every new amnesty as a further capitulation. The left protested at what it saw as the government's calculated indifference to police brutality.

The government, therefore, might have spared itself difficulties with a more coherent policy of public order. An early, full amnesty in the Basque country might have deprived ETA terrorists of most of their case and of the public support they continued to enjoy. A reform of the police was necessary for a non-authoritarian policy of law and order. The government feared that this might alienate the police forces and leave it at the mercy of extremists. The result was that police actions eroded the democratic credibility of the government without building a compensating image of authority and strength.

To many, the worst shortcoming of the Suárez government was its failure to face up to the serious economic situation. Politics had an almost obsessional priority. The government, fearing their

---

*For instance, the Civil Governor of Barcelona banned a demonstration on 23 October to commemorate the execution of Luis Companys, the President of the Catalan Generalidad during the Second Republic.

†A much publicised beating up was of a woman member of the Union of Technicians and Workers (UTT) in Tolosa. Photographs of her bruises appeared in magazines (cf. *Ya*, 1 May 1976).

impact on an electorate about to vote for the first time, refused to implement the austerity measures the Spanish economy urgently needed. The economic situation continued, therefore, to deteriorate in 1976 and 1977. The stock exchange fell dramatically. Investment ceased. Inflation ran at almost 30 per cent; unemployment reached unprecedented levels.[17] All this, as we have seen, was in large part a Spanish edition of the world crisis triggered off in 1974. Yet the government's passivity exasperated economists, entrepreneurs and workers alike.

All these circumstances qualified the success of Suárez. But even so, not even his enemies could dismiss him as a lucky opportunist equipped with personal and political charm. If, as prime minister in a 'pre-democratic' situation, he had most of the cards in his hands, he played them well. The key to his success lay in his political instinct; perhaps his period in television had given him sensitive antennae. He realised that a majority wanted an effective but peaceful evolution towards democracy, a smooth transition without uncertainties and political disorder. Suárez grasped the King's determination to give democratic legitimacy to his monarchy. He needed no special insight to see that a 'continuist' reform like that attempted by Arias would never be accepted either by the democratic opposition or by Western Europe. He also sensed the weakness of the opposition and, above all, its impotence to offer any alternative to the monarchy of Juan Carlos.

Suárez was not alone. He always had the King's support. In his many visits abroad, in his numerous meetings with Western leaders, Juan Carlos showed his determination to restore democracy. His role was crucial in winning the support of the army for a new political system, or at least in securing its neutrality. In the worst moments of the transition, Juan Carlos made the symbolic gesture — a speech, a meeting with senior officers — to appease the military. He faced the would-be 'putschists' in his army with an insurmountable dilemma: any attempt against democracy would be an attempt against the King, Chief of the Armed Forces and the symbol of the unity of the state.*

*Juan Carlos has always cultivated his relations with the army. He graduated in the three services — the navy, the infantry, the air force. His first act as king was his unexpected flight to the Sahara in 1975 to express his support for the army still stationed there. He always follows military manoeuvres with knowledgable enthusiasm. Like the founder of the constitutional monarchy, Alfonso XII, he is a soldier king. In 1976–7 Juan Carlos visited Colombia, Venezuela, France, Italy, Germany and the USA. He received in Madrid President Eanes of Portugal, Vice-President Mondale and Cyrus Vance of the USA, Willi Brandt and many others. All this was in sharp contrast to Franco's isolation.

Suárez could also count on Fernández Miranda, the President of the Cortes. 'It would be absurd,' the President argued 'that Spanish society, in spite of the changes that have taken place within it, should continue for ever to wear the juridical clothes of the Fundamental Laws.' The President's skills proved to be a decisive factor in bringing the Francoist Cortes to commit political hara-kiri by passing the Law of Political Reform in November 1976. He simplified both the text of the Law and the parliamentary procedures. He ignored the Mixed Commission devised by Arias and brought the Law to a full session of the Cortes. The Cortes was left with no alternative but to approve the reform or to reject it, thus opening a serious constitutional crisis. The Cortes refused to take such a responsibility. It could not ignore the fact that a majority of the Spanish people, the King, the church and the democratic world favoured reform. The government used this patent reality to put pressure on the deputies.

Though there were frequent alarmist rumours of an army coup, Suárez kept the army behind his reformist programme. On 8 September 1976 he held a meeting with senior army officers where he explained his plans for political reform and asked for their 'patriotic support'. The meeting was a skilful political move. The army gave Suárez the green light for his reform, a formidable reinforcement which allowed the government to overcome its first serious internal crisis: the resignation of Vice-President General Díaz de Mendívil who apparently opposed the legalisation of the Communist unions. Suárez replaced him with General Gutiérrez Mellado, a reformist and a liberal whose presence in the government was to be a guarantee to the army, a great impulse to democratic reform and a severe blow to the right's wild hopes of an army coup.*

Suárez, therefore, went to the Cortes with every trump in his

*See *Triunfo* (2 October 1976), which contains the reactions of the daily press to the Díaz de Mendívil crisis and the appointment of Gutiérrez Mellado. The crisis bears out our interpretation of the political theory of the army (see above, p. 5). The official communiqué on the 8 September meeting ran: 'No specific political option was considered because our Armed Forces,. permanent guarantee of the values of the fatherland in the eyes of the people from whom they proceed and whom they serve, feel a profound respect for whatever option which can be contained in the institutional order and its legitimate development', i.e. *provided* the new democracy was instituted via the Cortes the army would accept the 'general will'. *This meant the army vetoed the democratic break* – and this members of the opposition knew perfectly well. *El Alcazar*, the organ of the unreconstructed Francoist right, supported Díaz de Mendívil and Iniesta: they were 'as soldiers and Spaniards' faithful to the constitutional role of the army as guardian of Francoist legality when the government sought to subvert the constitution by 'substituting the State by another State'. (see Iniesta's letter in *Blanco y Negro*, 9 October 1976.)

hand. The Law of Political Reform was discussed on 18 November 1976. Miguel Primo de Rivera, the nephew of the founder of the Falange and a member of the *ad hoc* reporting committee, was the first to speak in its support. After two days of cliff-hanging negotiations in the bars and corridors of the Cortes the Law was passed by an overwhelming majority: 425 votes in favour, 59 against and 13 abstentions. The government had made only minor concessions to the right: there would be no proportional representation in the Senate elections — a provision the right believed would strengthen its position in the second Chamber. It would be hard to maintain that, under the new law, Spain would be a qualified democracy, a 'democracy with adjectives'. Francoism was dead. The old Falangist lion Girón had no doubts: the Law gave victory on a plate to the enemies of the Civil War. In spite of trimmings — for instance, royal nomination of Senators — the Law of Political Reform converted Spain into a democracy based on universal suffrage.

Suárez was convinced that the democratic opposition would have no alternative but to accept his 'reform from above', legitimised by the legal processes of the Francoist Constitution. To gain this acceptance he adopted tactics in his dealings with the opposition which stood in sharp contrast to those of his predecessor. Arias had attempted a pact with Francoism and failed. Suárez, instead, tried to reach a general consensus, to isolate the bunker and to open a dialogue with the democratic opposition, totally ignored by Arias. A month after his appointment, Suárez met Felipe González, the leader of the Socialist party (PSOE). Later he met the other leaders of the opposition; his Minister of Labour Relations, De la Mata, met the leaders of the illegal unions.[18]

These were not empty gestures. Suárez had realised that a democratic reform would not be possible if rejected by the democratic opposition. His policy of attraction bore fruit. The notion of a 'democratic break', that is, a democratic constitution imposed against the will of the government, became increasingly a less plausible tactic, and the 'negotiated break', a new settlement negotiated between government and opposition, increasingly attractive.

On 23 October the opposition had formally united in a single organisation: the Platform of Democratic Organisations which combined the Democratic Co-ordination, the Assembly of Catalonia and a number of regional parties.* Its programme was still the 'democratic break': the 'immediate formation of a government

---

*This new platform is not to be confused with the Platform of Democratic Co-ordination formed by the Socialists and moderate parties in the summer of 1975 and which had already united with the Democratic Junta in the Democratic Co-ordination.

of democratic consensus', a provisional government to preside over 'a constituent process' which implied the questioning of the monarchy as the form of government; the introduction of full democratic freedoms; the legislation of all parties; full amnesty for political prisoners; elections to a constituent assembly; the abolition of the remaining institutions of Francoism and the repeal of its legislation.[19]

What were the chances of forcing this programme on the government? Firstly, the formal 'unity' of the opposition was a misleading indication of its strength and its capacity to resist an accommodation with Suárez. Although only a minority of parties refused to join the new organisation, their absence damaged its credibility.* Moreover the presence of the more moderate parties was nominal.† Despite their formal adherence, Liberals, Christian Democrats and Social Democrats pursued independent lines. The Platform's notion of a 'democratic break' seemed an increasingly unreal strategy to the Christian Democrats – on paper still the strongest group in the opposition; the idea of negotiations between the government and the opposition appeared as increasingly attractive.** It was, apparently, Gil Robles who suggested the idea of negotiations with the government conducted by a 'committee of personalities' representing the main forces of the opposition.

The attitude of the more moderate forces within the opposition was decisive. The moderates did not regard negotiation as capitulation, and on 27 November a new 'summit' of the opposition accepted the Christian Democrats' view. The maximalist demands of the old Platform (provisional government, a constituent process) were dropped. Soon afterwards, a negotiating commission was formed with representatives of the five big parties (Liberals, Social Democrats, Christian Democrats, Socialists and Communists) together with the illegal unions and members of the Catalan, Basque and Galician oppositions.[20]

A majority of the opposition was by now convinced that Suárez' plans for reform could amount to a 'liquidation of Francoism', as the Socialist leader, Felipe González, told a Madrid newspaper in

---

*Neither the Christian Democrat parties led by Gil Robles and Álvarez de Miranda nor the liberal groups (with the exception of the Popular Democratic Party of Sr Camuñas) had joined the Platform.

†The Christian Democrat Democratic Left of Ruiz Giménez and the Social Democratic Union of Spain (USDE) had expressed many reservations towards the Platform's programme which they had signed.

**Ruiz Giménez was ready to accept a reshuffle of the cabinet by the incorporation of a few personalities with unsullied democratic credentials. Since Ruiz Giménez had himself served Franco as a minister, this presumably meant a politician whose opposition to Franco had been public for, let us say, a decade or so. See interview in *Blanco y Negro* (13 November 1976).

November 1976.[21] They doubted their own strength. A general strike called by the three main unions on 12 November was a relative failure.[22] Confronted with the possibility that the government might call the opposition's bluff and expose their weaknesses by granting a democratic reform and calling a general election, the moderate opposition and the Socialists thought it convenient to sever their links with the radical left. Condemnation of Suárez' reform would be a mistake even if it meant the end of the Platform and a precarious unity. In November and December 1976 it seemed evident that Liberals, Christian Democrats and Social Democrats would take part in the elections, provided the government could guarantee 'clean' elections with a fair deal over propaganda – especially the use of television, which all parties saw as a central issue.

This was also the position of the Socialists, both the small Popular Socialist Party (PSP) of Professor Tierno Galván and the rapidly growing Spanish Socialist Workers' Party (PSOE) led by Felipe González, which now claimed 75,000 members. The PSOE agreed to participate in the elections at a congress held in December 1976. The first public congress of the party in forty years, it took place in a smart four-star Madrid hotel with police protection, although the party was still technically illegal. The congress, with Willi Brandt (whose party was pouring money into the PSOE) on the platform and 350 journalists in the hall, resolved that the PSOE would not boycott the elections if all the preconditions demanded by the Platform of Democratic Organisations were met; but, on the other hand, the PSOE offered a 'constitutional compromise' which suggested that the Socialists were prepared to go to the polls even if not all parties had been legalised. González openly recognised that the Prime Minister's moves had thrown the opposition into 'a profound crisis' by dividing it and 'putting it in the ghetto'. But he told his intimates 'at times it's most revolutionary to be moderate' and stamped on the proposition of the Madrid Socialists to embody the dictatorship of the proletariat in the party programme.[23]

Negotiation with the government now appeared as the only path to democracy. Only one obstacle remained: the 'Communist question'. The Communists joined in the opposition's negotiating commission on its formation. But neither Suárez nor the other parties of the opposition were free of misapprehensions. Suárez had indicated that he would not negotiate with the Communists. The moderate opposition was not fully prepared to risk the whole process of democratisation for the sake of the Communists: some speculated with the idea of dropping the Communists from the negotiating commission, leaving them to contest the elections as 'independents', that is, not as a fully legalised party.

This left the Communists with no alternative but to force events. Santiago Carrillo appeared in Madrid on 10 December. This was a public challenge since his party was still illegal. Carrillo was arrested, but only for a few days. As in the case of other parties, the Suárez government was forced to recognise the *de facto* existence of the Communist party, even if legalisation had still to wait for several months. The repression of the Communists would have completely destroyed the democratic credentials of the government and made the Suárez reform programme unacceptable to the democratic opposition. However much the opposition may have cursed the Communists in private, they could not consent to their persecution in public.

The Communists made a sacrifice in their turn. They agreed not to be part of the delegation which would start the negotiations with the government. On 23 December Suárez met the representatives of the opposition, the Socialist Tierno Galván and the Catalan leader Jordi Pujol. The *ruptura* (the democratic break), the invention of the Communists and the historical dream of the anti-Francoist resistance, seemed definitively abandoned.[24]

Suárez entered into his negotiations with the opposition from a position of great strength. On 15 December 1976 the government's political reform was overwhelmingly approved in a referendum: 77.4 per cent of the electorate went to the polls; 94.2 per cent voted for the government, 2.6 per cent against; 22.6 per cent abstained. Yet a majority of the opposition had recommended abstention. This was a serious mistake. The referendum was a victory for the government in spite of the opposition's excuse that the result had been manufactured by the government's total control of television and radio and an expensive publicity campaign. So decisive a victory gave Suárez a powerful bargaining position.[25]

The negotiations between the commission which represented the government and the 'personalities' of the opposition took place in the first months of 1977. Despite difficulties and differences, a series of agreements was reached. In February the legalisation of political parties began. Under the new system, the parties had only to request registration, after submitting their statutes to the Ministry of the Interior. The Supreme Court would resolve controversial cases. In March the amnesty was extended.

The problem was, obviously, the legalisation of the Communist party. The democratic opposition could not accept its exclusion from political life − indeed they argued that the party's emergence from the mystery of clandestinity into the electoral field would expose its relative weakness. Since the end of the Civil War the suppression of 'Marxism' had been presented in the propaganda of the regime as its *raison d'être* and the legalisation of the PCE was still bitterly opposed by former reformists like Fraga. The Supreme Court, a stronghold of staunch Francoists, refused to pronounce on the case. The whole process of reform was in jeopardy and the political atmosphere at its tensest since July 1976. Suárez saved the day with a decree legalising the PCE on 9 April. This was a bold political move. It led to the most serious crisis in the process of transition from dictatorship to democracy.

Suárez had apparently promised the military at the meeting in September 1976 that the Communists would not be legalised, or at least that he would take no major political decision without consulting the army. His latest decision was known only to a few members of the cabinet. The Minister for the Navy, a loyal Francoist, resigned in protest. A few days later, the army leaders publicly expressed their dissatisfaction with the government's measure; they accepted it only out of 'patriotism', not out of obedience to the government. In an atmosphere reminiscent of the *ancien régime*, there were rumours that Spain had been on the verge of a military coup. If so, the King and Vice-President Gutiérrez Mellado must have played a substantial role in the appeasement of the military. Credit should also be given to the Communists themselves. They adopted the national flag and accepted the monarchy, in spite of their theoretical republicanism. Their moderation was decisive for the normalisation of the political situation.[26]

The crisis resolved, the commission of government and opposition agreed on an electoral law. The German model of proportional representation (the D'Hont system) was adopted, a system which favours a two-party structure. The government promised to dismantle the Movement and to give all parties equal access to television during the election campaign. The state would finance the elections; parties were entitled to refunds in proportion to their respective number of seats and votes.[27]

The road to the elections, therefore, seemed free from obstacles. Only in the Basque country were the elections in danger after serious clashes between police and demonstrators in May 1977. A further amnesty solved the question. Electoral participation in the Basque country was to be above the national average.

With the general election of 15 June 1977, the process of reform was completed. Suárez had achieved what many had thought an impossible task: the restoration of democracy through a gradual process and using the legal instruments inherited from Francoism. The opposition's acceptance of negotiation had played a crucial part. It had eluded a confrontation with the government by renouncing some of its most cherished demands: 'democratic rupture', a provisional government, and a referendum on the issue monarchy versus republic. It was not true that the opposition had no alternative. It could have rejected Suárez' reforms and tried to mobilise public opinion against them as some parties on the left wanted. For the opposition, if it did not hold the trump cards, had nevertheless a strong hand: it could have put stronger pressure on Suárez, since the government could hardly have claimed democratic legitimacy for its reforms without the consent of the democratic forces.

It is vain to speculate what might have happened. The opposition, including the Communists, chose negotiation and it paid a high price; but in so doing it made a splendid contribution to the restoration of democracy after forty years of dictatorship.

(c)
The 1977 elections

On 15 June 1977 the first free elections for forty years were held in Spain. The month-long electoral campaign was fought with every publicity device. There were mass meetings (4,000 hours per day) on a scale and with attendances inconceivable in Britain. All over Spain walls were plastered with political posters and the streets littered with handbills. Most parties approached the elections on radio and television as if launching a commercial product. Parties had their radio ditties like those advertising cornflakes or soap. Images counted more than party programmes.

Eighteen million people voted, 79.24 per cent of the electorate. Elections were peaceful, if confused. In Vallecas, a working-class district in Madrid, voting papers arrived two hours late. Long, patient queues stood outside the polling stations. Inside, the rooms were crammed with gossiping groups. The computerised system for the polling of the votes failed. The Minister of the Interior had promised final results at 8 a.m. on 16 June. It was several months before he was able to announce them.*

The elections were a triumph for moderation *and* for the desire for change. The electorate rejected Francoism. The extreme right, the 18 July National Alliance, polled less than 0.5 per cent of the popular vote. The neo-Francoist right − Popular Alliance (AP), a coalition of former Franco ministers led by Fraga Iribarne who

*But results with a 98 per cent accuracy were known in two days. See *Informaciones* (26 May 1977) for the parties' electoral programmes; *El País* (15 June 1977) for the election campaign; and R. Carr, 'Euphoria in Spain', *Spectator* (25 June 1977).

campaigned on anti-Communism and 'law and order' threatened by a government which set out to cure a 'cancer with aspirin' – won only 16 seats in a Congress of 350. It had based its electoral strategies on the supposed existence of what was called 'sociological Francoism', composed of those who had prospered in the past and were resistant to radical change. The opposition feared the forces of 'sociological Francoism'. It turned out to be a construct of sociologically minded journalists. AP polled a mere 8 per cent of the votes, even less than the Communists. Two months before the election, opinion polls gave AP around 20 per cent of the vote.*

The elections were also a failure as far as the Communists and the extreme left were concerned. The restrained Eurocommunism of Santiago Carrillo paid fewer electoral dividends than expected. The PCE won twenty seats, most of them in Catalonia, and polled a mere 9 per cent of the vote. Carrillo explained this relative failure by the fears created by Franco's forty years of exploitation of the Communist bogey. More probably, when all seemed touched by the glamour of youth, the party, like its leader, looked old and bound to the past.

The extreme left gained two seats, one in each Chamber and both in the Basque country, where left-wing nationalism made political capital out of seven years of violence and repression. But even in the Basque country the moderates won: of the 26 seats in Congress, the PSOE won 9, the PNV 8, and the Prime Minister's UCD 7. It was in Barcelona that the left scored its biggest triumph with the Socialists gaining 11 seats and the Communists 9, out of a total of 33.

The real winners were the Suárez coalition (UCD) and the Socialist party (PSOE) with 34.3 and 28.5 per cent of the vote respectively. The result was a personal success for the leaders of both parties, Adolfo Suárez and Felipe González. Their stylish, glamorous images seemed the symbol of the new Spain beside the tired appearance of the old men of politics like Ruiz Giménez, Gil Robles or Carrillo.[28]

The Socialist success was almost a political miracle. Three years before, the PSOE was a mere skeleton organisation. Foreign help, particularly from the German SPD, helped considerably in the Socialist comeback. Collective memory also played a part: the PSOE dated from 1879, it was the party of the venerated figures of the Spanish labour movement. But credit should be given mainly to the new, young leadership which took over control of the party

---

*AP was formed in the summer of 1976. Francoists joined in, despite their differences in the past. The disappointment of AP with the results was immediately apparent. Fraga did not arrive, as scheduled, to meet foreign journalists.

after 1972 from the exiles. The new PSOE filled a vacuum in the Spanish opposition. As a young and exciting party, it provided an alternative to both the respectability of the moderate opposition and to the 'ideological sclerosis' of the Communist party. The combination of a maximalist programme and pragmatic policies was a new edition of the party's traditional combination of revolutionary rhetoric on the platform and caution in practice. It allowed the Socialists to appeal to different sectors of the electorate. The PSOE won seats in forty-seven out of the fifty Spanish provinces.[29] González, in a lightning campaign, had campaigned as a democrat − 'A Vote for Socialism is a vote for Liberty' was the party's campaign slogan − carefully concealing what *El País* called the party's 'crisis of identity' caused by the presence in the party of both Marxists and reformist Social Democrats.

All efforts to unite the PSOE with Tierno Galván's PSP had failed. González, conscious of his growing strength, was unwilling to make any concessions to what appeared to the PSOE as a splinter party of intellectuals, a *tertulia* of notables with good connections with French journalists but no roots in the working class. Tierno and his group should have worked within the PSOE; the Socialists of the PSOE regarded their support of the Workers' Commissions as a blow below the belt delivered at the Socialist UGT. Tierno had been bamboozled by the Communist appeals for unity;[30] he should now join the PSOE unconditionally, since the ineffective exile leaders now fighting the old battles as a separate party in a rump called the 'Historic PSOE' had been replaced by a new, dynamic leadership. This he would not do and his party of respectable, non-revolutionary Marxists fought alone. His six seats were a tribute to his fine record as a consistent opponent of Francoism and to the curious prestige enjoyed by professors in Spain.*

The victory of UCD, the centrist coalition led by Suárez, surprised no one and had been confidently predicted by pollsters. In part a reflection of the enormous political prestige of Suárez himself, it proved that Spain was socially and economically ripe for a centre party. This had been one of the main arguments of the *aperturistas* in the last years of Francoism. Fraga was the father of the idea of 'centrism'; Areilza, the advocate of the 'civilised right'. Similar views were a commonplace among the democratic opposition. A government of the centre, but a liberal, democratic centre

---

*R. C. found that many whose first preference was for UCD or PSOE supported Tierno as a second choice. When a Communist taxi driver was asked why he would vote thus, he replied, 'Because he is a professor'. No English voter would vote for a professor as such − rightly.

under the hegemony of Christian Democracy, would be not only the most desirable but even the most likely solution to lead Spain from Francoism. Ruiz Giménez, Gil Robles, Álvarez de Miranda and other Christian Democrat leaders had once been regarded, by journalists and political scientists alike, as the De Gasperis of the future Spanish democracy.

If it was no surprise that a centre party emerged as the strongest party, what no one anticipated was that the winning coalition would be led not by Christian Democrats but by a politician with a Francoist past.

The Christian Democrats were literally smashed in the elections. Even Ruiz Giménez, the founder of *Cuadernos para el Diálogo*, failed to get a seat in the new parliament. 'The space' of the centre – political 'space' was one of the many pseudo-scientific neologisms of Spanish political journalism – had been occupied by UCD, the party of reform which was at the same time the party of government.

The emergence of UCD as the main party of the centre was partly the result of the success of reform and the failure of a 'democratic rupture'; partly the result of the division of the moderate opposition and a propensity for political in-fighting between the representatives of the different strands within it.

The moderate opposition failed to find a single answer to the choice between reform and rupture. Ruiz Giménez had been closer to the latter and his party, the ID (Democratic Left), had joined the Democratic Co-ordination in 1976 together with Socialists, Communists and the radical left. This damaged his political respectability on the right and put serious difficulties in the way of the creation of a single Christian Democrat party. A group led by Alvarez de Miranda split from ID in disagreement with the left-wing deviationism of its leader; by joining the UCD it avoided electoral annihilation.

Gil Robles' Popular Democratic Federation refused to join any of the different unitary organisms of the opposition. Gil Robles consistently advocated the idea of a united, independent Christian Democratic federation. Personal rivalries – and Gil Robles, at 78 the doyen of Spanish politicians, is a difficult, testy man – and fundamental differences on political strategy prevented it. Gil Robles himself stubbornly rejected co-operation with Christian Democrats who had served under Franco. Álvarez de Miranda thought it necessary to bridge the gaps between all the moderate parties, notwithstanding the political past of their leaders. He believed that this would pull 'sociological Francoism' away from AP and towards the democratic parties.

The unification of Christian Democracy proved impossible, and on the eve of the elections the Christian Democrat field looked like a labyrinth. Ruiz Giménez was prepared to join Suárez at the eleventh hour, as Álvarez de Miranda had already done. Gil Robles refused. He led Ruiz Giménez to an overwhelming electoral defeat.[31]

It was ironic that Ruiz Giménez himself had suggested the idea of a 'democratic centre'. But the initiative to form a 'democratic centre' with a liberal reformist programme had different origins.

The idea that was finally to crystallise in the UCD gained impulse in November 1976 with the creation of the Popular Party, a self-proclaimed liberal, Christian, democratic party launched by old *aperturistas* like Areilza, Pío Cabanillas and the *tácitos*. The PP saw itself as the catalyst of a great federation of the centre which would prevent the division of Spain into two antagonistic blocs. The idea seemed highly plausible. The presence of the *tácitos* made the government's support for the new party likely. The *tácitos* had been, as we saw, among the ablest advocates of the thesis of constitutional reform from within Francoist legality. Together with their close relatives from the UDE (Spanish Democratic Union), the *tácitos* formed the most prominent group of reformists in the Suárez government.*

It was the 'democratic centre' of the Popular Party that was the embryo of the future Union of the Democratic Centre. In January 1977 the Popular Party and UDE fused in the Democratic Centre to which the Popular Christian Democratic Party of Álvarez de Miranda and several small liberal groups immediately adhered. Soon afterwards, the Social Democrats of Fernández Ordoñez, the former president of INI and a member of the negotiating team of the opposition, joined the coalition.

The refusal of the Christian Democrats to become part of the nascent centre coalition was soon made known. On 24 January Gil Robles and Ruiz Giménez announced that the so-called 'Christian-Democratic Team of the Spanish State' would not adhere to the Democratic Centre. They would fight the elections on an exclusively Christian Democratic platform.† Gil Robles refused to

---

*Two *tácitos*, Oreja and Lavilla, were respectively ministers of Foreign Affairs and Justice. The ministers Osorio, De la Mata, Carriles and Reguera were members of UDE. Both groups were on close political and personal terms. It was argued that without Osorio's help Suárez could not have formed a government in July 1976. For *tácitos*, see above, pp. 200*ff*.

†The Christian Democratic Team (EDCEE) was formed by Gil Robles' Democratic Popular Federation, Ruiz Giménez's Democratic Left, the Basque national party (PNV) and the small Christian Democrat parties of Catalonia and Valencia.

co-operate with what he called 'reformed neo-francoism' as did the liberals led by another prominent figure of the democratic opposition, Joaquin Satrústegui.

The attitude of the Christian Democrats threatened to split the vote of the centre in the elections to the advantage of both Fraga's Popular Alliance and the left, thus opening up the prospect of polarised politics in post-Francoist Spain. It was also evident that only the support of Suárez could *guarantee* the victory of the centre. After a period of hesitation and the customary outpouring of political speculation, Suárez joined the Democratic Centre in March 1977. The integration of Suárez and 'his men' in the Democratic Centre implied its reorganisation. Areilza, the one man who could compete with Suárez for the leadership of the new Democratic Centre, was 'defenestrated'. The Minister of Public Works, Leopoldo Calvo Sotelo, left the government to take charge of the party.

On 3 May the new Union of the Democratic Centre (UCD) was officially baptised with the addition of twelve new parties. The UCD electoral lists revealed, however, the preponderent influence of the government in the coalition. There was a remarkable abundance among the prospective candidates of the 'men of Suárez' – third generation Falangists, most of them – who had not taken part in the early stages of the gestation of the Democratic Centre.

This caused internal frictions in UCD. But the incorporation of Suárez had the consent of a majority of members of the coalition. The presence of sincere liberals and democrats such as Álvarez de Miranda, Garrigues, Camuñas and Fernández Ordoñez gave UCD the democratic legitimacy which the 'blue' past of Suárez lacked. On his side the leader of the government brought the formidable prestige of his achievements in power.[32] On the final round of television performances he spoke with an authority no other party leader could match.

More than 6 million people voted for Suárez and UCD. Yet the party he had joined at the last moment and led to victory would not have an overall majority in the new democratic Cortes. Nor was it a modern mass party but an electoral coalition of heterogeneous groups, a fiction held together by the prestige of its leader, with neither a common programme nor a unitary organisation. The character of this coalition was well reflected in its election night party in a smart Madrid hotel: the bourgeoisie out in strength and smart clothes, presided over by a busty blonde.

(d)
The new parliamentary democracy

Spain came out of the elections with two large parties and in an atmosphere of widespread democratic consensus, an ideal combination for the stability of the new democracy. The monarchy of Juan Carlos seemed firmly established. His father, Don Juan of Borbon, had renounced his rights to the throne one month before the elections. No significant party advocated a republic, with the exception of the radical sectors of the PSOE. Even the Communists accepted the monarchy as the regime chosen by the Spanish people.

After the elections, Santiago Carrillo, the Communist leader, asked for a 'government of national concentration' to preside over the constituent period. The Socialists preferred to remain in opposition, as a future alternative government. Suárez formed a UCD government, aware that, without a parliamentary majority, he would be forced to make concessions. It was this minority government of electoral coalition rather than a disciplined party that must push through a new constitution, give some answer to the demand for regional autonomy, decide on where and how the municipal corporations should be democratically elected, 'solve' a severe economic crisis – and all this while terrorism and conflicts of public order persisted – to 'destabilise' democracy.[33]

Two problems needed urgent attention. The government must tackle the economic crisis if galloping inflation, rising unemployment and a growing trade deficit were not to discredit democracy. The government linked its future to the economic plan of the new Vice-President for Economic Affairs, Professor Fuentes Quintana. On 12 July the peseta was devalued. In August the new Minister of Finance, the social democrat Fernández Ordóñez, brought before parliament a Tax Law which increased direct taxation and attempted to stop the tax evasion so characteristic of Francoism.

The government knew, however, that this was not enough. No lasting solution to the economic crisis was possible without an austerity programme which would impose severe sacrifices on Spanish society. For both national and party reasons, Suárez must bring all parties together behind an economic programme of national recovery.

This is what was achieved in the so-called 'Moncloa Pact' signed in October 1977. The opposition agreed to a 20 per cent wage ceiling in 1978, severe credit restrictions, reductions in public expenditure and further tax increases; in exchange, the government promised structural reforms in the economic system and a number of political concessions: adultery would cease to be a crime and the public sale of contraceptives allowed; there would be a less restrictive regulation of the rights of assembly and demonstration, a reorganisation of police forces, and changes in the criminal law.[34]

The second most pressing problem was the need to find a provisional solution to the problem of regional autonomy before it could be definitely settled in the Constitution. As in the 1930s, the issue was particularly acute in Catalonia and the Basque country. In both regions, the elections had seen the victory of either nationalist parties or left-wing groups committed to autonomy.

In Catalonia, Suárez was skilled and lucky enough to secure the co-operation of Josep Tarradellas, the 78-year-old exiled president of the *Generalitat* (the Catalan self-government under the Autonomy Statute of 1932). An opportunist and skilled politician with a Gaullist *folie de grandeur*, Tarradellas negotiated with Suárez the formal reinstallation of the *Generalitat*, ignoring the recently elected Catalan parliamentarians who had formed themselves into an assembly and who might seem to constitute a more legitimate representation of Catalan democracy than the 'historic' claim of Tarradellas, like Gil Robles a relic of the Second Republic. Tarradellas returned in triumph to Barcelona on 23 October 1977 after thirty-eight years in exile. Catalan autonomy, he said, had cost 'neither a peseta nor a life'. But it was hardly a triumph for Catalonia's national aspirations. It was Suárez who had won: he had recovered the initiative lost in Catalonia in elections won by Socialists, Communists and nationalists. The new *Generalitat* was simply an empty symbol. It lacked any real power, at least in the first months of its existence.[35]

For the Basque country, Suárez could not find a Tarradellas. The Basque government-in-exile, even if favourable to an agreement with Madrid, preferred to leave the negotiations to the Basque deputies. Representatives of the three main Basque parties (PSOE, PNV, UCD) negotiated with the Minister of the Regions, Clavero Arévalo, the establishment of a Basque General Council which would have the functions of a Basque autonomous government. Negotiations were painful and long. A new amnesty had to be granted: on 9 December 1977 the last Basque detainee left jail, but ETA continued its terrorist activities to sabotage an autonomy which threatened its separatist and left-wing strategy. A new problem − or rather, a new version of an old problem − came near to wrecking the negotiations. The UCD of Navarre − a province only partially Basque − rejected the integration of Navarre in the future Basque government and wished to base self-government on the *Fueros*, the historic institutions spared by Franco as a reward for Navarre's loyalty in the Civil War, and which represented the notion of a separate Navarrese political contract with the Spanish state. New and complex negotiations were needed before the government, Basque delegates and Navarrese leaders agreed to a compromise: a referendum must be held to determine the future of Navarre.[36] On 29 December 1977 a royal decree created a General Council for the three provinces of Vizcaya, Alava and Guipúzcoa.

Chapter 11
Epilogue

1977 had been for Spain what a pompous rhetoric describes as a 'historical year'. The advent of democracy after forty years of dictatorship made it 'the most important year in the twentieth century'. The previous democratic experience, the Second Republic of 1931–6, had ended in the bloody Civil War of 1936–9. What are, in 1978, the prospects for the new Spanish democracy?

It was a sector of the army that on 18 July 1936 triggered off the Civil War which defeated the democratic Second Republic; it was the Catholic church that sanctified the war as a Crusade against 'those without God'. It is of some comfort that neither are now in a belligerent posture; nor are the democratic parties, as in the Second Republic, possessed with anti-militarist and anti-clerical furies. Azaña wanted to 'mash up [*triturar*] the army' and declared Spain to be no longer a Catholic nation; Santiago Carrillo flatters the army and calls the church 'a factor for progress'.

The army has publicly abandoned its role as the ultimate depository of the national will interpreted *by itself*, a sword hanging over any government that may seem to the officer corps as ceasing to represent the nation. 'I insist again,' declared the Captain General of Madrid 'that Armed Forces will only carry out what the government says.'[1] The extreme right is outraged at this 'treason' which denies it the remote hope of a right-wing coup or the means of bringing pressure on the legal government. Though the Armed Forces formally protested against the legalisation of the Communist party, they refused to become the defenders of the Francoist Constitution in the period of transition. Those officers who tried to assume that role were dismissed.[2]

This does not mean that 8,000 officers have suffered some conversion *en masse* to liberalism, though no doubt the fact that by 1986 no officer will have shared 'the spirit of the Crusade' as a combatant in the Civil War is significant. In a sense the Armed Forces are prisoner of their own political theory: the general will the Armed Forces profess to represent seems now determined on democracy.[3] In any country armies intervene only when – as in

1936 – the general will seems confused and military rebellion has the prospect of massive support in opinion.

By their rebellion in 1936 the victorious Armed Forces committed themselves to their Commander-in-Chief and his political system. They were consistently presented by committed Francoists as the backbone of the regime.[4] Now they are commanded by the king of a constitutional, democratic monarchy. 'The army,' according to the Chief of the General Staff, 'is not the fourth power.'[5]

The attitude of the army is paralleled by that of the church. Whatever their personal preferences, the episcopate refused to take a direct part in the June elections, whereas its political stance was clear during the Second Republic. It did not back the Christian Democrats in the June elections; this, as the Christian Democrat leader Ruiz Giménez confessed, would have been counter-productive 'because the shift towards secularisation in Spanish society is so radical'. The church has moved from the explicit commitment of national Catholicism to support of political pluralism without passing through the intermediate stage of supporting a confessional party.

There are limits to this neutrality and support of political pluralism and the democratic consensus both in the church and the army. Cardinal Tarancón, the *bête noire* of the right in the last agonies of Francoism, made what was called 'his step backwards' in November 1977. The new Constitution, he said, must respect 'sociological reality' as reflected in the wishes of 'the great Catholic majority of the country'; politically neutral it may be, but the church cannot be indifferent to the 'socio-political organisation of the country'.[6] This means – apart from opposing divorce and abortion – that the church must keep some of its control over secondary education and, until it can reorganise its finances, still retain the state subsidies without which its schools will go bankrupt. A frontal attack on church education will, in these circumstances, be a dangerous exercise in the traditional Jacobin anti-clericalism of the Spanish left.

Two factors may weaken the army's attachment to the new regime. Throughout its history the Spanish army has shown an undeviating attachment to the concept of its honour, reserving to itself the right to sanction those who 'insult' it. In December 1977 the Captain-General of Catalonia ordered the arrest of the manager and actors responsible for staging in Barcelona a play which pilloried in a crude fashion the barbarity of a military trial. This, it must be confessed, shows that Spain is not yet a 'democracy without adjectives'. It was an act of deliberate defiance of the civil authorities which had authorised the play. There were immediate strikes and protest demonstrations against which the police acted with a violence reminiscent of the *ancien régime*.

Such clashes are fraught with dangers and their consequences are the second factor making for disquiet in the Armed Forces. Liberals are outraged when a demonstrator is killed; soldiers and policemen when a member of the security forces is shot as a reprisal. The funerals of the victims become political acts. The deterioration of public order was, as we have argued, a main determinant of army intervention in July 1936. The police are being 'reeducated' but they still over-react in the course of duty. Each time they do, they are pilloried in the press or hauled over the coals in the Cortes.* It would be unfortunate if they became martyrs to the right and assassins to the left.

The enemies of democracy, on the right and on the left, hope to 'destabilise' political life by the exploitation of violence. The terrorism of the extreme left (GRAPO) and of the Basque nationalists (ETA) was used by the extreme right (which had its own terrorists) to discredit reformism. It is still a serious problem for democracy.† Although some sectors of ETA may be won over to legality by concession and negotiation there remains a hard core whose programme is non-negotiable and to whom terrorism has become a way of life, its continuance justified by reprisals for killings by the police. The political parties were over-cautious in condemning terrorism in the past when they needed to bring pressure on the government to move towards democracy. There can be no justification of terrorism in a democratic society where it constitutes the claim of a self-declared moral and political elite to impose its vision on citizens who can vote to express their opinions. There has always been a distrust of the ballot-box on the extremes of Spanish political life.** There has always been a hard right ready

---

*cf. the statement of General López Prieto in December 1977 after a civil guard had been killed. The Civil Guard, he stated, came from the people but would not be killed in the name of the people. One of the problems of the Civil Guard is that it lacks 'intermediate methods of defence' and therefore tends to shoot. A young Andalusian nationalist was shot in Malaga: in the Spanish tradition his funeral became a protest against the forces of public order.

†Terrorism was and still is a Basque problem: of the 36 civilian deaths between 1965 and 1975, 22 occurred in the Basque provinces. In January 1978 a bomb outrage killed 4 people in Barcelona. This was exceptional and the work of a Maoist group, not, as in the Basque provinces, of the extreme left of the nationalist movement.

**'Don't vote' was part of the anarchist creed. The *retraìmiento* (a refusal to participate in political life) was a device of the left-wing liberals and the Republicans under the monarchy. The *retraimiento* was partly a protest against manipulated elections, partly the *politique du pire* of parties that had no prospect of electoral success even in 'sincere' elections.

to point to any collapse of public order as a condemnation of democracy and democratic processes.

The first political debate in the Cortes took place on this very sensitive issue of public order after a Socialist deputy had been roughly treated by the Santander police. That the AP, in spite of its repeated cries for law and order and its consistent defence of the security forces, abstained thus allowing the government to escape a vote of censure, shows a determination to give democracy a chance.

There is a democratic consensus, a will to make democracy work, a determination shared by a king who will have more powers under the new Constitution than the remaining monarchs of Europe. The Constitution itself will not be, as all other Spanish Constitutions have been, the dogmatic imposition of a party; it has been hammered out in a committee that includes all the major parties. The politicians who will work it, though capable of party knock-about turns, work in an atmosphere of compromise. Fraga, the declared enemy of Marxism, invites Santiago Carrillo to lecture to his political club and chats with him in the corridors of the Cortes; when asked whether he would join a government of concentration with the men of AP Carrillo replies, 'Why not?' To Lister, the pro-Soviet Communist leader, this new democratic tolerance is one more sign that, under Carrillo, the party has ceased to be Marxist. 'You can call it liberal, it's not even a Social Democratic party.'

The Pact of Moncloa is the model of a new style of government which maximises the skills of Suárez as a negotiator and replaces confrontation by compromise: the pact was an extra-parliamentary agreement on a common programme to be later ratified in legislation by the Cortes. Carrillo calls this, approvingly, 'government Italian-style'.[7]

'Government Italian-style' is not without its critics. They see Spain governed by a clique of professional politicians who come to mutually convenient arrangements behind closed doors. As early as July 1977 political journalists were asking where 'open democracy' had vanished. Needless to say, the most prominent protesters are those excluded from the political game. Gil Robles thunders against a new 'great oligarchy' where government and opposition work in 'amiable collusion'.

Those who claim that the new style will alienate 'the people' from government, that the Cortes debates are as much a 'sham' as the old parliamentary exercises of Francoism, are perhaps mistaking a lowering of the political temperature for the growth of political apathy. The enthusiasms of 1976 and 1977, when ever

football was politicised, could not persist.* There is a decline in the
outpouring of political books, once a necessary guide to the maze
of parties — 158 in the elections. The circulation of political magazines is dropping off. The neighbourhood associations which a year
ago were pressure groups campaigning on political issues —
amnesty, for instance — have reverted to their original local concerns: housing, urban planning, pollution and prices. The frenetic
flag-waving street demonstrations in the Basque provinces, once the
favourite picture of Spain on foreign television, have subsided.

Political extremism is, at least for the moment, at a discount.
The extreme right is isolated in its rage. 'The State of 18 July,' its
ageing defenders declare, 'has capitulated without honour.'[8] They
profess themselves ready to 'die with their boots on' and engage in
punch-ups with radical Falangists. The extreme left made no
impression on the electorate — it gained two seats. Trotskyite,
Marxist and Anarchist 'groupuscules' continue to support social
revolution, sexual liberation and the 'incorporation of youth into
the political process'. But even in the university they are no longer a
force, and the graffiti on the walls are silent memorials to a student
revolution now moribund and buried under apathy and boredom.[9]

That the moderation of the Communist party has no attractions
for the new left is the price Carrillo pays for his Eurocommunism
and his declared willingness to accept pluralist democracy. The
party rejects direction from Moscow; it has abandoned Leninism
and the proletarian revolution. Carrillo assured American audiences that foreign investment will be safe in the new Spain.
Semprún and Claudín, once the party's leading intellectuals, protest against this desertion of Marxism, combined as it is with the
Secretary-General's 'Stalinist' management of the party. Carrillo's
new respectability makes his party less attractive to youth than the
Socialists. The youth movements of the extreme left campaign for
the legalisation of soft drugs: Carrillo denounces drug addiction
and 'teddy boys'. If collaborationism does not yield substantial
results — for instance, in wage settlements — it is hard to see how
the party will hold its ground against the PSOE.

Apart from the problem of 'destabilisation' through violence —
and for all democratic governments the dilemma is to combat
violence without destroying the fabric of democracy in the process — shadows lie over this scene of moderation and consensus: a

*The Committee of Barça (the Barcelona team) accused the Spanish Federation
of 'Fascist' tendencies. (*Cambio 16*, 6 March 1977.) As Fraga observed (*Blanco y
Negro*, 23 October 1976), the word 'Fascist' was used by the left as the same
blanket condemnation as 'red' had been used by Francoists.

return to an unstable party system, the exacerbation of the regional question, and the problematic implementation of the Moncloa Pact as a cure for the economic crisis.

We have argued that the elections of June 1977 produced what was in fact — though this was strenuously denied by the minor parties — a two-party democracy.[10] Its stability is therefore dependent on the cohesion of the Socialist PSOE and the 'centrist' UCD.

The UCD is still a conglomerate of groups rather than an organised party. It is composed of those who come from reformist Francoism — like Suárez himself — and of those who were active in the democratic opposition. It has its resolute believers in a market economy and its mild brand of Social Democrats. There are the Prime Minister's 'unconditionals' and those who resent his preponderant influence.

Will the centre hold? Is the UCD 'centre', 'centre right' or 'centre left'? Fraga believes that true conservatives will join AP, now presented as a British Conservative party, and the 'battle for the right' has replaced the battle for the centre of 1977. The UCD will probably hold — apart from minor desertions and hitherto innocuous cabinet crises — while it is in government. But will it hold as a party of the opposition if the Socialists win the next election? If its 'triumph' in June 1977 was a result, not of the appeal of its moderate conservative image to the electorate, but of governmental manipulation, will it fade away when it is no longer an 'officialist' party?[11] Although the opposition's charges of a resurrection of the old style of government electoral management were grossly exaggerated, the fact that Suárez was the Prime Minister undoubtedly gained his party votes in an electorate still, in many regions, unaccustomed to public politics.

If the UCD must hold on to its right, the problem of the PSOE is to consolidate its new strength on the left without alienating those who voted Socialist because they were attracted to its democratic image. The PSOE rejects any idea of a 'government of concentration' which it sees as the only device left to an inexpandable minority party — the PCE — if it is to get into government. Its present posture is a convenient one: if the Moncloa Pact does not work, it will bear no responsibility for economic disaster. It expects gains at the forthcoming municipal elections and a majority at the next general election. It is under pressure from its militants to live up to declarations that it is a Marxist party that believes in the 'class struggle as the motor of history', out not to 'touch up' capitalism by removing its most evident abuses, but to replace it by a Socialist system.[12] Will this pressure radicalise the party and polarise Spanish politics?

In our view it is the regional issue which has always been the most
intractable problem. The crucial change in Spanish democratic
politics was the support of regional autonomy by all the parties of
the Democratic Left, even if some of them do not escape the accusation, from enthusiastic regionalists, of *sucursalismo* (e.g. that the
Catalan PSOE is a 'branch' of the Madrid PSOE as a Catalan bank
is a branch of a bank whose central office is Madrid). This support
changed the whole basis of a Catalan regionalism: it has ceased to
be a predominantly middle-class concern and the working-class
parties are no longer indifferent or hostile to regional demands as
they tended to be in the Second Republic. Regionalism generally
has ceased to be dependent on regionalist parties: in Catalonia and
the Basque provinces the regionalist parties (the PNV and the
parties in the *Pacte Democratic per Catalunya*) were outvoted by
the Democratic Left.* The President of the General Council of the
Basque provinces is a veteran Socialist, Ramón Rubial, who cannot
speak Basque.†

As we have seen, Catalonia and the Basque provinces have their
'pre-autonomy'. The real struggle will come when pre-autonomy
becomes full autonomy. What will be the content of autonomy?
Will the government hand over the police to the autonomous
governments as the Basques demand? The right will fight hard to
preserve what it has always fought to preserve: the unity of Spain.
It already accuses the government of 'doling out autonomy statutes
by the handful'.** The autonomist movement is no longer confined to the Basque provinces and Catalonia: Assemblies of
Parliamentarians are demanding statutes for Galicia, Andalusia,
Valencia and the Canary Islands, demands which no one would
foresee from a scrutiny of the results of the election in which
regionalist parties failed to gain a seat.

Galicia and Andalusia are similar in that they are classic
depressed regions which see themselves confined in some sort of
colonial bondage. They are unlike in that Galicia has a distinct
culture and a language which enthusiastic nationalists are seeking

---

*In Catalonia the PSOE and the PSUC (the Catalan Communist Party) won
23 seats; the regionalists 11. In the Basque provinces the PSOE beat the PNV
by one seat. The UCD supported autonomy, not very enthusiastically. It gained
9 seats in Catalonia and 7 in the Basque provinces where its stronghold was
Navarre. The AP was the only party that opposed autonomy. It won only 1 seat
in Catalonia and 1 in the Basque provinces.

†The dominating presence of a non-nationalist party in the General Council
explains the lukewarm participation of the PNV. It still maintains the historic
legitimacy of the old exile Basque government.

**It accuses Suárez of excessive generosity to regionalist demands because he
needs the regionalist votes to sustain his parliamentary majority.

to raise from 'peasant' to 'bourgeois' status. Andalusia has only a dialect and its flamenco traditions, and the relative weakness of the demand from below is perhaps indicated by the newspaper headline 'The Assembly of Parliamentarians invites the people to demonstrate their support for autonomy'. The Galician and Andalusian demands for autonomy stem, therefore, from economic disadvantage – Andalusia has the highest rural unemployment levels in Spain. Here regionalist demands are contradictory: it will be difficult for a democratic government, however sincerely committed to autonomy, to reconcile competing claims when the Basque industrialist is seen as robbing Galicia of its savings via a banking system it (the government) controls, and of its hydro-electric resources via a national grid, and when Andalusia sees itself as a poor south, a reservoir of the cheap labour that is the basis of Catalan prosperity.

Immediate political stability depends on the success of the government's package in mitigating the economic crisis it neglected for over a year. Like all Western governments, it has to square the circle of curing inflation by austerity without aggravating an already serious problem of unemployment, especially amongst youth which at present has no vote and may be radicalised by desperation.[13] It has to bear the criticism of industrialists who want reflation and the pressure group of the small employers who want credit to survive in an inclement climate. It is confronted by an independent trade union movement divided still between the CC OO, the UGT and the independent unions. They must resist closures of uneconomic enterprises when the government is determined not to 'provide sick wards for ailing firms'; shipbuilding (the Cadiz yards are idle) and heavy engineering (the Babcock Wilcox firm which employs 6,000 men is bankrupt), are, as elsewhere, in serious trouble. The biggest concern of all, SEAT, seems to be on the way to becoming the Iberian British Leyland. The day labourers of Andalusia, with emigration closed to them, are becoming militant unionists.

It was the misfortune of the Republic of 1931–6 that it came into being at the time of the great slump. Now Spain's second experiment in democracy comes at a time of world recession and Francoism may appear, even to workers, as a golden age. Can a conservative government, whose strength lies in rural Spain, with little support in the great industrial cities, beat inflation without a confrontation with the unions? All the unions support *autogestión* (workers' control); all are competing for the same clientèle. They may be tempted to outbid one another in pushing against wage restraint and demanding a return to full employment.[14]

That the economy now seems set on the modest upturn of the European economies in general is a proof that Spain is part of the West, that her problems are the problems of Western Europe. Naturally enough Spain has her special problems in transition.

Every municipality in Spain is still presided over by mayors nominated 'by the finger' under Francoism: the result is an erosion of authority. This particular problem will be solved by the municipal elections for which all parties are preparing. Other problems will not vanish so easily. Television was a state-controlled, inflated bureaucracy; there is a bitter party struggle over its future between the PSOE, in favour of some form of nationalisation, and the UCD, which favours 'privatisation'. What will happen to the 5,000 former Professors of the Formation of National Spirit now unemployed?* How will the property of the official syndicates be handed over to the new, free unions?

These hangovers from an authoritarian past are symbolic. The deeper issue is how easily and painlessly a society formed by forty years of authoritarianism can adjust to the freedoms of democracy. Rejection of the political past appears overwhelming. Yet some Spaniards are shocked by the social implications of rapid change and the sudden appearance in Spain of the common problems of the West: pornography in the streets and in the cinema; squatters; the spread of hippy communes; the increase in violent crime and rape; common criminals, in the semantic confusion of the age termed 'social' prisoners, rioting in prisons all over Spain; a rash of strikes.

In the euphoria of June 1977 there was an assumption that democratic institutions solved problems by the simple fact that they existed; but the educational system remains a disastrous muddle; the social services ineffective and elephantine; urban planning unresponsive to the demands of city life. Democratic government presupposes a democratic society. It is the profoundest paradox of Francoism that the developments of the sixties and early seventies have at least laid the material preconditions for such a society; on such foundations the democracy of the Second Republic could not build.

---

*It was one of the characteristic phenomena of decaying Francoism that both television and the courses of the National Spirit were alleged to be infiltrated by the left-wing democratic opposition. Professors of the National Spirit, threatened with dismissal, claimed they had been teaching democratic principles. The presence of 'subversives' in television was one of the standard protests of the right — 'subversives' include the present editor of *Cambio 16*.

POSTSCRIPT – 1978

The Epilogue was written at the beginning of 1978. Then, if the economy looked in poor shape, the political horizons of Spanish democracy appeared, by and large, bright and clear. Eleven months later the first clouds have appeared, just as the formal stages of the transition from dictatorship to democracy have been completed. The Cortes passed a constitution which returned Spain to the 'inorganic democracy' of one man, one vote, by finally dismantling the political apparatus of the Francoist state.

The new constitution defines Spain as 'a social and democratic state ruled by law'. Its political form is a parliamentary monarchy (Art. 1). Article 2 guarantees the rights of the Spanish 'nationalities' to their autonomy, a dramatic departure from the rigid centralism of the Francoist régime.* Those bogies of the late Caudillo – trade unions and political parties – are given constitutional status and the fundamental freedoms for their operation are guaranteed. Voting age has been lowered to 18; the death penalty has been abolished. The state will have no official religion but it recognises 'the role of the Catholic Church in Spain' (Art. 16), a subtle formula to avoid the issue of the confessionality of the state. Article 32 opens the way to divorce. To Catholic hard-liners these clauses create an 'atheist' state. In spite of recognition in the text of the constitution of the legitimacy of free enterprise in a market economy, it has been labelled 'Marxist' by the far right.

The king becomes the head of state and commander-in-chief of the armed forces. While not responsible to the Cortes, his role as 'moderating power', to use the nineteenth-century phrase, is circumscribed compared with the powers he enjoyed under the Francoist constitution; he appoints the prime minister only after consultation with the party leaders and only if the Cortes gives a vote of confidence to the candidate. Even so, his powers – and his influence – are greater than those of English monarchs.

The Cortes has two chambers: a Congress, elected by universal

---

*Articles 143 to 158 develop the complicated procedures leading to devolution and define the powers of the state and the future autonomous regions. It recognises that the regions that enjoyed a Statute of Autonomy under the Republic (e.g. the Basque Provinces) constitute a special case.

suffrage and proportional representation, and a Senate with four senators per province. Both chambers will be elected for a four-year mandate.

Article 113 has been included to foster stable government when, given proportional representation, a strong government may not emerge from elections and when the legislators were aware of the debilitating effect of continued governmental crises in the years of the old constitutional monarchy and the Second Republic. Votes of no confidence must be sponsored by at least a tenth of the Congress and must include the nomination of an alternative prime minister; defeated signatories cannot present a new vote until the next session.

The new democratic constitution is long – 169 articles – complex, unnecessarily detailed, turgid and repetitive. However, it enjoys one important advantage over all previous Spanish constitutions as the first constitution in Spanish history that is neither the unilateral imposition of a party nor the expression of a single ideology. It attempts to synthesise divergent ideological viewpoints; its linguistic infelicities, not all of which were removed by the amendments of the novelist-senator Cela, derive from its synthetic nature.

Centrists, socialists, communists, Catalan regionalists and conservatives were included in the committee responsible for the original draft. In May 1978 a spectacular constitutional pact was engineered between the UCD, the PSOE, the PCE and the Catalan regionalists which allowed the constitution to pass both Chambers on 31 October without serious difficulties and in an atmosphere of self-congratulation. This was the high tide of the politics of consensus.*

Only two of the main parties – Popular Alliance (AP) of Fraga and the Basque Nationalist Party (PNV) – were excluded from the pact. It was from them that the main opposition to the constitution in the Cortes came.

Fraga's party objected to the use of the term 'nationalities' as a potential threat to the unity of Spain. Basque nationalists held that the constitution did not recognise the historic rights of the Basques as a nation. Interminable negotiations between the government and the PNV in the spring and summer of 1978 achieved nothing. The PNV asked for the simple recognition of the *fueros* (the Basque laws and institutions of self-government abolished in 1839 and 1876) as a basis for their new autonomous government. The

*The constitution was approved on 31 October. In Congress there were 325 votes in favour, 6 against and 14 abstentions; in the Senate, 226 in favour, 5 against, 8 abstentions.

government would grant the *fueros* only 'within the constitution' – a device to preserve the indivisibility of national sovereignty. In this sterile terminological confrontation the government was inept, the Basques were obstinate. The PNV finally decided to abstain in the vote on the constitution in the Cortes and, more important given the emphasis which other parties put on an enthusiastic 'Yes' as the final consolidation of a democratic monarchy, to recommend abstention in the referendum on the constitution to be held in December 1978.

It seems that the government feared that excessive concessions to the Basques might irritate the army and give an emotive rallying cry to the right as defenders of the unity of the *patria*. The PNV certainly feared to see its leadership of the Basque movement eroded if it 'capitulated' to Madrid over the *fueros*. Once again the Basque problem stands revealed as the worst, the most troublesome legacy of Francoism.

The concessions of Suárez in 1977 – including the pre-autonomous government of the Basque General Council – were not enough to halt terrorism and to open the way for the pacification of a much-troubled region. ETA has continued in 1978 its implacable terrorist campaign, aimed mainly at the security forces: between January and November 1978 political violence claimed fifty-three lives – most of them either policemen or members of the Civil Guard. ETA strategy aims at provoking indiscriminate repression against the Basque population in general, thus alienating opinion and creating water for the terrorist fish to swim in. Unfortunately, the security forces have played into the terrorists' hands by a violent over-reaction which has, on occasion, escaped the control of the civil authorities. Again, a police force used to unchallenged supremacy is a legacy from an authoritarian past.

While only a small fraction of Basques actively support ETA, terrorism is bringing the Basque Country to the verge of economic and moral collapse. Revolutionary taxation extorted by ETA from private enterprises and the general insecurity discourage investment. The local UCD, the PSOE and the communists have condemned terrorism outright. The PNV has taken a more ambiguous line: it has also condemned terrorism but it has made the intransigence and 'violence' of Madrid equally responsible for the deterioration of the situation in the Basque Provinces.*

---

*The PNV called for a demonstration against terrorism to be held in Bilbao on 28 October 1978. Later, it changed the slogan for one which read: 'Towards a free and pacified Euskadi [Basque fatherland].' Nevertheless, the demonstration was a success and an encouraging sign. *El Pais*, 29 October 1978.

This does not help to isolate terrorists. Meanwhile, terrorism is discrediting democracy and has helped in the revival of the neo-fascist authoritarian right in the second half of 1978. The funerals of policemen have been occasions for bitter right-wing demonstrations against Suárez and his ministers. In August, a police professional association issued a communiqué stating that they were 'fed up' with terrorist killings. In October, an armed police company mutinied in Bilbao. Terrorists have succeeded in one of their aims: a considerable part of the security forces has lost confidence in democratic procedures, even openly defying the government.

The extreme right demanded, in mass meetings and demonstrations, that the army should take power and install a strong 'national' government. On 17 November 1978 a lunatic military plot to k'idnap the king and his prime minister as the preliminary move in establishing a 'government of national salvation' was foiled in Madrid, and a general arrested in Cartagena for grossly insulting the Minister of Defence, General Gutierrez Mellado, as a traitor, 'a pig and a mason'. Both incidents, marginal in themselves, are indications of discontent, however limited in its incidence, within the army and security forces; there is a feeling of outrage at the deterioration of public order under the new régime and of frustration at the government's inability to master terrorism in the Basque Provinces. The Chiefs of the General Staff, however, expressed their continued determination not to be deflected from the duty to obey the king's government when, on 21 July, two senior officers were assassinated by ETA. We still believe that a majority of army officers, if not enthusiastic democrats, see the army's role as the defence of legality as embodied in the constitution and in the king; that the army will not intervene *directly* in politics unless officers come to believe once more, as they did in 1936, that the collapse of public order threatens the unity of Spain.

If the army has paid little attention to those who have urged it to seize power, the number of these right-wing extremists with their nostalgia for the *ancien régime* seems, in noise if not in number, to have increased in 1978. In November, Fuerza Nueva (New Force), the neo-fascist organisation, mobilised thousands of demonstrators against terrorism and the 'godless' constitution. The blue shirts and the fascist salute have once again appeared in the streets of Madrid; a minority of hard-line bishops and a handful of officers have joined the cry against the constitution as 'godless', the work of pro-abortionists, masons and Marxists.

Terrorism has therefore aided the resurgence of the extreme right. The conservative right, whose main party is Fraga's Popular Alliance (AP) has sought to make political capital out of the apparent weakness of the present government. Fraga, for all his violent and intemperate outbursts against the government and the ruling party (UCD) and despite his disagreements with some aspects of the constitution, has repeatedly defined himself as a conservative and democrat ready to play the parliamentary game. Hence his overtures in 1978 to figures of the 'civilised right': the former ministers Areilza and Osorio, both determined to launch a liberal-conservative alternative to UCD:* Once Fraga had sloughed off the most reactionary elements in AP, after their rejection of the constitution, the way was open for a pact with Areilza and Osorio. It was announced on 14 November.

Only future elections will show if Spain wants a 'new majority' as Areilza has repeatedly asserted.† These attempts to rearrange the Spanish centre-right – often inspired only by personal grudges – are not without risks. Democracy needs a stable party structure, a lesson which, so far, only the leaders of the Spanish left seem to have learnt. Attempts to form a 'new' conservative grouping can only weaken UCD as a party of the moderate right; both the socialist and communist leaders have warned against the dangers implicit in the weakening of the UCD, either as a ruling party or as the core of a future opposition.

Rumours about internal crises in UCD have been frequent throughout 1978, highlighting the tensions between its christian democrat and progressive wings. None the less, UCD has advanced considerably in 1978 towards consolidation as a unified party under Suárez. In line with the liberal, social democratic and christian ideals of its constituent groups UCD was defined, at its first congress in October, as an inter-class, progressive and reformist party.**

There is no doubt that UCD ideologues and managers think that this left-of-centre line reflects the mood of a majority of Spaniards in 1978. Just as the 'new majority' threatens UCD on its right, so UCD seems determined to invade the 'political space' of the moderate left, thus 'robbing' the Socialist Party (PSOE) of the votes of sincere liberals and democrats who supported the PSOE in June 1977 for want of a better alternative. In so doing UCD takes the risk of losing the support of conservative interests that voted for Suárez in 1977 because of their inert adherence to the government

---

*Areilza founded in January 1978 his own party, Acción Ciudadana Liberal (Citizens' Liberal Action). Both he and Osorio often talked of the need to define a 'great right' or a 'new majority'.
† See Areilza's views in *La Vanguardia*, 16 June 1978.
**El Pais*, 18-22 October 1978; and interviews with Arias Salgado in *La Calle*, 31 October-6 November 1978, and *El Pais*, 26 November 1978.

in power and because of the excessive Francoist overtones of other conservative forces.

The exercise of power has eroded the appeal of the UCD. With the right divided, this has benefited the main party of the opposition, the socialist PSOE. The creation of a unified socialist movement was completed when the small but influential group of Tierno Galvan joined the PSOE in April 1978. The PSOE won the two by-elections held in May. It is rumoured that the king would like to see a socialist government in a not-too-distant future. Enrique Múgica, one of the leaders of the party, seems to have established excellent relations with the army as president of the defence committee of the Cortes. The image of Felipe González – the PSOE secretary – is now that of an essentially moderate politician. The party's rhetoric has been toned down; it has accepted the monarchy and González has expressed his view that the party should reject Marxism.

The rejection of Marxism is one of the few turnabouts that the Spanish Communist Party (PCE) has not made in its attempts to change the party's image. At the Ninth Party Congress, held in April, the PCE abandoned Leninism, and Carrillo called the congress 'historic' in its recognition of democratic procedures within the party. Yet all the 'democratic procedures' displayed at the congress merely reinforced the control of Carrillo and his friends over the party bureaucracy, provoking only minor protests and discrepancies in Asturias and Barcelona. The congress ratified the bold Euro-communist line so enthusiastically sponsored by its secretary-general. As in 1977, so again in 1978 the PCE was the champion of moderation. Carrillo has been a main supporter of Suárez; the communists were second to none in their enthusiasm for the new constitution; they have been outspoken enemies of terrorism in the Basque Country.

A non-revolutionary left and a 'civilised' right are both prerequisites for the political stability and survival of democracy. So is a modicum of prosperity. Much must therefore depend on the performance of the economy. The outlook appears less gloomy in 1978 than it did in 1977. The Moncloa Pacts have worked reasonably well: inflation has been brought down from 26.4 to 16 per cent; tourism has done well, and there has been an export boom – how far Spain has moved from the old pattern is shown by the fact that cars are becoming the most important export. The deficit on visible trade has fallen; reserves have gone up. But the situation still remains delicate: 10 per cent of the labour force are without jobs and unemployment is particularly severe in the building industry and among the young. A credit squeeze to combat inflation has brought many firms to the verge of bankruptcy. Investment has reached an all-time low. Again, let us emphasise, Spain is not different: it shares the economic malaise of the West. Moreover, those who attribute the fall in the stock market – and it is some indication of the structure of the new Spain that one in three families holds shares – to the new political climate would do well to remember that the tumble began in 1973.

Largely because the economy has languished, democracy has not brought immediate material benefits to the mass of the Spanish population. This may help to explain the climate of disillusion that most observers have seen as a characteristic of the Spain of 1978 in contrast to the democratic euphoria revealed in the 1977 elections.* Democracy was seen by many as a purveyor of *individual* benefits, from better schools for their children to social security benefits on the levels of the advanced European economies. Perhaps this accounts for a new concentration – especially evident among the young – on individual liberties outside and beyond the conventional political concerns (e.g. abortion and 'free use of the body') rather than on collective issues, except when, as on environmental issues, these have a high individual content.

There are other reasons for a certain degree of political disenchantment. Consensus brings stability at a price; it invites political boredom and cynicism. It leaves the impression that offstage private agreements have become a substitute for open political debate and public, parliamentary control of government policies. These feelings of disenchantment have been reinforced by a noticeable increase – as in the rest of Europe – in crimes of violence, above all in the two great cities of Madrid and Barcelona which together account for half the violent crimes in Spain. These are seen by critics as the sequelae of the new democratic liberties. There is talk of 'terror in the streets' – rape, mugging, handbag snatching. To right-wing papers like *El Alcazar* Spain is in a 'state of war'. As in the case of the mushroom growth of the erotic cinema and pornographic literature, it is the contrast with the placid Spanish past and not the comparison with the rest of Western Europe that is commonly observed. The old cry first made in 1868, that democracy threatens the family and Christian values, is raised once more on the far right. To the descendants of those whom Unamuno called the 'troglodytes', a modern society is unacceptable. Whereas the Carlists looked back to the Spain of the sixteenth century, the dream world of modern reactionaries is located in the Spain of the forties and fifties. Like the less enlightened followers of William

---

*See *Cambio 16*, 25 June 1978, and the comments of the Spanish press one year after the 1977 elections: *El Pais*, 14 June 1978 and following issues.

Pitt they are always ready, in a changing society, to 'mistake dis-organisation for sedition'.

If elderly conservatives prefer 'the peace of Franco' to the style of the new democracy, the youngest generation shows signs of rejecting *all* cultural and political ideals or values. The universities, once the centres of ideological effervescence and political agitation, languish – victims of massification and mediocrity. The place of the Marxists of the sixties and the Maoists of the seventies has been filled in the late seventies by those who do not care, the *pasotas*.*

In the short run, Spanish democracy faces more urgent tasks than the reintegration of drop-outs. Carrillo, the communist leader, has repeatedly asked for the continuance of the consensus which produced the Moncloa Pacts and saw the constitution through the Cortes. A return to party government is, nevertheless, inevitable. A stable party system counts more than occasional party consensus in a democracy, especially in a country with scant historic experience of democratic processes and a tradition of fissi-parous parties. Even more important is the absence of 'de-stabilising' factors which might polarise politics and break down the unwritten conventions of civility upon which democracy rests – toleration based on an awareness of common values, respect between politicians for opponents within the 'rules of the game'. As 1978 draws to a close, the main concern is whether terrorism and the intricate Basque question might become such a 'de-stabilising' factor. The weekly *Cambio 16* put the issue drama-tically: 'Either the régime breaks ETA or ETA annihilates Spanish democracy.'

*See John Hooper's article on Spanish youth in the *Guardian*, 21 November 1978. *Pasotas* are those who pass in card games.

NOTES

INTRODUCTION

1 Juan Fernández Figueroa, 'La Izquierda: voto sin voz', *Indice* (1967), quoted Ludovico Garrucco, *Spagna senza miti* (1968), p. 361.
2 For Basque and Catalan regionalism see below, pp. 10-12.
3 The causes of Spain's late entry and the subsequent weakness of the industrial sector are the subject of some controversy. Some attribute it to the limited capacity for capital accumulation and the limited market provided by a 'feudal' agricultural system which could not modernise without threatening the existing structure of property; some to 'mistaken' investment, in the years after 1850, of scarce capital in railways and government stock instead of in 'productive' industry; some to the essentially ascetic, proud, conservative, unenterprising, anti-economic etc. characteristics of a traditional Catholic society.
4 See below, p. 161.

CHAPTER 1

1 This view neglected the fact that the empire had been lost by the most absolute of Spanish monarchs, Ferdinand VII. For the causes and consequences of the loss of empire see the brilliant analysis of J. Fontana, *La quiebra de la monarquía absolute* (1971).
2 Speeches of 4 December 1952 and 27 April 1967; cf. *Pensamiento político de Franco*, I, pp. 130−1: 'It is not an imperative condition of democracy that it must be worked through *artificial* parties of the nineteenth-century type.' This sort of statement is characteristic of the deliberate semantic confusion of Francoism.
3 The clearest exponent of this view was General Mola, the 'director' of the 1936 military conspiracy. See his *Obras Completas*, and generally R. Carr, 'Spain', in *Soldiers and Governments*, ed. Michael Howard (1957).
4 We do not mean to give the impression that Franco was a demagogue, but he interpreted crowd acclaim as legitimisation; cf. Francisco Franco Salgado, *Conversaciones privadas con Franco* (1976), p. 342; cf. his reactions to the crowds that welcomed Eisenhower: 'It has been a true plebiscite and a referendum supporting my foreign policy' (ibid., p. 274).
5 cf. his memoirs, *Entre el silencio y la propaganda. Memorias* (1977), ch. 6.

6 J. A. Girón, *Reflexiones sobre España* (1975), p. 23.

CHAPTER 2

1 It can be argued that a personal dictatorship is the most flexible of all forms of government because it is irresponsible. For an examination of the problem of decision making in an authoritarian regime see C. W. Anderson, *The Political Economy of Modern Spain. Policy Making in an Authoritarian System* (1970).

2 For the divisions of loyalty see R. Carr, *Spanish Tragedy*, pp. 67, 88: and Ramón Salas Larrazábal, *Historia del Ejercito Popular de la República* (1973), chs 1 and 2.

3 For a detailed analysis of the sociological structure of the officer corps see J. Busquets, *El militar de carrera en España* (1967).

4 There is a close parallel with the *Juntas de Defensa* of 1917 which originated in 'military syndicalism', i.e. protests over promotion prospects and pay eroded by inflation; but whereas the *Juntas* had serious political consequences, the UDM did not.

5 Military cabinet ministers: 1938–9, 5; 1939–41, 6; 1941–5, 3; 1945–51, 4; 1951–7, 5; 1957–62, 7; 1962–5, 7; 1965–9, 6; 1969–73, 4; 1973–4, 4; 1974–5, 3. From 1957 to 1969 the all-important Ministry of the Interior was held by a general – an indication of the importance of the issue of public order in those years. The political muscle of the army therefore varied considerably and tended to decrease. Obviously both Franco and his successor as Prime Minister, Admiral Carrero Blanco, were very close to and aware of army opinion.

6 cf. Jesús Infantes, *El ejército de Franco y de Juan Carlos* (1976), p. 113.

7 General García Valiño at the time of the Burgos Trials (1970), when the army was responsible for judging Basque terrorists. See E. de Blaye, *Franco and the Politics of Spain* (1976), p. 302.

8 Franco himself was aware of some of the counter-productive results of violent repression.

9 From a speech of a prominent right-wing general, Iniesta Cano, *Ya* (25 August 1972).

10 For the case of Queipo de Llano see Ricardo de la Cierva, *Historia del Franquismo* (1975), p. 65.

11 cf. Juan Benet *et al.*, *Dionisio Ridruejo: de la Falange a la oposición* (1976), pp. 31, 90. Ridruejo had been brave enough to speak his mind to Franco on the Decree of Unification.

12 *Conversaciones*, p. 230.

13 'Aspectos políticos del sindicalismo español de posguerra', in *Sistema*, no. 13 (1976).

14 See below, pp. 172-3.

15 For the letter see Dionisio Ridruejo, *Casi unas memorias* (1976), pp. 236–40. The 'conservative clans' comes from Ridruejo's letter to

Serrano Suñer who was himself sacked shortly after (see pp. 240–2).

16 *Conversaciones*, pp. 344, 253. He criticised General Alonso Vega for failure to pay attention to Falangist recommendations for political appointments.

17 See below, p. 174ff.

18 Pío Cabanillas was sacked as a result of a bitter attack on 'phoney liberals' by the old lion Girón in October 1974. See below, p. 200.

19 Antonio Castro Villacañas on the forty-first anniversary of the foundation of the Falange in Galicia. Quoted in *Doblón* (27 March 1976).

20 M. A. Aparicio Pérez, 'Aspectos politicos del sindicalismo español de posguerra', in *Sistema 13* (April 1976), pp. 55ff.

21 He also gave the church freedom from state censorship and a right to organise its own trade unions.

22 The integrists were the extreme right of the Spanish church which rejected liberal thought as sin and the liberal state as heretical.

23 Menéndez y Pelayo (1856–1912) was a polymath, much revered by the integrist extreme right. His main work was a history of Spanish 'heterodoxy' which rejected *in toto* the rationalism of the eighteenth-century Enlightenment as the fruit of the Lutheran heresy.

24 Father Ayala, the Jesuit who inspired ACNP, wrote a book called *Formación de Selectos*. A. Sáez Alba, *La otra 'cosa nostra'. La Asociación Católica de Propagandistas* (1974), pp. 11, 12.

25 The vows of chastity, poverty and obedience applied differently to various sectors of the Opus. But, as an embittered liberal told R. C. in 1958, if liberals had been willing to make the sacrifices in time and money that were made by the men of the Opus, then they might have won more influence. The argument, given the political convictions and police powers of the regime, is, of course, fallacious.

26 For his writings see Daniel Artigues, *El Opus Dei en España* (1968), pp. 71*ff*.

27 cf. the remarks of José Luis Aranguren in *Cuardernos para el Diálogo* (July 1962).

28 For the 'third force' see below, p. 171.

29 Quoted in Daniel Artigues, op. cit., p. 92. The Opus Dei was much more open to attacks of collective conspiracy, wire-pulling etc. For example, J. Ynfante, *La prodigiosa aventura del Opus Dei* (1970), takes the institution as a 'holy mafia'; A. Moncada's *El Opus Dei: una interpretación* (1974) contains the 'confessions' of a former member.

30 *Pueblo* (6 February 1968). He shared his master's obsession about masons and his distrust of ardent Falangists.

31 Benjamin Welles, *Spain. The Gentle Anarchy* (1965), p. 90.

32 For a bitter account of the disillusionment of the Liberal Monarchists see J. Ma. Gil Robles, *La Monarquía por la que yo luché (1941–54)* (1976).

33 See above, p. 7.

34 Quoted in Amando de Miguel, *Sociologiá del Franquismo* (1975), p. 180.

35 See below, p. 42.

36 Laureano López Rodó, *Política y desarrollo* (1970), pp. 38, 73.

37 See his *El crepúsculo de las ideologías* (1961) and below, p. 184.
38 For an excellent summary of the role of the civil service see K. N. Medhurst, *Government in Spain* (1973), ch. 6.
39 For the civil servants, see below, p. 36.
40 cf. the remarks of J. Tusell in *Oligarquía y Caciquismo en Andalucía (1850–1930)* (1976), pp. 267–7, on the predominance of lawyers in the reign of Alfonso XIII.
41 An early example of such rumours is the stories which surrounded the dismissal, in July 1939, of one of the heroes of the Civil War, General Queipo de Llano. See Ricardo de la Cierva, *Historia del Franquismo* (1976).
42 *Conversaciones*, p. 120.
43 M. Navarro Rubio, *El vacío político (1973)*, p. 168.
44 The new co-ordinating institutions did not relieve the cabinet of ultimate responsibility and they were regarded by the 'politicians' in government as mere devices to enhance the power of their creators — the technocrats of the Opus Dei and their patron Admiral Carrero Blanco. It was Carrero Blanco who in September 1956 asked López Rodó for a memorandum on administrative reform. All López Rodó's plans involved structures to be subordinated to the office of the presidency, Carrero Blanco's private fief. For this see K. N. Medhurst, op. cit., pp. 96–101.
45 For variations on this theme see *Pensamiento político de Franco*, ed. Ediciones del Movimiento (1975), nos. 673–799.
46 For a detailed analysis of the management of pressure groups over the new economic policy of the sixties see Anderson, *The Political Economy of Modern Spain* (1970).

CHAPTER 3

1 Text in *Bases Documentales de la España contemporanea*, Vol. XI, *La España de Franco 1939–73*, ed. Ma. Carmen García-Nieto and J. Ma. Donézar (1975), pp. 543–68.
2 L. López Rodó, *Política y Desarrollo* (1970).
3 The phrase was coined by Girón, long-serving Falangist Minister of Labour. See his *Reflexiones sobre España* (1975), p. 109.
4 For a few of Franco's many angry outbursts against Don Juan see General Francisco Salgado-Araujo, *Mis conversaciones con Franco* (1976), pp. 46, 52, 208, 237, 239, 250, 259.
5 For an appeal to Franco's patriotism see Carlos Iglesias Selgas, *Un régimen social moderno* (1969), pp. 67–8.
6 For the Fundamental Laws as modified by the Organic Law see L. Sánchez Agesta, *Los documentos constitucionales y supra nacionales con inclusión de las Leyes Fundamentales de España* (1972), pp. 196–256. The Fundamental Laws, promulgated piecemeal since 1945, were:

The Law of the Principles of the National Movement (LPMN May 1958) which set out the principles 'by their nature permanent and unalterable' which should inspire all acts of the state and which should be accepted on oath by all, from Franco's successor to the lowliest state employee;
The Fuero of Spaniards (FE July 1945) which set out their liberties and duties;
the Fuero of Work (March 1938) regulating the relations between capital and labour;
the Law constituting the Cortes (LC July 1942);
the Law of Succession (LS July 1947);
the Law of the Referendum (LR October 1945) governing the conditions for the popular sanction of important laws.

7   For interpretations of this future constitution see R. Fernández, Carvajal, *La constitución española* (1969), and especially J. de Esteban, *Desarrollo político y constitución española* (1973). For a general view of the political laws of the regime see J. Zafra Valverde, *Régimen político de España* (1973).

8   Support for the monarchical principle is set out in M. Herrero de Minón's *El principio monárquico: un estudio sobre la soberanía del rey en las Leyes Fundamentales* (1972). His views did not win general acceptance.

9   *Quién es quién en las Cortes* (1969), pp. 383*ff*.

10   cf. especially Jorge de Esteban, op. cit., pp. 127*ff*, 522*ff*.

11   For a full description of its composition and functions see Valverde, op. cit., pp. 233–61.

12   See below, p. 177.

13   For this see Xavier Tusell, *La oposición democrática al Franquismo,* pp. 388*ff*., and below, p. 165.

14   For an illuminating and perceptive short account of Linz's views and those of his critics see J. M. Maravall, *Dictatorship and Dissent. Workers and Students in Franco's Spain* (1978), ch. 1, where Linz's contributions are listed.

15   See below, p. 96, for a further examination of apathy.

16   cf. A. López Piña and E. L. Aranguren, *La cultura política de la España de Franco* (1976), pp. 55*ff*. As late as 1974 a poll found 53.3 per cent of Spaniards totally uninterested in politics.

17   Quoted by X. Tusell, op. cit., p. 410.

18   In *La cruz de la Monarquía española actual* (1974), p. 47.

19   For a brief criticism of the Linz arguments see J. Martínez Alier, 'El corporativismo católico. La ACNP y el Opus Dei', in *El Viejo Topo* (1977).

CHAPTER 4

1   It is important to realise that in large areas of rural Spain the proportion of the active population in agriculture remained very high; only this

explains emigration from the poorer provinces with a high level of underemployment.

2 H. París Eguilaz, *Evolución política y económica de España* (1969), p. 82.

3 For the protectionist zeal of Spanish industrialists during the First World War see S. Roldán, *et al.*, *La consolidación del capitalismo en España 1914–20* (1973).

4 For a critical review of autarky see J. Clavera *et al.*, *Capitalismo español: de la autarquía a la estabilización* (1973), Vol. 1.

5 L. A. Rojo in S. Paniker, *op. cit.*, p. 159.

6 See J. Clavera, op. cit., pp. 153–281.

7 For a strong statement of this view see F. Javier Paniagua, *La ordenación del capitalismo avanzado en España* (1977).

8 López Rodó, *Política y Desarrollo*, p. 44.

9 Kg consumed per capita: 1940, 30; 1975, 969. Production increased ten times in the same period.

10 For an account of INI's activities see J. Ma. López de Letona *et al.*, *La empresa pública industrial en España* (1973).

11 For a general treatment of industrialisation see J. B. Donges, *La industrialización en España. Políticas, logros, persectivas* (1976).

12 See the article in *Cuardernos para el Diálogo* (March 1975) quoted in R. Aracil and M. García Bonafé, *Lecturas de historia económica de España*, Vol. II, pp. 286–98.

13 Between 1960 and 1970 the contribution of agriculture to the GNP fell by *c*.10 per cent and that of industry remained stable, whereas that of the service sector rose from 41.6 per cent to 52.1 per cent.

14 C. W. Anderson, *The Political Economy of Modern Spain* (1970), p. 164.

15 For a full discussion and criticism of the pole strategy see H. W. Richardson, *Regional Development Policy and Planning in Spain* (1975), pp. 111–40. For a severe criticism see Lázaro Muñoz, 'El fracaso de una política económica', in *El Europeo* (April 1973).

16 For stop-go policies see *Objetivos e instrumentos de la política económica española 1957–69,* published by Servicio de Estudios en Barcelona Banco Urquijo (1973), pp. 121–36.

17 For a useful summary of such criticisms see Salustiano del Campo and Manuel Navarro, *Crítica de la planificación social española 1964–75* (1976).

18 *Plan de Desarrollo Económico y Social 1964–7*, p. 19.

19 *III Plan de Desarrollo Económico y Social 1972–5,* Sección Vivienda (1972), p. 36.

20 Quoted in J. Ma. García Escudero, *Dos Españas,* (1975), Vol. IV, p. 1883.

21 See Julio Alcalde, 'Razón para la congelación', *Cambio 16* (4 October 1976).

22 Salustiano del Campo, *Crítica*, p. 109.

23 *ABC* (30 April 1969).

24 cf. the *Informe Económico 1976* of the Banco de Bilbao, p. 237 and

passim. The Informe specifically criticises the failure to modernise legislation on holding companies.

25 For the position in 1975 see 'Aún existen dos Españas', in *Actualidad Económica* (2 September 1975).

26 This is an underlying thesis of *Barcelona. Génesis y problemática del area metropolitana* (Edit. Moneda y Crédito, 1972).

27 H. W. Richardson, *Regional Development Policy and Planning in Spain,* p. 90.

28 See *Estudio socioeconómico de Andalucía,* published by Escuela Nacional de Administración Pública (1970).

29 Quoted in F. Lara Sánchez, *La emigración andaluza* (1977), p. 72.

30 *Últimas tardes con Teresa* (1966), p. 81.

31 An article written in 1961 and republished in *Vivir al dia* (1968), p. 114.

32 For conditions in the *barracas* of Barcelona in the mid-sixties see F. Candel, *Los otros Catalanes* (1964).

33 See *Estudio Socioeconómico de Andalucía,* published in Estudios del Instituto de Desarrollo Ecónomico (1970), pp. 195−224. Thus emigration is higher in eastern Andalusia than in the relatively richer western Andalusia, and especially low in provinces like Huelva where there are local jobs in industry and mining.

34 The 'pirate' emigrants who did not use the state emigration bureau (so-called 'assisted emigratiòn') were the most harshly treated in Germany; they had no rights since they entered as tourists without an official contract. The suicide rate among emigrants is six times the Spanish rate. See C. del Pino, 'Aspectos psicopatológicos de la migración', in *España económica* (October 1969).

35 See M. Siguán, *El medio rural en Andalucía oriental* (1972).

36 For this see Antonio López Ontiveros, *Emigración propiedad y paisaje agrario en la campina de Córdoba* (1974).

37 For a passionate, if amateur, plea for those caught in the crisis of traditional farming see Javier Gorosquieta, *El Campo Español en crisis* (1973), pp. 119*ff.*

38 For the role of agriculture in early industrialisation see J. L. Leal *et al., La agricultura en el desarrollo capitalista español (1940−70)* (1975).

39 They are also unfair to the producers of export crops like oranges or wine faced with international prices. A rise in domestic price levels hits them unfairly.

40 For the problems of agricultural credit and the failure of credit institutions to reach the smaller farmer see *Conyuntura Económica* 3, published by the Confederación española de Cajas de Ahorro (1977), pp. 63−73.

41 cf. the comment of the Banco de Bilbao's *Informe Económico 1976*: 'The massive protest of the farmers is much more justified than that of any other sector of society'. But since they were producing only 8 per cent of the GNP and losing labour at the rate of 100,000 a year, their protest went unheeded.

42 For what follows see *Informe Económico 1976*, published by the Banco de Bilbao, and *Conyuntura Económica 5/6*, published by the Confederación española de Cajas de Ahorro.
43 cf. *Conyuntura*, p. 42.
44

	UK		Spain		France	
	1960	1974	1960	1974	1960	1974
Food etc.	37.6	31.2	53.8	36.7	42.5	25.8
Clothing	9.9	8.8	11.2	10.5	11.1	8.1
Housing	14.3	18.5	9.0	13.1	9.2	14.2
Household expenses	10.2	7.3	7.9	8.6	9.0	8.4
Other goods and services	28.0	34.2	24.9	31.1	28.2	43.5

45 Banco de Bilbao, op. cit., p. 206.
46 *Co yuntura*, op. cit., p. 113.

CHAPTER 5

1 See the perceptive remarks of Amando de Miguel, *Estructura*, pp. 369*ff*.
2 We follow here the analysis of Carlos Moya's *El poder económico en España* (n.d.).
3 ibid., p. 101.
4 cf. Carlos Barral, *Años de penitencia* (1975), p. 190.
5 D. Ridruejo, *Escrito en España* (1962), p. 134.
6 F. Franco Salgado, *Conversaciones*, p. 83.
7 *Los empresarios ante el poder publico.*
8 For instance, the Law of Banking Incompatibilities of 1968 was aimed at the more blatant connections between private banks and the state agencies.
9 'Pobre sudor de los españoles', *Actualidad económica* (20 January 1976).
10 For an analysis of the new middle class based on bank employees see J. F. Tezanos, *Estructura de clases en la España actual* (1975), especially pp. 75*ff*.
11 Especially *Miau* – the classic portrait of a *cesante*, a civil servant rendered unemployed by a political change.
12 For a detailed study of the complicated pay structure of the civil service see A. Nieto, *La retribución de los funcionarios en España* (1967).
13 For the development of this protest movement see the revealing book of Ciriaco de Vicente, *La lucha de los Funcionarios Públicos* (1977), especially pp. 185*ff*. The author took a leading part in the protest movement and was sanctioned for his activities.
14 Carrero Blanco's speech at the opening of the Centre de formación y perfeccionamiento de funcionarios (1960).
15 See Salustiano del Campo, *Análisis de la población de España* (1972), p. 81.
16 cf. Manuel García Ferrando, *Mujer y sociedad rural* (1977), pp. 184*ff*.

17 For Zúñiga see V. Pérez Díaz, *Pueblos y clases sociales en el campo español* (1974), pp. 58–125.

18 They often possessed a double status. In the local village they were the bigwigs; when they visited the local town they were members of the lower middle class.

19 Though all estimates (especially if the 'new middle class' of white-collar workers is included) reveal an expanding middle sector, estimates as to its absolute size vary very considerably. Some put the conglomerate middle class at 40 per cent of the active population; others put the 'old' middle class (professionals, artisans etc.) at 4 per cent and the new middle class (wage-earning professionals, office staff etc.) at 15 per cent. For a summary of the various estimates see José Cazorla, *Problemas de estratificación social en España* (1973), ch. 1, and Amando de Miguel, *Estructura,* ch. 4.

20 See *Estudio socioecónomico de Andalucía,* especially pp. 164–8.

21 cf. V. Perez Díaz, *Pueblos*, p. 125*ff.*

22 Francisco Candel, *Los que nunca opinan* (1971), p. 117.

23 See the calculations of the employers' magazine *Acción Empresarial* in *Cuadernos para el Diálogo* (25 September 1976). The legal minimum wage in 1975 was half that of France. (*Actualidad Económica*, 8 April 1975.)

24 This is the issue in e.g. Alfonso Carlos Comín and J. N. García Nieto's study of a Barcelona industrial satellite town in *Juventud Obrera y conciencia de clase* (1974).

25 F. Candel, *Ser obrero no es ninguna ganga* (1968), p. 43*ff.*, and *Inmigrantes y trabajadores (1976), pp. 131ff.*

26 Comín and García Nieto, op. cit., p. 100.

27 For the 1975 elections see I. Boix and M. Pujadas, *Conversaciones sindicales con dirigentes obreros* (1975), pp. 55, 69, 72, 83, 96*ff.*, 104–9.

28 F. Candel, *Los que nunca opinan*, p. 56.

29 For the early growth of Madrid as an industrial area see F. Quirós Linares, 'Getafe', *Estudios Geográficos,* XXX (1960), pp. 211*ff.*

30 For a vivid description of the poor suburbs of Barcelona see Candel, *Los otros Catalanes* (1964).

31 Ma. Gaviria, *Ecologismo y ordenación del territorio en España* (1976), p. 321. Gaviria's solution, typical of radical solutions, is nationalisation of the tourist industry and a tax of 5,000 pesetas per tourist!

32 For a severe Spanish criticism of the consumer society see *Triunfo* (22 December 1973). The arguments deployed are based on those of US radicals, e.g. Baran, Sweezy and Ralph Nader.

33 The title of the work from which this quotation comes is indicative of its content: *La Autopista como ideología* (1973) by M. Gaviria. For a detailed criticism of a motorway scheme see his *Libro negro sobre la Autopista de la Costa Blanca* (1973), and, generally, L. Marco, *Transporte en España* (1973).

34 Francisco Umbral, *Memorias de un niño de derechas* (1972), p. 37.

35 R. Fraser, *The Pueblo* (1973), pp. 77, 83 and *passim.*

36 *III Plan de Desarrollo Económico y Social* (1971), p. 33.

37 For an examination of attitudes see J. R. Torregrosa, *La juventud española* (1972), especially pp. 131*ff.*, 143, 148. As one would expect, the highest scores in indifference were reached by unskilled workers and in rural Spain. What is significant here is the high scores among the urban educated youth.

38 J. M. Maravall, *Dictatorship and Political Dissent. Workers and Students in Franco's Spain* (1978), p. 138, an interview with two student militants.

39 *Cambio 16* (26 December 1977).

40 For some perceptive comments see L. Garruccio, *Spagna senza miti* (1968).

41 E. Enciso, *La muchacha en el noviazgo,* quoted in A. Ferrandiz and V. Verdú, *Noviazgo y matrimonio en la burguesía española* (1974), p. 155.

42 *Triunfo* (1 May 1976).

43 cf. the interviews with various left-wing youth groups in *El País* (28 August 1977).

44 *Cambio 16* (28 November 1977).

45 Carlos Barral, *Años de penitencia* (1975), pp. 143, 167, 202.

46 See the analysis of A. López Piña and E. Aranguren in *La Cultura política de la España de Franco* (1976).

47 *Blanco y Negro* (27 March 1976).

48 J. M. Maravall, op. cit., p. 78.

49 I. Boix and M. Pujadas, *Conversaciones sindicales y dirigentes obreros* (1975), p. 30.

50 Carlos Barral, op. cit., p. 16.

51 Between 1966 and 1976, 20,000 people were killed on the roads.

52 Amando de Miguel, *Desde la España predemocrática* (1976), pp. 80–1, 97.

53 cf. 'Los ex de la religión', *Europeo* (15 February 1975).

54 The parish magazine of the Barcelona industrial suburb Cornellá, quoted in A. Carlos Comín and Juan N. García Nieto, *Juventud Obrera y conciencia Católica* (1974).

55 For the distribution of attendance at mass see Almerich *et al., Cambio social y religión en España* (1975), p. 137. cf. the pattern of German Catholicism.

56 *Estudio Socioeconómico de Andalucía,* p. 199.

57 J. López Pacheco, *Central Eléctrica* (1958). The novel was written between 1953 and 1956.

58 R. Fraser, *The Pueblo,* pp. 183, 190.

59 Newspaper readership is half that of France.

60 Interview with José María Iñigo in *Blanco y Negro* (30 October 1976).

61 cf. the history of the youth Tele Club of Ejica, an Andalusian town, in J. Yglesias, op. cit., pp. 182*ff.*

CHAPTER 6

1   For a brief account of their importance see *Spain: A Companion to Spanish Studies*, ed. P. E. Russell, pp. 416–8. All were born in the late nineteenth century or the early years of the twentieth.

2   For the activities of the 'other Spain' in Mexico see M. Fagen, *Exiles and Citizens: Spanish Republicans in Mexico* (1973).

3   For Marías see below, p. 111.

4   For Spain as a 'cultural desert' see J. L. Abellán, *La cultura en España* (1971); J. Marías, 'La vegetación del páramo', *La Vanguardia Española* (19 November 1976); J. L. Aranguren, *La cultura española y la cultura establecida* (1975) and *Reseña*, no. 100 (December 1976).

5   cf. F. J. Conde, *Contribución a la doctrina del Caudillaje* (1942), and J. Ma. Areilza and F. Ma. Castiella, *Reivindicaciones españolas* (1941).

6   See Carlos Castilla del Pino, 'La psiquitría española', in *La Cultura bajo el Franquismo* (1977), pp. 79*ff*.

7   C. Robles Piquer, 'La política cultural', in M. Fraga Iribarne (ed.), *La España de los años 70* (1974), Vol. III, no. 2, p. 627.

8   For D'Ors see E. Jardí, *Eugeni D'Ors. Vida i obra* (1967).

9   For the history of *Escorial* see J. C. Mainer, *Falange y Literatura* (1971), and *Literatura y pequeña burguesía en España* (1972).

10 In his book *Descargo de conciencia 1930–60* (1976).

11 See I. Martín's speech at the seventh Congress of CSIC in ABC (28 January 1947), and his *La Investigación Española* (1947).

12 On *Arbor*, see D. Artigues, *L'Opus Dei en Espagne* (1968), pp. 41–3 and 127–36; and A. Fontán, *Los Católicos en la Universidad española* (1961), pp. 90*ff*.

13 P. Laín Entralgo, *El problema de la Universidad* (1968), pp. 55–69; and C. París, 'De qué filosofía vivimos?', *Cuadernos para el Diálogo* (August 1974), p. 41.

14 Franco's speech of 21 June 1950, quoted in M. Tuñón de Lara, 'Historia', in *La Cultura bajo el Franquismo* (1977), p. 23. A few older monarchist historians (Fernández Almagro and Pabón) attempted a fair treatment of the period 1874–1923.

15 J. M. Jover, 'Corrientes historiográficas en la España Contemporánea', *Boletín Informativo de la Fundación Juan March* (March 1975). In the 1940s, of the 54 doctoral theses presented in Madrid University only 7 treated the contemporary period.

16 D. Sueiro, *La verdadera historia del Valle de los Caídos* (1977).

17 V. Bozal, *Historia del arte en España* (1972).

18 J. Marichal, *El nuevo pensamiento político español* (1966), p. 28.

19 See J. L. Aranguren, *Memorias y esperanzas españolas* (1969), pp. 69, 74*ff*, 113.

20 For various authors' views of the censorship see Antonio Beneyto, *Censura y política en los escritores españoles* (1975), especially pp. 35, 43, 47, 74, 134, 193.

21 *Jarama*, p. 153. Other practitioners of the 'objective' novel include Aldecoa, Carmen Martín Gaite and Fernández Santos.

22 For a short, perceptive account of the Spanish cinema see V. Molina Foix, *New Cinema in Spain* (1977).

23 For an English account see M. P. Holt, *The Contemporary Spanish Theatre* (1975), pp. 110*ff*.

24 *Cataluña a mediados del siglo XV* (1956), p. 9. Vicens was much frowned on by the official establishment and took to publishing to earn his living while waiting eight years for a chair. His early death was a great loss to history and Catalonia. The publication of the review he inspired, *Estudios de historia moderna,* represented in 1951 a breakthrough in Spanish historiography.

25 D. Ridruejo, *Escrito en España* (1962), pp. 176.

26 Franco himself wrote the script for *Raza* — a film in the heroic genre. He was as addicted to films as he was to football on television.

27 On Spanish cinema see D. Font, *Del azul al verde. El cine español durante el franquismo* (1976).

28 T. Moix, 'El filón del "Osú" ', *Nuevas Fotogramas* (10 May 1974).

29 F. Umbral, *Memorias de un niño de derechas* (1972), p. 63*ff*. For statistics of foreign films see *Anuario Español de Cinematografía* (1962), pp. 682*ff*.

30 For the theatre in this period see J. Monleón, *Treinta años de teatro de la derecha* (1971).

31 Juan F. Alvarez Macías, *La novela popular en España: José Mallorquí* (1972); and José Ma. Díez Borque, *Literatura y cultura de masas* (1972).

32 C. M. Gaite, 'Cuarto espadas sobre las coplas de posguerra', *Triunfo* (18 November 1972). See interview with Sautier in *Interviú* (21–27 April 1977). The best introduction to the culture of evasion is M. Vázquez Montalbán, *Crónica sentimental de España* (1971).

33 J. M. García, *El bisturí del fútbol español* (1975); '40 años de nacional-futbolismo', *El Pais* (27 February 1977).

34 E. Rodríguez Monegal, quoted in P. Gil Casado, *La novela social española* (1973), p. 119.

35 *Central Eléctrica*, p. 316; cf. p. 251 for a splendid take-off of the official 'triumphalist' language of the regime. Other writers of this so-called 'postwar realist generation' are Luis and J. A. Goytisolo, Hortelano, Valente, Grosso, A. González, Gil de Biedma, Barral. The critic J. M. Castellet was the theorist of the generation: see his *Un cuarto de siglo de poesía española* (1966); and P. Gil Casado, *La novela social española* (1968).

36 His essays are collected in two books: *Drama y sociedad* (1956) and *Anatomía del realismo* (1965).

37 Quoted in Farris Anderson, *Alfonso Sastre* (1971), p. 89.

38 Saura's films include a reflection on violence in Spanish society, *La Caza* (*The Hunt*, 1965), and subtle metaphors about personal relations *Peppermint Frappé* (1967) and *La Madriguera* (*The Den,* 1967). Patino's *Nueve cartas a Berta* (Nine Letters to Berta, 1965), a story about a young university student, was one of the first openly political films made in postwar Spain. The 'new Spanish cinema' declined after

1968; see C. Santos Fontenla, *Cine Español en la encrucijada* (1966).

39 Castilla del Pino published *Estudios sobre la depresión. Fundamentos de Antropología dialéctica* (1967), *Dialéctica de la personal dialéctica de la situación* (1968), *Psicoanálisis y marxismo* (1969) and many other titles. For Marxism and Christians, see J. Aguirre (ed.), *Cristianos y Marxistas: los problemas de un diálogo* (1969); and J. Dalmau, *Distensiones cristiano-marxistas* (1968).

40 F. Fernández Santos, 'Julián Marías y el liberalismo', *Ruedo Ibérico* (June/July 1965), pp. 63–9. According to F. Santos, Marías had excluded Gil Novales, Morodo, Elías Díaz, Jutglar, Goytisolo, Sacristán, Tamames, Tuñón de Lara, Sastre, Gil de Biedma, Martín Santos and many others. Marías' comment in J. Marías, *Los españoles* (1963), p. 234.

41 On the need for a new policy of information, see M. Fraga Iribarne, *Horizonte español* (1968), pp. 225*ff*.

42 Interview in *Triunfo* (23 December 1972).

43 On TVE finances see *El País* (2 January 1977). On TVE see J. Cueto, 'La otra fiesta nacional', *El País* (26 December 1976); *El Europeo* (12 April 1975); *YA* (15 February 1975, 24 April and 29 May 1976); *El País* (15 August 1976); J. M. Rodríguez Méndez, *Los Teleadictos* (1972); and M. Vázquez Montalbán, *El libro gris de Televisión Española* (1973).

44 A. Fernández Santos, 'Situación del teatro no-profesional en España', *Primer Acto* (December 1966), p. 5. See also R. Domenech, 'El teatro desde 1936', in *Historia de la literatura española* (1974), Vol. III, pp. 437*ff*.; and M. Bilbatúa, 'El teatro de Alfonso Paso', *Cuadernos para el diálogo, VI Extraordinario* (July 1967), pp. 63–7. The last year of Paso's dominance was 1969.

45 *Informaciones* (19 August 1976).

46 There were exceptions: Pablo Neruda and Gabriel García Márquez topped the best-selling list in 1974 and 1975. See *Anuario Económico y Social de España 1977* (1977), pp. 308–9.

47 *Cuadernos para el Diálogo* (September 1971), p. 24. On *fotonovelas,* see Manuel J. Campo, *Simplemente María y su repercusión entre la clases trabajadores* (1975); and A. Amorós, 'Fotonovelas', *Insula* (June 1969).

48 See his *Los Españoles* (1963), p. 216.

49 E. Díaz, *Pensamiento español 1939–73* (1974), pp. 246–59.

50 cf. the interview with José Yglesias in *The Franco Years* (1977), p. 78.

51 *Insula* (April 1969).

52 Benet's main novels are *Volverás a Región* (1967), *Una meditación* (1970), *Un viaje de invierno* (1972) and *La otra casa de Mazón* (1973). His novels describe the decadence of a country after a civil war.

53 The latest literary tendencies in Spain are represented in the work of Azúa, Molina Foix, Javiér Marías, Terenci Moix and F. Nieva.

54 The *Revista de Occidente* reappeared in 1963 under the guidance of Ortega's disciples.

55 See the contributions by C. Alonso de los Ríos and F. Umbral to *Anuario Económico y Social de España 1977* (1977). On the porn industry see A. García Pintado, 'Seudo-porno España S.A.', *Cuadernos para el Diálogo* (1 April(!) 1978), pp. 44*ff*.

56 *Si te dicen que caí (If they tell you that I fell)*, a picaresque novel set in Barcelona after the Civil War, full of embittered passion and written in a prose which combines realism and imagination. Among the new films: Jaime Chávarri's *El desencanto* (*The Disenchantment*, 1976) and *A un Dios desconocido (To an unknown God*, 1977); Jaime Camino's *Las largas vacaciones del 36* (*The Long Holidays of 1936*, 1975); R. Franco's *Pascual Duarte* (1975); Patiño's *Queridísimos Verdugos* (*Dearest Executioners*, 1976) and *Canciones para después de una guerra* (*Songs for after a War*, 1971, but not shown until 1976); Borau's *Furtivos* (1975) and Saura's two latest films, *Cría Cuervos* (*Crows*, 1975) and *Elisa, mía* (*Elisa, My Love*, 1977). This recovery was anticipated by Erice's *Espíritu de la colmena* (*The Spirit of the Beehive*, 1973), perhaps the most sensitive of them all.

57 See the interview in *El País* (19 February 1978). Miró refused to design posters in Castilian for the Socialist party.

CHAPTER 7

1 *Triunfo* (9 December 1972).
2 The siege of Numantia was a heroic resistance of the native inhabitants against the Roman armies
3 See below, p. 195.
4 Turnout in the November 1973 local elections was 35.74 per cent. In Madrid, in Barcelona and in the Basque country it was below 25 per cent. See *Informaciones* (14 November 1973 and in subsequent issues).
5 The Spanish phrase is 'asistencia social claramente mayoritaria'.
6 *Contestación* in the sense of protest is a new word: it does not appear as such in dictionaries until the 1970s.
7 These attitudes are abundantly illustrated in F. Franco Salgado-Araujo, *Conversaciones privadas*, e.g. pp 241, 248, 322, 346, 418, 438, 455–6, 468, 489.
8 On the OS see P. Lamata, *Teoría Sindical. Organización Sindical Española* (1970); C. Iglesias Selgas, *El Sindicalismo Español* (1974); M. Ludevid, *Cuarenta años de sindicato vertical. Aproximación a la Organización Sindical Española* (1976).
9 The attempt was made by Gerardo Salvador Merino, who was close to Ridruejo; he was forced to resign in 1941.
10 A. Rull Sabater, *La Seguridad Social en España* (1970–1); and J. Vergés, *La Seguridad Social española y sus cuentas* (1976)
11 On the new Spanish labour movement see F. Claudín, 'Le nouveau mouvement ouvrier', *Les Temps Modernes. Espagne 1976. Dossier*, no. 357 *bis* pp. 8–56.
12 A. García Barbancho, *Las migraciones interiores en España en*

1961 – 70 (1975); *Cuadernos para el Diálogo,* extra no. XL (May 1974).

13 J. M. Naredo and J. Leguina, 'Precios y salarios. Una difícil comparación, *Triunfo* (24 February 1973).

14 For the geography of strikes see J. M. Maravall, op. cit., pp. 44*ff.* See also his 'Modernization, authoritarianism, and the growth of working-class dissent: the case of Spain', *Government and Opposition,* vol. 8, no. 4 (Autumn 1973).

15 The exception is Asturias; but the output of the declining Asturian coalmines represented only a small part of Spanish total production and when the miners struck the government stepped up coal imports, including imports from the Socialist countries of Eastern Europe.

16 e.g. the Asturian strikes; the metallurgical strike in Madrid, the Basque provinces and Seville (Standard, Pegaso, Perkins, Marconi, Maquinista Terrestre y Marítima). After 1970 there were serious strikes in the automobile industry (SEAT in Barcelona, Citroen in Vigo, Renault in Valladolid and British Leyland in Pamplona). There were bad building strikes in Seville and Barcelona.

17 Vigo 1972; Pamplona 1973; Bajo Llobregat (Barcelona) 1974. See J. Amsden, *Collective Bargaining and Class Conflict in Spain* (1972); *Cuadernos para el Diálogo,* no. XXXIII (February 1973), and no. XLVII (June 1975).

18 J. M. García Nieto (ed.), *La Ley Sindical. Análisis de una protesta* (1970); C. Iglesias Selgas, *Comentarios a la Ley Sindical* (1971).

19 José Yglesias, *The Franco Years* (1977), p. 57.

20 On CC OO see N. Sartorius, *El resurgir del Movimiento Obrero* (1976), and *Qué son las Comisiones Obreras?* (1977); M. Camacho, *Charlas en prisión* (1977); M. Calamai, *Storia del Movimento Operaio Spagnolo dal 1960 al 1975* (1976); J. Ariza, *Las Comisiones Obreras* (1976).

21 A CC OO leader to the Italian writer Ludovico Garrucio, *Spagna senza miti* (1968), p. 278.

22 In the union elections of 1978, the first free union elections held in Spain since the Civil War, the results were as follows: CC OO, 54,238 shop stewards (35.15 per cent); UGT, 34,395 (22.2 per cent); USO, 5,449 (3.5 per cent); CSUT, 4,350 (2.82 per cent); SU, 2,662 (1.72 per cent); 27,766 with no clear affiliation and 18,771 independents. In the Basque country, the Basque nationalist union (ELA-STV) scored a great local success with 1,804 shop stewards elected. Results do not include the two largest Spanish firms, RENFE (railways) and the telephone company. See *El País* (30 March 1978).

23 P. Laín Entralgo, *Descargo de conciencia* (1975), pp. 385*ff.*

24 See the government's decree in *Boletín Oficial del Estado* (24 January 1969).

25 See above, p. 191.

26 See A. Peña, 'Veinticinco años de luchas estudiantiles', *Horizonte Español 1966* (1966), Vol. II, pp. 169*ff*; and 'Diez años de movimiento universitario', *Materiales* (March/April 1977).

27 cf. J. M. Maravall, op. cit., chs 6 and 7.

28   The Concordat text can be found in F. Díaz Plaja, *La España franquista en sus documentos* (1976), pp. 275–91.

29   In 1955 Mgr Pildain, Bishop of Las Palmas and a political conservative, declared that the OS was incompatible with Christian doctrine; in 1961 similar statements were made by the Suffragan Bishop of Valencia. In 1961 and 1962 the Bishop of Bilbao criticised low industrial wages, and the Archbishop of Seville the lamentable conditions of the Andalusian rural proletariat.

30   For a survey of modern episcopal life styles see Fermín Abolla, 'La ruptura episcopal', *El País Semanal* (12 February 1978). See also N. Cooper, 'The church: from Crusade to Christianity', in P. Preston (ed.), *Spain in Crisis* (1975); and S. Giner, 'Metamorfosis de la iglesia en diez Años', *Cuadernos para el Diálogo*, no. XXXVIII (December 1973).

31   R. Garriga, *El Cardenal Segura y el nacional-catolicismo* (1977).

32   J. Ruiz Giménez, 'En el arranque del camino', *Cuadernos para el Diálogo* no. VII (February 1968), p. 5.

33   On the influence of John XXIII on the Spanish Christian Democrats see *Cuadernos para el Diálogo* (July 1964).

34   F. Carrillo de Albornoz, *La Libertad religiosa y el Concilio Vaticano II* (1965).

35   *Iglesia y Sociedad en España 1939–75* (1977), p. 131.

36   See below, p. 205.

37   Besides the works quoted in previous notes, see J. Chao, *La Iglesia en el franquismo* (1976); and the collective publications of the hierarchy in Episcopado Español, *Mensajes al pueblo* (1975).

38   For a full account of the Burgos Trials see G. Halimi, *Le Procès de Burgos* (1971); and K. Salaberri, *El Proceso de Euskadi en Burgos* (1971).

39   *Berriak* (16 September 1976).

40   Terenci Moix in *El País Semanal* (24 July 1977). For a favourable account of Catalan culture of protest see J. Rossinyol, *Le problème national catalan* (1974), pp. 412*ff.*

41   For the effects of industrialisation on the *caserio* see Miren Etxezarreta in R. Aracil and M. García Bonafé, *Lecturas de Historia económica de España*, vol. II, pp. 357–79. On the modern Basque country see J. M. Azaola, *Vasconia y su destino* (1976); and L. Núñez, *La sociedad vasca actual* (1977).

42   It was anxious to prove that the kidnapping of the industrialist Huarte *helped* the strike movement and that the assassination of Carrero Blanco did not weaken a strike protest against the trial of the leaders of the Workers' Commissions. See Julian Agirre, *Operation Ogro* (trans. B. Solomon, 1975), pp. 18, 98, 176.

43   On ETA, see Ortzi, *Historia de Euskadi: el nacionalismo vasco y ETA* (1975); and J. Apalategui, 'Le mouvement basque aujourd'hui', *Les Temps Modernes*, no. 357 *bis* (1976), pp. 423–53.

44   Quoted in *Triunfo* (23 March 1974).

45   See *PSUC: Per Catalunya, la Democracia i el Socialisme* (1976).

46 It has been argued that the democratic institutions of the Republic had been eroded during the war. This happens to all democratic regimes in wartime. Nevertheless, with all its imperfections, before and after the war, the Second Republic represented the democratic tradition in Spanish politics.
47 R.C. made many inquiries in these years about pockets of guerrilla activities in Andalusia and Aragon. On the Spanish opposition see P. Preston, 'The Anti-Francoist opposition: the long march to unity', in P. Preston (ed.), *Spain in Crisis* (1976); and X. Tusell, *La oposición democrática al franquismo* (1977).
48 J. Ma. Gil Robles, *La monarquía por la que yo luché* (1976), p. 317.
49 For the exiles in Mexico see P. M. Fagen, *Exiles and Citizens. Spanish Republicans in Mexico* (1973).
50 For this controversy see Jorge Semprún's amusing and catty *Autobiografía de Federico Sánchez* (1977), especially pp 156, 268*ff*. Claudín and Semprún's quarrel with Carrillo involved other issues, e.g. the Stalinist nature of the party in the post-Stalin period. See also S. Carrillo, *Después de Franco, qué?* (1965), *Nuevos enfogues a problemas de hoy* (1967), *Demain L'Espagne* (1974); and F. Claudín, *Documentos de una divergencia comunista* (1978).
51 cf. Guy Hermet, *The Communists in Spain* (1971), pp. 171*ff*.
52 For a criticism of the exile leadership of Llopis see the collective work by F. Bustelo *et. al.*, *Partido Socialista Obrero Español* (1976).
53 For Tierno Galván's position see his *España y el socialismo* (1976); and F. Bobillo, *Partido Socialista Popular* (1976).
54 For instance the defence of the leaders of the CC OO in 1973. On the 'Munich affair' see, for example *ABC* (10 June 1962).
55 cf. the PCE declaration of June 1964.
56 'I ask those who accuse us of subjectivism, of not anticipating the rhythm of events hour by hour, year by year: if in 1939 the Party had said, "We will reach 1964 and Fascism will still exist in Spain", what would have happened?' Quoted in J. Semprún, op. cit., p. 212.
57 *Signo* (6 June 1966).
58 *ABC* (20 April and 21 July 1966).
59 *Informaciones* (20 May 1966).

CHAPTER 8

1 For a description of the families of the regime see above, p. 21 and *ff*.
2 For Serrano Suñer's account, see his *Entre el silencio y la propaganda. La Historia como fue: memorias* (1976), pp. 357–73.
3 See above, p. 113.
4 F. Franco, *Discursos y Mensajes,* p. 583.
5 For the splits in the monarchist camp see above, pp. 32–5. On relations between Don Juan and Franco, see X. Tusell, *La oposición democrática al franquismo (1939–62)* (1977); and J. M. Gil Robles, *La monarquía por la que yo luché*. See also V. Salmador, *Don Juan de Borbón. Grandeza y servidumbre del deber* (1976).

6 See above, p. 105.

7 See, for instance, his speech in Seville on 1 May 1956, in *Discursos y Mensajes*, p. 186.

8 On the 'third force' see R. Calvo Serer, *La fuerza creadora de la libertad* (1958), pp. 341*ff*.; R. Fernández Cuesta, *Continuidad falangista al servicio de España* (1955), p. 46; A. López Amo, *La monarquía de la reforma social* (1955); and *La Actualidad Española* (14 November 1974).

9 For the Falangist views, see E. Romero, *Cartas a un Príncipe* (1964) passim. For press attacks on the monarchy, Conde de los Andes "Condicionantes de la Monarquía", *España. Su Monarquía y el futuro* (1975) p. 82. Herrera Oria's view, in L. López Rodó, op. cit., p. 289.

10 Serrano Suñer's early views are in his *Entre Hendaya y Gibraltar* (1947), and his final version in *Entre el silencio y la propaganda. La Historia como fue: Memorias* (1976).

11 For Arrese's ideas in 1945, see J. L. Arrese, *Treinta años de política* (1966), pp. 619–641 and 1079–1108.

12 ibid., pp. 1128–45.

13 Carrero's speech is reproduced in *ABC* (16 July 1957). Carrero's speeches have been collected in L. Carrero Blanco, *Discursos y escritos* (*1943–73*) (1974).

14 Solís' speech is in J. Solís Ruiz, *Nueva convivencia española* (1959), pp. 13–39.

15 For Solís' 'political development' see J. Solís Ruiz, 'Monarquía, la presencia del pueblo en el Sindicalismo y en la política', in *España. Su Monarquía y el futuro* (1975), pp. 299–300; and E. Romero, *Cartas al Rey* (1973), pp. 157–95.

16 M. Fraga Iribarne, *Horizonte Español* (1965), p. 41; Franco's speech in 1962 is quoted in J. M. Gil Robles (ed.), *Cartas del pueblo español* (1967), p. 26; Franco's speech on 22 November 1966 is in *ABC* (23 November 1966).

17 Quoted in J. Solís, 'Monarquía...', p. 300. See J. Fueyo Álvarez, *Desarrollo político y orden constitucional* (1964).

18 For the limits of 'liberalisation' see I. Fernández de Castro and J. Martínez, *España hoy* (1963).

19 *ABC* (10 March 1963).

20 See above, p. 127.

21 E. Romero, *Cartas a un Príncipe* (1964).

22 For the reaction of the left, see E. García, 'La nueva izquierda falangista', *Cuadernos de Ruedo Ibérico* (April/May 1966).

23 L. M. Ansón, 'La Monarquía de todos', *ABC* (21 July 1966); for the policies of Calvo Serer and Pemán see R. Calvo Serer, op. cit., pp. 42, 55.

24 *El crepúsculo de las ideologías* (*The Twilight of Ideologies*) was the title of a book published by Fernández de la Mora in 1965. See R. Morodo, 'Los ideólogos del fin de las ideologías', *Cuadernos para el Diálogo* (August/September 1965).

25 For different views of the referendum (held on 14 December) see J. Meliá, *El largo camino de la apertura (Del Referendum a las asociaciones)* (1975), pp. 13–19; *Cuadernos para el Diálogo* (December 1966).
26 For a brief account of the failure to evolve see J. Valero, 'Voluntad de cambio y legislación posterior', *Documentación Social*, no. 18. For Ricardo de la Cierva's comments see *Gaceta Ilustrada* (30 March 1975).
27 *Cambio 16* (22–8 November 1976).
28 *Pueblo* (24 November 1966)
29 E. Romero, *Cartas al Rey* (1973), pp. 157–93, 286–8; J. Meliá, *El largo camino*, pp. 169–200.
30 For Carrero López Rodó, the crucial book now is L. López Rodó, *La larga marcha hacia la Monarquía* (1977).
31 J. Meliá, *El largo camino*, is a good analysis of *apertura* by one of its supporters. For a hostile view see J. Solé Turá, 'Los tecnócratas en la encrucijada', *España. Perspectiva 1972*, pp. 180–203. On the regime's 'third generation' see the comments of 'Argos' in *ABC* (3 March 1973) on Ortí Bordas' lecture on 'The Generation for the Transition'; and Luis Ma. Ansón, 'La generación del silencio', *ABC* (3 March 1973).
32 Equipo de Estudios, *Al filo de la crisis* (1975), pp. 125–52.
33 José Miguel Ortí Bordas, quoted in Amando de Miguel, *La herencia del Franquismo* (1976), p. 209.
34 For Fraga, see his books *El Desarrollo político* (1971), and *Legitimidad y Representación* (1973). See also M. Milián Mestre, *Fraga Iribarne, retrato en tres tiempos* (1975).
35 J. M. Areilza, *Escritos políticos* (1968), p. 182.
36 R. Chao, *Después de Franco, España* (1976), pp. 67–83. Areilza's articles are collected in *Cien artículos* (1971) and *Figuras y pareceres* (1973).
37 A. Alvarez Solís, *Qué es el bunker?* (1976); 'Familias y organizaciones politicas del bloque dominante', *Boletín HOAC*, extra no. 1 (1977); J. A. Girón de Velasco, *Reflexiones Sobre España* (1975).
38 See his 'Maeztu y la teoría de la Revolución', foreword to R. Maeztu, *Frente a la República* (1956), p. 105.
39 G. Fernández de la Mora, 'El Estado de Obras', *ABC* (1 April 1973). His book reviews have been collected in *Pensamiento Español 1963–7*, 5 vols (1964–8).
40 M. Jiménez de Parga, 'Política interior', *España Perspectiva 1968* (1968), p. 15.
41 The text of the law is in F. Díaz Plaja, *La España franquista en sus documentos* (1976), pp. 416–25. See also T. Luca de Tena, *Crónicas parlamentarias* (1967), p. 43.
42 J. Meliá, op. cit., pp. 89–98. On the Movement as 'communion' or as 'organization', see the editorial report in *Cuadernos para el Diálogo* (November 1968); Areilza's comments in *Escritos políticos* (1968), pp. 178–82; and J. A. González Casanova, 'Asociaciones políticas y Monarquía moderada', in *España. Perspectiva 1974*, pp. 103–22.

43 *Actualidad Econòmica* (4 February 1975) published a long report on the history of political associations. See also 'Las non natas asociaciones políticas', *Cuadernos para el Diálogo* (January 1970); and M. Herrero Miñón, 'El asociacionismo', in *España Perspectiva. 1970*, pp. 231–60.

44 *Actualidad Económica* (4 February 1975).

45 F. Bobillo, *Partido Socialista Popular* (1976), pp. 25–6; 'La oposición política en Cataluña', *Doblón* (17 January 1976).

46 P. Preston, 'The anti-Francoist opposition: the long march to unity', in P. Preston (ed.), *Spain in Crisis*, pp. 125*ff*; J. Benet *et. al.*, *Dionisio Ridruejo: de la Falange a la oposición* (1976); and X. Tusell, *La oposición democrática al franquismo 1939–62* (1976), *passim*.

47 S. Vilar, *Protagonistas de la oposición democrática. La oposición a la dictadura, 1939–69* (1969), pp. 729*ff*.

CHAPTER 9

1 For the 'Matesa affair' see E. Alvarez-Puga, *Matesa. Más allá del escándalo* (1974).

2 See C. Alonso Tejada, *La represión sexual en la España de Franco* (1977), and his article in *El Viejo Topo*, extra 1 (1977), p. 43.

3 *Pueblo* (7 November 1972); *Arriba* (8 November 1972). On Fernández Miranda see E. Romero, *Cartas al Rey*, pp. 168–80; and 'El Ministro del Movimiento habla', *Cuadernos para el Diálogo* (March 1972).

4 See Carrero's interview with Emilio Romero in 1968 in E. Romero, *Prólogo para un Rey* (1976), pp. 17–55.

5 E. Tierno Galván, 'Política Internacional', *España Perspectiva 1970*, pp. 61–6.

6 See above, p. 113.

7 J. N. García Nieto *et. al.*, *La nueva ley Sindical* (1970). See also the report on the new Syndical Law in *Cuadernos para el Diálogo* (November 1969).

8 A narrative of events is to be found in E. de Blaye, *Franco and the Politics of Spain* (1976), pp. 281*ff*. See also 'Hacia una política de endurecimiento', *Cuadernos para el Diálogo* (December 1971).

9 Quoted in 'Hemeroteca 73', *Triunfo* (27 January 1973).

10 J. M. Areilza, *Cien artículos* (1971), pp. 168–76, contains both his and Carrero Blanco's articles.

11 F. Silva Muñoz, 'Pluralismo y Participación', *ABC* (27 October 1972). See his lecture, 'La hora de la participación política', delivered on 26 November 1973, in *Ya* (27 November 1973). On the '1972 political articles' see L. González Seara, *España, en el umbral del cambio* (1975), p. 101.

12 R. Tamames, *La República. La Era de Franco* (1973). Cartoons by Perich, Mingote, Forges and others have been collected in book form and have sold thousands of copies.

13 P. Preston, 'General Franco's rearguard', *New Society* (29 November 1973).

14 *ABC, Ya, Arriba* (4–6 May 1973).
15 On 'Diego Ramírez' articles, see L. González Seara, op. cit., p. 162; and L. Carandell, *Democracia pero Orgánica* (1974), pp. 27–36.
16 S. Cruylles, 'Un refrán que no rige en política', *La Vanguardia* (7 February 1973).
17 The expression was coined by Fernández Miranda in a speech in Valladolid on 4 March 1971 and taken up by Emilio Romero in an article in *Pueblo* (4 September 1972). See 'Hemeroteca 72', *Triunfo* (16 September 1972), and P. Castellanos, 'Los nuevos socialistas', *Cuadernos para el Diálogo* (April 1971).
18 Quoted in *Ya* (10 October 1972).
19 For Franco's speech see *Informaciones* (2 January 1973), and *Ya* (5 January 1973); and *Tres discursos de Franco* (1973).
20 They would be known later as the 'group of 39'. Most of them came from the SEU, the Falangist Student Union. Prominent among them were Ortí Bordás, and the future Minister of the Interior under Suárez, Martín Villa.
21 *Informaciones* (2 March 1973).
22 See *El Alcázar* and *Pueblo* (14 May 1973).
23 On the new government, see the views of G. Cisneros in *Blanco y Negro* (23 June 1973).
24 For a detailed account see J. Agirre, *Operatión Ogro* (1975).
25 On the Arias period see E. Romero, *Prólogo para un Rey* (1976); J. Oneto, Arias entre dos crisis 1973–5 (1975), and *100 días en la muerte de Francisco Franco* (1975); and R. de la Cierva, *Crónicas de la transición. De la muerte de Carrero a la proclamación del Rey* (1975).
26 J. M. Ruiz Gallardón, 'El nuevo Gobierno. Un lustro en la politica del Régimen', *España. Perspectiva, 1974* pp. 87–100.
27 For the reaction in Spain, see *Ya* and *La Vanguardia* (30 January 1974).
28 J. Oneto, *Arias entre dos crisis 1973–5*, pp. 53–61.
29 E. Romero, 'Luz verde', *Pueblo* (19 June 1974).
30 P. Calvo Hernando, 'Opinión personal', *Gaceta Ilustrada* (11 May 1975).
31 It was even rumoured that the Pope had ready a decree excommunicating Franco and his government should they decide to expel Mgr Añoveros from Spain.
32 J. Oneto, op. cit., pp. 63–76.
33 ibid., p. 80.
34 *Arriba* (28 April 1974); J. Oneto, op. cit., pp. 85–95; E. Romero, *Prólogo para un Rey,* pp. 146–50.
35 See *Protagonismo del Movimiento. Discursos de Carlos Arias Navarro y José Utrera Molina, Barcelona 15 de Junio de 1974* (1974), pp. 27–41.
36 E. Romero, 'Luz Verde', *Pueblo* (19 June 1974).
37 'Hemeroteca 74', *Triunfo* (21 September 1974), contains a full account of Arias' press conference and of the reaction of the press.
38 Reproduced in full in E. Romero, *Prólogo para un Rey*, pp. 173–81. A number of well-known intellectuals and actors were arrested (Alfonso Sastre, Eva Forest, Lidia Falcón etc.). No charges could be

brought against them. The accusation against the Communist party was preposterous.

39 For Tácito see *Tácito* (1975), collected articles; and P. Calvo Hernando, 'Opinión personal', *Gaceta Ilustrada* (18 June 1975).
40 'Semana vasca', *Cambio 16* (7 April 1975).
41 For the new law and the reactions it brought, see 'Hemeroteca 75', *Triunfo* (6 September 1975); and *Cambio 16* (25 August 1975).
42 *La Actualidad Española* (26 December 1974–2 January 1975); *Cambio 16* (3–9 February 1975); and *Actualidad Económica* (4 February 1975).
43 Quoted in R. Tamames, 'La Era de Franco. 36 Años de la vida de España (1939–75)', *Tiempo de Historia* (January 1976), p. 30. See R. Chao, *Después de Franco. España* (1976), pp. 287–309.
44 Tierno had formed in 1967 a Socialist Party of the Interior (PSI) as an attempt to end the isolation of the PSOE in exile from the 'interior struggle'. In November 1974 the PSI became the Popular Socialist Party (PSP). Despite repeated negotiations, unification between PSP and PSOE did not materialise. See F. Bobillo, *PSP* (1976).
45 S. Carrillo, *Demain L'Espagne* (1974); R. Chao, op. cit., summarises the attitude of the different parties of the opposition in the months before Franco's death.
46 R. Chao, op. cit., pp. 311–16.
47 F. Bustelo *et al.*, *Partido Socialista Obrero Español* (1976), pp. 49–57.
48 For the Basques see 'Vascos y trece', *Cambio 16* (13–19 January 1975); for the Christian Democrat meeting, 'Valencia DC', *Cambio 16* (9–15 June 1975). See also 'El abanico catalán', *Cambio 16* (9–15 June 1975).
49 *Tácito* (1975), passim.
50 J. A. Ortega Díaz Ambrona, 'Es posible la evolución democrática?', in *España. Su Monarquía y el futuro* (1975), pp. 99–116; and F. Fernández Ordóñez, 'Mutaciones sociales y cambios politicos', ibid., pp. 217–29.
51 P. Calvo Hernando, 'Opinion personal', *Gaceta Ilustrada* 23 (30 March, 13 April and 11 May 1975); 'Listos para el partido', *Cambio 16* (3–9 February 1975). Silva, however, withdrew from the coalition and formed his own association, 'Democratic Spanish Union' (*Unión Democrática Española*, UDE) which was an attempt to disguise Silva's brand of Catholic Francoism under a Christian Democratic facade.
52 P. Calvo Hernando, op. cit.; J. Conte Barrena, *Las asociaciones politicas* (1976), pp. 79*ff*.
53 M. Fraga Iribarne, *Un objetivo nacional* (1975), p. 189. On FEDISA see J. Conte Barrena, op. cit., pp. 199–201. See also Godsa, *Llamamiento para una reforma democrática* (1976).
54 'El Juego asociativo', *Actualidad Económica* (20 September 1975).
55 'Huelga Superstar', *Cambio 16* (17–23 February 1975).
56 The government was confronted with a serious conflict in the Sahara. See 'Sahara', *Cambio 16* (27 October 1975).
57 J. L. López Aranguren, 'Política Nacional', *España, Perspectiva 1973* (1973), pp. 30–1.

CHAPTER 10

1 For a detailed account of Franco's agony see *Cuadernos de Vanguardia,* no. 1 (January 1976).

2 Moreover, another two 'men of Fraga' – his brother-in-law Robles Piquer and the liberal Martín Gamero – took over Education and Information. Villar Mir, a successful entrepreneur, was the new Minister of Finance. Another reformist, the pseudo-Christian Democrat Osorio, was the Minister of the Presidency. Two 'men of the Movement', Adolfo Suárez and Rodolfo Martín Villa, also entered the cabinet.

3 For the composition of the bunker see *Guadiana* (31 January 1976). Its best-known figures were Girón, Fernández de la Mora, Emilio Romero and General García Rebull.

4 *Guadiana* (3–9 January 1976).

5 J. M. Areilza, *Diario de un ministro de la Monarquia* (1977), p. 84.

6 On the events in Vitoria, see *Informaciones* (4–10 March 1976); *Triunfo* (13 March 1976).

7 J. M. Areilza, op. cit., pp. 124–5. Among those arrested was Marcelino Camacho, the leader of the Workers' Commissions.

8 Quoted in L. Carandell, 'El puente de los excombatientes', *Cuadernos para el Diálogo* (27 March 1976). See also 'El suicidio del bunker', *Posible* (12–18 February 1976); and 'En crisis', *Cuadernos para el Diálogo* (20–6 March 1976).

9 *Newsweek* (26 April 1976).

10 *Cuadernos para el Diálogo* (1–7 May 1976).

11 C. Elordi, 'Asesinatos en el monte sagrado', *Triunfo* (15 May 1976).

12 The assassination of a kidnapped Basque industrialist earlier in April had shocked public opinion. *Triunfo* (17 April 1976).

13 *Cuadernos para el Diálogo* (19–25 June 1976); *Triunfo* (10 and 17 June 1976).

14 See R. de la Cierva, 'La descomposición del franquismo', *Historia y Vida* (July 1976); and J. P. Villanueva, 'Los cien días del post-franquismo. El difícil reformismo', *Actualidad Económica* (24 February 1976).

15 On the July crisis, see *Cuadernos para el Diálogo* (10–16 July 1976); *Cambio 16* (25 July 1976); and *El País* (2 July and subsequent issues).

16 ETA killed four people in San Sebastián in October 1976. In December a mysterious left-wing group, GRAPO, kidnapped the former Minister of Justice, Oriol, and General Villaescusa, who were both rescued by the police. In January 1977 a neo-Fascist commando assassinated six Communist lawyers in Madrid; GRAPO retaliated by killing three civil guards. This marked the highest point of tension. The government and the opposition issued a joint communiqué condemning terrorism and ratifying their mutual determination to bring in democracy.

17 R. Tamames, 'Le economía española en 1976 y algunas reflexiones para 1977 y más allá', in *Anuario económico y social de España 1977* (1977), pp. 89*ff.*

18   Nicolás Redondo emerged as the main leader of the socialist UGT; Marcelino Camacho, Nicolás Sartorius, Julián Ariza were the leaders of the Communist-led Workers' Commissions (CC OO); J. M. Zufiaur and M. Zaguirre led the left-wing Catholic USO. UGT, CC OO and USO were the big three national unions in 1976−7.

19   *Triunfo* (11 September 1976, 30 October 1976).

20   *El País* (28−30 November 1976); *Triunfo* (4 December 1976).

21   *Informaciones* (6 November 1976).

22   *Triunfo* (20 November 1976); *El País* (13 November 1976).

23   For a full account of the Congress see *Cuadernos para el Diálogo* (11−17 December 1976) and *Cambio 16* (19 December 1976). Willi Brandt was a force for moderation and warned against the Communists by urging the Congress to look askance at those who did not practise democracy in their own ranks.

24   The best indication was that on precisely the same day (23 December 1976) the police announced the imprisonment of Carrillo and some of the main Communist leaders. They were released a few days later but the tactic of negotiation was not altered by these events.

25   *El País* (10−20 December 1976).

26   *El País* (10 April 1976 and subsequent issues); *Triunfo* (16 April 1976, 23 April 1976).

27   See the opinion of Pujol on the results of the negotiations in *Informaciones* (30 March 1977).

28   For the elections, see *Cambio 16* (27 June−3 July 1977); *Triunfo* (18 June 1977); H. Thomas, 'Renaissance in Spain', *New Statesman* (24 June 1977); *El País* (16 June 1977 and ff.).

29   For the PSOE electoral image, see A. Guerra, 'Socialismo es Libertad' *El País* (24 May 1977); F. González, 'Por qué socialismo, por qué PSOE' *El País* (12 June 1977); and *Diario 16* (4 June 1977).

30   For the differences between the PSP and the PSOE see Elías Díaz, 'Sobre los orígenes de la fragmentación actual del socialism español', *Sistema* no. 15 (October 1976).

31   See an interview with Alvarez de Miranda in *Triunfo* (21 May 1977); *Diario 16* (13 June 1977); *Informaciones* (7 May 1977); and 'El laberinto demócrata cristiano', *El País* (3 June 1977).

32   On UCD see C. Alonso de los Ríos, 'El centro propone; Suárez dispone', *Triunfo* (7 May 1977); 'UCD' *Diario 16* (10 June 1977); X. Tusell, 'El Centro no es franquismo', *Diario 16* (31 May 1977); Suárez' speech on 3 May 1977, in *El País* (4 May 1977); J. Garrigues Walker, 'Un compromiso histórico', *El País* (3 June 1977).

33   There were eleven victims of political violence in the six months after the elections. This is in sharp contrast to Portugal.

34   The Palace of Moncloa is Suárez' residence in Madrid. The Moncloa Pact severely restricted the money supply − the one element the government could control. Other factors, e.g. levels of employment, cannot be so easily managed and some, e.g. oil prices and the effect of the weather on harvests, are completely outside government control.

35   *La Vanguardia Española* (23−8 October 1977 and 5−10 December 1977).

36 *Deia* (25–9 November 1977, 7–15 December 1977, 31 December 1977); *El País* (31 December 1977). Killings by ETA took place in October and December 1977; two ETA members were killed by the police in Pamplona (Navarre) in January 1978.

CHAPTER 11

1 Declarations in *Vanguardia* (26 January 1977).
2 See above, p. 221.
3 cf. General Gutiérrez Mellado, Minister of Defence: 'We believe that our Armed Forces constitute a whole with society and are the defenders of the will of the citizens' (ibid.).
4 'The employment of the army as a tribunal for political offences and the use for non-military ends of images and values associated with it, inspires the erroneous belief in many citizens that the Armed Forces as such were the seat of power in Spain.' (Editorial in *El País*, 20 December 1977).
5 *Cuadernos para el Diálogo* (14 January 1978).
6 *Interviú* (17 December 1977).
7 It can also be seen as a shrewd move by Suárez to take the steam out of Carrillo's demand for an all-party 'government of concentration'.
8 Girón in *Diario 16* (28 March 1977).
9 On the decline of student activism see E. Bustamente, 'De la contestación al porro', *Cuadernos para el Diálogo* (4 March 1978). The Rector of the Law Faculty of Madrid (Complutense) who initiated a system by which students would vote for the professor under whom they wished to study – a sign of the times – confessed 'the moment has passed when the University was the pioneer in the struggle for democracy'.
10 UCD 47 per cent of total seats; PSOE 33.7 per cent.
11 cf. the characteristically bitter – and largely unjustified – comments of the defenestrated José María de Areilza in *El País* (21 June 1977).
12 Declaration of 4 March 1978.
13 For instance, Barcelona, where UCD obtained 18 per cent of the vote and Bilbao only 25 per cent. Obviously the UCD was weakened by its relative indifference to regionalist demands. In Madrid the UCD was beaten by the left. It scored its most decisive victories in Galicia, León, the two Castiles, Extremadura. Andalusia is the only backward rural area where the UCD was defeated.
14 In our view the Moncloa Pact is most likely to be threatened by union uneasiness about unemployment. The Spanish economy has a poor record in job creation. During the boom of the sixties, when the GNP was growing at around 7 per cent, the total number of jobs created rose at only 0.9 per cent a year. The problem is now aggravated by the end of foreign emigration; in 1976 net emigration turned negative.

INDEX